स्वयम्भूपुराणम्
Svayambhūpurāṇam

स्वयम्भूपुराणम्

आङ्ग्लभाषानुवादसहितम्

पुराणसम्पादकौ आङ्ग्लानुवादकौ च

काशीनाथ न्यौपाने

मालवीय पीठाचार्य – भारतीय ज्ञान परम्परा

केन्द्रीय संस्कृत विश्वविद्यालय, नई दिल्ली

एवं

शारदा पौडेल

सह-आचार्य

लुम्बिनी बौद्ध विश्वविद्यालय, नेपाल

DK®

PRINTWORLD

भारतीय परम्पराओं के प्रकाशक

Cataloging in Publication Data — DK

[Courtesy: D.K. Agencies (P) Ltd. <docinfo@dkagencies.com>]

Puranas. Svāyambhūpurāṇa.

Svayambhūpurāṇam : original text with English translation / edited and translated in English by Kashinath Nyaupane, Sharada Poudel.

pages cm

Sanskrit and English.

Added title page title: Svyambhūpurāṇam : Āṅglabhāṣānuvādasahitam.

ISBN 9788124612507 (Hb)

1. Buddhist shrines – Nepal – Kathmandu Valley. I. Nyaupāne, Kāśīnātha, editor, translator. II. Poudel, Sharada, editor, translator. III. Puranas. Svāyambhūpurāṇa. English. IV. Title. V. Title: Svyambhūpurāṇam : Āṅglabhāṣānuvādasahitam.

LCC BQ5755.N35P87 2024 | DDC 294.3435095496 23

प्रथम संस्करण, 2024

ISBN : 978-81-246-1250-7 (सजिल्द)

लेखक – काशीनाथ न्यौपाने (b.1966) और शारदा पौडेल (b.1978)

मुद्रक एवं प्रकाशक

डी०के० प्रिण्टवर्ल्ड (प्रा०) लि०

पंजीकृत कार्यालय : "वेदश्री", एफ-395, सुदर्शन पार्क

(मेट्रो स्टेशन : ई०एस०आइ० हॉस्पिटल), नई दिल्ली - 110015

फोन : (011) 4172 2626, 98713 94815

ई-मेल : indology@dkprintworld.com

वेब : www.dkprintworld.com

Svayambhūpurāṇam

Original Text with English Translation

Edited and translated in English by

Kashinath Nyaupane
M.M. Malaviya Chair Professor,
Central Sanskrit University, New Delhi

and

Sharada Poudel
Associate Professor of Buddhist Studies
Lumbini Buddhist University, Nepal

DK PRINTWORLD
Publishers of Indian Traditions

Cataloging in Publication Data — DK
[Courtesy: D.K. Agencies (P) Ltd. <docinfo@dkagencies.com>]

Puranas. Svāyambhūpurāṇa.
Svayambhūpurāṇam : original text with English translation / edited and translated in English by Kashinath Nyaupane, Sharada Poudel.
pages cm
Sanskrit and English.
Added title page title: Svyambhūpurāṇam : Āṅglabhāṣānuvādasahitam.
ISBN 9788124612507 (Hb)

1. Buddhist shrines – Nepal – Kathmandu Valley. I. Nyaupāne, Kāśīnātha, editor, translator. II. Poudel, Sharada, editor, translator. III. Puranas. Svāyambhūpurāṇa. English. IV. Title. V. Title: Svyambhūpurāṇam : Āṅglabhāṣānuvādasahitam.

LCC BQ5755.N35P87 2024 | DDC 294.3435095496 — 23

First published in India in 2024
ISBN: 978-81-246-1250-7 (Hb)

Authors – Kashinath Nyaupane (b.1966) and Sharada Poudel (b.1978)

Printed and published by:
D.K. Printworld (P) Ltd.
Regd. Office: F-395, Sudarshan Park
(Metro Station: ESI Hospital), New Delhi 110015
Phones: (011) 4172 2626, 98713 94815
e-mail: indology@dkprintworld.com
Web: www.dkprintworld.com

Dedicated to

Bhagavān Śrī Ṣaṇmukha Anantha Nātha

Preface

All that is gold does not glitter.
– JRR Tolkien

In the bustling streets of Kathmandu, *circa* 1995, I embarked on a casual stroll. Freshly appointed as a lecturer at the Nepal Sanskrit University, my return from India had brought with it a sense of homecoming. As I meandered through the vibrant city, an encounter awaited me that would resonate through time.

Amidst the numerous alleyways (*gallīs*) and the chaotic symphony of the city, I stumbled upon a beggar, one among the many that inhabit the streets of Kathmandu. His presence was unremarkable amidst the sea of humanity, yet one thing set him apart – the vessel he held out as he begged, a tarnished golden pot, the gleam of its purity now obscured by layers of dirt and grime.

Driven by curiosity, I approached the beggar, and with a compassionate smile, I inquired about the origins of his unusual beggar's bowl. The man's eyes, worn by life's hardships, held an air of bewilderment as he began to recount its story. It was a relic from his family, an heirloom passed down through generations, a vessel to which he had been tethered by fate. However, the beggar remained oblivious to its true nature, ignorant of the treasure that had been clutched within his soiled fingers.

Intrigued by his tale and sensing the potential value of this seemingly ordinary pot, I decided to act. With a gentle determination, I suggested that we pay a visit to a local goldsmith, a venerable craftsman skilled in discerning the authenticity and worth of precious metals.

At the goldsmith's humble workshop, the beggar relinquished his cherished pot. The old goldsmith, with an expert eye honed by years of discerning authenticity, meticulously examined the vessel. His verdict was unequivocal – the beggar's humble pot was indeed crafted from gold.

Stunned and overcome with emotions he had never known, the beggar's life was drastically changed. The golden pot, a silent testament to the legacy of his family, now held the promise of a better life. It was traded for a sum that the man had never ever dreamt of.

With newfound wealth, the beggar transitioned from the dusty, worn streets of Kathmandu to a life of comfort and security. He embraced opportunities that once seemed distant dreams, and in doing so, proved that fate, when coupled with unexpected kindness, could rewrite the chapters of one's life in the most remarkable ways. The begging pot, once understood to be gold beneath its layers of grime, had become the catalyst for an extraordinary transformation.

⁂

Now, the question naturally arises: why, at this particular moment, does this tale re-emerge from the halls of my memory? The answer, I dare say, lies in the very text that graces the pages of this volume, i.e. our *Svayambhū Purāṇa*. It, too, languished in a condition akin to the beggar's pot, concealed and unimposing due to the veils of accumulated grime and neglect, at least in philology's eye. The manuscripts and their earlier Sanskrit renditions, tainted by layers and layers of textual inaccuracies and corruptions, rendered this inherently valuable text into an object seemingly bereft of literary value.

Yet, as fate would have it, our dearest friend from China, the esteemed Madam Dongmei Zhang from the Chinese Academy of Social Sciences recognized the true gold concealed within those seemingly flawed verses of the text. She had understood that there lied an inherent value and richness in the text; and as such, her heart was set on unveiling its treasures to a broader audience through a Chinese translation.

Therefore, with the intent of translating it into Chinese, Madam Zhang came to Kathmandu around 2018 to study the *Svayambhū Purāṇa* with me; but we had only finished studying the first two chapters, when she had to return to China. So we tried, for a while, to continue our study online, but various occupations made it difficult to make much progress. Of course, Madam Zhang, given her years of devoted Sanskrit study, is quite capable of translating standard Sanskrit texts on her own, but this text, with all the layers of textual corruption and the apparent anomalies in the language and meter, presented quite a challenge even to the seasoned Sanskritist. So we agreed that our team in Nepal, i.e. myself and Dr Poudel, would work with the text and translate it into English, while Madam Zhang and Professor Weiguang Ma in China, would translate the Sanskrit into Chinese, using our English version to verify the translation at each step. Both the English and the Chinese translations were completed, on an initial level, during 2019. The Chinese translation has been meticulously curated by Madam Dongmei Zhang and Professor Weiguang Ma, and will soon be published from China.

The present volume contains only the Sanskrit text and the English translation, for it is primarily intended for audience in the Indian subcontinent and for other interested individuals, who read in English and/or Sanskrit. Nevertheless, it is to be acknowledged that it sprang forth, like a branch, from that large collaborative project, which is why our primary thanks are owed to Madam Dongmei Zhang and Professor Weiguang Ma, without whom this book would have probably never existed.

***

This book has been dedicated to the highly esteemed and dear Bhagavān Śrī Ṣaṇmukha Anantha Nātha, for two reasons.

The first is the very fact that the primary translation was completed in the beautiful island of Ko Pha Ngan, located in the Thai Sea, where Bhagavān's wonderful *āśrama* was then situated. Actually, Bhagavān and I had lost contact for two decades, until one of his students came to Nepal and suddenly discovered my whereabouts – such was her happiness at having finally located her teacher Bhagavān's old friend that she immediately shed tears of joy, which not only attests to her own deep-rooted empathy and humanity, but also to Bhagavān's fondness and benevolence towards me, which he seemed to have transmitted even to his students! Some months later, during summer time, I and my family went to visit Bhagavān in his *āśrama* (where *yoga* of very high level is masterfully taught and practised), and we stayed in the idyllic island as his guests; that is when (and where) the main portion of this translation was completed.

Hence, our deepest gratitude goes to Bhagavān Śrī Ṣaṇmukha Anantha Nātha, and to his whole team of students and collaborators at the Śrī Kālī Āśrama, especially to Ms. Natalia Temnova and Ms. Lavanya Rao, whose hospitality, generosity, and kindness we shall forever cherish and fondly remember.

The second reason for the dedication is that it may be a symbol of my regards for him, and of our sincere hope to collaborate on numerous projects in the future: Bhagavān is one of the very few remaining experts of the Vedic and Yogic sciences, as well as the traditions of Āgama, Tantra and related disciplines. Together, we wish to work on numerous texts and translations of the old texts, in order not to let these old traditions simply fade away and vanish.

⁂

Special thanks are due to Mr Aanandavardhan Nyaupane, for his notable contributions to the present volume. I am also very grateful to Mr Riccardo Paccagnella – a very promising young scholar in the field of Indology – who was kind enough to proofread the entire translation. Likewise, my heartfelt gratitude to Ācārya Śrī Tapan Kumar Panda and Dr Subodh Kumar Shukla, for their constant and tireless support.

Lastly, my sincere gratitude goes to Śrī Susheel Mittal ji, the Director of DK Printworld, for his immense patience and unwavering support throughout the production of this volume. This book would have been published two or three years ago, if not for my own delays in the various stages of proofreading. Nevertheless, Mittal ji and the entire team of DK Printworld demonstrated their saintly patience, alongside their remarkable dedication and flexibility, by accommodating to my schedule and kindly offering extensions. I look forward to numerous other collaborations with DK Printworld!

Kathmandu, Nepal
July 2023

Kashinath Nyaupane

Contents

Introduction

The Svayambhū Purāṇa and Its Date of Composition

THE *Svayambhū Purāṇa* (henceforth referred to as the *SvP*) is a text of utmost importance in Nepalese Buddhism, focusing on the magnification of the shrine of Svayambhū, which serves as one of the central points of veneration for Buddhists in Kathmandu. Perched atop a hill west of Kathmandu, this majestic shrine draws thousands of worshippers who offer prayers and donations throughout the year.

Historians maintain that the Svayambhū shrine had acquired paramount importance among Buddhists by the onset of the Malla period in the thirteenth century. In fact, historical records indicate that even as early as 1041 CE, during the era of the renowned monk Atīśa, the Svayambhū pilgrimage served as a compelling excuse for monks to depart from their monastic abodes and embark on a prolonged journey to the Nepal Valley. This attests to the enduring significance and allure of the Svayambhū as a sacred and revered pilgrimage site for at least the last 1,000 years.

Given the millennium-long glory of the Svayambhū, it is safe to believe that there must have been various legends surrounding the revered shrine, most likely circulating orally for generations. However, a written form was needed to bestow the sanctity and authority of the Buddha's word upon the celebrated legends. This is where the *Svayambhū Purāṇa* comes in, with its rich tapestry of local lore, religion and anthropology woven into a grand cosmic context.

This text of the *Svayambhū Purāṇa* claims to have been delivered as a sermon by Śākyamuni Buddha on Mañjuśrī Hill. However, some scholars believe that it was actually written (or compiled) during the reign of King Yakṣa Malla, at the beginning of the fifteenth century, shortly after Kathmandu became a separate city state. Others push the date of composition towards the sixteenth century, contextualizing the work against the backdrop of the Mughal invasion of India. They argue that, in the wake of the dissolution of Buddhism's Indian stronghold, the Nepal Valley (present-day Kathmandu) became a haven for the practice of Sanskrit-based Buddhism. Subsequently, Newārs, the inhabitants of the Nepal Valley, were faced with the intricate task of localizing and recalibrating the grand Buddhist lineage, now severed from its Indian pilgrimage sites, erudite academies, maritime trade routes, and political patronage. Such an argument might simultaneously explain the *Svayambhū Purāṇa*'s *raison d'être* and its collocation in the time frame of the sixteenth century. An evidence in favour of this argument is the fact that the oldest extant copy of the text dates back to the 1558 CE. Nevertheless, no decisive answer has been provided to the elusive question of the *Svayambhū Purāṇa*'s date of composition.

Key Themes of the Svayambhū Purāṇa

While the *Svayambhū Purāṇa* exists in numerous versions and recensions, each with its own unique features, it accommodates some central thematic cores that form the heart of the work. Here is a synopsis of these nuclear elements, recurring in the majority of the recensions:

1. The *Svayambhū Purāṇa* unfolds the narrative of the self-generated birth of the Svayambhū shrine (*caitya*), with the Śākyamuni Buddha serving as the narrator.
2. There is mention of the Vipaśvi, a primordial Buddha, who lived near the Great Lake that then filled the Nepal Valley, and foretold the rise of the Svayambhū.
3. During Śikhi Buddha's era, a radiant and bejewelled lotus emerges from the dark waters of the lake, foreshadowing the eventual manifestation of the Buddha's shrine (*caitya*) at its core.
4. A substantial portion of the text is devoted to delineating devotional practices and the outcomes of veneration, offering profound insights into religious observance.
5. Central to the cosmic drama of Nepal Valley's civilization is Mañjuśrī, emerges from his Five-Peaked Mountain home in China during the time of Viśvabhū Buddha. Mañjuśrī, accompanied by his two consorts, played a pivotal role in shaping the destiny of the

region. He is attributed with several significant actions, including draining the primordial lake, infested with serpents, that once filled the Valley, and rendering the Svayambhū shrine accessible for worship by humankind.

6. The narrative advances as the Valley starts to be populated during Krakucchanda's era, marking a pivotal juncture in the text.
7. In accordance with the Purāṇic genre's tradition, the *Svayambhū Purāṇa* includes an extensive excursus, delving into other sacred sites in the Valley, encompassing the *tīrtha* and *upatīrtha* sites.
8. In the Kanaka era, the revered monk Dharmaśrīmitra receives instructions from the Bodhisattva Mañjuśrī on a section of the *Mañjuśrīnāmasaṅgīti*, emphasizing the veneration of Mañjuśrī's names, credited with enabling the inhabitation of the Valley.
9. Kāśyapa's time sees the Vajrācārya Śāntaśrī (or Śāntikara) enshroud the Svayambhū *caitya* with a *stūpa*, safeguarding it from potential harm.
10. In Guṇakāmadeva's era, Śāntideva, sometimes referred to as the Śāntaśrī, successfully eradicates drought through a ceremonial act of appeasing the serpents (*nāga-sādhanā*).

The narrative within the *Svayambhū Purāṇa* is made intricate by multiple layers embedded within one another. The outermost frame consists of the discourse delivered by the Bhikṣu Jayaśrī to the Bodhisattva Jineśvara. This discourse recounts the sermons originally imparted to King Aśoka by the Bhikṣu Upagupta, who, in turn, relays the teachings of the Śākyamuni Buddha to Maitreya.

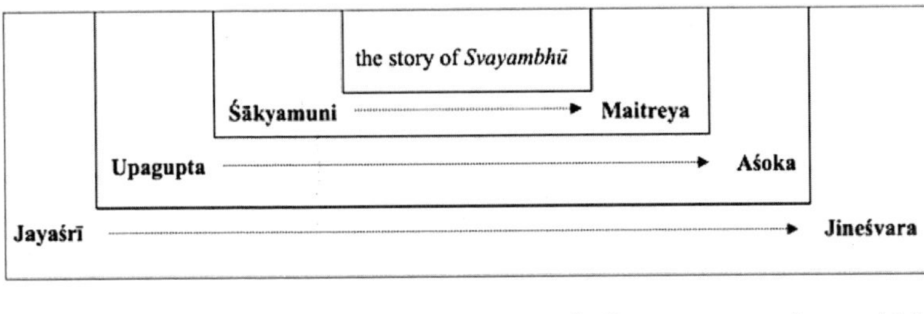

As illustrated in the above diagram, each discourse envelops within itself the narration of an older discourse, forming a layered sequence

which ultimately culminates in the story of the Svayambhū and the core themes of our Purāṇa. This structure cleverly allows the oral tradition to be traced back to the Śākyamuni Buddha, thereby conferring upon the *Svayambhū Purāṇa* its apparent validation and authenticity within the Buddhist context.

In conclusion, the *Svayambhū Purāṇa* not only stands as a testament to the rich spiritual and cultural heritage of the medieval Nepal Valley, but also unveils the sophisticated nature of Newār Buddhist Sanskrit literary output of the fifteenth century. It brings to life a vivid panorama of legends, each contributing to the religious identity and historical narrative of the region. Even today, the *Svayambhū Purāṇa*'s enduring influence continues to shape the religious beliefs and practices of the Newar Buddhist community.

Manuscripts

The groundbreaking study led by the late Horst Brinkhaus, a German professor of Indology, distinguished the manuscripts of the *Svayambhū*

Purāṇa in four distinct recensions or versions, each possessing its own distinctive features. Successive scholarship, notably of the erudite Min Bahadur Shakya, identified a fifth version, possibly unknown to the German scholar. Following Brinkhaus' and his successors' footsteps, we may classify the manuscripts as such:

Recension	*Version*	*Language & Style*	*Chapters*	*Length**
I	IA	Sanskrit (prose)	8	410 *śloka*s
	IB	Sanskrit (verse)	8	280 verses
II	IIA	Sanskrit (verse)	8	4,100 verses
	IIB	Sanskrit (verse)	8	4,600 verses
III	IIIA	Sanskrit (verse)	10	1,750 verses
	IIIB	Newārī (prose)	10	–
IV	–	Sanskrit (mixed)	12	3,600 *śloka*s
V	–	Sanskrit (prose)	13	5,380 verses

* Length of the versions in prose is measured with the *śloka* unit, whereby each *śloka* consists of 32 syllables and corresponds to an Anuṣṭubh verse quatrain.

The text in the present volume is primarily based on IIIA, the Sanskrit prose version with ten chapters and around 1,750 verses. For the purpose of recension, facsimile editions (of MSS: A 923/3; B 101/4; D 36/2) were consulted. Although the titles present in the manuscripts were either *Svayambhūcaityabhaṭṭārakoddeśa* or *Svayambhūcaityasamutpattikathā*, for this book, we have preferred to retain the conventional title *Svayambhū Purāṇa*, so that it may be recognized by non-specialists as well.

Our Edition and Translation

Our version of the *Svayambhū Purāṇa* represents a notable enhancement in the accessibility of the text. First and foremost, we have adopted a bilingual approach, presenting both Sanskrit and English text together. This approach allows readers to engage directly with the original Sanskrit verses while simultaneously comprehending the English translation. This dual-language presentation is especially valuable for scholars and those seeking an in-depth exploration of the text.

And as such, our book fills a notable gap in the existing literature. Before our work, there was a notable absence of a complete English translation for each verse of the *Svayambhū Purāṇa*. While there were summaries and translated blocks of monolingual prose available, a comprehensive bilingual edition was missing, not just in English, but in any modern language at all, except for Newārī. Our version addresses this gap by presenting the Sanskrit verses alongside their English translations, and thereby not only catering to the curious Sanskritist but also making the text more accessible to a broader audience.

Throughout the text, readers will encounter a predominantly literal translation, maintaining the faithfulness to the original Sanskrit (to the extent possible). However, every now and then, the keen reader will notice instances of more explanatory or interpretative translations to certain verses. The supercilious philologist might label this approach as inconsistent, but the kinder reader will understand that a versatile strategy had to be adopted to ensure that the readers, especially those new to the text, are not left perplexed. Thus, some translations have been made more explanatory to offer context and clarifications for verses where the Sanskrit might present obscurity or cultural specificity. In this way, our approach strikes (or at least, attempts) a balance between honouring the original text's integrity and making it more accessible and comprehensible to a wider audience.

⁂

Our edition of the text deviates itself from some of its predecessors in the disposition and numbering of certain verses. As is usual with Purāṇa literature, the metre of the concerned text is the Anuṣṭubh, which consists of two hemistiches (let us call them "lines", for the reader's convenience) coupled together to make one verse (*śloka*) of thirty-two syllables. Usually, the second line of the verse responds to and concludes the first line, so that the verses stand as isolated and self-contained units in terms of their meaning.

Now, for the most part, the conventional disposition and numbering of the verses found in previous editions of the *Svayambhū Purāṇa* worked quite well. But there were some instances where the second line of one verse was tied in meaning with the first line of the subsequent verse. Likewise, this pattern continued, with the second line of the latter verse seamlessly connected to the first line of the following one, and so forth.

It is most probable that this type of issue arose due to the insertion of a spurious line in the middle of the text, which triggered the domino effect that would, alas, only be settled at the end of the concerned chapter.

Such a phenomenon, frequently found in the previous editions, not only disrupted the internal harmony of each verse by separating the two syntactically and semantically interconnected hemistiches, but also presented a challenge (or rather, an impossibility) to the translator willing to provide a coherent rendering of each isolated verse. Therefore, to remedy this awkward issue, we have, at times, counted three lines as one verse – a small act to render all the subsequent verses coherent and self-contained. Other times, to the same effect, we have removed the blatantly spurious hemistich, thereby automatically restoring all remaining hemistiches to their rightful partners.

But whenever there was a genuine (syntactic and semantic) connection of the verses and they did not easily lend themselves to isolation, we grouped them together without interposing the translation; instead, we placed the translation after the two or three verses that belonged together.

These and some other tactics had to be employed in order to edit and translate a text that was somewhat corrupt in its textual tradition. And yet, despite our efforts, various shortcomings and inadvertent errors may yet be lingering in the volume. But we trust the kind reader to forgive us and contemplate, instead, the brilliance of the *Svayambhū Purāṇa*. May the light of Svayambhū enlighten all of our minds!

With Metta,

Sharada Poudel

॥ स्वयम्भूपुराणम् ॥

अथ प्रथमोऽध्यायः
(Prathama Adhyāya)

Origin of Svayambhū

ॐ नमः श्रीधर्मधातुवागीश्वराय। ॐ नमः सर्वबुद्धधर्मबोधिसत्त्वेभ्यः।

Salutations to the Dharmadhātu Vagīśvara. Salutations to the Buddha, the *dharma*, and the Sangha of Bodhisattvas.

श्रीमता येन सद्धर्मस्त्रैलोक्ये[1] संप्रकाशितः।
श्रीघनं तं महाबुद्धं वन्देऽहं शरणाश्रितः[2] ॥ १ ॥

Dwelling in his protection, I bow down to Śrīghana, the great Buddha, by whom the true *dharma* has been illustrated in all three worlds.

नत्वा त्रिजगदीशानं धर्मधातुं जिनालयम्।
तत्स्वयम्भूसमुद्देशं वक्ष्यामि शृणुतादरात्॥ २ ॥

Bowing down to the protector of all three worlds, I am about to tell the story of the origin of Svayambhū, which is the mine of *dharma*. Come, listen with devotion.

श्रद्धया यःशृणोतीमां स्वयम्भूत्पत्तिसत्कथाम्।
परिशुद्धत्रिकायोऽसौ बोधिसत्त्वो भवेद् ध्रुवम्॥ ३ ॥

The one who listens to the true story of Svayambhū with devotion shall attain purity in all three bodies and definitely become a *bodhisattva*.

तद्यथाभूत्पुराभिज्ञो जयश्रीः सुगतात्मजः।
बोधिमण्डविहारे स विजहार ससांघिकः॥ ४ ॥

---

1 त्रिलोके इति कपाठः। त्रलोक्ये इति गपाठः।

2 गतः इति कपाठः।

The story begins this way:

Once upon a time, the Sugata's son was a great *bodhisattva* named Jayaśrī, who lived in a *vihāra* (monastery) named Bodhimaṇḍa in the Saṅgha.

तत्र जिनेश्वरो नाम बोधिसत्त्वो महामतिः ।
श्रद्धया शरणं गत्वा जयश्रियमुपागमत्[3] ॥ ५ ॥

In that very monastery lived another wise monk named Jineśvara, who took refuge in Jayaśrī and served him full of devotion, asking him for knowledge and wisdom.

तदा धीमाञ्जयश्रीः स सर्वसत्त्वहितार्थवित् ।
सद्धर्मस्योपदेशाय[4] सभासने स्थितोऽभवत्[5] ॥ ६ ॥

Consequently, for the welfare of all the living beings, Jayaśrī, who knew the secrets to the welfare of humanity, took the highest seat at the assembly of the monks in order to teach the true religion.

तत्र सर्वे महासत्त्वा बोधिसत्त्वा जिनात्मजाः ।
अर्हन्तो भिक्षवश्चापि श्रावका ब्रह्मचारिणः ॥ ७ ॥

In the assembly, all *mahāsattva*s (great beings), Buddha's disciples, *bodhisattva*s, *arhant*, *bhikkhu*, *brahmacārī* and *Śrāvaka*s.

भिक्षुण्यो ब्रह्मचारिण्यो व्रतिनश्चाप्युपासकाः ।
उपासिकास्तथान्येऽपि गृहस्थाश्च महाजनाः ॥ ८ ॥

*Bhikkhuṇī*s, *brahmacāriṇī*, *upāsaka*s and *upāsikā*s, householders and wealthy laymen,

ब्राह्मणाः तीर्थिकाश्चापि यतयश्च तपस्विनः ।
राजानो मन्त्रिणोऽमात्याः सैन्याधिपतिपौरिकाः ॥ ९ ॥

Brāhmaṇas, Jainas, Hindu monks, ascetics, kings, ministers,

---

3 उपाश्रयेत् इति गपाठः ।

4 उपादेष्टुं इति खपाठः ।

5 समाश्रयेत् इति कपाठः ।

secretaries, armies and their generals, as well as the public (townsmen and townswomen) were present.

ग्राम्या जानपदाश्चापि तथान्यवासिनो जनाः ।
तत्सद्धर्मामृतं पातुं श्रद्धया समुपागताः ॥ १० ॥

Countrymen and countrywomen, villagers, city folks and forest dwellers alike, to drink the sweet nectar of true religion, were present in the assembly, full of devotion.

तत्र सभासमासीनं तमर्हत्श्रीजयश्रियम् ।
अभ्यर्च्य सादरं नत्वा तत्सभायां यथाक्रमम् ॥ ११ ॥

कृतांजलिपुटाः सर्वे परिवृत्य समन्ततः ।
पुरस्कृत्य समुद्विक्ष्य समाश्रय-समाहिताः ॥ १२ ॥

तान् सर्वान् समुपासीनान् सद्धर्मश्रवणोत्सुकान् ॥
दृष्ट्वा श्रीजिनराजाऽसौ बोधिसत्त्वः समुत्थितः ॥ १३ ॥

उद्वहन्नुत्तरासंगं सांजलिः पुरतःस्थितः[6] ॥
जानुभ्यां भूतले धृत्वा सम्पश्यन्नेवमब्रवीत् ॥ १४ ॥

Having seen the mass of the devotees encircling Jayaśrī, who, standing with their hands joined, were worshipping, serving and being completely immersed into the Bodhisattva Jayaśrī, the wise Jineśvara understood that everyone present was very keen and enthusiastic on listening to the preaching of the true religion. Subsquently, Jineśvara dropped on his knees, arranged his upper robe and looking at Jayaśrī, humbly said:

भदन्त! [7]अहमिच्छामि चरितुं बोधिसंवरम् ।
तदादौ किं व्रतं धृत्वा संचरेयं समाहितः ॥ १५ ॥

"O *bhadanta*! I am willing to take on the path of the *bodhi*. For that, what am I to do? Which austere vow should I start at first? How do I achieve concentration?

---

[6] समुपाश्रितः इति कपाठः ।

[7] भदन्तोहंषमि. कपाठः ।

तद् भवान् समुपादिश्य सर्वानस्मान् प्रबोधयेत् ॥
बोधिमार्गे समायुज्य चारयितुं शुभेऽर्हति ॥ १६ ॥

Therefore, O dear God! enlighten us all present here and make us walk the *bodhi* way – the path that is auspicious."

इति संप्रार्थितं तेन श्रुत्वा स सुगतात्मजः ।
जयश्रीस्तं महासत्त्वं समामन्त्र्यैवमादिशत् ॥ १७ ॥

Upon hearing the requests and prayers of the wise Jineśvara; the Bodhisattva Jayaśrī commandingly addressed the mass as such:

शृणु वत्सास्ति ते वाञ्छा सम्बोधिसम्वरे यदि ।
यथाक्रमं प्रवक्ष्यामि संबोधिव्रतसाधनम् ॥ १८ ॥

"O my dear children! listen carefully. If your true desire is to walk down the *bodhi* path, I shall teach you so gradually. The practice of this path is excellent and essential.

यो वाञ्छत्यत्र[8] संसारे चरितुं बोधिसंवरम् ॥
स आदौ शरणं गत्वा सद्गुरुं समुपाश्रयेत् ॥ १९ ॥

The one who, despite living in the mortal realm, desires to practice the *bodhi* ways, needs to submit himself to the enlightened *guru* and serve him well.

[9]गुरोराज्ञां समालभ्य तन्निर्दिष्टपथे तथा ।
तदुपदेशमासाद्य यथाविधि समाहितः ॥ २० ॥

Thenceforth, he needs to walk in the path as shown by the *guru*, with focus and concentration, procedurally, according to the *guru*'s teachings.

तीर्थे स्नात्वा विशुद्धात्मा त्रिरत्नशरणं गतः ।
यथाविधि समभ्यर्च्य संबोधिनिहिताशयः ॥ २१ ॥

---

[8] यो वाञ्छातत्र. इति कपाठः ।

[9] द्वितीयापंक्तिरेव लब्धा प्रथमा पङ्क्तिर्नास्ति ख पुस्तके ।

To begin, one needs to bathe in the holy place to attain purity. After attaining such purity, one needs to take refuge in the *tri-ratnas* (three gems); and having worshipped the Buddha procedurally, with the hope of gaining knowledge in mind, one has to devote himself into the practice of *bodhi*."

उपोषव्रतमाधाय समाचरेज्जगद्धिते ।
एवं यश्चरते नित्यं संबोधिमानसः सुधीः ॥ २२ ॥

Having focus of mind and a resolution to make the world's welfare, a scholar should practice austerity with the hope of knowledge.

परिशुद्धःत्रिकायः स बोधिसत्त्वे मतिर्भवेत्[10] ।
बोधिसत्त्वो महासत्त्वः सर्वसत्त्व-हितार्थभृत् ॥ २३ ॥

The one who engages in such austere ways is completely purified. His mind, speech and body are cleansed. His intellect and mind both turn towards the *buddhahood*. He then transcends into the *mahāsattva* and eventually the *bodhisattva* state, and becomes ready to work for the welfare of the world.

क्रमात्संबोधि-संभारं पूरयित्वा[11] समाहितः ।
एतत्पुण्याभियुक्तात्मा चतुर्ब्रह्मविहारधृक् ॥ २४ ॥

Subsequently, the person attains the state of *sambodhi*. He becomes focused, full of merits and virtues. Eventually, he proceeds to dwell in the four *brahma-vihāras*.

[12]सर्वदुःखविनिर्मुक्तः सर्वचिन्ताविनिर्गतः ।
निःक्लेशो जरयन् मारान् संबोधिं समवाप्नुयात् ॥ २५ ॥

He becomes free of all grief, agony and anxiety. He gets rid of *kleśa* and earthly mundane desires. Thus, he becomes enlightened.

---

10 ... सत्त्वे भवेद् इति खपाठः ।

11 संपूरयेत् इति गपाठः ।

12 द्वितीयापंक्तिरेव विद्यते कपुस्तके ।

एवं सर्वत्र लोकेषु सद्धर्मं संप्रकाशयन्।
समाप्य सौगतं कार्यं सुनिर्वृत्तिमावाप्नुयात्॥ २६॥

In this way, he starts promoting the true religion. Having promoted it, he then proceeds into *nirvāṇa* (ultimate freedom).

ततोऽहं सुगतो भूत्वा सर्वान् सत्त्वान् प्रबोधयन्।
बोधिमार्गे प्रतिष्ठाप्य परमार्थं समालभेत्[13]॥ २७॥

After that, he pledges to become Buddha and to spread enlightenment in the entire world.

"I shall establish people onto the path of *bodhi* and show them the reality of this world", he vows.

एवं सर्वेऽपि संबुद्धाः येऽतीता अप्यनागताः।
वर्त्तमानाश्च ते ह्येतद् व्रतपुण्यविपाकतः॥ २८॥

In this way, all the *buddhas*, who have ever existed, are existing and will exist, owe to the fruit of their austerity.

बोधिं प्राप्यजिना[14]जाता भविष्यन्ति भवन्त्यपि।
एवं सर्वे महासत्त्वा बोधिसत्त्वा जिनात्मजाः॥ २९॥

After attaining *buddhahood*, they became Buddha, are becoming Buddha and will become Buddha. This is how all *bodhisattvas*, *mahāsattvas* and the disciples of Buddha came into existence.

अर्हन्तोऽपि यथा सर्वे परिशुद्धत्रिमण्डलाः।
बोधिं प्राप्य सुनिर्वाणं याता यास्यन्ति यान्त्यथ[15]॥ ३०॥

Similarly, the *arhants* came to be. All these liberated beings are pure in three dimensions: in their body, mind and speech. Thereby, after the attainment of *buddhahood*, they all reach the ultimate state of *nirvāṇa*.

एवं यूयं परिज्ञाय यदीच्छथ सुनिर्वृतिम्।
त्रिरत्नशरणं गत्वा संचरध्वमिदं व्रतम्॥ ३१॥

13 संवृत्तौ संप्रचारये कपाठः।

14 आसन् गपाठः।

15 यान्त्यतः खपाठः।

Therefore, having understood the path of *bodhi*, if you wish for your own welfare, take up the solemn vow of *bodhi*, in the refuge of the *tri-ratna*.

इति तेन समादिष्टं श्रुत्वा स सुगतात्मजः ।
जिनेश्वरं तमर्हन्तं सम्पश्यन्नेवमब्रवीत् ॥ ३२ ॥

After the great Jayaśrī instructed everyone so, the disciple of Buddha Jineśvara, with the image of Buddha in his mind, asked:

भदन्त श्रोतुमिच्छामि तद्व्रतस्थानमुत्तमम् ।
एतद् व्रतं चरेत्कुत्र तद्देशं समुपादिश ॥ ३३ ॥

"O, Lord! Which auspicious location should be chosen for the vow of *bodhi*? How do I partake in this vow, and where? Pray, tell me."

इति संप्रार्थिते तेन जयश्रीः स महामतिः।
जिनेश्वरं महासत्त्वं तं पश्यन्नेवमादिशत्॥ ३४ ॥

Upon hearing the question, Jayaśrī, the disciple of Buddha, looked at Mahāsattva Jineśvara and answered:

शृणु वत्स समाधाय व्रतस्थानमनुत्तमम्[16] ।
मुनीश्वरैर्यथाख्यातं तथा वक्ष्यामि तेऽधुना ॥ ३५ ॥

"I will answer the question you have raised. I will tell you the proper place to start the vow, as Buddha himself once told me.

पुण्यक्षेत्रेषु तीर्थेषु विहारे सुगताश्रमे ।
बुद्धानां निर्वृतानाञ्च[17] चैत्येषु प्रतिमासु च ॥ ३६ ॥

The places are many: sacred *bihāra*s, *āśrama*s, shrines of the Buddha, holy places where other attained *bodhisattva*, *caitya*s, all are locations where the vow of *bodhi* can be upheld.

बुद्धक्षेत्रेषु सर्वत्र व्रतस्थानं समुत्तमम् ।
एतेष्वपि समाख्यातं स्वयंभूचैत्यमुत्तमम्[18]॥ ३७ ॥

---

16 समुत्तमम् कपाठः ।

17 निवृतानाम् गपाठः ।

18 चैत्यम् उत्तमम् घपाठः ।

The vow can be taken in any place of the Buddha. But, among all sacred places, the place where the Svayambhū *caitya* lies is the holiest and most appropriate.

एवं विज्ञाय यो धीमान्व्रतं चरितुमिच्छति ।
स स्वयंभूजिनक्षेत्रमाश्रित्य चरतात् व्रतम् ॥ ३८ ॥

With this knowledge, any wise person that seeks the path of *bodhi*, can take residence near Svayambhū.

स्वयंभूक्षेत्रमाश्रित्य व्रतं यो चरति मुदा ।
लभते सुमहत् पुण्यमक्षयं बोधिसाधनम् ॥ ३९ ॥

The one, who, in Svayambhū, upholds this vow with a pure heart, attains the greatest merit and indestructible *bodhi sādhanā*.

एतत् पुण्यविशुद्धात्मा भद्रश्रीसद्गुणाश्रयः ।
बोधिसत्त्वो महाभिज्ञो भवेज्जिनात्मजो ध्रुवम् ॥ ४० ॥

He who upholds this solemn vow will reach the highest purity of the mind and the soul, be full of merit, endowed with welfare, virtues and all great qualities, and will eventually become a *bodhisattva*, *mahāsattva*, and ultimately equal to the son of Buddha.

दुर्गतिं न व्रजेत् क्वापि संसारे स कदाचन ।
सदा सद्गतिसम्पन्नो[19]बोधिचर्याव्रतं चरेत् ॥ ४१ ॥

Such a person would never find themselves in a state of despair, would never be wretched, never get entangled in the worldly devices, would always walk the path of welfare and good fortune by upholding the *bodhicaryā* vow.

एवं स संसरल्लोके कृत्वा सर्वत्र भद्रताम् ।
संबोधिप्रणिधिं धृत्वा संचरेत तज्जगद्धिते ॥ ४२ ॥

The one, who puts himself in the path of welfare as such, with the devotion to knowledge and to the welfare of the world, must walk the earth with purpose.

---

19 गतिसंजाती इति गपाठः ।

एवं च बोधिसंभारं पूरयित्वा यथाक्रमम् ।
त्रिविधां बोधिमासाद्य निर्वृतिपदमाप्नुयात् ॥ ४३ ॥

Having performed the *bodhi vrata*, three types of *bodhi* must be attained by the person before he moves on to the path of *nirvāṇa*.

एवं यूयं परिज्ञाय स्वयंभूस्थान आश्रिताः ।
त्रिरत्नशरणं गत्वा संचरत[20]व्रतोत्तमम् ॥ ४४ ॥

Thus, with the understanding of the ways of *bodhi*, go to Svayambhū and devote yourself to Buddha, the Dharma and the Saṅgha, to partake in this great *vrata*."

एतत्तेनार्हतादिष्टं श्रुत्वा स सुगतात्मजः ।
जयश्रियं तमर्हन्तं सम्पश्यन्नेवमब्रवीत् ॥ ४५ ॥

Hearing the wise words of the Arhant Jayaśrī, Jineśvara looks at him and says:

भदन्त भवतादिष्टं श्रुत्वा मे रोचते मनः ।
स्वयंभूचैत्यमाराध्य चरितुमिष्यते व्रतम्[21] ॥ ४६ ॥

"O *bhadanta*! having heard your *upadeśa*, my heart is gladdened. Now I want to devote myself to Svayambhū and perform this vow of Bodhi.

स्वयंभू-चैत्यराजःश्रीधर्मधातु-जिनालयः ।
कुत्रास्त्यत्र महीलोके तत्समादेष्टुमर्हति ॥ ४७ ॥

O Lord! Svayambhū is the king of all *caitya*, the *dharmadhātu*, the home of the Buddha. But where is it on this earth? Pray, tell me."

इति सप्रार्थितस्तेन श्रुत्वा सोऽर्हन् यतिः सुधीः ।
जयश्रीस्तं महासत्त्वं समालोक्यैवमादिशत् ॥ ४८ ॥

Jayaśrī, having heard the prayers of the *Mahāsattva* Jineśvara, looked at the *mahāsattva* and said so:

---

20 संचरथ इति कपाठः ।

21 चरितुं व्रतमाभवम् इति खपाठः ।

विद्यतेऽत्र महीलोक उत्तरस्यां हिमालये ।
नेपाल इति विख्यातो गोपुच्छाख्यो नगोत्तमः ॥ ४९ ॥

"Look, it is in the northern part of the earth, in the laps of the Himalaya. There is a mountain range shaped like a cow's tail. That land is known as Nepal."

तद्गिरेर्नाम चातुर्ध्यं चतुर्युगेषु वर्तते ।
तद्यथाभूद्युगे सत्ये पद्मगिरिरिति स्मृतः ॥ ५० ॥

The mountain has had four names in the four ages. In Satya age, the mountain was known as Padmagiri.

त्रेतायां वज्रकूटाख्यो गोशृंगो द्वापरे स्मृतः ।
इदानीं तु कलौ लोके[22]गोपुच्छ इति विश्रुतः ॥ ५१ ॥

In the Tretā age, the mountain was known was Vajrakūṭa; in Dvāpara as the Gośṛṅga and now in the Kali age, it is known as Gopuccha.

सोऽपि शैल इदानीन्तु लौकैर्नेपाल देशकैः ।
सम्हेगुरिति[23]चाख्यातस्तथा संप्रथितो भुवि ॥ ५२ ॥

The mountain, among Nepali people, is famous as the Samhegu.

स सर्वधातुरत्नादि-सर्वद्रव्यमयोत्तमः ।
अश्वत्थप्रमुखैः सर्वैः पादपैः संप्रशोभितः ॥ ५३ ॥

On that famed mountain of Nepal, there exist precious minerals, gems and elements. There are many beautiful and exotic trees, and there are many jungles with such trees covering the area beautifully.

सर्वत्र कुसुमैःकान्तः सर्वौषधिफलद्रुमैः ।
सर्वपक्षिविरावैश्च भ्रमद् भ्रमरनिस्वनैः ॥ ५४ ॥

The land is decorated with flowers, fortified with many types of medicinal herbs. The trees are strange and beautiful, almost hard to describe, with large birds residing there, whose words echo in the air. And the insects buzz around.

---

22 कलौऽसौ इति क पाठ ।

23 विख्यात इति कपाठः ।

जन्तुभिः सकलस्नेहनिवद्धमैत्रमानसैः ।
तपस्विवृद्धया भद्रचारिण्या[24] सन्निषेवितः ॥ ५५ ॥

The beings there, animals and humans exist in perfect harmony. Sages, full of the highest merit and virtue, such as Bhadracāra, meditate in that land.

अष्टांग-गुणसंपन्न-संशुद्धामृतनिर्भरैः ।
शोभितःपुष्पगंधादि[25] सुवासितैः समीरणैः ॥ ५६ ॥

Complete with all eight of the highest qualities, and full of springs with water like elixir, fragrant with the scent of flowers lingering in the air, such a country served by the wind is strange.

आराधितः सदा दिव्यमहासत्त्वैः समादृतः[26] ।
सर्वलोकाधिपैर्नित्यं संसेवितः समादरात् ॥ ५७ ॥

Divine beings like gods and sages, who are usually invisible to the mundane eye, for the welfare of the world, live there respecting one another.

तत्र रत्नमयः पद्मः कर्ण्णिकायां समाश्रितः ।
दिव्य-स्फटिक-रत्नाभ-ज्योतिरूपो निरञ्जनः ॥ ५८ ॥

It is the place with forests full of bejewelled lotuses. Such forests are home to divine swans and fishes with celestial gems such as crystals illuminating the land.

एकहस्तः[27]प्रमाणोच्चैश्चैत्यरूपो जिनाश्रयः ।
स्वयंभूः सर्वलोकानां भद्रार्थं समवस्थितः ॥ ५९ ॥

There lies a *caitya*, a hand tall in height, which is the residence of Lord Buddha, called the Svayambhū. It exists for the welfare of the whole world.

---

24 भद्रचारिभिः इति गपाठः ।

25 गन्धाधि इति खपाठः ।

26 महोत्साहैर्विराजितः । समादरैः इति गपाठः ।

27 प्रमान इति गपाठः ।

ब्रह्म-शक्रादिभिर्देवैः [28]सर्वलोकाधिपैरपि ।
सर्वैर्दैत्याधिपैश्चापि नागेन्द्रैर्गरुडैरपि ॥ ६० ॥

The place is served by gods like Brahmā and Indra, lords of many dimensions, *daitya*s, serpents and divine falcons.

सिद्धैर्विद्याधरैः साध्यैर्यक्षगन्धर्वकिन्नरैः ।
राक्षसेन्द्रैश्च रुद्रैश्च ग्रहैस्तारागणैरपि ॥ ६१ ॥

All types of divine demi-gods, such as *sādhya*s, *yakṣya*s, *gandharva*s, *kinnara*s, demons, Indras, Rudras, *graha*s (planets) and *tārā*s (stars) are also in service of the holy place.

वसुभिश्चाप्सरोभिश्च सर्वैश्च त्रिदशाधिपैः ।
ऋषिभिर्यतिभिः सर्वैर्योगिभिर्ब्रह्मचारिभिः ॥ ६२ ॥

Similarly, celestial nymphs (*apsaras*es), lords of the heaven, sages, *guru*s, *brahmcārī*s and other divine beings also dwell in the land of Nepal, near Svayambhū.

सर्वैश्च तीर्थिकैर्विज्ञैस्तापसैश्चापि सज्जनैः ।
दिवानिशं चतुःसन्ध्यं दृष्ट्वा स्मृत्वा प्रवन्दितः ॥ ६३ ॥

All kinds of pilgrims, Vedic sages, learned ones, meditators, pious men and women, in the morning, day, evening and the night, in all four periods of the day, worship the *caitya*, the Svayambhū, and receive goodwill and happiness.

नित्यकाले समायाते समभ्यर्च्य समादरात् ।
[29]स्तुतिभिश्च महोत्साहैः संमानितोऽभिवन्दितः ॥ ६४ ॥

The constant worshipping of the *caitya* by such special beings, with respect and enthusiasm, earns them piousness and spiritual gratification.

---

28 सर्वैल्लोका इति घपाठः ।

29 संस्तुभिः इति कपाठः।

एवं स त्रिजगन्नाथः स्वयंभूर्धर्मधातुकः ।
सर्वलोक-हितायैव संभाषयन् समास्थितः ॥ ६५ ॥

As such, the Lord Buddha, whose body is the Dharmadhātu, is Svayambhū himself. He resides there as Svayambhūnātha for the good of the world, to teach the world the path of enlightenment.

इदानीन्तु कलौ लोका दुष्टाःक्रूराशयाःशठाः ।
दृष्ट्वेमं श्रीधर्मधातुं[30]हरिष्यन्ति न संशयः ॥ ६६ ॥

But this is the Kali age, where many people are cruel and wicked, cunning and evil, and the sight of Dharmadhātu, which resides as a beautiful bejewelled lotus, arises greed and wrong intentions in their hearts.

इत्यमूं[31]शिलयाछाद्य गुप्तिं कृत्वाप्रकाशितः ।
तदुपरीष्टीकाभिश्च विधाय चैत्यमुत्तमम् ॥ ६७ ॥

Thus, Lord Buddha, having foreseen the Kali age's evil, to protect the shrine from theft, hid the Dharmadhātu deep inside the earth, and covered it with bricks and stones and soil, and built a *caitya* on top of it.

छत्र-ध्वजैः पताकाभिरलंकृत्याप्यधिष्ठितम्[32] ।
तत्रापि सर्वलोकैश्च सर्वलोकाधिपैरपि ॥ ६८ ॥

The *caitya* is decorated by flags and symbols. And the ones who arrive there only see the outer structure of the *caitya*, and do not see the hidden interior of the Dharmadhātu.

समागत्य समाराध्य समभ्यर्च्याभिवन्दितः ।
सत्कारैश्च महोत्साहैः स्तुतिप्रदक्षिणादिभिः ॥ ६९ ॥

The people who arrive with devotion worship the *caitya* with their hands joined in reverence, chanting the prayers respectfully, walking around clockwise.

---

30 धर्मधातुम् । हि इति कपाठः ।

31 इत्यसौ । गुप्तिकृत्वा इति खपाठः ।

32 ध्यतिष्ठितम् इति घपाठः ।

प्रणामैश्च समाराध्य सेवितो मानितोऽर्चितः ।
एवं स त्रिजगन्नाथो[33] धर्मधातुर्जिनालयः ॥ ७० ॥

With different salutations and bows, the *caitya* that stands there is worshipped by many; and it is equivalent to the worshipping of the Dharmadhātu that resides inside of it.

सर्वसत्त्व-शुभार्थेन संशोभितो व्यवस्थितः ।
तत्र ये शरणं यान्ति[34]शुद्ध-बुद्ध्याशया मुदा ॥ ७१ ॥

The *caitya* resides there for the welfare of the entire world, and the people who worship it get purified and go home with newfound happiness and inner peace.

दुर्गतिं ते न गच्छन्ति संसारेऽत्र कदाचन ।
सद्गतावेव [35]धर्मश्रीर्जायन्ते संघशोभिताः ॥ ७२ ॥

Such people shall never walk the path of evil; they shall only walk the path of good and right, and are filled with respect for the *dharma*, that protects them.

बोधिसत्त्वा महासत्त्वाः परिशुद्धत्रिमण्डलाः ।
भद्रश्री-सद्गुणाधाराः सर्वसत्त्वहितंकराः ॥ ७३ ॥

*Bodhisattva*s, *mahāsattva*s, great beings from all three dimensions and people filled with the intentions of welfare reside around the *caitya*.

बोधिचर्याव्रतं धृत्वा संचरन्ति जगद्धिते ।
एवं यूयमपि ज्ञात्वा श्रद्धया शरणं गताः ॥ ७४ ॥

Near Svayambhū, many people practise the *bodhicaryā vow*, for the world's welfare. Thus, you must do the same.

स्वयंभूचैत्यमाराध्य संचरध्वं व्रतं सदा ।
एवं कृत्वात्र संसारे भद्रश्री-सद्गुणाश्रयाः ॥ ७५ ॥

---

33 श्रीजगन्नाथः इति गपाठः ।

34 गत्वा । शुद्धयामुदा इति कपाठः ।

35 संजाती इति कपाठः ।

Having worshipped the Svayambhū *caitya*, you all shall walk the world with good feelings. The evil of the world should never come to you, only good. Thus, you will become *bodhisattvas*, *mahāsattva*s and the children of Buddha.

बोधिसत्त्वा महासत्त्वा जिनात्मजा भविष्यथ ।
ततः संबोधिसंभारं पूरयित्वा यथाक्रमम् ॥ ७६ ॥

In this way, having received the *bodhi*, *dharma* and *jñāna*, you all shall become filled with knowledge and will be established into the path of Buddha."

त्रिविधां बोधिमासाद्य संबुद्धपदमाप्स्यथ ।
इति तेन समादिष्टं[36]निशम्य स महामतिः ॥ ७७ ॥

When he gave such instructions, the Mahāmati *bodhisattva* looked at the Lord, and spoke with hands joined in reverence:

शास्तारं प्रणिपत्यैव पुनरेवमयाचत ।
भदन्त श्रोतुमिच्छामि श्रीस्वयम्भूर्जिनालयः[37] ॥ ७८ ॥

"O Lord! I want to hear from your divine lips, when did the Dharmadhātu *caitya* originate and how did such a divine event come to occur?"

कदा स्वयं समुत्पन्नः कथं तदिति ब्रूहि नः ।
इति संप्रार्थितस्तेन[38]श्रुत्वा सोऽर्हन् यतिः सुधीः ॥ ७९ ॥

Having heard his prayers, the scholastic Jayaśrī, looking at the sage Mahāmati, answered descriptively:

जयश्रीस्तं महासत्त्वं संपश्यन्नेवमादिशत् ।
साधु शृणु महाभाग यथा मया श्रुतं गुरोः ॥ ८० ॥

"Very well. I will tell you exactly as my *guru* once told me. I shall tell you the story of the origin of Svayambhū.

---

36 समालोक्यं । अवोचत इति कपाठः ।

37 परस्वयम्भू जिनालयः । चतदुपादिश इति खपाठः ।

38 संप्रार्थितम् इति कपाठः ।

तथाहं ते प्रवक्ष्यामि स्वयंभूत्पत्तिसत्कथाम् ।
तद्यथा पाटलीपुत्रे पुरेऽशोको नराधिपः ॥ ८१ ॥

A long time ago, in a city called Paṭaliputra, there was a great king called Aśoka.

सद्धर्म-साधनोत्साही त्रिरत्नसेवकोऽभवत् ।
स तत्र कुक्कुटारामे विहारे सुगताश्रमे ॥ ८२ ॥

The King Aśoka was a great devotee of Buddhism and with great enthusiasm, he constantly served the Buddha, Dharma and Saṅgha. One time, he went far from his capital, in search for knowledge, to a *vihāra* called Kukkuṭa.

उपगुप्तं महाभिज्ञं वन्दितुं समुपागमत्[39] ।
तदा सोऽर्हन् महाभिज्ञः सर्वसंघपुरस्कृतः ॥ ८३ ॥

There, in a monastery, lived a respected monk-scholar called Upagupta. The humble king then bowed down and touched the feet of the monk. In reciprocation, he welcomed the king that had arrived at his doorstep.

सभामध्यासनासीनस्तस्थौ ध्याने[40] समाहितः।
तमर्हन्तं सभासीनं सर्वसंघपुरस्कृतम् ॥ ८४ ॥

The *bhikkhu*, after he welcomed the king, called forth an assembly. He took the central seat at the assembly, and he focused his eyes around to see that many members of the Saṅgha were sat encircling him, looking back at him eagerly and with joy.

दृष्ट्वाऽशोकः स भूमीन्द्रो मुदितः समुपागतः ।
तत्र स सहसोपेत्य साञ्जलिरर्हतो यतीन् ॥ ८५ ॥

King Aśoka was filled with joy as he saw the *bhikkhu* seated at the high seat. He, then, stood up and, with hands joined in reverence, prayed to the Bhikkhu Upagupta.

39 उपाचरत् इति कपाठः ।

40 ध्यात्वा इति कपाठः ।

सर्वान् नत्वोपगुप्तं तञ्चाष्टांगैः[41]प्रणमन्मुदा ।
ततस्तं गुरुमर्हन्तं वीर्यवान् स यथाविधि ॥ ८६ ॥

He used eight different bodily positions (*aṣṭāṅga*), to bow down and show respect to the *bhikkhu* and slowly gained proximity to the *bhikkhu* whom he was affectionately bowing down to.

तमभ्यर्च्य[42]प्रणम्यैव धर्मं श्रोतुमुपाश्रयत् ।
तथा तन्मन्त्रिणः सर्वे सामात्यसचिवा जनाः ॥ ८७ ॥

Having bowed down to the Upagupta, the king sat down with a desire to listen to words of *dharma*. His entourage, his ministers and his subjects sat down as well.

तमर्हन्तं यतिं नत्वा तत्रैकान्तमुपाश्रयन् ।
ततः सोऽर्हन् महाभिज्ञो दृष्ट्वा सर्वान्[43] समाश्रितान् ॥ ८८ ॥

As the king and ministers sat around him, the scholar Upagupta was happy to see everyone present in the assembly.

आदि–मध्यान्तकल्याणं सद्धर्मं समुपादिशत् ।
तत्सद्धर्मामृतं पीत्वा सर्वे लोकाःप्रबोधिताः ॥ ८९ ॥

The *bhikkhu* proceeded to tell everyone about the first *kalyāṇa*, middle *kalyāṇa* and the final *kalyāṇa* of Buddhism. Having taken the elixir of such good *dharma*, everyone present was very pleased.

धर्मविशेषं विज्ञाय तैर्बोधिव्रतमीप्सितम् ।
ततः सोऽपिमहाराजःश्रुत्वा तद्धर्ममुत्तमम् ॥ ९० ॥

They understood the special *dharma* and sought to walk the path of *bodhi*. And having heard about the highest *dharma*, the king spoke to the *bhikkhu*.

---

41 तमष्टांगैः । महोत्साहैः । यथाविधिम् इति खपाठः ।

42 समभ्यर्च्य । प्रणत्वा इति खपाठः ।

43 सर्वा इति गपाठः ।

सम्बोधिसाधनाचर्यां समैच्छत् चरितुं मुदा[44] ।
ततः स नृपती राजा साञ्जलिः पुरतःस्थितः ॥ ९१ ॥

तमर्हन्तं महासत्त्वं नत्वा पश्यन्[45]मुदावदत् ।
भदन्त! श्रोतुमिच्छामि संबोधिसाधनं व्रतम् ॥ ९२ ॥

Even the king developed a strong desire to gain the highest *dharma*, and thus, with hands joined, the king said to the superior *bhikkhu* seated there, "O *bhadanta*! what is the *vrata* for the ritual to gain knowledge? I want to hear it from you.

कुत्र पुण्यतमं क्षेत्रं[46]यत्राशु सिध्यति व्रतम् ।
तद् भवान् समुपादिश्य सर्वान् लोकान् प्रबोधयेत् ॥ ९३ ॥

And, O Lord! where does such pious land exist, where fulfilment of the *bodhi vrata* is granted? Everyone who seeks welfare might go to that land.

बोधिमार्गे समायोज्य संचारयितुमर्हति ।
इति संप्रार्थिते राज्ञा श्रुत्वा सोऽर्हन् महामतिः ॥ ९४ ॥

In this way, on the path of *bodhi*, everyone could fulfil their vows." Having heard this prayer, the *bhikkhu* started to answer:

तमशोकं महीपालं सम्पश्यन्नेवमब्रवीत् ।
साधु शृणु महाराज यथा मे गुरुणोदितम् ॥ ९५ ॥

The *bhikkhu* facing the king said "O King! Listen carefully. I will tell you how my teacher once told me about the *bodhi vrata* which shall bring welfare to all.

तथाहं ते प्रवक्ष्यामि बोधिव्रतं यदीष्यते ।
सर्वक्षेत्रोत्तमं राजन्नुत्तरस्यां हिमालये ॥ ९६ ॥

---

44 संचरितुं समैच्छत । समुपाश्रितः इति कपाठः ।

45 पश्यम् इति खपाठः ।

46 क्षत्रम् । सिद्ध्यते । सर्वाल्लोकान् । प्रबोधयन् इति कपाठः ।

नेपाल[47]इतिविख्यातं यत्राशु सिध्यति व्रतम्।
तत्राप्यतिमहत्पुण्यक्षेत्रं बुद्धैः प्रशंसितम्॥ ९७॥

स्वयंभूचैत्यराजस्य धर्मधातोः समाश्रयः।
तत्र यद्यत्कृतं कर्म तत्तत्संसिध्यति द्रुतम्॥ ९८॥

Among all lands, the superior land lies towards the north, in the Himalayas, called Nepal. Such is the might of the land that any vow practised is easily fulfilled.

Within that land lies a very important and pious area, which is lauded by Buddha himself. It is Svayambhū, king of all *caitya*s. It is the residence of the Dharmadhātu. It is the place that grants fulfillment to all vows practised there.

इतिक्षेत्रं महासत्त्वैः संसेवितं जिनैरपि।
इति विज्ञाय राजेन्द्र सम्बोधिं यदि वाञ्छसि॥ ९९॥

Hence, all beings that walked the *bodhi* path, disciples of Buddha, learned ones and scholars have all served this place. With this information, O King, if you do seek knowledge, go to that land.

तच्चैत्यशरणं गत्वा संचरस्व सुसंवरम्।
एतत्पुण्यविशुद्धात्मा भद्रश्री-सद्गुणर्द्धिमान्॥ १००॥

In the refuge of the *caitya*, you shall fulfil your vows. The ones who do so will be purified – filled with merit, virtuous, and full of wisdom and knowledge.

बोधिसत्त्वो महाभिज्ञो भवे सर्वहितार्थभृत्।
ततःक्रमेण[48] सम्बोधिसंभारं परिपूरयन्॥ १०१॥

You might go there to become *bodhisattva*, holder of all knowledge and to work for the welfare of all life and finally, in the end, having crossed all the levels of *jñana* to reach the highest level of enlightenment.

---

47 नेपाले इति कपाठः।

48 क्रमेना इति कपाठः

निःक्लेशोऽर्हञ्जगन्नाथो भूत्वा सम्बोधिमाप्स्यसि।
इति तेनार्हतो[49]वाक्यं निशम्य स नृपो मुदा ॥ १०२ ॥

You shall get rid of all *kleśa* and obstacles and misery. O king! you shall reach Buddhahood." Having heard these words of the *bhikkhu*, the king was ecstatic.

उपगुप्तं गरुं नत्वा पप्रच्छैवं समादरात्।
भदन्त! श्रोतुमिच्छामि स्वयंभूत्पत्तिसत्कथाम् ॥ १०३ ॥

After hearing this from the Upagupta, the king asked the *bhikkhu*, O Lord! I want to hear the story of the origination of Svayambhū.

कदा स्वयं समुत्पन्नस्तद् भवान् वक्तुमहर्ति।
इति संप्रार्थितो राज्ञा श्रुत्वा सोऽर्हत् यतिः सुधीः ॥ १०४ ॥

अशोकं तं महीपालं सम्पश्यन्नेवमब्रवीत्।
साधु राजन् यथाप्रोक्तं गुरुणा मे श्रुतं तदा ॥ १०५ ॥

When did the Svayambhū originate? Pray, tell me. Answering the devoted king's prayers, the *bhikkhu* says: "O king! I shall tell you what my *guru* once told me.

तथाहं संप्रवक्ष्यामि शृणु त्वं चावधानतः।
तदाचासौ जगच्छास्ता शाक्यमुनिस्तथागतः ॥ १०६ ॥

I shall tell you exactly how I heard it. For in that time, there was Lord Śākyamuni Buddha, who gave wisdom to the whole world.

सर्वज्ञो धर्मराजोऽर्हन् मुनीश्वरो विनायकः।
स सर्वसांघिकैः सार्धं जनान्तिकेषु संचरन् ॥ १०७ ॥

The Buddha was the omniscient, king of *dharma*, versed in all forms of knowledge, superior among sages, the destroyer of all obstacles and misery. In his time, he used to dwell among *his bhikkhus*.

एकस्मिन् समये तत्र नेपाले समुपागतः।
गोपुच्छपर्वतपार्श्वे पश्चिमे श्रीस्वयम्भूवः ॥ १०८ ॥

---

49 तेनार्हतादिष्टम् इति गपाठः।

While wandering with his *bhikkhus*, he once reached Nepal, which existed in the lap of Gopuccha. Towards the west of the mountain range, he reached a place called Svayambhū.

पुच्छाग्राऽभिधचैत्यस्य सन्निधौ सुगताश्रमे ।
सर्वसत्त्वहितायैव पूर्णेन्दुरिव भासयन् ॥ १०९ ॥

Towards the west of the mountain range shaped like the tail of the cow, was the *caitya* of Svayambhū. Near that was an *āśrama*, where Buddha started to reside. Since he got there, the place looked as bright as the sky during a full moon.

सद्धर्मस्योपदेशाय[50]विजहार ससांघिकः ।
यथा स भगवाञ्छास्ता सत्त्वानां धर्मवृद्धये ॥ ११० ॥

Lord Buddha, then, with the intention of making the world's welfare, resided there for preaching of the Bauddha Dharma.

सद्धर्मस्योपदेशाय[51] सभासनं समाश्रयत् ।
भगवन्तं विलोक्यैव मञ्जुश्रियः शुभाश्रमे[52] ॥ १११ ॥

Once he sat in the centre of the courtyard, on the highest seat, to teach the Bauddha Dharma, surrounded by his disciples. The *āśrama* was built by Mañjuśrī, who was also present there.

विहारे वासिनी चूडाभिधानी ब्रह्मचारिणी ।
अर्हन्ती भिक्षुणी भद्रा सद्धर्मगुणवाञ्छिनी ॥ ११२ ॥

In that *āśrama*, was a *bhikkhuṇī*, known as Cūḍā. She was chaste, learned, and always ready to walk the path of welfare. She was a mine of merits and virtues, constantly trying to gain more virtues.

सुप्रसन्ना भक्तिमती[53]काषायचीवरावृता ।
दिव्यपूजोपचाराणि गृहीत्वा श्रद्धयान्विता[54] ॥ ११३ ॥

50 समुपादेष्टुं इति कपाठः ।

51 सधर्म्म समुपादेष्टुं इति कपाठः ।

52 तं दृष्ट्वा तदा तत्र मञ्जुश्रियः समाश्रमे इति गपाठः ।

53 श्रया शुद्धा इति कपाठः ।

54 समादायप्रमोदिता इति कपाठः ।

She was very glad to see Lord Buddha. Thus, clad in her monastic robes, she gathered divine materials for worship and approached the Buddha.

तत्सद्धर्मामृतं पातुं तत्राशु समुपागमत् ।
तदा तत्र महासत्त्वा बोधिसत्त्वा जिनात्मजाः ॥ ११४ ॥

With the intention of worshipping him to gain knowledge and wisdom, she walked towards him, past the *bodhisattva*s and the *mahāsattva*s.

मैत्रेयप्रमुखाः सर्वे तद्धर्मं श्रोतुमागताः ।
अर्हन्तो भिक्षवश्चापि श्रावका ब्रह्मचारिणः ॥ ११५ ॥

Another prominent *bodhisattva* called Maitreya, along with other *bodhisattva*s, *arhant*s, *śrāvaka*s and disciples, was also present.

भिक्षुण्यो ब्रह्मचारिण्यःचैलका व्रतिनोऽपि च ।
त्रिरत्नशरणासीनाश्चोपासका उपासिकाः ॥११६ ॥

Bhikkhu, *brahmacāriṇī*, *brahmacārī*, disciples clad in one cloth and the disciples clad in two pieces of cloths, practitioners of austere vows, and the ones who were in the refuge of Buddha, Dharma and Saṅgha, the laymen and laywomen in service of the Buddha, were all present there.

बुद्धभक्तिरताः सर्वे तद्धर्मश्रोतुमागताः ।
सर्वे ते समुपायातास्तत्र सभासने स्थितम्[55] ॥ ११७ ॥

As Buddha was sat there, his devotees gathered, full of affection and devotion, to gain knowledge.

संबुद्धं तं समालोक्य मुदिताःबोधिमानसाः[56] ।
ते सर्वेऽभ्यर्च्य तं नाथं नत्वा साञ्जलयो मुदा ॥ ११८ ॥

तत्सद्धर्मामृतं पातुं तत्सभायां समागताः[57] ।
ब्रह्मशक्रादयो देवाः सर्वे लोकाधिपा अपि ॥ ११९ ॥

55 श्रितं इति घपाठः ।

56 समुपाचरन् इति गपाठः ।

57 समाश्रयन् इति खपाठः ।

At the sight of Buddha, everyone was filled with devotion and happiness. Everyone worshipped the Buddha, prayed to him with hands joined and was eager to drink the elixir of *dharma*.

Not only humans, divine beings too were present there. Brahma, Indra, gods and the lords of all realms, were present.

ग्रहास्तारागणाश्चापि सिद्धा विद्याधरास्तथा ।
साध्या रुद्राश्च गन्धर्वा यक्षगुह्यककिन्नराः ॥ १२० ॥
दैत्येन्द्रा राक्षसेन्द्रा च नागेन्द्रा गरुडा अपि ।
एवमन्येपि लोकेन्द्राः सर्वे तत्र मुदागताः ॥ १२१ ॥

*Graha*s, *tārā*s, *siddha*, *vidyādhara*, *yakṣya*, *gandharva*, *kinnara*, all sorts of demi-gods, as well of demon-lords, serpents, falcons, lords of worlds, had all come to listen to Buddha's words.

तं मुनीन्द्रं समभ्यर्च्य पौनपुण्येन संस्थिताः[58] ।
हारिती यक्षिणी चापि बोधिसत्त्वानुपालिनी ॥ १२२ ॥

Among the crowd was a demi-goddess named Hāriṇī, who was walking the path of *bodhisattva*, also eager to gain knowledge.

भगवन्तं प्रणम्यैव तत्सभायां समाश्रिता[59] ।
अथ स भगवाञ्छास्ता दृष्ट्वा सर्वान् सभाश्रितान् ॥ १२३ ॥

The demi-goddess approached the Lord, prayed to him and sat down in a corner of the assembly in the courtyard. In that assembly, as everyone was gathered around him

मैत्रेयं समुपामन्त्र्य सम्पश्यन्नेवमब्रवीत्[60] ।
मैत्रेयेमं जगन्नाथं स्वयम्भूवं जिनालयम् ॥ १२४ ॥

The Lord said to Maitreya, whom he invited closer, O Maitreya! Behold! This is Svayambhū, the lord of the world. I am the Buddha, and this is my refuge.

---

[58] सत्वा तत्र समाश्रयन् इति कपाठः ।

[59] समश्रित इति खपाठः ।

[60] विशत् इति कपाठः ।

धर्मधातुं त्रिरत्नाख्यं पश्येत यूयमादरात्।
भजेध्वं श्रद्धया नित्यं गत्वात्र शरणं मुदा ॥ १२५ ॥

And this *caitya* is the *dharmadhātu*. It is ultimate goal of the *tri-ratna*. Serve this *caitya*, seek asylum in it", he said to Maitreya.

बोधिचर्याव्रतं धृत्वा हिताय जगतां सदा[61]।
श्रद्धया ये भजन्त्यत्र शरणं समुपाश्रिताः ॥ १२६ ॥

"The people who, practicing *bodhi*, live in the shadows of the *caitya* would always have welfare and walk the path of knowledge with a fast pace.

बोधिचर्याव्रतं धृत्वा हिताय जगतां सदा।
सर्वे विमुक्तपापास्ते परिशुद्धत्रिमण्डलाः ॥ १२७ ॥

Upon completion of the *bodhi vrata*, the people will be freed of all sins and worldly desires and will be established into the *tri-maṇḍala*.

बोधिसत्त्वा महाभिज्ञा भवेयुः सद्‌गुणाश्रयाः।
भद्रश्रीसुखसम्पन्नाश्चतुर्ब्रह्मविशारदाः ॥ १२८ ॥

The *bodhisattva*s, *mahāsattva*s, and all the learned ones, who worship Svayambhū and Dharmadhātu, shall always have good fortune, welfare and ultimately will reach the highest knowledge and will be established in the four steps of divine knowledge and enlightenment.

सर्वसत्त्वहितोद्युक्ताः संबोधिव्रतधारिणः।
न क्वापि दुर्गतिं यायुः सदा सद्‌गतिसंभवाः ॥ १२९ ॥

For the welfare of all beings, the ones practising the *vrata* of *bodhi* shall never reach a state of doom or despair and are always found in the highest state of being.

त्रिरत्नभजने लग्नाः सद्धर्मसाधनोद्यमाः।
ततःप्रव्रज्यया बुद्धशासने शरणं गताः ॥ १३० ॥

People who are devoted to the service of the *tri-ratna* and to Buddha

---

61 संचरन्ते जगद्धिते इति कपाठः।

Dharma ultimately become *bhikkhu* and *bhikkhuṇī* and come into the jurisdiction of Buddha and attain enlightenment.

ब्रह्मचर्यव्रतं धृत्वा संचरेयुः समाहिताः ।
ततस्ते निर्मलात्मानो निःक्लेशा विजितेन्द्रियाः ॥ १३१ ॥

O *bhikkhus*, go to this Svayambhū, and do the *vrata* of *bodhi*, with purity and chastity, and with focus and concentration, to gain control over your organs; all misery will be destroyed, your mind will be pure.

त्रिविधां बोधिमासाद्य सम्बुद्धपदमाप्नुयुः ।
एवं विज्ञाय ये मर्त्या वाञ्छन्ति सौगतं पदम् ॥ १३२ ॥

The one who serves Svayambhū gets established in *bodhi* and attains Buddhahood; so the people that seek knowledge and Buddhahood must go there.

ते भजन्तु सदात्रैव श्रद्धया शरणाश्रिताः ।
इत्यादिष्टं मुनीन्द्रेण तन्निशम्य सभाश्रिताः ॥ १३३ ॥

And with devotion to the *caitya*, worship and serve the *caitya*.

On hearing such words of the Buddha, everyone present there was astonished.

सर्वे प्रमुदिताः सन्तस्तथा भजितुमीच्छिरे ।
मैत्रेयः स ततो धीमान् बोधिसत्त्वो मुदा ततः[62] ॥ १३४ ॥

Along with surprise, everyone was also pleased, for they were eager to serve the Svayambhū *caitya*. Maitreya, who was also overjoyed by this information, wanted to ask something to Lord Buddha.

समुत्थाय मुनीद्रं तं पुरतः समुपागमत् ।
उद्वहन्नुत्तरासंगं नत्वा तत्र मुनीश्वरम् ॥ १३५ ॥

He rose from his seat, bowed down in front of the Buddha, arranged his robes, and then addressed him.

---

62 हि मोदितः इति गपाठः ।

जानुभ्यां भुवि संधाय साञ्जलिरेवमब्रवीत् ।
भगवन्! नाथ सर्वज्ञ धर्मधातुजिनालयः ॥ १३६ ॥

With his knees on the ground, and hands joined, he spoke "O Lord! O Dharmadhātu Jinālaya! O omniscient one! …

कदायं स्वयमुत्पन्नस्तद् भवान् वक्तुमर्हति[63] ।
इति संप्रार्थिते तेन मैत्रेयेण महात्मना ॥ १३७ ॥

O Buddha! When did the Svayambhū *caitya* originate? Pray tell me." In this way, Maitreya begged for answers.

भगवान्! तं महाभिज्ञं संपश्यन्नेवमादिशत् ।
साधु शृणु समाधाय मैत्रेय त्वं स्वयंभुवः ॥ १३८ ॥

As he asked with respect and reverence, the Lord looked at Maitreya and said "O Maitreya! you have asked a good question. Listen, I shall tell you how it originated.

समुत्पत्तिकथां वक्ष्ये लोकबोधाय साम्प्रतम्[64] ।
पुराभूद् भद्रकल्पेऽत्र विपश्वी नाम सर्ववित् ॥ १३९ ॥

The story is a very amazing and mysterious one and will bring good to the world. A long time ago, during the *bhadrakalpa* (*bhadra* age), there was an omniscient Buddha named Vipasvī.

जगच्छास्ता मुनीन्द्रोऽर्हन् धर्मराजस्तथागतः ।
अशीतिवर्षसाहस्र्यं परमायुर्यदा नृणाम् ॥ १४० ॥

Among all sages the lord of *dharma* was Vipasvī Buddha, he would be the one to bring knowledge to the world. The lifespan of humans was 80,000 years then, so that would give humans freedom to seek knowledge.

तदाहं सत्यधर्माख्यो बोधिसत्त्वोऽभवं किल ।
यदा स भगवाञ्छास्ता बन्धुमत्याः पुराऽन्तिके ॥ १४१ ॥

---

63 तन्समादेष्टुमर्हति इति खपाठः ।

64 सर्वलोकाभिबोधने इति कपाठः ।

I, too, was present in that age. But I was not a Buddha yet, I was a *bodhisattva*, under the Buddha Vipasvī, who would give teachings for the welfare of the world.

विहारे धर्ममादिश्य विजहार ससांघिकः ।
तदाहं तं जगन्नाथमाराध्य समुपस्थितः ॥ १४२ ॥

Once, as he was sitting in the *Vihāra* preaching the *dharma* among the *saṅgha*, I was also present to worship him.

तदात्राभूत् सप्तकोश-व्याससंविस्तरो ह्रदः ।
तदनुशासनं धृत्वा प्राचरं बोधिसम्बरम् ॥ १४३ ॥

There was a large pond there, which was spread in seven *kośa*s and was located near Vipasvī Buddha's residential *āśrama*.

अष्टांग-गुण-सम्पन्नो जलाशयो नगावृतः ।
पद्मोत्पलादि-सौगन्धिनानापुष्पप्रशोभितः ॥ १४४ ॥

The water body, complete with eight virtues, was inhabited by serpents. And it was decorated by lotuses and various other flowers.

हंस-सारस-काडम्ब-प्रमुख-पक्षिमण्डितः ।
तीरोपान्तनगारुह-सर्वर्तु-पुष्पितैर्द्रुमैः ॥ १४५ ॥

In that pond swam swans, ducks, cranes: all the greatest birds of the world. In the bank grew tall and mighty trees that were full of flowers and fruits in all seasons.

फलौषधादिवृक्षैश्च समन्तात् परिमण्डितः ।
मीनकच्छपमण्डूकप्रमुख-जलवासिनाम् ॥ १४६ ॥

There were fruits, and medicinal trees in abundance nearby. Fishes, turtles, frogs were all present in the water.

जन्तूनां निलयोऽगाधः सर्वनाथाधिपालयः ।
तत्र सर्पाहिराजेन्द्रःकर्क्कोदकाभिधो महान् ॥ १४७ ॥

The pond was the residence of different aquatic lives, especially serpents. There existed a great serpent known as Karkaṭa, king of all serpents.

एवं तदा महत् तीर्थं पुण्यामृताश्रयो बभौ ।
सदा ते त्रिदशाःसार्धमप्सरोभिःप्रमोदिताः ॥ १४८ ॥

That was the holiest spot, full of merit. All men, gods, and even *apsaras*es (celestial nymphs) seeking *dharma* visited.

स्नात्वा संक्रीडमानाः सत्सौख्यं भुक्त्वा दिवं ययुः ।
तथा ब्रह्मादयः सर्वे महर्षयस्तपस्विनः ॥ १४९ ॥

Many sages, gods, men came to the place, meditated, prayed, chanted the sacred hymns, bathed in the holy waters, and, with realization of purity and happiness, returned to their homes. Even Brahmā and Indra came occasionally, to gain absolute purity.

स्नात्वा संध्यादिकं कर्म कृत्वा संसेविरे सदा ।
एवं लोकाधिपाश्चापि स्नात्वात्र सर्वदा मुदा ॥ १५० ॥

People bathed, performed the evening and morning rituals; in this way, the great lords of the world came there to rinse off their sins and gain holiness.

स्वे स्वे कुले समभ्यर्च्य महोत्साहैर्निसेविरे ।
एवमन्येपि लोकाश्च व्रतिनो ब्रह्मचारिणः ॥ १५१ ॥

Those who were the greatest among their kin came there with enthusiasm to bathe and serve and worship the great pond.

स्नात्वात्र संबरं धृत्वा पूतात्मानो दिवं ययुः ।
बोधिसत्त्वाः तथानैके स्नानदानव्रतं मुदा ॥ १५२ ॥

Having bathed and purified themselves there, some people reached the heavens, others became *bodhisattva*s, and many people donated lavishly, or fulfilled their *vrata* and went back with a purified soul for the welfare of the world.

कृत्वात्र विमलात्मानो लोकहिताय चागमन्[65] ।
एवं सर्वैर्मुनीन्द्रैश्च स्नानव्रतादि यत् फलम् ॥ १५३ ॥

---

65 समाचरञ्जगद्धिते इति कपाठः ।

All these sages, having received the ultimate fruit of ablution and devotion, went on with their lives.

महत्पुण्यतरं श्रेष्ठमाख्यातं बोधिसाधनम् ।
यत्र स्नात्वा त्रिरत्नानां शरणे समुपागताः ॥ १५४ ॥

That land was the greatest land for earning merit, and paramount for attaining *bodhi*. Bathing there, and gaining refuge in Buddha, Dhamma and Saṅgha, freed men of their worldly attachments and led them to *nirvāṇa*.

बोधिचर्याव्रतं धृत्वा जगद्धिताय तेऽगमन्[66] ।
त आशु विमलात्मानो भद्रश्रीसद्गुणान्विताः ॥ १५५ ॥

Having fulfilled the *bodhicaryā vrata*, they would spread everywhere for the welfare of the world. They would be filled with all purity and virtues.

बोधिसत्त्वाःमहासत्त्वा अभूवन्[67] सुगतात्मजाः ।
केचिन्निक्लेशितात्मानो भवकार्ये[68] च निस्पृहाः ॥ १५६ ॥

*Bodhisattva*s, *mahāsattva*s and disciples of Buddha would all be freed of their misery and their attachments would get dissociated from the mortal realm.

श्रावका बोधिमासाद्य बभूवुर्ब्रह्मचारिणः ।
केचिच्च निर्मलात्मानो संसारे विरतास्तथा ॥ १५७ ॥

The *śrāvaka*s (minor disciples) then became *bodhisattva*s and for some, their worldly attachments were over.

प्रत्येकबोधिमासाद्य सुनिर्वृतिं समाययुः ।
केचित् संबोधिचित्तं च प्राप्य सद्धर्मलालसाः ॥ १५८ ॥

*Pratyekabuddha*s (a lower stage of Buddhahood) also then attained a higher stage of Buddhahood and thus reached the path of

66 प्राचरन्त जगद्धिते इति कपाठः ।

67 अभूवन् इति घपाठः ।

68 भवसंचारे इति खपाठः ।

enlightenment and *nirvāṇa*. While some people reached *bodhicitta*, some gratified their lives and others gained *dharma*.

बोधिचर्याव्रतं धृत्वा हिताय जगतां ययुः ।
केचित्तु सर्वतो भुक्त्वा दिव्यकायसुखान्यपि ॥ १५९ ॥

Some people practised *bodhicaryā* and travelled the world for its welfare through promotion of the *dharma*. Others, having fulfilled their service, were able to achieve divine bliss.

सद्धर्मगुणसंरक्ताःप्राचरन् सर्वदा शुभे ।
केचित् सर्वे महीपालाः सुनीति–धर्मचारिणः ॥ १६० ॥

Desiring to understand the quality and the merits of Bauddha Dharma, many people from far and wide travelled to that place. Kings, pilgrims, diplomats, everyone went to that place.

कृत्वा सत्त्वहितं कर्म ययुरन्ते निजालयम् ।
अहमपि तदा तत्र स्नात्वाचरं व्रतं मुदा[69] ॥ १६१ ॥

A desire for welfare of the world grew in the hearts of anyone who went there. In that trend, I too went to that sacred place and practised the *vrata*. O Mahāmati! listen:

एतत्पुण्यविशुद्धात्मा द्रुतं सम्बोधिमाप्तवान् ।
यैश्चाप्यस्य जलं पीतं तेऽपि निर्मुक्तपातकाः ॥ १६२ ॥

Having been to that pure land, hearts are purified. Mine was as well. As for the ones who drink water from the divine pond, their sins are all washed away.

परिशुद्धाशया भद्रा बभूबुर्बोधिभागिनः ।
एवमेदद् महातीर्थं सर्वैरपिमुनीश्वरैः ॥ १६३ ॥

Everyone who goes there definitely gains knowledge and welfare. It is the ultimate pilgrimage, served by all sages and men.

समधिष्ठापितं नूनं प्रशंसितं महीतले ।
तत्र पश्चात् स्वयं धर्मधातुरुत्पत्स्यते ध्रुवम् ॥ १६४ ॥

---

69 सदा इति कपाठः ।

That place is still intact to this day. It is the most lauded spot on this earth. And in that very spot, will arise the Dharmadhātu;" said the Vipasvī Buddha.

इत्यादिश्य मुनीन्द्रोऽसौ भूयोऽपि चैवमादिशत्।
तदा तत्र समुपन्ने धर्मधातौ जिनालये ॥ १६५ ॥

Having given this knowledge to everyone, the Vipasvī Buddha further told us that when the Dharmadhātu originated there, it would be the supreme pilgrimage for everyone, and all would travel there with a desire to have a glimpse of it.

निरुत्पातं शुभोत्साहं प्रवर्तिष्यति सर्वदा।
सर्वे लोकाश्च तं दृष्ट्वा धर्मधातुं स्वयम्भूवम् ॥ १६६ ॥

After the origin of the Dharmadhātu, all obstacles would be destroyed, everything would be auspicious, realms would be happy, and finally the entire world would shower in welfare.

श्रद्धया शरणं गत्वा प्रभजिष्यन्ति सर्वदा।
तदेतत्पुण्यलिप्तास्ते सर्वे लोकाःशुभेन्द्रियाः ॥ १६७ ॥

The person who, with devotion, lived there and worshipped the shrine would be subject to merit; his organs would be pacified and he would be led to bliss.

भद्रश्रीसत्सुखं भुक्त्वा यास्यन्त्यन्ते जिनालयम्।
इत्यादिष्टं मुनीन्द्रेण विपश्विना निशम्यते ॥ १६८ ॥

He shall feel happiness and welfare there, and ultimately reach the realm of the *buddhas*." This is what the Vipasvī Buddha preached to the assembly, where I was present.

सर्वे सभागता लोकाः प्राभ्यनन्दन् प्रबोधिताः।
इति विपश्विना शास्ता समादिष्टं श्रुतं मया ॥ १६९ ॥

Everyone present in the assembly stood up in reverence to the Vipasvī Buddha and thanked him for his great teaching.

तथा युष्मत्प्रबोधार्थं समाख्यातं प्रबुद्ध्यताम् ।
इत्यादिष्टं मुनीन्द्रेण श्रीघनेन निशम्यते ॥ १७० ॥

मैत्रेयादि-सभालोकाः सर्वेऽपि संप्रसेदिरे ।
[70]भगवद्भासितं श्रुत्वा प्रानमन् सुगतं हि ते ॥ १७१ ॥

And thus, O Maitreya! I have given you the knowledge that I once received. Having heard this, every being present there bowed to the Lord.

॥ इति श्रीस्वयम्भूधर्मधातुसमुत्पत्तिनिदानकथायां प्रथमोऽध्यायः सम्पूर्णः ॥

And thus, the first chapter on the origin of Svayambhū ends.

70 नास्तिपाठः इति खपाठः ।

अथ द्वितीयोऽध्यायः
(Dvitīya Adhyāya)

Practising the Worship of Svayambhū

अथ श्रीमान् महासत्त्वो मैत्रेयः स जिनात्मजः ।
भगवन्तं पुनर्नत्वा साञ्जलिरेवमब्रवीत् ॥ १ ॥

Maitreya, the *mahāsattva* son of Buddha, again, with hands joined in reverence, started to thus address the Buddha.

भगवञ्छ्रोतुमिच्छामि स्वयम्भूत्पत्तिसत्कथाम् ।
तद्भवान्समुपाख्यातुं लोकानां बोधिप्राप्तये[1] ॥ २ ॥

"O Lord! I seek to hear the story, the greatest story of all, which shall bring good into the world. I want to hear the story of the origin of Svayambhū."

इति संप्रार्थितं तेन मैत्रेयेण सुधीमता ।
भगवान् तान् सभालोकान् सम्पश्यन्नेवमब्रवीत्[2] ॥ ३ ॥

While the wise Maitreya thus prayed to him, the Lord, looking at the members seated in the assembly, said:

साधु मैत्रेय सर्वेऽपि सभालोकाः समादरात् ।
शृणुत संप्रवक्ष्यामि स्वयम्भूत्पत्तिसत्कथाम् ॥ ४ ॥

"O Maitreya! your curiosity is commendable. The entire audience, of all the realms, the members seated in this assembly, I ask all of you to listen carefully to this story, with reverence and with respect.

---

1 संप्रबोधने इति कपाठः ।

2 दिशत् इति कपाठः ।

तद्यथा निर्वृतिं याते विपश्विनि मुनीश्वरे।
चिरकालान्तरेणात्र जगच्छास्ताऽभवत् पुनः ॥ ५ ॥

TheVipasvī Buddha, who lived in those ages, liberated himself from the realm of death. Only after a long period of time, another Buddha originated to rule the knowledge in the world.

शिखी नाम मुनीन्द्रोऽर्हन् धर्मराजस्तथागतः।
सर्वज्ञः सुगतः सर्वविद्याधिपो विनायकः ॥ ६ ॥

The Śikhī Buddha was his successor; he was the king of all sages, king of *dharma*, the *tathāgata*, omniscient, master of all knowledge, filled with humility and magnificence.

तदा सप्ततिवर्षाणां सहस्रायुर्नृणामभूत्।
अहं क्षेमकरो नाम बोधिसत्त्वोऽभवं किल ॥ ७ ॥

During those times, the lifespan of men was 70,000 years. It was in that period when I was born as the *bodhisattva* named Kṣemakara.

यदा स भगवाञ्छास्ता शिखीधर्माधिपो जिनः।
अरुणाख्यपुरोपान्ते व्यहरत् सौगताश्रमे ॥ ८ ॥

The Buddha named Śikhī was the teacher of the highest *dharma*. He lived in his *āśrama* in the outskirts of a city named *Aruṇā*.

तदा सर्वे महासत्त्वा बोधिसत्त्वा जिनात्मजाः।
शिखिनस्तस्य वै शास्तुःप्राभजन् समुपस्थिताः।
अहमपि तथा तस्य शिखिनस्त्रिजगद्गुरोः ॥ ९ ॥

In that age, all *bodhisattva*s, *mahāsattva*s, disciples of Buddha, were gathered near his *āśrama*. I was among the gathered crowd, turning to the Śikhī Buddha.

शरणे समुपस्थाय प्राभजं सर्वदा मुदा।
तत्रैकसमये सोऽर्हन् भगवान् सर्वविच्छिखी ॥ १० ॥

सद्धर्मस्योपदेशाय सभासने समाश्रयत्।
तद्वीक्ष्य भिक्षवः सर्वे श्रावका ब्रह्मचारिणः ॥ ११ ॥

In his refuge, I served him most gladly. During my time of service, the omniscient Śikhī Buddha decided to give *upadeśa* to us.

In his heart, he had a wish to preach the Buddha Dharma, and so he seated at the heart of the assembly; as the *bhikkhus*, *śrāvakas* and disciples all gathered around him.

भिक्षुण्यो व्रतिनः सर्वे उपासका उपासिकाः ।
तत्सद्धर्मामृतं पातुं समागत्य च तं मुनिम् ॥ १२ ॥

Bhikṣuṇī, vrata holders, laymen, laywomen, everyone came closer to the Śikhī Buddha eager to drink the elixir of the good *dharma.*

नत्वा साञ्जलयस्तत्र परिवृत्य समाश्रयन् ।
तदा ब्रह्मामरेन्द्रादि-त्रिदशाश्च समागताः ॥ १३ ॥

There, everyone bowed to the Buddha, from all directions. Among the crowd encircling him were Brahmā, Indra and the other gods.

सर्वे लोकाधिपाश्चापि धर्मं श्रोतुं ययुर्मुदा[3] ।
सिद्धा विद्याधराः साध्या यक्ष-गन्धर्व-किन्नराः ॥ १४ ॥

The lords of all realms had arrived to drink the elixir of Buddha's wisdom. Among them were demi-gods like *yakṣa, gandharva, kinnara, vidyādhara, sādhya.*

गरुडा राक्षसेन्द्राश्च दैत्या नागाधिपा अपि ।
ऋषयो ब्राह्मणाश्चापि तीर्थिकाश्च तपस्विनः ॥ १५ ॥

Mythical falcons, demon-lords, *daityas*, serpent-lords, sages, brāhmaṇas, Vedic brāhmaṇas and meditators, were all present.

यतयो योगिनश्चापि निर्ग्रन्थाश्च दिगम्वराः ।
राजानो क्षत्रिया वैश्या अमात्या मन्त्रिणो जनाः ॥ १६ ॥

Yogī, *digambaras* (of the Jaina community), kings, kṣatriyas, vaiśyas, ministers and the public were also present.

---

[3] समागताः इति खपाठः ।

शिल्पिनो वणिजः सार्थवाहादयो महाजनाः ।
पौरा जानपदा ग्राम्यास्तथान्यदेशवासिनः ॥ १७ ॥

Carpenters, merchants, businessmen, city folk, villagers, foreigners and everyone else, also gathered around the Buddha.

तत्सद्धर्मामृतं पातुं संहर्षिताः समागताः ।
तत्र ते समुपागत्य समीक्ष्य तं मुनीश्वरम् ॥ १८ ॥

The mass, full of joy, approached him, bowed to him, and sat around him in the anticipation of the divine elixir that was the Buddha Dharma.

यथाक्रमं समभ्यर्च्य कृत्वा चापि प्रदक्षिणाम् ।
कृत्वाञ्जलिपुटा नत्वा परिवृत्य समन्ततः ॥ १९ ॥

The Buddha was subjected to the ultimate respect from the mass; with reverence, worship, bows and such.

पुरस्कृत्य समुद्वीक्ष्य समादरादुपाश्रयन् ।
तान् सर्वान् समुपासीनान् दृष्ट्वा स भगवाञ्छिखी ॥ २० ॥

The crowd gathered around the Śikhī Buddha in all cardinal directions; the front, the back, the left, the right, with hands joined in devotion, as he looked at them and spoke:

आदिमध्यान्तकल्याणं सद्धर्मं समुपादिशत् ।
तत्सद्धर्मामृतं पीत्वा सर्वे लोकाःप्रबोधिताः ॥ २१ ॥

I would like to preach the path of *dharma* that brings initial, intermediate and the ultimate welfare to all. Having drunk the elixir of the greatest *dharma*, you all shall rise beyond your mortal attachments and mental turmoil induced by them.

सद्धर्मसाधनोद्युक्ता बभूवुर्बोधिभागिनः ।
तस्मिन् हि समये तत्र पुण्यजलाश्रये ह्रदे ॥ २२ ॥

With the practice of the highest *dharma*, many people become enlightened." In the meantime, at the lake of pious waters….

मणिनालं महद्दीप्तिहीरकेशरमुत्तमम् ।
पंचरत्नमयं दीव्यसरोजराजकर्णिकम् ॥ २३ ॥

प्रादुर्भूतं महापद्मं सहस्रदलकाशितम् ।
तस्य रत्नसरोजस्य कर्णिकामध्यमण्डले ॥ २४ ॥

श्रीस्वयम्भूसमुत्पनो धर्मधातुर्जिनालयः ।
एकहस्तप्रमाणांशः शुभ्ररत्नमयोज्वलः ॥ २५ ॥

A lotus, brilliant, radiant with the sparkle of a diamond, filled with the five gems and divine, arose.

The great lotus was of a thousand petals; with its centre being the Dharmadhātu – the residence of the Buddha, the embodiment of all knowledge of the *buddha*s. The Dharmadhātu was a feet tall, and filled with gems and diamonds, and the dazzle of the gems illuminated the entire area.

सम्बोधिश्रीगुणाधारः सर्वलक्षणमण्डितः ।
ज्योतिरूपो जगज्ज्येष्ठः पंचतथागताश्रयः ॥ २६ ॥

The Dharmadhātu was the epitome of all knowledge, all virtues and merits. It was the embodiment of energy. And it was the residence of the five *buddha*s.

जगदीशो जगन्वन्द्यो जगत्पूज्यो जगत्प्रभुः ।
अनादिनिधनोऽजीर्णो मान्यः सर्वशुभार्थभृत् ॥ २७ ॥

The Dharmadhātu was the Lord of the world; it was worthy of reverence from the entire world; it was worthy of worship; it did not have a beginning or an end, it was unaffected by senescence; it was respected by the whole world; it was the assimilation of all that was auspicious.

समन्तभद्ररूपोऽग्रः श्रेष्ठः सद्धर्मरत्नभृत् ।
त्रैलोक्य-सद्गुणाधीशश्चतुर्वर्ग-फलप्रदः ॥ २८ ॥

It would bring welfare to all; and was superior to all. It was jewel of *dharma*, and contained the virtues of all three realms. It gave the bliss of *dharma*, *artha* (wealth), *kāma* (desire) and *mokṣa* (liberation) all at once.

तस्मिंश्चैत्ये समुत्पन्ने साब्धिनगा समन्ततः[4] ।
[5]चचाल वसुधा नूनं चैत्योत्पत्तिप्रभावतः ॥ २९ ॥

दिव्यसुगन्धपुष्पाणि संनिपेतुः सुरालयात् ।
सुरन्दुन्दुभयो नेदुःदिशः सर्वाः प्रसेदिरे ॥ ३० ॥

Flowers of divine aroma were started to appear around it as there was a shower of flowers from the heaven. Celestial music started to echo through the entire universe, alerting it of the appearance of the Dharmadhātu.

वह्नयो दक्षिणावर्ता भद्राभाः संप्रजज्जलुः ।
सुशीतला गन्धवहा[6]धीरं ववुः समीरणाः ॥ ३१ ॥

With this appearance flames started to dance on its right.

Kalyāṇa was heard everywhere.

Everyone was quiet. The winds were cool, gentle and fragrant. There was a divine scent in the air, which alerted everyone of the divine incident.

ववर्षुः तत्र चाम्बूनि मेघ गम्भीरनिश्वनाः ।
ग्रह–तारेन्दुचन्द्राभाः सभासिता विरेजिरे ॥ ३२ ॥

The gods showered it with waters from the celestial river. The clouds chanted a solemn melody of reverence, and in its bliss, released rain. The planets, moon and stars shone brighter than ever.

स्तुतिमङ्गलसंगीतिशब्दा व्योम्नि प्रचेदिरे ।
सर्वत्रापि सुमाङ्गल्यमहोत्साहं निरन्तरम् ॥ ३३ ॥

Words, hymns and melodies echoed through the skies; auspiciousness floated everywhere.

---

4 रसाचलत् इति गपाठः ।

5 नास्तिपाठः इति ग पुस्तके ।

6 सुगन्ध्याद्या इति गपाठः ।

सुभिक्षं श्रीगुणाधारं सद्धर्मभद्रसाधनम्।
निरुत्पातं शुभाचारं प्रावर्तत समन्ततः ॥ ३४ ॥

Fertility spread through the soil; the rains were perfect; grains grew in plenty, harvests were good. And along with crops, good qualities and virtues grew in the ground. *Dharma* was practised by everyone; there were no strife, no evil and no mishaps.

तमेवं स्वयमुत्पन्नं धर्मधातुं जिनालयम्।
समीक्ष्येशादयः सर्वे आरुप्यभुवनाश्रिताः ॥ ३५ ॥

Lords from all over the universe were surprised at the rise of self-originated Dharmadhātu, which was the residence of Buddha.

योग-ध्यान-महानन्द-सौख्येऽपि विरतोत्सवाः।
स्वयम्भूवं तमीशानं वन्दितुं समुपाचरन्॥ ३६ ॥

Even the ones who were in a state of meditation, the ones in a state of pleasure, the ones in a state of celebration, all stopped what they were doing and came to catch a glimpse of the Dharmadhātu.

तथा ब्रह्मादयः सर्वे मुनयो ब्रह्मचारिणः।
एवं स्वयम्भुवं द्रष्टुं मुदिताः समुपाचरन्॥ ३७ ॥

Brahmā, the creator of the universe, arrived; and so did the other gods, sages, *brahmacārī*s and maidens; and all those who came experienced divine ecstasy.

एवं शक्रादयः सर्वे त्रिदशाः साप्सरोगणाः।
पूजाङ्गानि समादाय द्रष्टुमेनं मुदाययुः ॥ ३८ ॥

Indra, the king of heaven, landed; followed by his entourage of gods and demi-gods and heavenly nymphs; and they did not come empty handed. They came prepared, with worship materials in their hands. And when they worshipped the Dharmadhātu, they felt divine gratification.

तथाग्नि-धर्मराजोऽपि नैऋतो वरुणो मरुत्।
श्रीदो भूताधिपश्चैव सर्वे लोकाधिपा अपि॥ ३९ ॥

Similarly, the god of fire, the god of death, the god of wind, the god of wealth, the god of time, and lords of all realms paid a visit.

स्वस्वपरिजनैः सार्द्धं महोत्साहैः प्रमोदिताः ।
एवं स्वयम्भुवं चैत्यं संद्रष्टुं समुपाययुः ॥ ४० ॥

The visitors did not come alone. They came with their kins. Some came with their wives, some with their husbands, and all with joyous hearts, avid to see the Dharmadhātu.

धृतराष्ट्रो महाराजो गन्धर्वैः सह मोदितः ।
संगीतिवादनोत्साहैः स चैनं द्रष्टुमाययौ ॥ ४१ ॥

King of the *gandharvas* realm, Dhr̥tarāṣṭra, came with his group of *gandharva* demi-gods, and brought with him a festival of music and melodies, only to catch a glimpse of the Svayambhū.

विरुढको महाराजःकुम्भाण्डसहितो मुदा ।
स्वयम्भुवं तमालोक्य मुदा वन्दितुमाययौ ॥ ४२ ॥

The king of Viruḍha came with Kumbhāṇḍa, and having worshipped Svayambhū, achieved absolute joy and bliss.

विरुपाक्षोऽपिनागेन्द्रैः सर्वैर्नागाधिपैः सह ।
रत्नपूजोपहाराणि धृत्वैनं द्रष्टुमाययौ ॥ ४३ ॥

King Virupākṣa also arrived, and brought with him serpents and serpent-lords, who brought with them gems and crystals, and worshipped the Svayambhū.

कुवेरो यक्षराजोऽपि यक्षिणीभिः समन्वितः
नानाद्रव्योपहाराणि धृत्वैनं द्रष्टुमाययौ ॥ ४४ ॥

Lord Kubera, king of all wealth and *yakṣa* demi-gods, arrived, accompanied by a group of *yakṣiṇīs*, with many materialistic offerings for the Svayambhū.

वज्रपाणिश्च गुह्येन्द्र–सर्वगुह्यक–संयुतः ।
दिव्यभोग्योपहाराणि धृत्वैनं द्रष्टुमाययौ ॥ ४५ ॥

Lord Vajrapāṇi himself came. So did Lord Guhyendra, who came with demi-gods and demi-goddesses, with divine gifts of pleasure as offerings to the Svayambhū.

द्रुमःकिन्नरराजोऽपि सर्वैः सह हयाननैः ।
तूर्यसंघोषणोत्साहैः सहैनं द्रष्टुमाययौ ॥ ४६ ॥

Druma, king of semi-gods, came with his servants, and played the *tūrya* instrument, whose melody brought pleasure to everyone's ears.

तथा सर्वार्थसिद्धाख्यः सर्वविद्याधराधिपः[7] ।
दिव्यपूजोपहाराणि धृत्वैनं द्रष्टुमाययौ ॥ ४७ ॥

Mythical omnipotent demi-gods, and their king Sarvārthasiddha, came with divine offerings, to worshipped the Svayambhū.

गरुडः पक्षिराजोऽपि सर्वैः पक्षिगणैः सह ।
स्व-स्वर्द्धिश्रीमहोत्साहैरेनं संद्रष्टुमाययौ ॥ ४८ ॥

The king of all birds, the divine falcon flew in along with all other birds that brought with them their fortune, joy and glory and sang hymns to the Svayambhū.

एवं सिद्धाश्च साध्याश्च वसवश्च ग्रहा अपि ।
सर्वे तारागणाश्चापि सर्वाश्चाप्सरसोगणाः ॥ ४९ ॥

Siddha, *sādhya* and *vasu* demi-gods all arrived Planets also came, so did the stars and their systems, and groups of celestial nymphs also arrived.

एवं दैत्याधिपाः सर्वे स्व-स्व-परिजनैः सह ।
महासमृद्धिप्रोत्साहैः सहसा समुपाचरन् ॥ ५० ॥

Kings of *daitya*s came, with their kinsmen; and as they did, they saw festivities and celebrations happening.

एवं लोकाधिपाः सर्वे दशदिक्षु व्यवस्थिताः[8] ।
दृष्ट्वा तं स्वयमुत्पन्नं वन्दितुं सहसाचरन्[9] ॥ ५१ ॥

---

[7] धरानृपाः इति खपाठः ।

[8] अव्यवस्थिताः इति कपाठः ।

[9] सहसैवेतितत् इति खपाठः ।

Lords of the world, who would be informed of all that occurred in all directions, also came. As they caught a glimpse of the Svayambhū, they experienced divine pleasure.

सर्वेऽपि ते समागत्य दृष्ट्वा तं जगदीश्वरम् ।
संहर्षिताशया दूरात् प्रणम्य समुपाचरन् ॥ ५२ ॥

Everyone else who came to see the Dharmadhātu had their desires satisfied; even a glimpse from afar gave them fulfilment.

ततस्ते श्रीजगन्नाथं सर्वेऽभ्यर्च्य यथाक्रमम् ।
अष्टांगैः प्रणितिं कृत्वा प्राभजन्त समादरात् ॥ ५३ ॥

All, who arrived, worshipped the Svayambhū taking turns, bowed down in eight positions, and sat down nearby with devotion.

केचिद्दिव्यसुगन्धैस्तं प्राभिलिप्याभजन् मुदा ।
केचिन्नानाविधैः पुष्पैः केचिद्धूपैर्मनोहरैः ॥ ५४ ॥

Some persons worshipped the Svayambhū with scented incense, some applied fragrant lotions on his body, and some adorned the Svayambhū with flowers.

केचिच्च पुष्पमालाभिः केचिच्च दिव्यचीवरैः ।
केचिच्च दीपमालाभिः केचिदारतिदीपनैः ॥ ५५ ॥

Some people offered divine garlands, some clad him in divine *cīvara*, some lit candles all around the Svayambhū and some even performed the *āratī*.

केचिद्दिव्यामृतैर्भोग्यैः केचिद्दिव्यौषधैरपि ।
केचिन्नानाविधैर्दिव्यरत्नालंकारभूषणैः ॥ ५६ ॥

Some offered nectar, others offered him divine ambrosia, some offered multitudes of jewellery and gems.

केचिच्छत्रध्वजैर्वलिव्यजनैश्च वितानकैः ।
केचित् संगीतिसंवाद्यैर्मृदङ्गमुरजादिभिः ॥ ५७ ॥

Some offered umbrellas to give him shade; some offered fans and fanned him with gentle winds. Some used drums and flutes to please the Lord Svayambhū with their melodies.

केचित् तौर्यत्रिकैर्वंशैः शंखैः शृङ्गैश्च केचन ।
काहारैश्च तथा केचित् वीणादिततवादनैः ॥ ५८ ॥

Some people played ancient instruments, some played medieval wooden instruments, some blew conch shells and some blew horns as trumpets. Some played different other instruments, some played the stringed instruments. In this way, everyone played to please the Svayambhū.

तालादिघनवाद्यैश्च भेर्यानकविमर्दलैः ।
तथा नानाविधैर्मड्डुर्डिण्डिम-झर्झरादिभिः ॥ ५९ ॥

Some clapped their hands, some played instruments that sounded like the thunder, some played the *ḍamaru*, some played the *bherī* instrument. Everyone played the instruments they were well versed with, in order to please the Svayambhū.

केचिन्नृत्यैश्च गीतैश्च हाहाकारैश्च केचन ।
एवं नानाविधोत्साहैः प्राभजन्त जिनालयम् ॥ ६० ॥

Some people danced, some sang. Some prayed with words, some chanted hymns. Everyone was intent on pleasing the Svayambhū.

केचित् प्रदक्षिणान्येव कृत्वाऽभजन् सहस्रशः ।
केचिच्च धारणीविद्या-जपस्तोत्रादिभिर्मुदा ॥ ६१ ॥

Some people walked in clockwise direction, thousands of times, around the Svayambhū. Some chanted the Dhāraṇī *mantra*s, others chanted *stotra*s to please the Lord.

एवं नानाप्रकारैस्ते सर्वे लोका द्विजादयः[10] ।
श्रद्धया समुपाश्रित्य प्राभजन् तं स्वयम्भुवम् ॥ ६२ ॥

In their own different ways, even the brāhmaṇas, kṣatriyas (warrior

---

[10] रसाचलत् इति गपाठः ।

race) and vaiśyas (merchant race), with full devotion, worshipped the Svayambhū.

एतद्दिव्यमहोत्साहैः संप्रवृत्तिं प्रसारिताम् ।
श्रुत्वा सर्वे सभालोका विस्मयं समुपाययुः ॥६३ ॥

It was a divine festival, the word of which travelled far and wide. The men of the world were astonished by the news of such a great occurrence.

तत् समीक्ष्य महासत्त्वो रत्नपाणिः पुरःस्थितः[11] ।
शिखिनं तं मुनिं नत्वा साञ्जलिरेवमब्रवीत् ॥ ६४ ॥

In Śikhī Buddha's ongoing court, the Ratnapāṇi Buddha also heard. He stood up, joined his hands, and addressed the Lord.

भगवन् या मही सर्वा कम्पिता दिव्यमुत्सवम् ।
प्रसारितं च कस्येदं कारणं कृपया वद[12] ॥ ६५ ॥

"O Lord! the entire planet is vibrating with the waves of celebration that are spreading. What happened? How did it come to occur? Pray tell me."

इति संप्रार्थितं तेन सुधिया रत्नपाणिना ।
स शिखी भगवान् पश्यन् रत्नपाणिं तमब्रवीत् ॥ ६६ ॥

After the wise Ratnapāṇi thus prayed to the Lord, the Lord Śikhī Buddha addressed the scholar and replied:

साधु शृणु महासत्त्व यत् सर्वा चलिता मही ।
दिव्योत्साहैः प्रवृत्तं च तद्धेतुः संनिगद्यते ॥ ६७ ॥

"O Ratnapāṇi! you have asked a good question. Listen carefully, the reason for the vibration of the entire world is the worship of the Svayambhū with divine enthusiasm.

तद्यथात्रास्ति भूलोक उत्तरस्यां हिमालये ।
अष्टाङ्गगुणसम्पन्नपुण्यजलाश्रयोह्रदः ॥ ६८ ॥

---

11 पुरोगतः इति खपाठः ।

12 हेतुं तत् समुपादिशः इति कपाठः ।

Perhaps you know of this. In the northern part of the mortal realm, in the Himalayas, filled with all eight qualities, lies a huge body of water.

तत्र रत्नमये पद्मे सरोजराजकर्णिके[13] ।
स्वयमेव समुत्पन्नो धर्मधातुर्जिनालयः ॥ ६९ ॥

In that very pond filled with jewels and bejewelled lotuses, Dharmadhātu Jinālaya, the home of the Buddha, has originated in itself.

तदुत्पन्ने मही सर्वा रचिता संप्रमोदिता[14] ।
सर्वत्रापि शुभोत्साहं प्रावर्तत भवालये ॥ ७० ॥

As the Svayambhū self-originated, the entire earth is elated. Celebrations have commenced everywhere, the waves of which have shaken the entire world.

तं समीक्ष्य महेशान-ब्रह्मशक्रादयो ऽमराः ।
ग्रहास्ताराश्च सिद्धाश्च साध्या विद्याधरा अपि ॥ ७१ ॥

After seeing it, great and mighty gods like Brahmā, Śiva, Indra, and planets, stars, *siddha*s, *sādhya*s and demi-gods were all ecstatic.

महर्षयश्च सर्वे ऽपि विस्मयेन प्रमोदिताः ।
सर्वे लोकाधिपाश्चापि दैत्या नागाः खगेश्वराः ॥ ७२ ॥

Venerable sages were all gladdened and surprised. Not only them, lords of many realms, birds and serpents, everyone was filled with awe.

यक्ष-किन्नर-गन्धर्व-गुह्यकराक्षसा अपि ।
एतत्प्रभृतयः सर्वे समीक्ष्य तं स्वयंभूवम् ॥७३ ॥

Yakṣa, kinnara, gandharva, guhyaka, were all awestruck, for they understood the magnificence and the might of the Lord Svayambhū.

संहर्षिताः समागत्य प्राभजन्त महोत्सवैः ।
एतत्पूजामहोत्साहसंप्रवृत्तिः प्रसारिता ॥ ७४ ॥

---

13 कम्पिते इति कपाठः ।

14 हर्षते इति कपाठः ।

All of them with divine happiness came to the spot where the Lord Svayambhū originated, and they all partook in the worship of Svayambhū. This is the cause of such loud vibrations in the earth.

एतस्येदं महद्भाग्यनिमित्तं संप्रजायते[15] ।
इत्यादिष्टं मुनीन्द्रेण शिखिना संनिसंम्य सः ॥ ७५ ॥

Thus, when Śikhī Buddha revealed the mystery of these events to Ratnapāṇi, he was also awestruck and filled with wonder.

रत्नपाणिमहासत्त्वः विस्मयाच्च प्रमोदितः ।
सुप्रबुद्धमुखाम्भोजो महासंहर्षिताशयः ॥ ७६ ॥

Ratnapāṇi was instantly filled with joy and happiness at this news, and he became the epitome of happiness. He then entered a state of joyous trance.

भूयस्तं शिखिनं नत्वा साञ्जलिरेवमब्रवीत् ।
भगवन्! तद्विजानीयां यन्मनो मे समीच्छति ॥ ७७ ॥

Again, the Ratnapāṇi, with joined hands, spoke to the Lord. "O Lord! I would like to ask of you the wish in my heart.

तदनुज्ञां प्रदायात्र संप्रसादितुमर्हति ।
अहमपि च शास्तारं[16]स्वयम्भूवं तमीश्वरम् ॥ ७८ ॥

श्रद्धया समुपाश्रित्य प्रभजामि महोत्सवैः ।
इति संप्रार्थिते तेन श्रुत्वा स भगवाञ्छिखी ॥ ७९ ॥

I would like to visit the Svayambhū, and devote myself to him, and chant hymns eagerly to worship him. I ask your permission to depart to see the Svayambhū".

रत्नपाणिं महासत्त्वं संपश्यन्नेवमादिशत् ।
कुलपुत्र प्रयाहि त्वं यद्याशु बोधिमिच्छसि ॥ ८० ॥

As the Ratnapāṇi prayed to the Lord Śikhī, he looked at him and spoke

15 सञ्जातम् इति कपाठः ।

16 जगच्छास्तु इति कपाठः ।

"O Son! you may instantly go that place. If you seek knowledge, it is necessary that you pay a visit to the Svayambhū.

श्रद्धया समुपाश्रित्य प्रभज तं जिनालयम् ।
ये तत्र समुपाश्रित्य भजेयुःश्रद्धया मुदा ॥ ८१ ॥

Go and devote yourself to the Svayambhū. Your devoted worship of the Svayambhū will bring you great welfare.

त आशु प्राप्य संबोधिं सम्बुद्धपदमाप्नुयुः ।
इत्यादिष्टं मुनीन्द्रेण रत्नपाणिर्निशम्य सः[17] ॥ ८२ ॥

Should you worship the Lord, meditate of him, encircle him and pray to him with reverence, you shall receive instant *bodhi*-hood, and all knowledge shall be yours." Hearing the Śikhī Buddha say this, Ratnapāṇi was duly pleased.

साञ्जलिस्तं मुनिं नत्वा मुदितः प्राचरत् ततः ।
ततस्तेन सहानेके बोधिसत्त्वा जिनात्मजाः ॥ ८३ ॥

Having received this permission from his Lord Śikhī Buddha, he prayed to his Lord, encircled him and finally set out for the worship of the Svayambhū. He was then accompanied by many *mahāsattva*s, *bodhisattva*s, and other disciples of Buddha.

श्रावका भिक्षवश्चापि भिक्षुण्यश्चाप्युपासिकाः ।
उपासका भक्तिमन्तो व्रतिनः पुण्यलालसाः ॥ ८४ ॥

In his company were initiates, *bhikkhu*s, *bhikkuṇī*s, laymen and laywomen, devotees of the Svayambhū, the people who desired merit and virtues, who all departed for the Svayambhū.

ऋषयो ब्राह्मणाश्चापि यतयो योगिनोऽपि च ।
तीर्थिकास्तापसाश्चापि निर्ग्रन्था ब्रह्मचारिणः ॥ ८५ ॥

Sages, monks, ascetics, brāhmaṇas, *yogī*s, Vedic followers, Jainas and celibates all accompanied the Ratnapāṇi.

---

17 अवाप्यइति इति कपाठः ।

राजानः क्षत्रिया वैश्या अमात्या मन्त्रिणो जनाः ।
शिल्पिनो वणिजः सार्थवाहाश्चापि महाजनाः ॥ ८६ ॥

Kings, warriors, businessmen courtiers, carpenters, merchants, tradesmen with caravans, and every important person departed for the Svayambhū.

पौरा जानपदा ग्राम्या स्तथान्यदेशवासिनः ।
एवमन्येपि लोकाश्च सद्धर्मगुणलालसाः[18] ॥ ८७ ॥

Townsfolk, villagers, foreigners, general public, all who desired welfare from the Svayambhū also went.

सर्वे तत्र महोत्साहैस्तेन सार्द्धं मुदाऽचरन् ।
एवं स रत्नपाणिस्तैः सर्वैर्लोकैः समन्वितः ॥ ८८ ॥

Everyone went with great enthusiasm, and walked with joy, led by Ratnapāṇi. The company's journey was filled with great celebration and festivities.

पूजाङ्गानि समादाय महोत्साहैर्मुदाचरन् ।
एवं सप्रवरः श्रीमान् सर्वान् लोकान् विनोदयन् ॥ ८९ ॥

All had carried worship materials in their hands, and enthusiasm in their hearts. They had offerings of their capacities with them, to offer to the Lord Svayambhū.

As they went, they also encouraged the bystanders to journey to the Svayambhū along with them.

सहसा तत्र प्रागत्य ददर्शेमं जिनालयम् ।
दृष्ट्वैनं स महासत्त्वः मुदितः समुपागमत्[19] ॥ ९० ॥

As they reached the Svayambhū, they saw the *jinālaya* (home of the Buddha). A glimpse of the Svayambhū led them to commence further worship.

---

18 वाञ्छिनः इति कपाठः ।

19 सरन् इति कपाठः ।

यथाविधि समभ्यर्च्य प्रणम्य प्राभजन्मुदा ।
एवं सर्वेऽपि ते लोकाः सहायाः पूजनेऽभवन्[20] ॥ ९१ ॥

They worshipped the Svayambhū procedurally, and bowed down to him. To guide them through their worship procedure, sages were already present on the spot.

यथाविधि समभ्यर्च्य महोत्साहैर्मुदाभजन् ।
एवं ते सकला लोकाः स्तुत्वा जप्त्वा च धारणीम् ॥ ९२ ॥

They gradually chanted hymns for the Svayambhū, and indulged in worship through chanting of his names, bowing down, prayers, Dhāraṇī *mantra*, with lots of enthusiasm.

प्रदक्षिणाः तु कृत्वाष्टौ प्रणम्य प्राभजन् मुदा ।
एवमन्ये महासत्त्वा बोधिसत्त्वा जिनात्मजाः ॥ ९३ ॥

Everyone did revolutions around the Svayambhū in eight ways, while they saluted the Svayambhū with folded hands. In this way, *bodhisattva*s and *mahāsattva*s all took part in the worship.

दशदिग्भ्यः समागत्य प्राभजन्जिनमीश्वरम् ।
अहमपि तदा तेन समेत्य रत्नपाणिना ॥ ९४ ॥

As a part of Ratnapāṇi's company, I witnessed everyone worshipping the Svayambhū from all ten directions", said Buddha to Maitreya.

श्रद्धया समुपाश्रित्य मुदा प्राभजमीश्वरम् ।
एतत् पुण्यानुभावेन बोधिं प्राप्य कलावपि ॥ ९५ ॥

Although it was the age of evil (Kali age), everyone devotedly worshipping the Svayambhū received merit and the ultimate knowledge.

जीत्वा मारगणान् सर्वान् धर्माधिपोऽभवं तदा ।
य एनं समुपाश्रित्य भजेयुःश्रद्धया मुदा ॥ ९६ ॥

My prayers helped me emerge victorious against my bodily

20 तस्यमहर्षयः इति खपाठः ।

desires (*māra*). That is the common destiny of all who worship the Svayambhū.

ते ते सर्वेऽपि संबोधिं प्राप्य स्युः सुगता द्रुतम् ।
एवं महत्तरं पुण्यं सेवासमुद्भवं मतम्[21] ॥ ९७ ॥

All who went received immediate *jñāna* and a large amount of merit. In service of the Svayambhū, everyone experienced divine ecstasy.

भद्रश्रीसद्गुणापन्नं सम्बोधिज्ञानसाधनम् ।
इति सर्वैर्मुनीन्द्रैश्च समाख्यातं समन्ततः ॥ ९८ ॥

An amazing quality of pleasure was seen in everyone present. Similarly, everyone attained knowledge; and this fact was noticed and consequently discussed by the sages, monks and laymen present in the masses gathered around the newly emerged Svayambhū.

यूयमपि परिज्ञाय भजतैनं[22] समादरात् ।
मुनीन्द्रा अपि तत्रैव चतुःसन्ध्यं दिवानिशम् ॥ ९९ ॥

You all too understand and devote yourself to the Lord Svayambhū, as the sages and monks pray in remembrance of the Lord in all four periods of the day, in order to bring welfare to all.

दृष्ट्वा ध्यात्वा स्मृतिं कृत्वा[23]प्राभजन् तं समादरात् ।
भजन्ति साम्प्रतं सर्वे बुद्धाः सर्वदिगाश्रिताः ॥ १०० ॥

The sight of Lord Svayambhū, and his profound meditation, remembrance, devotion, and respectful service, grants instant Buddhahood to all. Such *buddha*s are present today, and will continue to exist in the future.

अनागताश्च सर्वेऽपि भजिष्यन्ति तथा सदा ।
अस्य दर्शनमात्रेण प्रदुष्टा अपि पापिनः ॥ १०१ ॥

---

21 नास्ति इति खपाठः ।

22 भजतास्य इति गपाठः ।

23 धृत्वा इति घपाठः ।

In the future, the sinful and the wicked, who catch of the glimpse of the Svayambhū will be rid of all their sins.

निर्मुक्तपातका ह्याशु भवेयुर्निर्मलेन्द्रियाः ।
ततस्ते निर्मलात्मानो निःक्लेशा ब्रह्मचारिणः ॥ १०२ ॥

Even the highest sinners, those that are doomed to the ultimate punishment, in the mercy of Lord Svayambhū will be removed from their misery; they shall join the path of goodness, purity, merit and chastity.

दुर्गतिं नैव गच्छेयुः कुत्रापि हि कदाचन ।
सङ्गतावेव संजाता भद्रश्रीसद्‌गुणाश्रयाः ॥ १०३ ॥

They shall not have to endure further degradation and misery and would be established into the path of *mokṣa.*

बोधिसत्त्वा महासत्त्वा भवेयुः सुगतात्मजाः ।
ततस्ते बोधिसम्भारं पूरयित्वा यथाक्रमम् ॥ १०४ ॥

Those people will become *bodhisattva*s, *mahāsattva*s, and the disciples of Buddha. They will reach the upper level of knowledge and ultimately become candidates for *mokṣa.*

त्रिविधां बोधिमासाद्य निर्वृतिं पदमाप्नुयुः ।
इति मत्वा सदाप्यस्य कृत्वा दर्शनमादरात् ॥ १०५ ॥

After receiving the three types of knowledge, they will be established into the path of liberation. Thus, the ones who behold, chant and worship Svayambhū shall have no wish unfulfilled.

अनुमोद्याभ्यनुस्मृत्वा ध्यात्वानुभाव्य सर्वदा ।
नामापि च समुच्चार्य श्रद्धया बोधिवाञ्छिभिः ॥ १०६ ॥

The people who want to receive knowledge this way have to remember, revere, worship and sing hymns and even when they are in no state to do so, they should chant his name and remember him with devotion, to bring themselves into the path of knowledge.

यथाशक्ति प्रकर्तव्या भक्तिसेवा सदादरात् ।
इत्यादिष्टं मुनीन्द्रेण श्रीघनेन निशम्यते ॥ १०७ ॥

"Thus, energetic devotion to the Lord Svayambhū should bring you greatness", said the Buddha as he commanded the assembly to devote themselves to the Svayambhū.

मैत्रेयप्रमुखाः सर्वे सभालोकाः प्रबोधिताः ।
तथेत्यभ्यनुमोदन्तो धर्मधातोः स्वयंभुवः[24] ॥ १०८ ॥

Having heard this, the crowd, including Maitreya, had their spirits raised. They expressed their gratitude for the knowledge of the Svayambhū.

श्रद्धया समुपाश्रित्य संभजितुं समीच्छिरे ।
अथ सर्वे सभालोका धर्मधातोः स्वयंभुवः ॥ १०९ ॥

They were quick to devote themselves to the Svayambhū and meditated with remembrance of him in their pleased minds. They wanted to worship and follow the Svayambhū.

पूजाफलविशेषाणि संश्रोतुं पुनरीच्छिरे ।
तन्मत्वा स महासत्त्वो मैत्रेयः सुगतात्मजः ॥ ११० ॥

Maitreya Bodhisattva, having heard all of this, gathered special types of fruits, flowers and materials, with an inherent desire to worship the lord. But he wanted to know about the most appropriate offerings and worship materials to do so.

भगवन्तं मुनीन्द्रं तं प्रार्थयेदेवमानतः ।
भगवन्नस्याःपूजाया विशेषफलविस्तरम् ॥ १११ ॥

"O Lord of all sages! I pray to you. How do we acquire the highest benefits of worship? What is the procedure of Svayambhū worship? And what are the necessary materials for worship?

सर्व इमे सभालोकाःश्रोतुमिच्छन्ति साम्प्रतम् ।
तद् भवान् समुपादिश्य पूजाफलविशेषताम् ॥ ११२ ॥

---

24 स्वयं तदा इति गपाठः ।

The assembled all seek the knowledge of the special procedure of worship, and the benefits of it.

इमान् सर्वान् सभासीनान् संबोधयितुमर्हति[25] ।
इति संप्रार्थितं तेन मैत्रेयेण निशम्य सः ॥ ११३ ॥

Everyone present here wants to know; do grant us this knowledge". Having said this, Maitreya sat down quietly.

भगवान् तान् सभालोकान् सम्पश्यन्नेवमादिशत् ।
शृणुत सकला लोका अस्य पूजाफलं महत् ॥ ११४ ॥

Having heard this, the Lord said to the devout assembly: "Listen carefully, I shall tell you of the extent of the benefits and procedure of this worship."

विशेषेण प्रवक्ष्यामि सर्वेषां बोधनाय वै[26] ।
पञ्चामृतैः सहाम्भोभिः संशोभितसुनिर्मलैः ॥ ११५ ॥

As I tell you, I grant knowledge to the entire world. The use of *pañcāmṛta* is paramount, along with water and flowers. (*Pañcāmṛta* is a concoction of butter, honey, sugar, milk and yogurt, and often described as a form of elixir accessible to mankind.)

ये मुदा स्नापयन्तीमं धर्मधातुं जिनालयम् ।
मन्दाकिन्यां सदा स्नात्वा ते विशुद्धत्रिमण्डलाः ॥ ११६ ॥

The people who happily shower the Dharmadhātu with *pañcāmṛta*, must go on to bathe in the Mandākinī River that flows nearby to achieve immeasurable merit.

दिव्यसुखानि भुंजानः प्रान्ते यान्ति जिनालयम् ।
सुरम्यद्रव्यसंयुक्तं यत्र चैत्ये स्वयंभुवे ॥ ११७ ॥

As a result, they will achieve divine bliss, within and out of this world. Finally, they will reach the dimension of Buddha. Thus, this form of worship of Svayambhū, is certain to grant one the path of liberation.

---

25 ससंबोधेत् इति गपाठः ।

26 लोकाभिबोधने इति कपाठः ।

मोदयन्तो जगच्चित्तं धूपयन्ति मुदा सदा ।
ते सुगंधितसौम्याङ्गा मान्या देवसुरैरपि ॥ ११८ ॥

श्रीमन्तः सुखसंपन्ना भवन्ति रत्नसन्निभाः ।
पंचगन्धैर्मुदा यत्र धर्मधातो जिनालये ॥ ११९ ॥

Such people, full of joy, shall radiate happiness in the outer world. Their bodies become fragrant as a result of the worship. Even gods and demons shall respect such people. They shall acquire riches beyond measure, shall have all the gems and jewels.

In this manner, there is nothing that the worship of Lord Svayambhū with *pañcāmṛta* will not grant them.

लिप्याराध्य समाश्रित्य प्रभजन्ति सदादरात् ।
सप्तरत्नसमेतास्ते भद्रश्रीसद्गुणाश्रयाः ॥ १२० ॥

The ones who with absolute focus do the worship will be filled with jewels and gems; and good virtues and qualities will come into their lives.

सर्वे लोका हितोद्युक्ता भवन्ति क्षितिपाधिपाः[27] ।
ये चात्र मुनिराजेन्द्रा विचित्रचीवराम्बरैः ॥ १२१ ॥

They shall be ready to do the welfare of all. The people who, in their worship, offer the *cīvara* to the Svayambhū shall receive whatever they desire.

प्रवार्य श्रद्धया भक्त्या संभजन्ते समादरात् ।
ते दिव्यभव्य-कौशेय-रत्नाभरणभूषिताः ॥ १२२ ॥

With devotion, the ones who offer silk shall have plenty of silk and all luxury will be theirs.

सुज्ञा धर्माधिपाः सन्तो भवन्ति भद्रचारिणः ।
ये चैवं कुसुमैः सर्वैर्जलैः स्थलगतैरपि ॥ १२३ ॥

If they worship the Lord with terrestrial and aquatic flowers, their lives shall progress into success. They become wealthy, wise and healthy.

27 क्षितीतलाः इति कपाठः ।

अर्चयित्वा समाश्रित्य संभजन्ते प्रमोदिताः ।
महीन्द्रश्रीसमृद्धास्ते शक्राधिपप्रभान्विताः ॥ १२४ ॥

They shall be matched with Indra, the king of the gods, in both influence and prosperity.

भद्रश्रीसुखसंपन्ना भवन्ति बोधिभागिनः ।
ये चैनं पुष्पमालाभी रचिताभिर्मनोहरैः ॥ १२५ ॥

The ones who offer great flowers and garlands shall be subject to boundless happiness.

सर्वपुष्पैः प्रलम्बाभिः शोभयित्वा भजन्ति च ।
भवन्ति श्रीसमृद्धास्ते धर्मकामाः सुराधिपाः ॥ १२६ ॥

The gods who desire great bliss, and offer special garlands to the Svayambhū, shall be granted their wish.

सत्कीर्त्तिगुणसंरक्ताः शुभगा बोधिचारिणः ।
ये च पुष्पाणि सर्वाणि मुदात्र सुगतालये ॥ १२७ ॥

Their fame will spread far and wide. Their actions shall become good. Slowly, they will start pacing on the path of knowledge. Thus, even with the worship through simple flowers, all wishes are granted.

अवकीर्य समाराध्य भजन्ति शरणाश्रिताः ।
तेऽपि देवाधिपा स्वर्गे गता पृथ्व्यां[28] नृपाधिपाः ॥ १२८ ॥

The kings who shower the Svayambhū with flowers and worship with devotion shall be rewarded with extended time in heaven.

महच्छ्रीगुणसम्पन्ना भवन्ति बोधिभागिनः ।
घृतसुगन्धितैलादिसंप्रदीप्तां तमोऽपहाम् ॥ १२९ ॥

The ones who with butter, oil and other fragrant oils light the *dīpa*, shall receive all the worldly happiness and then move on with the ultimate knowledge to the path of liberation.

28 मह्यां इति कपाठः ।

ज्वालयन्ति मुदा येऽस्मिन् धर्मधातौ जिनालये[29] ।
सुदृष्ट्यः सुरूपास्ते ज्ञानदीपतमोपहाः ॥ १३० ॥

The ones who light the *dīpa* around the Dharmadhātu with delight would be granted stronger eyesight, gentler appearance and greater knowledge.

भूपार्चितपदाम्भोजा भवन्ति बोधिभागिनः ।
प्रणीतं सुरसं भोज्यं दीव्यगन्धसमन्वितम् ॥ १३१ ॥

Offering aromatic food to the Svayambhū shall earn men reverence from kings; and they will receive knowledge.

ये चास्मिन्नुपढौकित्वा प्रभजन्ति समादरात् ।
ऋद्धिमन्तो नृपेन्द्रास्ते सप्तरत्नसमन्विताः[30] ॥ १३२ ॥

Offering different types of things shall grant people prosperity of riches and *ratnas*.

स्वर्गे देवाधिपाश्चापि भवन्ति बोधिभागिनः ।
ये चास्मिन् सुरसंपानं सुवर्णगन्धसंयुतम् ॥ १३३ ॥

The gods, who reside in heaven, who have come to earth to offer to him the nectar that they ingest, shall be introduced into the path of liberation.

उपढौक्य समाराध्य प्रभजन्ते समाहिताः ।
ते बलिष्ठा महीपेन्द्राःश्रीसमृद्धा निरोगिणः ॥ १३४ ॥

The ones who offer many offerings, with devotion and focus, shall retain the strength of kings and similar prosperity and will never be disturbed by ailments or diseases.

स्वर्गे गताश्च देवेन्द्रा भवन्ति बोधिभागिनः ।
ये चास्मिन् स्कन्दमूलानि बीजपत्रफलानि च ॥ १३५ ॥

The gods of heaven are bound to walk the path of liberation should they come to Svayambhū and offer him fruits from the forest.

29 स्वयंभुवे इति खपाठः ।

30 गन्धरत्नाश्च इति कपाठः ।

श्रद्धया समुपस्थाप्य संभजन्ते समाश्रिताः ।
ते प्रभुज्य यथाकामं भोग्यानि विविधान्यपि ॥ १३६ ॥

The ones who offer different types of foods will get whatever in the world they desire.

सद्धर्मसाधनारक्ताः संयान्त्यन्ते[31]जिनालयम् ।
ये चास्मिन् सुगताधारं पथ्यौषधगणान्यपि ॥ १३७ ॥

The ones, indulged in the practice of Bauddha Dharma, who offer foodstuff and medicine to the Svayambhū, will ultimately receive liberation.

समर्प्य श्रद्धया नित्यं प्रसेवन्ते समादरात् ।
ते बलिष्ठा सुपुष्टाङ्गाः सौम्येन्द्रिया निरामयाः ॥ १३८ ॥

Others who offer food with constant devotion to the service of Svayambhū shall have beauty, control over their organs and shall carry no disease in their bodies.

राज्यश्रीसुखमाभुज्य संयान्त्यन्ते सुखावतीम् ।
ये चाप्यत्र जिनाधारे धर्मधातौ स्वयम्भुवि ॥ १३९ ॥

Constant worship of the Lord Svayambhū shall grant them royal prosperity, and save them a seat in the realm of bliss (*sukhāvatī*).

वितत्योच्चैर्वितानं च संसेवन्ते समादरात् ।
धन्यास्ते गुणिनो वन्द्याःशुद्धवंशा विचक्षणाः ॥ १४० ॥

The ones who place tall flags near Svayambhū and pieces of sacred fabric nearby, shall become respectable, virtuous, venerable and their legacy will be purified, and they will be granted wisdom.

सर्वार्थसिद्धिसम्पन्नाः प्रयान्त्यन्ते जिनालयम्[32] ।
ये चास्मिन् सुगतावासे विचित्रानुच्छ्रितान्ध्वजान् ॥ १४१ ॥

The ones who go there, worship and position beautiful flags in all

[31] संत्यजन्ति इति कपाठः ।

[32] गृहालयम् इति कपाठः ।

directions shall receive all the powers and ultimately reach the realm of Lord Buddha.

अवरोप्य महोत्साहैः संभजन्तेऽभिनन्दिताः ।
श्रीसद्गुणसुख धारा भूत्वा भूपाधिपा भुवि[33] ॥ १४२ ॥

The ones who erect tall pillars and hang flags on top, and worship the Svayambhū as such, will be filled with good qualities and become the kings of their lands.

स्वर्गे देवाधिपाश्चान्ते संप्रयान्ति जिनालयम् ।
सौवर्णरत्नपुष्पादि-छत्राणि विविधानि ये ॥ १४३ ॥

The gods of heaven that come to the Svayambhū and offer him golden jewels, golden flowers and golden umbrellas shall reach the land of Buddha and achieve liberation.

आरोप्याऽत्र महोत्साहैः संभजन्ते प्रमोदिताः ।
ते नरेन्द्राः सुरेन्द्राश्च छत्रोपमाः सदा भवे ॥ १४४ ॥

The ones who come to Svayambhū and offer tall umbrellas, flags and gems, and worship the lord so; if they desire, can attain kingship in earth and heaven; and they will be higher than others as an umbrella is higher than others.

महत्सुखानि भुक्त्वान्ते संप्रयान्ति जिनालयम् ।
ये चास्मिन् सुगतावासे पताकाःपञ्चरङ्गिकाः[34] ॥ १४५ ॥

The ones who offer five coloured pieces of cloths stringed together like a banner (*patākā*) shall experience ultimate bliss and finally reach *jinālaya*, the residence of Buddha.

समावलंवयित्वापि संसेवन्ते[35]महोत्सवैः ।
ते भूत्वात्र महीपालाः सदा देवाधिपा अपि ॥ १४६ ॥

---

33 भूमौ इति घपाठः ।

34 पञ्चकामदा इति कपाठः ।

35 संभन्द्रन्ते इति कपाठः ।

The ones who come to Svayambhū, and hang cloths, leaves, and different plants, and thus celebrate, shall become kings on the earth or reside forever in the god's realm if they desire.

भद्रश्रीसत्सुखं भुक्त्वा संयान्त्यन्ते जिनालयम्।
ये चास्मिन् विविधैर्वाद्यैः संगीतिमुरजादिभिः ॥ १४७ ॥

The ones who play instruments, and sing hymns, chant prayers, songs, shall receive optimum bliss and finally walk the path of *mukti.*

तौर्यवंशादिभिश्चापि संसेवन्ते महोत्सवैः ।
ते मनोज्ञस्वना दिव्यश्रीश्रीश्रीसद्गुणाश्रयाः ॥ १४८ ॥

The ones who play different kinds of bamboo instruments and *tūrya* instrument and serve and please the lord by celebration, will become rich in mind and knowledge and will be famed and granted immeasurable riches and wealth thricefold.

सद्धर्मसाधनं कृत्वा व्रजन्ति सुगतालयम्।
सलाजाक्षतपुष्पाणि ये चास्मिन् सुगतालये ॥ १४९ ॥

प्रक्षिप्य श्रद्धया भक्त्या संभजन्ते समादरात्।
दुर्गतिं ते न गच्छन्ति संजाताः सद्गतौ सदा ॥ १५० ॥

The ones in practice of *dharma* that visit the Svayambhū and worship using the grains of paddy flower, and other flowers, will directly walk the path of *nirvāṇa.*

The ones who with devotion offer *lājā*[36] in Svayambhū shall never reach a state of misery and always be in a state of success.

सर्वसत्त्वहितं कृत्वा संप्रयान्ति जिनालयम्।
सधातुद्रव्यरत्नादि-दक्षिणा यत्र ये मुदा ॥ १५१ ॥

The ones who offer gems and different other materials, shall bring great welfare to beings in the world and will later reach the realm of Buddha.

---

[36] Fried rice.

श्रद्धया परिढौकित्वा संभजन्ते सदादरात् ।
दिव्यश्रीसुखभुञ्जाना भद्रश्रीसद्गुणाश्रयाः ॥ १५२ ॥

Similarly, offering commodities consumed by the mortals to Svayambhū shall bring divine bliss into the mortal world, and take the person to the heaven filled with virtues and merits.

सर्वसत्त्वहितं कृत्वा संप्रयान्ति जिनालयम् ।
ये चापि स्तुतिभिस्तथ्यैरेनं बुद्धालयं मुदा ॥ १५३ ॥

In Svayambhū, chanting of hymns and sincere prayer shall bring welfare to the world and take you to the realm of Buddha eventually.

पद्यैर्गद्यमयैश्चापि स्तुत्वा भजन्ति सादरम् ।
बहुरत्नसमृद्धास्ते सर्वविद्याविचक्षणाः ॥ १५४ ॥

Prayers to Svayambhū in poetry and prosody, would grant anyone prosperity of riches and make them well-versed in all arts and knowledge.

भूपाः स्वर्गाधिपाश्चापि भूत्वान्ते यान्ति सौगतम् ।
श्रद्धयैनं जगन्नाथं समाश्रयन्ति श्रद्धया[37] ॥ १५५ ॥

The men who take refuge in Svayambhū with devotion become kings in this world, and when their time here ends, they shall reach the realm of the Buddha.

नत्वाष्टांगैः प्रसन्ना ये संभजन्ते समादरात् ।
सप्तरत्नसमेतास्ते नृपाधिपा महर्द्धिकाः ॥ १५६ ॥

The ones who bow down to the Buddha in eight different bodily positions, pray to him with reverence and devotion, shall receive all eight jewels on earth, become kings and become filled with fortune.

सद्धर्मसाधनारक्ता भवन्ति बोधिचारिणः ।
ये चैनं चैत्यराजेन्द्रमनेकशःप्रदक्षिणाम् ॥ १५७ ॥

The ones, who having worshipped and revolved around the Svayambhū, indulge in Buddha Dharma, will finally receive knowledge.

---

37 स्वयंभुवं इति खपाठः ।

कृत्वा ध्यात्वाप्यनुस्मृत्वा नामोच्चार्य भजन्त्यपि ।
जातिस्मराश्चिरायुष्का मतिमन्तः सुवर्णिनः ॥ १५८ ॥

The one who remember Svayambhū and chant its name will be famous among their kin, have a long life full of wisdom and prosperity.

वन्द्याःपूज्याश्च मान्यास्ते भवेयुर्बोधिचारिणः[38] ।
शुद्धाश्च भस्मसंक्षालैः समालिप्य समन्ततः ॥ १५९ ॥

The ones who in Svayambhū with pure heart offer ashes shall earn respect in their world, and finally receive the *bodhi* knowledge.

समभ्यर्च्य सहोत्साहैर्ये भजन्त्येनमीश्वरम्[39] ।
शोक-क्लेशाग्निसंताप-विवर्जिताश्चिरायुषः ॥ १६० ॥

Thus, the ones who worship and celebrate the Svayambhū shall have their miseries, sorrows and distress removed to have a long life.

नीरोगाः सुखिनो देवा भवेयुर्भूमिपाश्च ते ।
ये च निर्माल्यमाकृष्य शोधयित्वात्र सर्वतः ॥ १६१ ॥

The ones who pray to the Svayambhū, and clean the surrounding and tidy the place, shall be healthy, wise, and may become kings or gods.

समुपाश्रित्य सेवन्ते सम्बुद्धभक्तिमानसाः ।
निर्मुक्तक्लेश-शोकास्ते दर्शनीयाःशुभेन्द्रियाः[40] ॥ १६२ ॥

They who, with great reverence for Buddha in their hearts, worship the Svayambhū shall be freed of their mortal misery and be enriched in beauty, and will receive *nirvāṇa*.

श्रीमन्तःपुण्डरीकास्या भवेयुर्बोधिचारिणः ।
जीर्णे शीर्णे विभग्नेऽस्मिन् प्रतिसंस्कृत्य ये मुदा ॥ १६३ ॥

They who renovate the old and broken structures around the Svayambhū shall be granted a golden lotus and receive knowledge.

---

38 ज्ञानिनः इति कपाठः ।

39 गौरवम् इति घपाठः ।

40 शुभाज्ञया इति गपाठः ।

प्रतिष्ठाप्य महोत्साहैः संभजन्ते समादरात्।
सर्वसम्पत्समृद्धास्ते पुष्टेन्द्रिया निरामयाः ॥ १६४ ॥

They who replace the damaged buildings with renewed buildings and shrines (*caitya*s), shall receive great respect, prosperity, development in their organs and freedom from all diseases.

धर्मकामाः शुभाचारा भवेयुर्बोधिचारिणः।
जल्पित्वा यस्य मन्त्राणि धारणीश्च समाहिताः[41] ॥ १६५ ॥

Those who chant the Buddhist hymns such as the Dhāraṇī *mantra* shall be religious in all their lives, filled with goodwill and knowledge equivalent to the Buddha.

ध्यात्वा स्मृत्वा समुच्चार्य नामापि प्रभजन्ति च।
तेऽपि सर्वे महासत्त्वाः परिशुद्धत्रिमण्डलाः ॥ १६६ ॥

Those who practice profound meditation in the Svayambhū and chant his name in remembrance shall become *mahāsattva*s, pure in all three worlds.

भद्रश्रीसद्गुणाधारा भवेयुर्बोधिचारिणः।
एवं महत्तरं पुण्यमस्मिन् धर्माधिपालये ॥ १६७ ॥

They who worship the Svayambhū so will attain *bodhi* and be filled with boundless merit – that cannot be expressed in words.

श्रद्धाभजनसंभूतमित्यादिष्टं मुनीश्वरैः।
मयैतत्पुण्यसंक्षिप्तमात्रं तु कथ्यतेऽधुना ॥ १६८ ॥

The ones who with sincere devotion worship and serve the Svayambhū shall receive an unimaginable quantity of fruits, merit and blessings.

I have only summarized the benefits of Svayambhū worship.

समग्रं विस्तरेणात्र समाख्यातुं न शक्यते।
एवं मत्वास्य सत्कारपूजाफलं महत्तरम् ॥ १६९ ॥

In essence, all the merit and virtues received from the worship of

41 समन्ततः इति कपाठः।

Svayambhū is indescribable. Thus, with this knowledge, you all must worship and devote yourself to the Svayambhū to the best of your abilities.

श्रद्धया शरणं गत्वा कर्तव्यं भजनं सदा ।
येऽप्यस्मिञ्छरणं गत्वा श्रद्धया समुपाश्रिताः ॥ १७० ॥

Go to the Svayambhū, pray, chant, take refuge there, worship the Lord, so there will not be anything that you shall not have received.

सुप्रसन्नाशया भक्त्या भजन्ति बोधिमानसाः ।
न ते गच्छन्ति कुत्रापि दुर्गतिं च कदाचन ॥ १७१ ॥

With pure and gentle heart, devoted worshippers of the Svayambhū shall never be found in a state of misery or distress, and shall always walk the path of good and welfare.

संजाताः सद्गतिष्वेव भवेयुर्बोधिचारिणः ।
सदा ते सुकुले जाता बोधिसत्त्वा विचक्षणाः ॥ १७२ ॥

Those that have taken the path of good, through the Svayambhū worship, shall be favoured in their *bodhicaryā* vows for the welfare of the entire world. If they are born again, their birth shall be in a noble household, and they will have been *bodhisattva*s since birth.

सर्वसत्त्वहिताधानं[42] चरेयुर्व्रतमाभवम् ।
ततस्ते बोधिसंभारं पूरयित्वा यथाक्रमम् ॥ १७३ ॥

Those born in their clans shall walk the path of knowledge again, and will take part in the welfare of the world and cross the three steps of *bodhi* to reach the path of liberation.

त्रिविधां बोधिमासाद्य निर्वृतिपदमाप्नुयुः ।
न हि चित्तप्रसादस्य स्वल्पा भवति दक्षिणा ॥ १७४ ॥

After attaining three types of *bodhi*, they will start on the path to liberation (*nirvāṇa*).

---

42 हितायात्र इति कपाठः ।

But the one who does not have goodwill and joy in his heart will receive very little fruit.

तथागतेषु सद्धर्मे संबुद्धे श्रावकेष्वपि ।
एवं ह्यचिन्त्याः संबुद्धा बुद्धा धर्माश्च निर्मलाः ॥ १७५ ॥

अचिन्त्यो हि प्रसन्नानां विपाकश्च महत्फलः ।
एवं मत्वा त्रिरत्नेषु भक्तिपूजा-फलं महत् ।
कार्या भक्तिः सदात्रैव धर्मधातौ जिनालये ॥ १७६ ॥

Those who pay attention and concentration to the words and *dharma* imparted by the *tathāgatas*, *buddhas* and *śrāvakas* will have their devotion increased and their actions purified. Their productivity, welfare and bliss shall increase unimaginably. With this understanding, the one who devotes himself to the worship of *tri-ratna* shall gain unimaginable and indescribable merit.

इत्यादिष्टं मुनीन्द्रेण श्रुत्वा सर्वे समाश्रिताः ।
लोकास्तथेति विज्ञाप्य प्रीत्यानन्द-प्रबोधिताः ॥ १७७ ॥

Having heard the commands of the great sage, all those present agreed with bliss and affection, and were filled with joy.

इति मे गुरुणादिष्टं श्रुतं मया तथोच्यते ।
त्वमप्येवं सदा राजन् भज तत्र जिनालयम् ॥ १७८ ॥

Thus, I have told the command that I had heard from my teacher. You too, then, O King! always serve the Jinālaya

तत्पुण्येन ते भद्रं निरुत्पातं सदा भवेत् ।
बोधिचित्तरसं प्राप्य बोधिसत्त्वो भविष्यसि[43] ॥ १७९ ॥

With that merit, may you always have good auspices and no disasters. You will then receive the taste of the enlightened mind and become a Bodhisattva.

ततः सम्बोधिसंभारं पूरयित्वा तथाक्रमम् ।
मारान्निर्जित्य संबोधिं प्राप्य बुद्धपदं लभेः ॥ १८० ॥

---

43 भवेरपि इति कपाठः ।

Then, after gradually completing the steps of enlightenment, after defeating desire, after attaining *sambodhi*, you may attain Buddhāhood.

इति शास्त्रार्हतादिष्टं संगम्यैष नराधिपः ।
अशोकः ससभालोकःप्राभ्यनन्दत् प्रबोधितः ॥ १८१ ॥

Thus, having understood the command of the Master Arhanta, King Aśoka along with the assembly, praised him and was illuminated.

॥ इति श्रीस्वयंभूत्पत्तिकथायाःश्रीस्वयंभूभट्टारकोद्देशपूजावर्णनं
नाम द्वितीयोऽध्यायः सम्पूर्णः ॥

Thus, within the story of its origin, the second chapter on the description of Svayambhū worship ends here.

अथ तृतीयोऽध्यायः
(Tṛtīya Adhyāya)

Story of the Origin of Svayambhū

अथाशोको महीपालः साञ्जलिः पुरतःस्थितः[1] ।
तमर्हन्तं यतिं नत्वा प्रार्थयेदेवमादरात् ॥ १ ॥

On that occasion, King Aśoka, with hands joined in reverence and humility, addressed the Bhikkhu Upagupta to ask him:

भदन्त! श्रोतुमिच्छामि तद्भूमेः सत्कथां शुभाम्[2] ।
तत्सम्यक् समुपादिश्य संबोधयतु नो भवान् ॥ २ ॥

"O Bhante! I want to listen to the good story of the pious land, the Svayambhū. Bless me by telling me the story."

इति संप्रार्थिते राज्ञा सोऽर्हन् यतिर्महामतिः ।
उपगुप्तो नरेन्द्रं तं सम्पश्यन्नेवमब्रवीत्[3] ॥ ३ ॥

As the king prayed like this, the wise Upagupta Bhikkhu, facing the king, replied:

साधु शृणु महाराज! यथा मे गुरुणोदितम् ।
तथाहं ते प्रवक्ष्यामि लोकबोधाय साम्प्रतम्[4] ॥ ४ ॥

"O great king! you have asked a great question. Listen carefully. I shall tell you just like my *guru* once told me; and this shall bring welfare to the world.

---

1 पुरः आश्रितः इति गपाठः ।

2 नास्ति इति कपाठः ।

3 दिशते इति खपाठः ।

4 सर्वलोकाभिवोधने इति खपाठः ।

तद्यथायं महासत्त्वो मैत्रेयः स जिनात्मजः।
भगवन्तं पुनर्नत्वा साञ्जलिरेवमब्रवीत्॥ ५॥

See, king, this is the same story that Maitreya then, with joined hands in devotion, had asked Lord Buddha.

भगवन्! ज्ञातुमिच्छामि महाजलाशयो ह्रदः।
कदा भूमिप्रदेशोऽत्र कथं जलाशयोऽभवत्॥ ६॥

He had asked the Lord, "O Lord Buddha! the large body of water that once was, is dry land now. How and when did this come to happen?

कस्य वा समये देशे ग्रामादयः प्रवर्तिताः।
तत्सर्वं समुपादिश्य सर्वानस्मान् प्रबोधय॥ ७॥

Did the countries and villages exist during those times? Tell us this, for our welfare."

इति संप्रार्थिते तेन मैत्रेयेण सः सर्ववित्।
भगवन्तं महासत्त्वं सम्पश्यन्नेवमादिशत्॥ ८॥

After the Maitreya thus prayed the Lord, the omniscient Buddha, looking at the *mahāsattva*, answered:

साधु शृणु महासत्त्व ! यदत्राभूद् महीतले।
तत्प्रवृत्तिं समाख्यापि लोकज्ञानाय सम्प्रति[5]॥ ९॥

"O Maitreya! listen to what I tell you carefully; this land was once a large body of water, a pond, which was then drained out. I shall tell you all about it. Listen with attention.

तद्यथा भूविलोकानां वर्षषष्टिसहस्रकम्।
परमायुस्तदा शास्ता विश्वभूर्नाम सर्ववित्॥ १०॥

It was at the age when human lives spanned 60,000 years. Then the Buddha had incarnated as the Viśvabhū.

धर्मराजो मुनीन्द्रोऽर्हन् तथागतो विनायकः।
सर्वविद्याधिपस्तायी संबुद्धः सुगतो जिनः॥ ११॥

---

[5] सर्वलोकाभिवोधने इति कपाठः।

Hc was the Lord of *dharma*, superior to all sages, who knew the truth, he was the destroyer of obstacles, the residence of all knowledge, learned, enlightened and victorious.

सो ऽनुपमा नामपुर्यामुपकण्ठे जिनाश्रमे।
सर्वसत्त्व-हितार्थेन विजहार ससांघिकः ॥ १२ ॥

The Viśvabhū lived in his *āśrama* near a city called Anupamā. He sat in there, thinking about the welfare of all humanity and intent on helping anyone who came to him with their troubles.

मैत्रेयोऽहं तदाऽभूवं विश्वभूव उपासकः।
पर्वताख्यो महासत्त्वो बोधिसत्त्वो हितार्थभृत् ॥ १३ ॥

O Maitreya! I was a follower of the Viśvabhū. My name at that time was Parvata and I was a *bodhisattva* and *mahāsattva* and I was concentrated on the welfare of all beings.

तत्र स भगवाञ्छास्ता संभासयन् सुधांशुवत्।
सद्धर्मं समुपादेष्टुं सभासने समाश्रयत् ॥ १४ ॥

At one instance, the *śāstā* (teaching name of the Buddha) with the knowledge of everyone's wishes, in order to give the teachings of the Buddha Dharma, took the high seat in the assembly, just as the moon takes the high seat in the sky.

तं दृष्ट्वा भिक्षवः सर्वे श्रावकाब्रह्मचारिणः।
प्रत्येक-सुगताश्चापि बोधिसत्त्वाश्च चैलकाः[6] ॥ १५ ॥

भिक्षुण्यो ब्रह्मचारिण्यो यतयो ऽयोगिनो ऽपि च।
त्रिरत्नभजनासक्ता उपासका उपासिकाः ॥ १६ ॥

Seeing the Lord thus, all the *bhikkhus*, *bhikkhuṇīs*, *śrāvaka*, *brahmacārī*, *brahmacāriṇī*, *pratyeka-buddhas*, *sugatas*, *bodhisattvas*, *cailakas*, maidens, *yatis*, *yatinīs*, *yogīs*, *yoginīs* and all who were devoted to the Buddha, Dharma and Saṅgha, such as *upāsaka* and *upāsikās* all gathered in the assembly.

---

[6] कौलिका इति गपाठः।

एवमन्येऽपि लोकाश्च सद्धर्मगुणलालसाः ।
भद्रश्री–सद्गुणारक्ताः संबुद्धदर्शनोत्सुकाः ॥ १७ ॥

Similarly others, who desired to gain the knowledge of the good *dharma* and merits, virtues and prosperities and wished to receive an auspicious audience of the Buddha, also went.

तत्सुधर्मामृतं पातुं समेत्येनं मुनीश्वरम्[7] ।
यथाक्रमं समभ्यर्च्य नत्वा साञ्जलयो मुदा ॥ १८ ॥

Thus, everyone who arrived to drink the nectar of the good *dharma* approached the Buddha and gradually worshipped him, with hands joined in reverence.

परिवृत्य पुरस्कृत्य समुद्विक्ष्य समादरात् ।
तत्सभायां समाश्रित्य संनिषेदुः समाहिताः ॥ १९ ॥

They all spread in four directions in respect of the Buddha, some opposite to the Buddha, some facing the Buddha with respect; everyone who arrived at the assembly took seats they saw vacant.

एवं ब्रह्मादयः सर्व ऋषयो ब्रह्मचारिणः ।
तीर्थिका अपि सर्वे तत्सद्धर्मं श्रोतुमागताः ॥ २० ॥

Even Brahmā, Viṣṇu and other gods, many sages, *brahmacārī*s, Vedic scholars and the special scholars, to hear the mystery of *dharma*, arrived there.

शक्रदयो ऽपि देवाश्च सर्वलोकाधिपा अपि ।
ग्रहास्तारागणाः सिद्धाः साध्या विद्याधरा अपि ॥ २१ ॥

Indra and his council of gods, devils, lords of the world, planets, stars, *siddha*s, *sādhya*s and *vidyādhara* demi-gods also arrived.

सर्वेऽपि ते समागत्य भगवन्तं यथाक्रमम् ।
समभ्यर्च्य नमस्कृत्य[8] सभायां समुपाश्रयन् ॥ २२ ॥

---

7 कम्पिते इति इति कपाठः ।

8 प्रणत्वातत् इति कपाठः ।

All who arrived saluted the lord, worshipped him, did *pradakṣiṇā* (by respectfully walking around him) and sat down at the assembly.

एवं च ब्राह्मणा विज्ञा राजानः क्षत्रिया अपि[9] ।
वैश्याश्च मन्त्रिणो ऽमात्या गृहस्थाश्च महाजनाः ॥ २३ ॥

Similarly, brāhmaṇa scholars, kṣatriya kings, vaiśya courtiers and secretaries, householders and merchants, also went.

शिल्पिनो वणिजश्चापि सार्थवाहाश्च पौरिकाः ।
ग्राम्या जानपदाश्चापि तथाऽन्ये देशवासिनः ॥ २४ ॥

Carpenters, tradesmen, caravan merchants, townsfolk, villagers and other residents of the country all arrived.

सर्वे ते समुपागत्य भगवन्तं यथाक्रमम् ।
समभ्यर्च्य नमस्कृत्य कृत्वा[10]प्रदक्षिणान्यपि ॥ २५ ॥

All approached the lord gradually, worshipped him, bowed to him and did the *pradakṣiṇā.*

गुरूकृत्य पुरस्कृत्य परिवृत्य समन्ततः ।
सत्सद्धर्मामृतं पातुमुपतस्थुः समाहिताः ॥ २६ ॥

Their arrival increased the glory of the Lord, as they bowed to him, circled around him and to taste the elixir of wisdom that the Lord would grant, sat down around him.

तान्दृष्ट्वा समुपासीनान् विश्वभूर्भगवाञ्जिनः ।
आदि-मध्यान्त-कल्याणं सद्धर्मं समुपादिशत् ॥ २७ ॥

When the Lord Viśvabhū saw everyone gathered around him, full of devotion, he decided to teach the method for the initial, intermediate and final welfare of all.

तत्सद्धर्मामृतं पीत्वा सर्वे लोकाः सभाश्रिताः ।
धर्मविशेषमाज्ञाय प्राप्यानन्द-प्रबोधिताः ॥ २८ ॥

As the Lord granted the elixir of *dharma*, everyone present was able

[9] अथ इति कपाठः ।

[10] प्रणत्वाच इति खपाठः ।

to understand the special *dharma*, which ignited divine bliss inside of them and brought them internal awakening.

तस्मिन्क्षणे मही सर्वा चचाल सह पर्वतैः[11] ।
सुप्रसन्ना दिशः सर्वा रेजू रवीन्द्र-वह्नयः ॥ २९ ॥

When the Lord preached so, the entire planet shook with pleasure; even the mountains moved a little; all the cardinal directions were ecstatic; sun, moon and fire were all pleased and illuminated brighter in their energy.

सुरदुन्दुभयो नेदुर्निपेतुःपुष्पवृष्टयः ।
निरुत्पातं महोत्साहं प्रावर्तत समन्ततः ॥ ३० ॥

Suddenly, the divine drums of gods played and the gods showered flowers from the heaven. There was only celebration and joy everywhere on earth.

तद् विलोक्य सभालोकाः सर्वे ते विस्मयान्विताः ।
श्रोतुं तद्धेतुं सर्वज्ञमुद्वीक्ष्य तस्थुराद्रिताः ॥ ३१ ॥

When the people in the assembly noticed this divine happening, they were ecstatic, full of joy. They were curious about the reason of it all.

तदा गगनगञ्जाख्यो बोधिसत्त्वः समुत्थितः ।
उद्वहन्नुत्तरासंगं पुरतः समुपस्थितः[12] ॥ ३२ ॥

In that moment, a *bodhisattva*, named Gaganagañja (sound of the sky), stood up from his seat and arranged his fallen robes above his shoulders and addressed the Lord.

सर्वज्ञं तं महाभिज्ञं धर्मराजं विनायकम् ।
विश्वभुवं मुनिं नत्वा साञ्जलिरेवमब्रवीत् ॥ ३३ ॥

As he stood up, with hands joined in reverence and bowed to the Lord of *dharma*, the omniscient, destroyer of obstacles, the Viśvabhū, he asked:

---

11 सपर्वताः इति कपाठः ।

12 श्रितः इति खपाठः ।

निमित्तं भगवन् चैतत्[13]कस्येदं जायते ऽधुना ।
तद् भवान् समुपादिश्य संबोधयतु नो गुरोः ॥ ३४ ॥

"O Lord! what is the cause of all that is happening now? Master, please tell us what it is."

इति संप्रार्थिते तेन भगवान् स मुनीश्वरः ।
गगनगञ्जमालोक्य तां सभां चैवमब्रवीत् ॥ ३५ ॥

When he prayed to the Lord so, the Munīśvara (Lord of Sages), the Buddha, then addressing the Gaganagañja, facing the assembly, answered so:

कुलपुत्र! महद्भद्रनिमित्तमिदमाचरत् ।
तदहं संप्रवक्ष्यामि शृणुत यूयमादरात् ॥ ३६ ॥

"O Son of Noble Family! a great and auspicious welfare is destined to happen. The omen that we witnessed hints at an occurrence of a great event. Listen carefully, I shall tell you about it.

तद्यथा त्रिगुणाभिज्ञो मंजुश्रीः सुगतात्मजः ।
उत्तरस्यां विहरति महाचीने नगाश्रमे ॥ ३७ ॥

As it were, there is a great person, also titled as the son of Buddha, called Mañjuśrī, who is well versed in all three qualities and lives in an āśrama called Naga which lies in the Mahācīna[14] (China in present day).

तस्य भार्या उभे ज्येष्ठा केशिनी श्रीवरप्रदा ।
विद्या-सद्गुण-संभर्त्री द्वितीया चोपकेशिनी ॥ ३८ ॥

Mañjuśrī has two wives: the first one, called Keśiṇī, is able to grant prosperity while the second one, called Upakeśiṇī, is able to grant wisdom and virtue.

13 भगवन्तद्रनैमित्यं इति कपाठः ।

14 Based on the texts, it is evident that Mañjuśrī was of Chinese origin（基于文本，可以证明文殊师利来自中国。——英文译者）. Mahācīna, 意为“大中国”.

एकस्मिन् समये तत्र मंजुश्रीः सद्गणोदधिः ।
लोकसंदर्शनं नाम समाधिं विदधे मुदा ॥ ३९ ॥

At one time, Mañjuśrī, full of virtues, entered a state of trance known as Lokasaṁdarśa (where one can see the world) and was filled with happiness.

ध्यानदृष्ट्या ददर्शात्र महाह्रदसरोरुहे[15]।
रत्नमयं समुत्पन्नं धर्मधातुं जिनालयम् ॥ ४० ॥

In his trance, as he delved deeper, he saw a mysterious scene: a large lake floating with lotuses made of gems, which, he understood, was the house of the Dharmadhātu itself.

स्वयंभुवं तमालोक्य मंजुदेवः सुसन्मतिः ।
संहर्षितःपुनर्ध्यात्वा मनसैवं व्यचिन्तयत् ॥ ४१ ॥

Thus, having seen the self-originating Svayambhū, the wise Mañjuśrī was filled with joy, and meditating again, he thought in his mind.

अहो!! स्वयं समुद्भूतो धर्मधातुर्जिनालयः[16] ।
निर्जने सुजल-ज्योतिरूपः संभासयन् स्थितः ॥ ४२ ॥

"O the Dharmadhātu! home of the Buddha has arisen on its own. It lies alone in the pious waters, and its luminous form is filled with light.

तत्तथाहं करिष्यामि गत्वा तत्र महाह्रदे ।
शोषयित्वा तदम्भांसि यथा पृथ्वीतलो भवेत् ॥ ४३ ॥

So I shall do this: after going to the great lake, I shall drain the water out, so land might appear.

तदा तत्र महीभूते निर्जले सुप्रतिष्ठिते ।
शिलोच्चये प्रतिष्ठाप्य भजिष्यामि तमीश्वरम् ॥ ४४ ॥

When the water is thus removed, I shall pick the Dharmadhātu, raise it and establish it on the high ground on top of a rock and having done that, I shall worship the shrine thus formed.

15 जिनलयम् इति कपाठः ।

16 स्वयंभुवः इति गपाठः ।

तथा तत्र महीभूते ग्रामादि-वसतिर्भवेत्।
तदा सर्वे ऽपिलोकाश्च भजेयुस्तं जिनालयम्॥ ४५॥

After the water is removed and the Lord has been placed on top of the mountain, the ground that appears can be housed and populated by those devoted to the worship of the Lord.

तथा तत्पुण्यभावेन सर्वदा तत्र मंगलम्।
निरुत्पातं भवेन्नूनं लोकाश्च स्युः सुभाविनः॥ ४६॥

When I do this, all merit will be available there; everything will be auspicious; nothing shall perish; and the world shall have tranquillity.

ततस्ते मानवाः सर्वे तमेव शरणाश्रिताः।
यथाशक्ति महोत्साहैः प्रभजेयुः सदा मुदा॥ ४७॥

The people that live there would take refuge in the Svayambhū full of devotion and please the Lord by worshipping him to the best of their abilities.

ततस्तत्पुण्यशुद्धास्ते सद्धर्म-गुणलालसाः।
महासत्त्वा बोधिसत्त्वाश्चरेयुर्बोधिसंवरम्॥ ४८॥

Through the merit earned by the worship of the Svayambhū, they shall be purified and take the path of the good *dharma*, the Buddha Dharma, whose practice shall make them *bodhisattva*s, *mahāsattva*s and practitioners of the *bodhi* vow.

ततस्ते बोधिसंभारं पूरयित्वा यथाक्रमम्।
त्रिविधां बोधिमासाद्य निर्वृतिपदमाप्नुयुः॥ ४९॥

As they climb the three steps to enlightenment, they will complete their vows and be established in the path of liberation.

एवं कृत्वा महत्पुण्यं प्राप्याहं त्रिजगत्स्वपि।
कृत्वा धर्ममयं कृत्यं निर्वृतिपदमाप्नुयाम्॥ ५०॥

In this way, I shall earn merit that shall promote the *dharma* and bring me fame in all three worlds. And having performed an act as pious, I shall walk the path of liberation.

इति ध्यात्वा विनिश्चित्य मञ्जुश्रीः स जिनात्मजः ।
मंजुदेवाभिधं चारुरूपं धृत्वा महर्द्धिमान् ॥ ५१ ॥

Having thought so, Mañjuśrī assumed a strong and beautiful form full of great strength and thus proceeded to depart for the Svayambhū.

केशिनी वरदा नाम मोक्षदा चोपकेशिनी ।
भूत्वानेकैर्महासत्त्वैः सर्वैः सह समागमत्[17] ॥ ५२ ॥

His two wives Keśiṇī and Upakeśiṇī, along with many *mahāsattvas*, accompanied him.

ततश्चरन् सभार्योऽसौ मंजुदेवः ससांघिकः ।
सर्वत्र भद्रतां कुर्वन्[18]महोत्साहैः समागमत्[19] ॥ ५३ ॥

Mañjuśrī then became strong and with his strength and desire for welfare, finally reached the place of Svayambhū.

तत्र ते समुपागत्य दूरतः संप्रभास्वरम् ।
महाह्रदाब्जमध्यस्थं ददृशुस्तं जिनालयम् ॥ ५४ ॥

He first saw the Dharmadhātu from afar, in the middle of the pond, thanks to its energy illuminating all that surrounded it.

तत्र ते तं समालोक्य ज्योतीरूपं समुज्वलम् ।
प्रणम्य[20] सहसोपेत्य कृत्वा प्रदक्षिणानि च ॥ ५५ ॥

After he saw the luminous Svayambhū, he saluted it, and then approached it, and performed the *pradakṣiṇā*.

तत्तीरे पर्वते रम्ये सर्वेऽपि ते समाश्रिताः ।
तं चैत्यमेव संवीक्ष्य न्यवसन् ते प्रमोदिताः ॥ ५६ ॥

As he reached close to the hills in that beautiful spot, his company

---

17 सहसर्वोऽपिनेचरत् इति कपाठः ।

18 कृत्वा इति घपाठः ।

19 चरत् इति खपाठः ।

20 प्रणत्वा इति गपाठः ।

gathered around him and at the joyous sight of the Svayambhū, was filled with awe and admiration.

ततः प्रातः समुत्थाय मञ्जुदेवः स ऋद्धिमान् ।
भक्त्या परमयास्तौषीज्जिनालयं स्वयंभुवम् ॥ ५७ ॥

They spent the night there and when the dawn arrived, Mañjuśrī full of prosperity and devotion, started to chant hymns to worship the Svayambhū.

ज्योतीरूपाय चैतन्यरूपाय भवते नमः ।
अनादि-निधनाय-श्रीदात्रे प्रणवरूपिणे ॥ ५८ ॥

He said, "O Luminous Lord! I salute you. You are full of wisdom; you have no beginning or end; you provide welfare to all; your form is like the *oṁkāra*; I bow to you.

विश्वतोमुखरूपाय स्वाहास्वधास्वरूपिणे ।
पृथ्व्यादिभूतनिर्मात्रे महामहस्वरूपिणे ॥ ५९ ॥

O Lord! you have multiple forms and faces; Svāhā and Svadhā are your own forms, you are the creator of the five elements (earth, along with wind, fire, energy and light); I bow to you, the greatest in the world.

जगत्स्रष्टे जगत्पात्रे जगद्धर्त्रे नमो नमः ।
जगद्वन्द्याय जगतामाराधाय च ते नमः ॥ ६० ॥

O Great One! the creator of the world, the fosterer of the world, the sustainer of the world, the one whom the world loves, prays and salutes, I bow to you.

अतिस्थूलाय सूक्ष्माय विकाराय विकारिणे ।
निराकृतिकृते तुभ्यं सच्चिदानन्दमूर्तये ॥ ६१ ॥

Your form is prominent and it is subtle; it is the formation and it is what forms; it is what frees the world from the misery. You are the form of all three – existence, bliss and mind; I bow to you.

वषट्कारस्वरूपाय हुतभुजे स्वयं नमः ।
होत्रे हवनरूपाय होमद्रव्याय ते नमः ॥ ६२ ॥

I salute you, who embody the Vedic rituals. You are fire in the oblation, you are the offering in the oblation and you are also who offers in the oblation.

भक्तिलभ्याय सौम्याय भक्तवत्सलाय नमः[21] ।
ध्यानगम्याय ध्येयाय चतुवर्गप्रदायिने ॥ ६३ ॥

You are what can be achieved through devotion. You have a gentle form; you are full of love to your devotees. You can be understood through *dhyāna*, you are also the one that does *dhyāna*. You are who grants *dharma, artha* (wealth)*, kāma* (desire) and *mokṣa* (liberation). I bow to you.

अग्ररत्नाय निःसीममहिम्ने सर्वदा नमः ।
गुणातीताय योगाय योगिने च सदा नमः ॥ ६४ ॥

You are the superior jewel of all; you are limitless, beyond the three qualities. You are all eight forms of *yoga* and you are also the *yogī* that practises them. I bow to you.

एवं स्तुत्वा मंजुदेवःपुनःक्षमार्थतां व्यधात्[22] ।
प्रसीद भगवन् तावद् ह्रदं संशोषितुं यते ॥ ६५ ॥

Having prayed such to the Lord, he also apologized, "O Lord! please forgive me for draining the pond that submerges you and grant me the permission to do so."

इत्युक्त्वा चन्द्रहासं स सज्जीकृत्य समन्ततः ।
त्रिधा प्रदक्षिणीकृत्य समन्ततो व्यलोकयत् ॥ ६६ ॥

After he prayed to the Lord so, Mañjuśrī then raised his sword and after performing *pradakṣiṇā* thrice, he studied the hills surrounding the valley in all directions.

---

21 भक्तवत्सले नमःइति कपाठः ।

22 कृत इति गपाठः ।

विलोक्य स महासत्त्वो याम्यदिशावृतं नगम्[23] ।
चन्द्रहासेन खड्गेन छित्वा जलाशयं व्यधात् ॥ ६७ ॥

Having surveyed all the directions, the strong Mañjuśrī, with his shiny blade, cut the hill that stood in the southern direction, in order to drain the water out of the valley.

तच्छिन्नशैलमार्गेण तज्जलानि समन्ततः ।
प्रनिर्गत्याशु सर्वाणि गंगासंगममाययुः ॥ ६८ ॥

As he cut the mountain, the rocks that dammed the waters were removed, so all the water that was inside the pond, flowed through, outward to the Ganges and the sea.

तदारभ्य नदा नद्यो बभूवुर्भूतले ह्रदाः ।
दिग्विदिक्ष्वमलांभोभिस्तद् द्वीपैः परिपूरिताः ॥ ६९ ॥

Beginning that day, great rivers, rivers and ponds were formed in that land. Isles filled with beautiful water were also seen in all directions.

तत्र निरुध्य येऽम्बुनि यत्र ये नु शिलाःस्थिताः ।
तत्र तत्र स तान् सर्वाञ्च्छित्वा जलं ह्यवाहयत्[24] ॥ ७० ॥

He also noticed a few other hills and rocks blocking the water drainage, so he severed them in hundreds of pieces with his blade, in order to drain all water out of the valley.

एवं स सर्वतःछित्वा कृत्वा तज्जलनिर्गमम् ।
त्रिरात्रेण जलानिच सर्वाणि निरचारयत् ॥ ७१ ॥

Through three days and three nights, he stood there witnessing the water leave the valley. Yet, the waters were still not completely gone; he noticed there was still another disturbance obstructing his mission. He investigated into the matter with his divine sight to discover the source.

---

23 याम्यदिशिकृतम् इति कपाठः ।

24 चारयेत् ।

तज्जलाधानमेकन्तु ह्रदं धनादहाभिधम्।
कर्कोटकस्य नागस्य वासस्थानमभूत्ततः[25] ॥ ७२ ॥

With his divine sight, he discovered the reason there, in one corner of the pond, was a great serpent known as the Karkoṭa, who was stopping the water, his habitat, from flowing away.

सिंहेनोपद्रुता यद् वद् गजेन्द्रा भयविह्वलाः।
महारावै रुदन्तो वै विद्रुवन्ते दिशो दशः ॥ ७३ ॥

He then attacked the serpent with the ferocity of a lion, with his shiny blade. The children of the great serpent fled in all directions, producing great noises of screams and wails.

एवं तज्जलसंघातश्चन्द्रहासासिछेदनात्।
मार्गान्तरान्निरगमत् पंकशेषं यथाभवत्॥ ७४ ॥

Almost all the serpents and other minor obstructions, were then removed from the valley and finally all water was completely drained out, leaving only a land of mud and quagmire.

तज्जलाधानमेकन्तु ह्रदं धराद्रहाभिधम्।
कर्कोटकस्य नागस्य समस्थापयदाश्रयम्॥ ७५ ॥

However, the Karkoṭa serpent requested asylum to the Mañjuśrī, so he circumscribed a small area of water for the great serpent to live within.

ततस्तस्मिन् जले शुष्के यदाधारसरोरुहः।
तदेव पर्वतीभूय धर्मधातुर्व्यवस्थितः ॥ ७६ ॥

When the water drained out, there was mud and mire everywhere. Mañjuśrī gathered all the golden bejewelled lotuses of the pond and stacked them on top of one another to form a hill. Then he placed the Dharmadhātu on top of the so formed hill.

मंजुदेवानुभावेन स सर्वपर्वतोत्तमः।
अभेद्यो वज्रवत्तेन वज्रकूट इति स्मृतः ॥ ७७ ॥

---

25 समस्थापयदाश्रमं।

With the glory of the Mañjuśrī, the hill thus formed from gold lotuses was strong, unyielding and indestructible, just as diamond. Thus, the hill was named Vajrakūṭa.

तदिदं भूतलं रम्यं समन्ततो नगावृतम्।
उपछन्दोह इत्याख्यो हिमालयोऽपि चोच्यते ॥ ७८ ॥

Thence, the land became habitable and beautiful, surrounded by hills in all directions; it was known as the "Upachandoha".

सुदुर्जया स्वरूपाभूः प्रज्ञाज्ञानानुभाविनी।
हेरुकमण्डलाकारा भूत्वा समवतिष्ठते ॥ ७९ ॥

Fortified with unconquerable mountains surrounding it, the land was extremely fertile, full of *prajnā*. Knowledge would follow anyone who went there. It is as bright as a gold earring. Such a land exists on earth.

तत्रापि च प्रधानाश्रीर्महादेवीखगानना।
धर्मोदया समाहुता संतिष्ठते जगत्कृते[26] ॥ ८० ॥

In that land lives a Goddess, with a mouth like a bird, named Khagānanā, also known as Dharmodayā, who is the protector of the land, its patron deity, residing there for the welfare of the whole world.

तां दृष्ट्वा स महाचार्यो मञ्जुदेवो महर्द्धिमान्।
बोधिसत्त्वो महासत्त्वःभूयश्चा[27]नन्दितोऽभवत् ॥ ८१ ॥

At the sight of the Goddess Khagānanā, Mañjuśrī was filled with bliss and bowed to her.

ततः सतां महादेवीं समालोक्य प्रमोदितः।
उरसा शिरसा दृष्ट्वा वचसा मनसा तथा ॥ ८२ ॥

पद्भ्यां कराभ्यां जानुभ्यामष्टांगोऽयमिति स्मृतः।
अष्टांगैः प्रणतिं कृत्वा सांजलिः समुपाश्रयत् ॥ ८३ ॥

As he saw the mighty Goddess, he was filled with bliss. Then, he saluted her with his chest, his head, his sight, his words, his mind,

26 द्धिते इति कपाठः।

27 भूयश्चा इति कपाठः।

his feet, his knees and with his hands. Thus, he saluted her with eight bodily positions, in eight ways. He then stood up.

सुप्रसन्नमुखाम्भोजः सुप्रबुद्धः शयाम्बुजः ।
संपश्यन् तां महादेवीं स्तोत्रैरेवं मुदाभजत् ॥ ८४ ॥

His face reflected the immense joy he felt in his heart, for his knowledge had increased, his ability to read minds had developed and with this realization, he then chanted a hymn in reverence of the Goddess.

महादेवि भगवति भवत्याः शरणं व्रजे ।
वन्दे पादाम्बुजे नित्यं भजामि तत्प्रसीदतु ॥ ८५ ॥

"O Great Goddess! I am in your asylum. I bow to your feet. O Mother! please be pleased for I am in your eternal service.

जननी सर्वबुद्धानां त्वमेव बोधिदायिनी ।
सर्वेषां बोधिसत्त्वानां माता हितानुपालिनी ॥ ८६ ॥

You are the mother of all *buddhas*; you are the one who grants them knowledge, you are the one that raises and fosters all *bodhisattvas* like a mother.

सर्वहितार्थ–संसक्ता[28] सर्वपापविशोधिनी ।
दुष्टमारागणा क्षोभा महानन्दा सुखप्रदा ॥ ८७ ॥

You bring welfare to all; you remove the sins of your devotees; you destroy their enemies; you remove their obstacles; you are the embodiment of all pleasure; and you grant happiness and bliss.

सद्धर्म–साधनोत्साह–वलवीर्य–गुणप्रदा ।
निःक्लेशस्तिमित–ध्यान–समाधि–सुखदायिनी ॥ ८८ ॥

You are the one who grants bravery and strength to people practising the *dharma*; you remove their miseries and grant them focus, concentration and happiness.

---

28 संभक्तिं इति गपाठः ।

प्रज्ञागुण-महारत्न-श्री-समृद्धिप्रदायिनी ।
तव भक्त्या पदाम्भोजशरणस्थो भजाम्यहम् ॥ ८९ ॥

You are the qualities of knowledge, you are the supreme jewel among jewels; you are prosperity and the granter of prosperity; you grant welfare to those who worship you. I wish to come into your asylum and worship you so, Mother."

इति संप्रार्थ्य स प्राज्ञो मंजुदेवः स शम्बरी ।
तस्या भक्तिप्रसन्नात्मा समाराधितुमैच्छत ॥ ९० ॥

As he prayed to the Great Goddess, the wise Mañjuśrī, intent on worshipping her, was filled with excitement.

अथ तत्र स आचार्यः सगणः संप्रमोदितः ।
मार्गशीर्षे सिते पक्षे[29]नवम्यां रविवासरे ॥ ९१ ॥

प्रातः स्नात्वा विशुद्धात्मा शुचिवस्त्रावृतः सुधीः ।
उपोषधव्रतं[30] धृत्वा देवीमाराधयन् स्थितः ॥ ९२ ॥

He prepared himself for the worship. He bathed to purify himself, clad himself in good clothes and along with his company, he, in the month of Mārgaśira, in the ninth day of the *kṛṣṇa-pakṣa* fortnight on Sunday, sat down to worship the Goddess.

रात्रौ जागरणं कृत्वा धारणी-मन्त्र जल्पनैः[31] ।
स्तुतिभिश्च समाराध्य प्राभजच्च जिनेश्वरीम् ॥ ९३ ॥

He stayed awake all night, chanting Dhāraṇī *mantra* and other *stotra*s, in devoted prayer to the Goddess Guhyeśvarī.

ततःप्रातःदशम्यां स स्नात्वा गन्धोदकैर्मुदा ।
दत्वा दानं यथाकामं परिशुद्धत्रिमण्डलः ॥ ९४ ॥

In the morning of the tenth day, he ablated to purify his appearance,

29 शितैः पक्षैः इति घपाठः ।

30 पोषधसम्बरं इति घपाठः ।

31 जल्पने इति कपाठः ।

mind and soul and then he offered sandalwood, water and flower to the Mother.

यथाविधि समभ्यर्च्य तां देवी परमेश्वरीम् ।
महोत्साहैः स्तुतिं कृत्वा त्रिधा प्रदक्षिणानि च ॥ ९५ ॥

He, who was in her refuge, was devoted to her procedural worship. Filled with excitement, he prayed to her with chanted hymns and thrice performed *pradakṣiṇā* around her.

सुप्रसन्नमुखाम्भोजः सद्धर्मगुणमानसः ।
भूयोऽष्टांगैः प्रणम्यैवं प्रार्थयत् साञ्जलिर्मुदा ॥ ९६ ॥

He was extremely elated – his face bloomed like a lotus, he was filled with virtues. So after he bowed again to her in eight positions, he finally addressed her with hands joined in reverence.

प्रसीदतु जगन्मात भर्वत्याः समुपाश्रयात् ।
सम्बोधिसाधनोत्साहो भजामि सर्वदा मुदा ॥ ९७ ॥

"O Mother! I worship to please you. You are the practice of acquiring knowledge. I pledge my eternal devotion to you. Mother, I pray I may be able to gain knowledge."

इति संप्रार्थ्य स प्राज्ञो नत्वाष्टांगैर्मुदा च ताम् ।
तत्पद्मामृतमादाय त्रिधा ह्यञ्जलिनाऽपिबत् ॥ ९८ ॥

As the wise Mañjuśrī prayed so, he again worshipped the Goddess in eight ways. Then, he picked up the elixir in her feet and drank it in three parts.

तदमृतं निपीयासौ संविशुद्धत्रिमण्डलः ।
अष्टाक्षणविनिर्मुक्तः संबुद्धक्षणमाप्तवान् ॥ ९९ ॥

As he drank the water of her feet that was equal to nectar, he was absolutely purified. The eight flaws of a human – he was rid of them. And he instantly reached a state where he would be able to attain Buddhahood.

एवं कृत्वा स आचार्य देव्या भक्तिपरायणः ।
संबुद्धक्षणमासाद्य सर्वधर्माधिपोऽभवत् ॥ १०० ॥

Having done that, he was devoted to the worship of the Goddess. In that moment, the light of knowledge broke out inside of him, wisdom dawned in his mind and he became the lord of *dharma*.

ततःश्रीमान् स आचार्यो बोधिसत्त्वो जगत्कृते ।
ससंघश्चावसत् तत्र भर्मधातोरुपाश्रमे ॥ १०१ ॥

Mañjuśrī, then, in the form of an *ācārya*, *bodhisattva*, started to reside in an *āśrama* near the Dharmadhātu, where he lived with the Saṅgha he formed, for the welfare of the world.

तस्य तत्र स्थितत्त्वेन[32]प्रदेशःश्री मनोहरः ।
स्यात्सर्वत्रापि मंजुश्रीपर्वत इतिविश्रुतः ॥ १०२ ॥

The place of his residence, from where he granted all knowledge, was in a hill, which is beautiful and still stands there, famous as the Mañjuśrī Parvata, in his name and memory.

तत्र स्थितः सदा चासौ धर्मधातोरुपासकः ।
सर्वसत्त्वहितार्थेन प्राभजत् स जिनात्मजः ॥ १०३ ॥

He resides there, perpetually in devotion to the Dharmadhātu, for his devotion is to bring welfare to the entire world. With this intent, he still worships the Dharmadhātu.

तत्समीक्ष्यामला सर्वे ब्रह्मेन्द्र-प्रमुखा अपि ।
सर्वे लोकाधिपाश्चापि मुदा तत्र समागताः ॥ १०४ ॥

Seeing Mañjuśrī living in his *āśrama*, practising austerity for the welfare of the entire world, Indra, Brahmā and all the gods and lords of all realms, pleased, approached him.

तत्रैवोपोषधं धृत्वा कृत्वा जागरणं निशि ।
जपित्वा[33]धारणी-मन्त्रान् ध्यात्वा तां श्रीजिनेश्वरीम् ॥ १०५ ॥

---

32 तत्समभ्यषितत्वात् इति खपाठः ।

33 उषित्वाइति इति कपाठः ।

यथाविधि समभ्यर्च्य कृत्वा प्रदक्षिणानि च ।
कृत्वाष्टांगप्रणामानि स्तुतिभिश्चाभजन् मुदा ॥ १०६ ॥

They who arrived there, including Brahmā and Indra, brought offerings with them and stayed awake all night in devotion. They chanted the Dharaṇī *mantra* and prayed to the Goddess Jineśvarī. Then they performed the *pradakṣiṇā*, and salutations with eight bodily positions, and enriched their worship with devoted chanting and prayers.

एवं तस्या महादेव्याः सर्वे ते शरणाश्रिताः ।
धर्मश्रीगुणसंपत्ति-महर्द्धिसिद्धिमाप्नुवन् ॥ १०७ ॥

As they went to the refuge of the Goddess, they acquired prosperity of *dharma* and were granted divine powers.

ततस्ते चामराः सर्वे सेन्द्र-ब्रह्मादयो ऽधिपाः ।
वज्रकूटं नगाब्जं तं समीक्ष्यन्ते जिनालयम् ॥ १०८ ॥

Thus, those who had come, including Brahmā and Indra, took refuge at the Vajrakūṭa Mountain where the Dharmadhātu was situated, in devotion to him.

अनुमोद्याभिनन्दन्ते तस्यापि शरणं गताः ।
महोत्साहैः समभ्यर्च्य प्राभजन्त समादरात् ॥ १०९ ॥

During their residence, they were in constant devotion, prayer and worship of the lord and chanted great hymns and prayers in his reverence.

ततः सर्वे ऽमरास्तावत् सर्वे लोकाधिपाश्च ते ।
अस्यापि मंजुदेवस्य वज्राचार्यस्य सद्गुरोः ॥ ११० ॥

शरणं समुपासृत्य दिव्यपूजोपहारकैः ।
समभ्यर्च्य महोत्साहैः प्राभजन्त प्रमोदिताः ॥ १११ ॥

Then all those gods and lords of the realms, came to the refuge of the good teacher Mañjuśrī, and offered divine materials and worshipped him full of energy and enthusiasm.

एवं मन्वादयः सर्वे मनुयोऽपि महर्षयः ।
यतयो योगिनश्चापि भिक्षवो ब्रह्मचारिणः ॥ ११२ ॥

Great sages such as Manu, great monks, *saṁnyāsī*, *bhikkhu*s and *brahmacārī*s, all came to that place.

चैलका बोधिसत्त्वाश्च महासत्त्वा जिनात्मजाः ।
ते सर्वे समुपागत्य तस्या देव्या उपासकाः ॥ ११३ ॥

*Cailaka*s, *bodhisattva*s, *mahāsattva*s, children and disciples of Buddha and the able-bodied all came there for the worship of the Goddess Guhyeśvarī.

यथाविधि समभ्यर्च्य प्राभजन्त प्रमोदिताः ।
ततस्ते धर्मधातुञ्च सर्वेऽपि शरणाश्रिताः ॥ ११४ ॥

All who came worshipped in proper order and filled with happiness, having worshipped the goddess, proceeded to fully devote themselves to the Dharmadhātu Svayambhū.

समभ्यर्च्य महोत्साहैर्नत्वा कृत्वा प्रदक्षिणाम् ।
सुप्रसन्न-मुखाम्भोजाः प्राभजन्त प्रमोदतः[34] ॥ ११५ ॥

Those that worshipped the Dharmadhātu and performed *pradakṣiṇā* were filled with bliss and blessed with knowledge.

ततस्ते च महासत्त्वं मञ्जुदेवं महर्द्धिकम् ।
आचार्यं च समुत्साहैः समर्चयन् प्रमोदिताः ॥ ११६ ॥

Again they went to the Mañjuśrī and in acceptance of him as their *guru*, worshipped him enthusiastically.

प्रत्येक-सुगताश्चापि सर्वे तत्र समागताः ।
तां देवीं धर्मधातुं तमाचार्यं च समर्चयन् ॥ ११७ ॥

Novice disciples of Buddha, *bodhisattva*s and those in line for Buddhahood, all arrived there and worshipped the goddess, the Svayambhū and finally the Ācārya Mañjuśrī.

---

[34] प्रमोदितनः इति कपाठः ।

सर्वे तथागताश्चापि पूजामेघमहद्धनैः[35] ।
तां देवीं धर्मधातुं तमाचार्यं च समर्चयन् ॥ ११८ ॥

*Tathāgata buddha*s came with large amount of offerings that they offered there. They worshipped the Goddess, the Dharmadhātu and finally the *guru*.

एवमन्येऽपि लोकाश्च दृष्ट्वैव समुपागताः ।
तां देवीं धर्मधातुञ्च तमाचार्यं च प्राभजन् ॥ ११९ ॥

Thus, all those who came there, were filled with joy as they worshipped the three: the goddess, the Dharmadhātu and the teacher.

एतत्पुण्यानुभावेन चलिता सानुगा मही ।
पुष्पवृष्टिःशुभोत्साहः प्रावर्तत समन्ततः ॥ १२० ॥

Due to the influence and merit of the worship of the three, the entire world shook. This is why the flowers showered from the heavens and the celestial drums were played."

इत्यादिष्टं मुनीन्द्रेण विश्वभूवा निशम्यते ।
सर्वे सभाश्रिता लोका विस्मयं समुपाययुः ॥ १२१ ॥

After the Viśvabhū Buddha, greatest among the sages, quenched the curiosities of the assembly; everyone was filled with wonder and awe.

ततः सर्वेऽपि ते लोकास्तां देवीं श्रीमहेश्वरीम् ।
धर्मधातुं तमाचार्यं द्रष्टुमभिववाञ्छिरे ॥ १२२ ॥

They all then desired to visit the Great Goddess, the Svayambhū and the Mañjuśrī Ācārya.

तदाशयं परिज्ञाय गगनगञ्ज उत्थितः ।
भगवन्तं प्रणम्यैव साञ्जलिः पुनरब्रवीत्[36] ॥ १२३ ॥

Having heard the words of the Viśvabhū, the Bodhisattva Gaganagañja, rising from his seat, with hands joined in reverence, prayed to the lord.

35 सर्जनैः इति गपाठः ।

36 भगवन्तन्तमानस्पश्यन्नेवमब्रवीत् इति कपाठः ।

भगवन्! सर्व इच्छन्ति द्रष्टुं तां सुखगेश्वरीम्।
धर्मधातुं तमाचार्यं तदनुज्ञां ददातु नः ॥ १२४ ॥

And said, "O Lord! O Buddha! everyone present here wishes to pray to the Goddess, the Svayambhū and the *ācārya*. Please grant us permission to do so."

इति संप्रार्थितं तेन भगवान् स मुनीश्वरः ।
गगनगञ्जमात्मज्ञं तं पश्यन्नेवमादिशत् ॥ १२५ ॥

After the sage prayed, the Lord Viśvabhū, looking at the *bodhisattva* who had just asked him permission, commanded him thus:

साधु साधु महादेवीं खगाननां जिनेश्वरीम्[37] ।
धर्मधातुं तमाचार्यमपि द्रष्टुं यदीच्छथ ॥ १२६ ॥

तत्र हिमालये गत्वा तां श्रीदेवीं खगाननाम् ।
धर्मधातुं तमाचार्यं संभजध्वं यथाविधि ॥ १२७ ॥

"Good. You all must go. If you wish to worship the Goddess Khagānanā Jineśvarī, the Dharmadhātu Svayambhū and the Ācārya Mañjuśrī, you must travel to the place near the Himalaya, where they reside, and devote yourselves to their service."

इत्यादिष्टं मुनीन्द्रेण विश्वभुवा निशम्यते ।
सर्वे लोका महोत्साहैरत्रायुः प्रमोदिताः ॥ १२८ ॥

As the Lord of all sages, the Viśvabhū commanded the assembly so, the assembled masses present, in divine happiness, proceeded to depart for the a forementioned land.

अहमपि मुनीन्द्रस्य प्राप्यानुज्ञां प्रमोदितः ।
तैः सार्द्धं प्रस्थितो दूरात्पश्यन्निमं समागतः[38] ॥ १२९ ॥

I too, having received the Sage-lord's permission, was filled with joy. So, along with everyone else, I started on the journey. Finally, I saw the place from afar.

---

37 मिहेश्वरी इति कपाठः ।

38 समाययौ ।

अत्र प्राप्तः समालोक्य धर्मधातुमिमं मुदा ।
समभ्यर्च्य महोत्साहैस्तैर्लोकैः सह प्राभजम् ॥ १३० ॥

Having reached there, I relished at the sight of the Dharmadhātu. I enthusiastically chanted hymns for him. And along with everyone else, I served him.

श्रद्धया शरणं गत्वा कृत्वा चैनां प्रदक्षिणाम् ।
स्तुत्वाष्टांगैःप्रणम्यैव[39]प्रार्थयं बोधिसम्वरम् ॥ १३१ ॥

I sought his refuge, full of devotion. I performed *pradakṣiṇā*, chanted praises, bowed to him in eight ways and prayed to him to grant me knowledge.

ततोऽहं मंजुदेवाख्यं तमाचार्यं समीक्ष्य च ।
समभ्यर्च्य महोत्साहैः प्राभजं च सहानुगैः ॥ १३२ ॥

Then, I went where the Mañjuśrī lived and beheld him, worshipped him, offered him my offerings and served him.

ततस्तस्योपदेशेन तां श्रीदेवीं खगाननाम् ।
यथाविधि समाराध्य महोत्साहैः समर्चयम् ॥ १३३ ॥

Similarly, as the Buddha had commanded me previously, I went to the Goddess. I procedurally prayed to her and full of enthusiasm, worshipped her.

कृत्वा प्रदक्षिणां चापि नत्वाष्टांगैः प्रमोदितः ।
स्तुत्वा ध्यात्वा च संबोधिं संप्रार्थयं जगत्कृते ॥ १३४ ॥

I did the *pradakṣiṇā* and in eight ways bowed to her, sang hymns for her and devoted myself to her meditation. I prayed to her to grant me knowledge that would bring welfare to the world.

एतत्पुण्यानुभावेन परिशुद्धत्रिमण्डलः ।
अष्टाक्षणविनिर्मुक्तो बोधिसत्त्वोऽभवं कृती ॥ १३५ ॥

Due to the merit received by the worship, my words, mind and actions

---

39 प्रणत्वाच ।

were purified, and I was freed of the eight human flaws and thus became a *bodhisattva.*

ततः सम्बोधिसंभारं पूरयित्वा यथाक्रमम् ।
जित्वा मारगणान् अर्हन् कलावपि जिनोऽभवम् ॥ १३६ ॥

Then I climbed the steps of *bodhi*, conquered the bodily desires and, even in the Kali age, I became a *jinaḥ*.

एवमस्या महादेव्या ये ये शरण आश्रिताः ।
यथाविधि समाराध्य भजेयुर्बोधिमानसाः ॥ १३७ ॥

Similarly, everyone else who takes the refuge of the Goddess and ritually worships her shall receive the *bodhi* knowledge.

ते ते सर्वे महासत्त्वाः परिशुद्धत्रिमण्डलाः ।
बोधिसत्त्वा महाभिज्ञा भवेयुस्त्रिगुणाधिपाः ॥ १३८ ॥

And those *mahāsattva*s, *bodhisattva*s, who have purified their hearts, words and actions become great wise ones and the lords of the three worlds.

कुत्रापि ते न गच्छेयुर्दुर्गतिञ्च कदाचन ।
सदा सङ्गतिसंजाता भवेयुःश्रीगुणाश्रयाः ॥ १३९ ॥

They will never reach a bad state anywhere. They will always be in good state – full of all prosperity.

यथाभिवाञ्छितं द्रव्यं दत्वार्थिभ्यो समादरात् ।
यथाकामं सुखं भुक्त्वा सञ्चरेयुर्जगत्कृते ॥ १४० ॥

Those people will be able to grant all wishes to others and will walk the earth as they wish until their time here ends.

ततो विशुद्धशीलास्ते चतुर्ब्रह्म-विहारिणः[40] ।
बोधिसम्बरमाधाय संचरेयुः सदा शुभे ॥ १४१ ॥

Their morals will be purified and they will experience the four steps of bliss and then, established in bodhihood, shall act as *bodhisattva*s.

---

40 महोरगा इति कपाठः ।

ततस्ते स्युर्महासत्त्वाः सद्धर्मसुखलालसाः ।
स्वपरात्महिताधारक्षान्तिव्रतसमारताः ॥ १४२ ॥

Then such *mahāsattva*s, in the desire of the happiness obtained by the Buddha Dharma, will live to practice the *bodhi* vow for the welfare of themselves and others.

ततस्ते सद्‌गुणाधारा वीर्यवन्तो विचक्षणाः[41] ।
सद्धर्मसाधनोद्युक्ता भवेयुस्त्रिगुणाधिपाः ॥ १४३ ॥

Then they will be filled with virtue and full of glory in the practice of *dharma* and will eventually be the lords of three worlds.

ततस्ते सुधियो धीरा निःक्लेशा विजितेन्द्रियाः ।
समाधिगुणसम्पन्ना भवेयुर्बोधियोगिनः ॥ १४४ ॥

Then those people, firmly rooted in *bodhi*, will be wise, resilient, shall conquer misery, and be able to enter trance.

ततस्ते विमलात्मानः सर्वविद्या-गुणाधिपाः ।
प्रज्ञाश्रीरत्नसम्प्राप्ता भवेयुः सुगतात्मजाः ॥ १४५ ॥

Then those people will be purified from within; all knowledge will enter them; and they will attain perfected wisdom. Filled with the jewel of wisdom, they will eventually turn into children of Buddha.

ततश्च ते महासत्त्वाः सर्वे सत्त्वाहितोत्सुकाः ।
सर्वोपायविधिप्राज्ञा भवेयुस्त्रिगुणाधिपाः ॥ १४६ ॥

Thus, the *mahāsattva*s and *bodhisattva*s will be indulged in the welfare of the world. And with the knowledge of all ideas and procedures and with all their wisdom, they would be the lords of three worlds.

ततस्ते बोधिसंभार-प्रणिधिरत्नसागराः ।
सर्वसत्त्वहितं कृत्वा संचरेयुः सदा शुभे ॥ १४७ ॥

They will understand the secret to the attainment of *bodhi*. They would swim in the ocean of knowledge and auspiciousness, for the welfare of the whole world.

---

41 भजन्ति च इति खपाठः ।

ततश्च ते महाभिज्ञाः भद्रश्री-सद्गुणान्विताः ।
बलिष्ठा दुष्टजेतारो भवेयुस्त्रिभवेश्वराः ॥ १४८ ॥

Consequently, they, filled with great knowledge, prosperity, good virtues, great strength and the ability to defeat the evil and wicked, will live as the lords in the world.

ततस्ते त्रिविधां बोधिमासाद्य भद्रचारिणः ।
सम्बोधिज्ञानसद्रत्नसमृद्धाः स्युर्मुनीश्वराः ॥ १४९ ॥

Thus, having attained the three types of *bodhi*, those that walk the path of welfare, should be filled with highest level of wisdom and will live as superiors even among sages.

ततस्ते सुगता बुद्धा दशभूमीश्वरा जिनाः ।
बोधिमार्गे प्रतिष्ठाप्य कुर्युः सर्वान्सुधार्मिकान् ॥ १५० ॥

Then they will be the Sugata, omniscient, beyond the ten *bhūmi*, established in the *bodhi* path and as such, they will preach *dharma* to all.

एवं धर्ममयं कृत्वा सर्वत्र भुवनेष्वपि ।
सुनिर्वृतिपदं प्राप्य संप्रयायुर्जिनालयम् ॥ १५१ ॥

Thus, having preached the words of *dharma* and having filled the three worlds with *dharma*, they will walk the path of liberation and upon reaching the realm of *buddha*s would live there as *buddha*s.

एवमस्या महादेव्या भजनात् प्राप्तमुत्तमम्[42] ।
पुण्यं महत्तरं सिद्धं सम्बुद्धपदसाधनम् ॥ १५२ ॥

Thus, those who pray to the Great Goddess earn tremendous merit, become divine and finally reach Buddhahood.

इति सत्यं समाख्यातं सर्वैरपि मुनीश्वरैः ।
विज्ञायास्या महादेव्या भजध्वं शरणे स्थिताः ॥ १५३ ॥

I have told these truths, as the sages have been telling forever. It is advisable to go to the refuge of the Goddess in devotion.

---

42 हूतमुक्तमं इति कपाठः ।

अस्यापि धर्मधातोश्च भजनोद्भूतमुत्तमम् ।
पुण्यं महत्तरं सिद्धं सम्बुद्धपदसाधनम् ॥ १५४ ॥

अस्यापि मञ्जुदेवस्य भजनोद्भुतमुत्तमम् ।
पुण्यं महत्तरं सिद्धं सम्बुद्धपदसाधनम् ॥ १५५ ॥

मत्वेति यदि वो वाञ्छा विद्यते सौगते पदे[43] ।
सर्वे यूयं समाधाय भजतात्र जिनालये ॥ १५६ ॥

The worship of the Svayambhū Dharmadhātu will grant greatness, divine powers, merit and Buddhahood. Upon worshipping and offering great items to the Mañjuśrī, a person will collect immense merit enough to grant them Buddhahood. Hence, all of you who seek Buddhahood must worship the Dharmadhātu.

खगाननामहादेव्याः शरणे च समाश्रिताः ।
ध्यात्वा स्मृत्वा समुच्चार्य नामापि भजताभवम् ॥ १५७ ॥

Taking the refuge of the Great Goddess, remember her, meditate on her, chant her names and pray to her.

य एषां शरणे स्थित्वा ध्यात्वा स्मृत्वा समाहिताः ।
नामापि समुदाहृत्य भजन्ति सर्वदा भवे ॥ १५८ ॥

Those that receive her asylum and focus and meditate on her and chant her names and devote to her prayers forever, shall be subject to eternal welfare.

ते सभद्रा न गच्छन्ति दुर्गतिं च कदाचन ।
सदा सद्गतिसंजाता भवेयुःश्रीगुणश्रयाः ॥ १५९ ॥

Those gentle people shall never reach a miserable state and will always be in a good state. They will be filled with virtues and qualities.

बोधिसत्त्वा महासत्त्वा सद्धर्मबोधिचारिणः[44] ।
सर्वसत्त्वहितोद्युक्ता भवेयुः सुगतात्मजाः ॥ १६० ॥

---

43 च गुरुपदे इति खपाठः ।

44 बोधिकामनात् इति खपाठः ।

Those that pray so will become *bodhisattva*s, *mahāsattva*s, users of the Buddha Dharma and will be vying for the welfare of all and ultimately become sons of Buddha.

एवं तेषां महत्सौख्यं भद्रश्रीसद्गुणान्वितम् ।
सर्वदापि नीरुत्पातं प्रवर्तते समाहितः ॥ १६१ ॥

They (who pray to the Goddess, the Svayambhū and the *guru*) shall receive divine bliss, prosperity and good virtues, shall never reach a state of misery, and shall always be calm, focused and full of tranquillity.

दैवोत्पातभयस्तेषां विद्यते न समन्ततः ।
एतान् दृष्ट्वा सुराः सर्वे रक्षन्तीन्द्रादयो मुदा ॥ १६२ ॥

Those who chant hymns for them will never be subject to the wrath of the gods; and gods would always gladly appear near them to give them protection.

अग्न्युत्पातभयं तेषां विद्यते न कदाचन ।
ते तान्दृष्ट्वा प्रसीदन्तो रक्षेयुर्वह्नयः सदा ॥ १६३ ॥

They need not ever fear fire or danger from arson, for fire himself would gladly appear to protect them.

अकाल-मरणाद् भीतिस्तेषां न विद्यते क्वचित् ।
यद्यमोऽपि समालोक्य रक्षति तां प्रसादतः ॥ १६४ ॥

They will never die before their time, for the god of death himself would intervene to prevent it.

राक्षसस्य भयं तेषां विद्यते न समन्ततः ।
यद् वायवोऽपि तावीज्य रक्षेयुः सर्वदानुगाः ॥ १६५ ॥

They need not fear demons, for the winds would provide them divine fortification against evil.

यक्षस्यापि भयं तेषां विद्यते न सदा क्वचित् ।
यक्षाः समीक्ष्य रक्षेयुः सर्वे यक्षाधिपा अपि ॥ १६६ ॥

They would never have to fear *yakṣa* demi-gods, for the demi-gods would appear themselves to protect such people.

भूतेभ्योऽपि भयं तेषां विद्यते न समन्ततः ।
यदीशानो ऽपि तान्पश्यन् संरक्षेत् संप्रमोदितः ॥ १६७ ॥

They would never have to fear ghosts and spirits, because Lord Śiva – the Iśāna himself would gladly appear to protect them.

गन्धर्वोत्पाततो भीतिस्तेषां न विद्यते क्वचित् ।
धृतराष्टो ऽपि तान्पश्यन् संरक्षेत्संप्रसादितः ॥ १६८ ॥

They would not have to fear *gandharva* demi-gods, because the king of *gandharva* demi-gods would gladly appear to prevent any harm.

कुम्भाण्डेभ्यो ऽपि नास्त्येवं भयं तेषां कदाचन ।
विरूढको हि तान् पश्यन्नभिरक्षेत् प्रसादतः ॥ १६९ ॥

They will not have to fear the *kumbhāṇḍa* demi-gods, because the Lord of *kumbhāṇḍa* called Virūḍhaka, would personally protect them.

नागेभ्योऽपिभयं तेषां विद्यते न सदा क्वचित् ।
विरूपाक्षो हि सम्पश्यन्तान् रक्षेत् सम्प्रसादितः ॥ १७० ॥

They were in no danger of the serpents, for the king of the serpents – Virūpākṣa would gladly protect them from any serpentine harm.

यक्षेभ्योऽपि सदा तेषां विद्यते न भयं क्वचित् ।
कुवेरो हि समालोक्य संरक्षेत् तान् प्रसादितः ॥ १७१ ॥

They need not fear the *yakṣa*s, for Lord Kubera himself would gladly protect them of any danger from *yakṣa*-kind.

भयं न किन्नरेभ्योऽपि तेषामस्ति कदाचन ।
द्रुमो हि तान् महासत्त्वान् संवीक्षेच्च प्रसादितः ॥ १७२ ॥

Kinnara semi-gods will also pose no danger to them, for the king of *kinnara*s, Drumakinnara, would provide full protection.

गुह्यकेभ्योऽपि नास्त्येव भयं तेषां सुधर्मणाम् ।
वज्रपाणिर्हि तान् वीक्ष्य प्रसादितो भवेत् सदा ॥ १७३ ॥

They would not have to fear *guhyaka*s, for Vajrapāṇi, who carries a *vajra* in his hand, would protect them.

तथा विद्याधरेभ्योऽपि भयं तेषां न विद्यते ।
यतः सर्वार्थसिद्धोऽपि सम्पश्यन् तान् प्रसीदति[45] ॥ १७४ ॥

Vidyādhara demi-gods also pose no threat; because Sarvārthasiddha Vidhyādhara would protect them of any danger.

ग्रहोत्पातभयस्तेषां विद्यते न कदाचन ।
ग्रहाधिपा हि सर्वेऽपि संरक्षेयुः प्रसादतः[46] ॥ १७५ ॥

They need not fear the planets, for the lords of the planets would come to protect those people.

तथा तारागणोत्पातभयं तेषां न विद्यते ।
सर्वास्तारा हि तान् वीक्ष्य रक्षयेयुः प्रसादतः[47] ॥ १७६ ॥

They will have no danger of the stars and constellations, for in all times, the lords of the stars would protect them.

सिद्धाः साध्याश्च रुद्राश्च वीक्ष्यावेयुः सदापि तान् ।
तत्तेभ्योऽपि भयं क्वापि तेषां नास्ति कदाचन ॥ १७७ ॥

They will have no fear for *siddha*, *sādhya*s or *rudra*s, for such demi-gods would also come to their protection when called upon.

तथा च मातृकोत्पातं भयं नास्ति कदाचन ।
सर्वा हि मातृका दृष्ट्वा रक्षेयुस्तां प्रसादिताः ॥ १७८ ॥

A group of demi-goddesses, called the *Mātṛikā*s, will not be a threat; for they would also protect them.

महाकालो गणेशोऽपि स्कन्दश्च भैरवा अपि ।
सर्वदा तात्समालोक्य रक्षेयुस्तान् प्रसादिताः ॥ १७९ ॥

Mahākāla, Gaṇeśa, Skanda and Bhairava themselves will protect these people from all miseries incoming from all directions.

---

45 वेत्सदा इति कपाठः ।

46 समीक्ष्यतानवेत्सदा इति खपाठः ।

47 सर्वत्रा वेयुराभवं इति कपाठः ।

प्रेता भूताःपिशाचाश्च वेताला डाकिनीगणाः ।
अपि तान् सर्वदालोक्य संरक्षेयुः प्रसादिताः ॥ १८० ॥

Ghosts, phantoms, demons, vampires, sirens, witches will bring no fear to them. Such evil spirits will flee at the sight of such *mahāsattvas*. Moreover, Mahākāla, Gaṇeśa, Skanda would also provide protection.

एतेभ्योऽपि भयं तेषां विद्यते न कदाचन ।
सर्वेऽपि ते सहायाः स्युः सम्बोधिधर्मसाधने ॥ १८१ ॥

They will have no fear from any of the aforementioned groups. Everyone would be supportive to the practitioners of *dharma.*

सिंहादिसर्वजन्तुभ्यः पक्षिभ्योऽपि समन्ततः[48] ।
सर्पादिकृमिकीटेभ्यो भयं तेषां कदापि न ॥ १८२ ॥

Lions and other beasts, evil birds, snakes and insects will pose no threat.

दुष्टप्रत्यर्थिकेभ्योऽपि तस्करेभ्योऽपि सर्वतः ।
शत्रुभ्योऽपिभयं तेषां विद्यते न समन्ततः ॥ १८३ ॥

The wicked, hostiles, thieves, enemies and robbers will impose no fear on such people.

यदेतत्पुण्यलिप्तान् तान् समीक्ष्य ते प्रसादिताः ।
सर्वे मैत्रीकृपास्नेहनिबद्धाः स्युर्हितार्थिनः ॥ १८४ ॥

Thus, having seen such pious people, may everyone be bound by friendship, welfare, and charity for the good of all beings.

एवं सर्वेऽपि सत्त्वास्तान् दृष्ट्वा ते संप्रसादिताः ।
स्निग्धचित्ताः प्रसान्नास्याःपश्येयुर्मैत्रीभावतः ॥ १८५ ॥

All beings of the world will approach them with happiness and perceive them with a friendly attitude, for the sight of those who worship the trio would soften their hearts.

---

48 कदाचन इति खपाठः ।

राजानोऽपि च तान् दृष्ट्वा मैत्रीस्नेहसभाविताः ।
सुप्रसन्नाशयाःप्रीता मानयेयुः सदा मुदा ॥ १८६ ॥

Even kings, at the sight of them, would be filled with joy, affection and a desire to befriend such men.

मन्त्रिणोऽपि सदा तेषां मैत्रीस्नेहसुभाषिताः ।
मानयेयुःयथाकामं सद्धर्मव्रतसाधनम्[49] ॥ १८७ ॥

At the sight of such people, even courtiers and ministers would be happy and treat them with kindness, compassion and respect and would support their *vrata*.

ब्राह्मणा अपि सर्वे च तेषां सद्धर्मसाधनम् ।
दृष्ट्वानुमोदितात्मानो दद्युर्भद्राशिषं सदा ॥ १८८ ॥

Even brāhmaṇas, at the sight of their practice of *dharma*, would be pleased and support them and bless them into welfare.

ऋषयोऽपि तथा सर्वे ते दृष्ट्वा संप्रसादिताः ।
पश्यन्तः कृपया दृष्ट्वा मोदयेयुः शुभाशिषा ॥ १८९ ॥

Even sages, at the sight of these people, would be happy. With the perspective of welfare, they would impose goodwill and blessings on these people.

एवं च योगिनः सिद्धा यतयो ब्रह्मचारिणः ।
तीर्थिकास्तापसाश्चापि व्रतिनश्चाप्युपासकाः ॥ १९० ॥

Similarly, *yogī*s, *siddha*s, *saṁnyāsī*, *brahmacārī*s, Vedic scholars, ascetics, *vrata* holders, *upāsaka*s and *upāsikā*s would all bless them and show support.

चैरका भिक्षवश्चापि भिक्षुण्यश्चाप्युपासिकाः ।
अपि तान् सदृशान् दृष्ट्वा नन्दयेयुःशुभाशिषा ॥ १९१ ॥

*Cailaka*s, *bhikkhu*s, *bhikkhuṇī*s and all followers of Buddha, would all be pleased at the sight of them and would give them blessings.

---

49 कदाचन इति खपाठः ।

एवं च श्रावकाः सर्वे प्रत्येकसुगता अपि ।
बोधिसत्त्वाश्च सर्वेऽपि तान् दृष्ट्वा संप्रसादिताः ॥ १९२ ॥

Novices and initiates of the Buddha Dharma, *bodhisattva*s, would all, at the sight of these people, be pleased and offer blessings.

कृपा–दृष्ट्यानुपश्यन्तो मैत्रीस्नेहसुभाविनः ।
रक्षित्वा बोधिमार्गेषु नियोजेयुः सदा भवम् ॥ १९३ ॥

All the aforementioned people would look at these people with friendliness, affection, protectiveness and would always be helpful to those walking the path of *bodhi*.

एवं सर्वेऽपि संबुद्धा दृष्ट्वा तान् संप्रसादिताः ।
सर्वदा तान् रक्षयेयुश्चारयेयुर्जगत्कृते ॥ १९४ ॥

Those that have attained Buddhahood will be filled with a desire to bless at the sight of these people, and shall work to further propel these people into the path of welfare.

एवं तेषां महत्पुण्यं सम्बुद्धपदसाधनम्[50] ।
भद्रश्रीगुणसंपत्तिसमृद्धिसिद्धिसंपदम् ॥ १९५ ॥

These people will have immeasurable merit, enough to grant them Buddhahood. Wealth of virtues, prosperity and divine powers would all come to these people.

एवं यूयमपि ज्ञात्वा सर्वदा शरणाश्रिताः ।
यथाशक्ति समभ्यर्च्य भजतैतान्त्रिरत्निकान् ॥ १९६ ॥

Understand this. You must go to the asylum of the three gems to worship them to the best of your abilities, which will bring you welfare.

स्मृत्वा ध्यात्वापि नामापि समुच्चार्य सदा मुदा ।
एषामेव त्रिरत्नानां भजेध्वं शरणे स्थिताः ॥ १९७ ॥

50 व्रतकारणात् इति कपाठः । गोपनं इति खपाठः ।

Remember them, meditate on them, utter their names; for they are the three gems – receive their asylum.

एतत्पुण्यविलिप्ता ये परिशुद्धत्रिमण्डलाः ।
भद्रश्रीगुणसंपन्ना भवेयुस्ते शुभाशयाः ॥ १९८ ॥

Having gotten the merit by worship of the trio, your mind, words and actions will be purified; you shall have good thoughts; and you shall see plenty of paths for welfare.

दुर्गतिं ते न गच्छेयुः सदा सद्गतिसंभवाः ।
बोधिसत्त्वा महासत्त्वा भवेयुर्भद्रचारिणः ॥ १९९ ॥

You will never reach a state of misery. Instead, you shall always walk the path of good and ultimately become *bodhisattva*s, *mahāsattva*s and work for the welfare of the world.

ततस्ते सर्वसत्त्वानां हितार्थं साधनोद्यताः ।
सुधीरा बोधिसम्भारं पूरयित्वा यथाक्रमम् ॥ २०० ॥

You all should work for the welfare of all beings, attain *bodhi* and profound resilience, and proceed further into Buddhahood.

ततो मारगणाञ्जित्वा निःक्लेशा विजितेन्द्रियाः ।
अर्हन्तः त्रिविधां बोधिं प्राप्य यायुर्जिनालयम् ॥ २०१ ॥

After that, you shall conquer the army of bodily desires, to be in control of your organs, freed of all your miseries; you shall become *arhant*s, cross the three steps of *bodhi* and finally dwell the land of Buddha.

एतत्सर्वं मयाख्यातं सर्वैरपि मुनीश्वरैः ।
श्रुत्वानुमोदनां कृत्वा प्रचरेत सदा शुभे ॥ २०२ ॥

I have told you the secrets – words accepted and heeded by the greatest of the sages. You all must propagate these words far and wide to promote auspiciousness."

इत्यादिष्टं मुनीन्द्रेण निशम्य ते सभाश्रिताः ।
सर्वे तथानुमोदन्तः प्राप्यानन्दं प्रबोधिताः ॥ २०३ ॥

As the great sage Upagupta commanded them so, everyone seated in the assembly had marked his words and, full of bliss, had awakened.

॥ इति श्रीस्वयंभूत्पत्तिसमुद्देशमहाह्रदशोषणधर्मधातुपद्मगिरिसंप्रास्थापनो नाम तृतीयोऽध्यायःसम्पूर्णः ॥

The third chapter, called the origin of Svayambhu, is thus completed.

अथ चतुर्थोऽध्यायः
(Caturtha Adhyāya)

Vītarāga Tīrtha

अथात्रासौ महासत्त्वो मैत्रेयः सुगातात्मजः ।
भगवन्तं प्रणम्यैव[1]प्राहैवं साञ्जलिर्मुदा ॥ १ ॥

Upon hearing the words of the Lord, the Maitreya, who was like a son to Buddha, with hands joined in prayer, addressed the Lord.

कदात्र भगवन् जाता ग्राम-नगरपङ्क्तयः ।
प्रवर्तिता महाराष्ट्राः तत्समादेष्टुमर्हति ॥ २ ॥

"O Lord! after Mañjuśrī severed the hill to drain the water out of the pond, when did the landmass get populated? When did villages, groups of cities and the country settle here?"

इति संप्रार्थिते तेन मैत्रेयेण निशम्य सः ।
भगवान् तं महाभिज्ञं समालोक्यैवमादिशत् ॥ ३ ॥

When the Buddha heard the prayers of Maitreya, he looked at the *bodhisattva* and answered so:

साधु शृणु महासत्त्व! मैत्रेय! त्वं समाहितः ।
तत्कालं संप्रवक्ष्यामि यदात्र वसतिरभूत् ॥ ४ ॥

"Listen to my words carefully, O Mahāsattva Maitreya! and I will tell you when people started living here."

यदायूंषि नृणां वर्षचत्वारिंशत्सहस्रकम् ।
धर्मराजो जगन्नाथः क्रकुच्छन्दो[2]मुनीश्वरः ॥ ५ ॥

---

1 मानंम्य इति खपाठः ।

2 ककुच्छन्दः इति खपाठः ।

When the lives of men spanned 40,000 years, there lived a Buddha called *Krakucchanda*, he was the Lord of *dharma*, Lord of all sages, Lord of the world.

सर्व-विद्याधिपः शास्ता त्रैधातुक-विनायकः ।
सर्वज्ञोऽयं[3]महाभिज्ञ[4]स्तथागतो जिनोऽभवत् ॥ ६ ॥

The Krakucchanda Buddha was the Lord of all knowledge, ruler of the world, protector of the three realms, the omniscient, the *tathāgata* and the enlightened.

स सम्बुद्धो जगल्लोकहितार्थाय[5] ससांघिकः ।
क्षेमावत्या महापुर्या ह्युपारामे मनोरमे ॥ ७ ॥

The Buddha named Krakucchanda, for the welfare of the world, lived with his Saṅgha in an *āśrama* in the outskirts of the large city of Kṣemāvatī.

विहारे सौगतावासे सद्धर्मं समुपादिशत् ।
आदिमध्यान्तकल्याणं विजहार प्रभासयन्[6] ॥ ८ ॥

At the *vihāra*, which was his residence, the Lord gave the teachings of the good *dharma*, which ensured welfare to all in the beginning, middle and end.

तदा संबोधिसत्त्वोऽहं ज्योतिः-पालाभिधः सुधीः।
शास्तारं तं क्रकुच्छन्दं समाराध्य सदाभजम् ॥ ९ ॥

During that time, I was a *bodhisattva* named Jyotipāla. I was a great scholar with a sharp mind. I was in service of the Krakucchanda Buddha, to whom I prayed and whose wisdom I heeded.

सदा स भगवाञ्छास्ता क्रकुच्छन्दो जगत्कृते ।
जानपदेषु सद्धर्मं समुपादेष्टुमैच्छत ॥ १० ॥

---

3 हं इति खपाठः ।

4 मभिज्ञ इति घपाठः ।

5 येन इति कपाठः ।

6 प्रदृष्टिसः इति कपाठः ।

The Lord Krakucchanda, for the welfare of the world, wished to preach the *dharma* to the public in villages and towns.

ततः स भगवान् शास्ता सर्वसंघैः समन्वितः ।
सर्वत्र भद्रतां कृत्वा संभाषयन्समाचरत् ॥ ११ ॥

After that the Lord Krakucchanda, with his Saṅgha following behind him, started to wander the land, teaching the Buddha *Dharma*.

एवं स सञ्चरञ्छास्ता सर्वज्ञो धर्ममादिशत् ।
क्रमेणेह समायातः सन्ददर्श समन्ततः ॥ १२ ॥

दृष्ट्वेमं धर्मधातुं संप्रज्वलितं जिनालयम्[7] ।
ससंघं समुपाश्रित्य प्राभजद्विधिना मुदा ॥ १३ ॥

The Krakucchanda Buddha wandered from one town to other, one village to the next, travelling with the purpose of preaching *dharma*, in all places, in all directions. As he approached the sight of the illuminating Dharmadhātu, he joyfully went on to procedurally worship the Svayambhū along with his Saṅgha.

ततः स प्रस्थितोऽत्रैव शंखाभिधे शिलोच्चये ।
महच्छुद्धशिलायां स विजहार ससांघिकः ॥ १४ ॥

The Krakucchanda Buddha then settled on top of a rock on the Śaṅkha Parvata (the conch-shaped hill).

तत्र तं त्रिजगन्नाथं क्रकुच्छन्दो मुनीश्वरम् ।
सभामध्यासनासीनं भिक्षुसंघैः पुरस्कृतम् ॥ १५ ॥

Being the master of all knowledge, the Lord of the world, the Krakucchanda Buddha assumed the highest seat at the centre of the assembly; and he was surrounded by his Saṅgha.

समालोक्य महासत्त्वा जिनात्मजाः समन्ततः[8] ।
तत्सद्धर्मामृतं पातुं संहर्षिताः समागताः ॥ १६ ॥

---

7 महोरगम् इति खपाठः ।

8 नास्ति इति कपाठः ।

When they saw the Krakucchanda Buddha sitting there, everyone from *mahāsattva*s to honorary sons of Buddha gathered around, expecting the nectar that are his words.

भिक्षुण्यपि शुशीलाद्याश्चैलकाश्चाप्युपासकाः ।
चैलका व्रति नश्चापि सर्वे उपासिका अपि ॥ १७ ॥

बोधिसत्त्वा महासत्त्वा सद्धर्मगुणलालसाः ।
तत्सद्धर्मामृतं पातुं सर्वे ते समुपागताः ॥ १८ ॥

As he started preaching, the *bhikkhuṇī*s, *cailaka*s, *upāsaka*s, monks, vow practitioners, *bodhisattva*s, *mahāsattva*s, laymen and laywomen and all those who sought to drink the elixir of *dharma* gathered around.

भगवन्तं समभ्यर्च्य कृत्वा प्रदक्षिणान्यपि ।
नत्वा साञ्जलयस्तत्र पश्यन्तः समुपाश्रयन्[9] ॥ १९ ॥

They approached the Lord Buddha to worship him, perform the *pradakṣiṇā* and with their hands joined in salutation, went to his refuge.

तथा ब्रह्मादयश्चापि महर्षयस्तपस्विनः ।
यतयो योगिनश्चापि मुनयो ब्रह्मचारिणः ॥ २० ॥

Brahmā and the gods, sages and the austere, *yogī*s and monks, celibates and hermits, all arrived there.

एवं शक्रादयो देवाः सर्वे लोकाधिपा अपि ।
ग्रहास्तारागणाःसिद्धा साध्या विद्याधरा अपि ॥ २१ ॥

Similarly, Indra and his council of gods, lords of the worlds, planets, stars and constellations, demi-gods such as *siddha*s, *sādhya*s, *vidyādhara*s, all arrived.

गन्धर्वा किन्नरा यक्षा गुह्यका राक्षसा अपि ।
दानवा गरुडा नागास्तथान्येह समागताः ॥ २२ ॥

भगवन्तं ससंघं तं समभ्यर्च्य प्रमोदिताः ।
नत्वा धर्मामृतं पातुमुपतस्थुः समाहिताः ॥ २३ ॥

---

[9] समतस्थिरे इति खपाठः ।

Demi-gods such as *gandharvas, kinnaras, yakṣyas* and *guhyakas*, as well as demons, serpents and falcons, they all came to receive audience of the Lord Buddha. They worshipped him as he sat there and then returned to their respective seats, waiting to drink the elixir of *dharma* that came from him.

एवं च ब्राह्मणा विज्ञा राजानः क्षत्रिया अपि ।
वैश्याश्च मन्त्रिणोऽमात्याः सैन्या भृत्या जनाधिपाः[10] ॥ २४ ॥

Similarly, brāhmaṇas, scholars, kings, merchants, ministers, courtiers, warriors and soldiers, servants, arrived at the place.

गृहस्था धनिनःश्रेष्ठाः साधवश्च महाजनाः ।
शिल्पिनो वणिजश्चापि सार्थवाहाश्च पौरिकाः[11] ॥ २५ ॥

Householders, rich men, businessmen, monks, noblemen, tradesmen with caravans, townsfolk, everyone came.

प्रजा जानपदाःश्राम्याः कार्पटिकाश्च पौरिकाः ।
एवमन्येऽपि लोकाश्च सर्वदिग्भ्यः समागताः ॥ २६ ॥

भगवन्तं समालोक्य प्रणम्य[12] समुपागताः ।
यथाक्रमं समभ्यर्च कृत्वा प्रदक्षिणान्यपि ॥ २७ ॥

The general public, labourers, craftsmen, menial workers, everyone came from all directions. They approached the Lord, worshipped him and performed *pradakṣiṇā* around him.

कृत्वाष्टांग-प्रणामाँश्च कृतांजलिपुटा मुदा ।
तत्सद्धर्मामृतं पातुं तत्सभायां समन्ततः ॥ २८ ॥

परिवृत्य पुरस्कृत्य समाश्रित्य समाहिताः ।
गुरूकृत्य मुनीन्द्रास्तं समुद्वीक्ष्य निषेविरे ॥ २९ ॥

Those who came saluted the Lord Krakucchanda with eight bodily positions, gladly joining their hands in his reverence. Sitting around

---

10 धिपाः इति खपाठः ।

11 ब्राह्मणा इति खपाठः ।

12 प्रणम्य इति कपाठः ।

the Lord in all directions, with the desire to hear the words of *dharma* like elixir that he would teach the assembly, they looked above at him expectantly, knowing the Lord would grant knowledge and words of wisdom.

ततः स भगवान् दृष्ट्वा सर्वान् तान् समुपस्थितान् ।
आर्यसत्यं समालक्ष्य सद्धर्मं समुपादिशत् ॥ ३० ॥

When the Lord saw everyone gathered there with devotion in their hearts and a strong desire to hear the *dharma*, he started to preach – starting with the noble truths.

तत्सद्धर्मामृतं पीत्वा सर्वेऽपि ते प्रबोधिताः ।
बोधिचर्याव्रतं धर्तुं समैच्छन्त प्रसादिताः ॥ ३१ ॥

As they drank the nectar (in the form of the Krakucchanda's words) everyone awakened. With happy hearts, they desired to practise the *Bodhicaryā* (*bodhi* vow).

तदाशयं परिज्ञाय भगवान् स मुनीश्वरः ।
समागतान् बोधिसत्त्वान् सम्पश्यन्नेवमादिशत् ॥ ३२ ॥

Having understood the intent of everyone present, the Lord willed everyone to become *bodhisattva*s and to practise the *bodhicaryā*. He addressed them so:

कुलपुत्रा मुदा येऽपि श्रद्धया सौगते वृषे ।
प्रव्रजितुं समिच्छन्ति तत्र प्रव्रजिताद्रिताः ॥ ३३ ॥

"O sons and daughters! please heed my words with devotion. You should follow your desire to practise monkhood and ordinance, for it is a good path."

अत्र ये ह्युपछन्दांसि सर्वधर्मार्थसिद्धये ।
प्रव्रज्या-शासने बौद्धे चरन्ति बोधिसंवरम् ॥ ३४ ॥

Everyone present here, for the access to the essence of the true *dharma* must practise the *bodhicaryā* with discipline.

ते सर्वे पातकाद् मुक्ताः परिशुद्धत्रिमण्डलाः ।
निःक्लेशा विमलात्मानो बोधिसत्त्वा जितेन्द्रियाः ॥ ३५ ॥

Those people that practise *bodhi* are cleansed of their sins; they are purified in their actions, words and bodies; their miseries are destroyed; their souls are purified; they can claim victory and control over their organs and finally attain *bodhi*.

जित्वा मारगणान् दुष्टान् हन्त! ते ब्रह्मचारिणः ।
त्रिविधां बोधिमासाद्य सम्बुद्धपदमाप्नुयुः ॥ ३६ ॥

They then defeat the bodily desires, overcome the wicked, become celibate and pure, and are established onto the three steps of *bodhi* to ultimately walk the path towards Buddhahood.

इति मत्वात्र संसारे ये वांछन्ति सुनिर्वृतिम् ।
तत्र प्रव्रज्यया बौद्धं चरन्तु श्रद्धया व्रतम् ॥ ३७ ॥

With this knowledge, those who desire to free themselves from this world, must become monks and practise their vows faithfully, as preached by the Buddhas.

इत्यादिष्टं मुनीन्द्रेण निशम्य ते प्रबोधिताः ।
सभासीना महासत्त्वा ऐच्छन् प्रवजितुं तदा[13] ॥ ३८ ॥

Having heard these words of the Krakucchanda Buddha, everyone present there including the *mahāsattva*s and *bodhisattva*s, desired to practise the Buddhist ordinance.

ततो गुणध्वजादीनां ब्राह्मणानां चतुःशतम् ।
तथाभयं ददौ नाम क्षत्रियाणां शतत्रयम् ॥ ३९ ॥

तथानेके महासत्त्वा वैश्याःशूद्राश्च सज्जनाः ।
सर्वेऽपि सुप्रसन्नास्त ऐच्छन् प्रव्रजितुं तदा ॥ ४० ॥

The assembly of 400 brāhmaṇas that exhibited signs of virtue, 300 kṣatriyas, many vaiśyas and śūdras, many *mahāsattva*s and gentlemen and all, who were present, were gladdened with the desire to become monks.

---

13 प्रव्रजितुं समीच्छिरे इति खपाठः ।

ततस्ते सर्व उत्थाय साञ्जलयः पुरागताः ।
भगवन्तं प्रणम्यात्राब्रूवन्नेवं समादरात्[14] ॥ ४१ ॥

So, everyone rose from their seats, joined their hands in front of the Lord, saluted him and prayed to him so:

भगवन्! नाथ सर्वज्ञ धृत्वाज्ञां भवतो वयम् ।
प्रव्रज्याशासने बौद्धे चर्तुमिच्छामः संवरम्[15] ॥ ४२ ॥

"O Omniscient One! we are all avid to follow your words and to practise the wisdom recommended by you, to accept monkhood and practise the *bodhicaryā*.

भगवन्! तद् भवानस्मान् सर्वान् पश्यन् कृपा दृशा ।
समन्वागत्य सद्धर्मं नियोजयितुमर्हति ॥ ४३ ॥

O Lord! bless us with your benevolence, inaugurate us into the Buddha Dharma, with the knowledge of *dharma*."

इति तैः प्रार्थिते सर्वैर्भगवान् स मुनीश्वरः ।
सर्वान् तान् सन्मतीःपश्यन् कृपया[16] चैवमादिशत् ॥ ४४ ॥

When the assembly requested the Lord so, he looked at them, who were all wise and filled with devotion, and thus commanded them:

यद्यत्र सौगते धर्मे प्रव्रजितुं समिच्छथ ।
एतत् प्रव्रज्य सर्वत्र चरत सौगतं व्रतम् ॥ ४५ ॥

"All present here, who desire to be inaugurated into the *dharma*, practise ordinance and dwell without fear."

इत्यादिश्य स संबुद्धःपाणिना तच्छिरःस्पृशन् ।
तान् सर्वान् सौगते धर्मे समन्वाहरदादरात् ॥ ४६ ॥

As he commanded the mass so, the Krakucchanda Buddha gradually

---

14 तमानस्यप्रार्थयन्नेवमादरात् इति कपाठः ।

15 व्रते इति गपाठः ।

16 समामन्थ्यै इति कपाठः ।

* Foods

put his hands on their heads and ordained everyone present there into the Bauddha Dharma.

ततोऽवतार्य ते केशान् रक्त-चीवर-प्रावृताः ।
खिखिरी-पात्रमाधाय सर्वे ते भिक्षवोऽभवन् ॥ ४७ ॥

Everyone then shaved their heads, wore red robes, held a bowl for *bhikṣā* (food) and thus became monks and nuns (*bhikkhus*–*bhikkhuṇīs*).

ततः स भगवान् तेभ्यो यतिभ्यो बोधिपाक्षिकान् ।
सद्धर्मान् समुपादिश्य प्रददौ बोधिसम्वरम् ॥ ४८ ॥

Then the Lord preached all types of *dharma*'s knowledge to the newly ordained *bhikkhus* and taught the way of *bodhi*.

ततस्ते विमलात्मानो निःक्लेशा विमलेन्द्रियाः ।
सत्कार-लाभ-निःकांक्षा वीतसङ्गा निरंजनाः ॥ ४९ ॥

Everyone present there was purified, their minds were cleansed, obstacles destroyed, organs purified; their desire for personal welfare and gain vanished, they became free from all attachments.

स्वपरात्म-समाचाराः संसारगतिनिःस्पृहाः ।
मारचर्या-निरासक्ताः समलोष्ट-सुवर्णकाः ॥ ५० ॥

They did not differentiate between themselves and others, friends or enemies. They were freed of their worldly desires and attachment to mundane lives. Their greed was also pacified, so much so that they valued gold the same as stones or soil.

क्लेशनिर्गतमात्मानो परिशुद्ध-त्रिमण्डलाः ।
अर्हन्तो भद्रकाचारा बभूवुर्ब्रह्मचारिणः ॥ ५१ ॥

Their sorrows came to an end. Their souls were purified. Their three *maṇḍalas* (mind, word and body) were also purified. They became *arhants*, *bhadrakas* and *brahmacārīs*, with the ability to reach out and help everyone.

ततः सर्वेऽपि ते बौद्धा यतयो बोधिचारिणः ।
सर्वसत्त्वहितं कृत्वा संप्राचरन् सदा शुभे ॥ ५२ ॥

On the path of the Buddha Dharma, those *bhikkhus*, able to contain the *bodhi* knowledge, walked the earth with good actions for the welfare of all beings.

ततस्ते विशुद्धात्मानःपंचाभिज्ञमहर्द्धिकाः ।
वन्द्याःपूज्याः सदेवानां लोकानां गुरवोऽभवन् ॥ ५३ ॥

Purified, they were all filled with five kinds of knowledge. All prosperity found its way to them, due to their lack of desire for it. They became teachers worthy of respect, worship and reverence from gods and men.

तस्मिँश्च समये तत्र गिरेः शंखस्य मूर्द्धनि ।
वज्रसत्त्व-कराङ्गुष्ठान्निश्चचाराम्बु निर्मलम् ॥ ५४ ॥

In the meantime, on top of the Śaṅkha mountain, water materialized from the thumb of a *bodhisattva* named Vajrasattva.

तदेतदभवद् रम्यं[17]पुण्यतीर्थमहासरित् ।
यदभूत् सर्वलोकानां चतुवर्गफलप्रदा ॥ ५५ ॥

The water thus emerged was extremely pure and rendered the emanating river holy. The river was able to grant *dharma*, *artha*, *kāma* and *mokṣa* (the bliss of *dharma*, wealth, desire and liberation) to everyone and thus, came to be a great pilgrimage.

भूयोऽपि सा नदी[18]तस्य ऋकुच्छन्दस्य तायिनः ।
सद्धर्म-देशनावाक्याद् बभूवातिपवित्रिता ॥ ५६ ॥

The pure river was further purified by the words of the Krakucchanda Buddha, to the point that it attained the ability to quench and purify everyone.

तेनासौ सर्वतीर्थाग्रे [19]वाग्वतीतिप्रसिद्धिताम् ।
अभवद्[20]गुणसंभर्त्री सर्वपापविशोधिनी ॥ ५७ ॥

17 तदेमान्वद्भूति स्पन्दं इति कपाठः ।

18 सादिदि इति गपाठः ।

19 वाग्मतीति इति खपाठः ।

20 भद्रश्री इति खपाठः ।

Thenceforth, the river, foremost among the pilgrimages, came to be known as the Vāgvatī (Vāgmatī in present day). Those who bathe in the river are wholly purified: for it grants virtues and destroys all evil.

ये तत्र विधिना स्नात्वा पितृ-देवादितर्पणम् ।
कृत्वा[21]दानादिकं दत्त्वा व्रतं चापि प्रकुर्वते ॥ ५८ ॥

ते संघविमलात्मानो भद्रश्रीसद्गुणान्विताः ।
यथाकामं सुखं भुक्त्वा[22]संप्रयान्ति जिनालयम् ॥ ५९ ॥

Those who ablute in the Vāgvatī, provide offerings and perform rites for ancestors and donate lavishly to the poor, become absolutely purified, filled with virtues and enjoy the pleasures in this realm before they dwell the realm of Buddha, in liberation.

इति मत्वा सदा तत्र स्नात्वा पित्रादितर्पणम्[23] ।
दानादि-संवरं कृत्वा संचरन्तां जगत्कृते ॥ ६० ॥

Thus, having understood this, you must provide offerings and perform rites, give donations and practise vows, in the sacred pilgrimage of Vāgmatī.

तस्या दर्शनमात्रेण पीताम्बु-विमलात्मके ।
स्पर्शनादपि नश्यन्ति सर्वाणि पातकान्यपि ॥ ६१ ॥

The auspicious sight of the river, the touch of its water and its intake frees one of the greatest of sins.

प्रक्षाल्यापि च तत्रास्यं गंगास्नानफलं भवेत्[24] ।
शिलासिंचन-मात्रेण शुद्धानि चेन्द्रियाणि षट् ॥ ६२ ॥

The one who washes his body in the Vāgmatī receives merit equal to that of a bath in the Ganges. Even a sprinkle of the water on the head purifies all their sense organs and mind.

---

21 स्नानादिकम् इति खपाठः ।

22 सुरे भूत्वा इति कपाठः ।

23 देवादितर्पणम् इति गपाठः ।

24 लभेत् इति कपाठः ।

एवं महत्तरं पुण्यं वाग्वती-भजनोद्भवम् ।
सर्वतीर्थोत्तमं ख्यातं तेनासौ वाग्वती मता ॥ ६३ ॥

Thus, by the worship of the Vāgmati, great piety arises. Therefore, it came to be known as the Vāgmati and the greatest pilgrimage of all.

इति मत्वात्र संसार इच्छन्ति ये सदाशुभम् ।
वाग्वतीं श्रीसुखाधारां भजन्तु सर्वदापि ते ॥ ६४ ॥

Having understood this, those who desire welfare, must always touch and worship the pure holy waters of the Vāgmatī.

भूयोऽप्येषा सरिज्जाता तस्यैव करसंभवा ।
सापि पवित्रतां याता[25]क्रकुच्छन्दस्य वाक्यतः ॥ ६५ ॥

Similarly, another river originated as the Lord Krakucchanda was giving his sermon, from the hand of the Vajrasattva Bodhisattva.

तत्र प्रव्रजितानां यत् श्मश्रुकेश-नखानि च ।
कृत्वा भागद्वयं तत्र भागमेकं प्रचिक्षिपुः ॥ ६६ ॥

The newly-ordained monks who had shaved their hair and beards, trimmed their nails, then disposed half of their hair in the newly-originated river.

तदा केशावतीत्यासीत् प्रसिद्धा सा महानदी ।
एको भागस्तु तत्रैव संस्थापितःशिलातले ॥ ६७ ॥

Because of this, the newly-originated river was named *Keśavatī* (since *keśa* means hair) and the river became greatly famous. The other half of their hair was left on the rock on top of the mountain.

यावन्ति श्मश्रु-केशानि तावन्त्यपि शिलातले ।
प्रादुर्भूतानि चैत्यानि तान्यद्यापि लसन्ति[26] हि ॥ ६८ ॥

Each strand of hair on the rock gave rise to a *caitya*. Thus, the thousands of strands of hair gave rise to thousands of new *caitya*s on the rock.

---

[25] पवित्रिताभूतो इति कपाठः ।

[26] वसति इति घपाठः ।

सापि नदी महातीर्थं वाग्वतीव प्रसिद्धताम्[27] ।
तेषां प्रव्रजितानां हि जाता पुण्यानुभावतः ॥ ६९ ॥

The river, just like Vāgmatī, came to be very pure and became a great holy spot. Since the merit achieved by the newly-ordained monks went to that river, it also came to be known as the Puṇyaśālī River.

तेषां प्रव्रजितानाञ्च भिक्षूणां ब्रह्मचारिणाम् ।
तदा पुण्य-महाकीर्ति-शब्दः सर्वत्र प्रासरत् ॥ ७० ॥

The merit received by the mass of newly-ordained monks spread and along with the merit, spread the news of the origination of the rivers.

तदनन्तरमष्टौ च वीतरागा निराश्रयाः ।
ज्योतिरूपा निराकाराः प्रादुर्भूता जगत्कृते ॥ ७१ ॥

Then emerged eight *vītarāga*, who were devoid of worldly attachments, who had no refuge or basis; they were in the form of pure energy and light; and they were there for the welfare of the world.

एकःशंखगिरेः पार्श्वे मणिचूडाश्रमान्तिके ।
मणिलिङ्ग इति ख्यातः सोऽद्यापि संप्रतिष्ठते ॥ ७२ ॥

On the hill named Śaṅkha, was an *āśrama* named Maṇicūḍā and there originated the first *vītarāga* as the Maṇiliṅga, which still lies there.

द्वितीयोऽभूच्च गोकर्णस्थले ज्योतिर्मया कृतिः ।
चारुगिरौ तृतीयश्च कुम्भतीर्थे चतुर्थकः ॥ ७३ ॥

पंचमः फणिशैले च षष्ठश्च गर्तकस्थले ।
सप्तमो गन्धवत्यां च ह्यष्टमो विक्रमस्थले ॥ ७४ ॥

एते ह्यष्टौ महादेवाः वीतरागा निरञ्जनाः ।
ज्योतिरूपा निराकाराः प्रादुर्भूता जगद्धिते ॥ ७५ ॥

The second one lay at the Gokarṇeśvara, which existed in the form of light. In the mountain named Cāru lived the third one. The fourth, in the Kumbha pilgrimage, existed in the form of light. The fifth was

27 प्रसीद्धता इति गपाठः ।

situated on the Phaṇi Mountain, the sixth in the Gartaka, the seventh in the Gandhavatī and the eighth Vikrama. These eight are the forms of Mahādeva; they are devoid of desires; they have no beginning and only exist in form of light.

अत्रैषां वीतरागाणामनुभावात् समन्ततः।
मनोरमा महीजाता सर्वपीठोक्तमावनौ ॥७६ ॥

The eight *vītarāga*, due to their influence and glory, adorned the entire earth such that all places became beautiful.

तदा योऽभूद् महातेजा महासामन्त-वंशजः।
कृपाकारुण्य-भद्रात्मा बोधिसत्त्वो नृपोऽभवत् ॥ ७७ ॥

In that time, from the lineage of *Mahāsāmanta*, was born a great king, who had become a *bodhisattva*, filled with immense compassion and desire for welfare of all.

तत्र स नृपराजेन्द्रः क्रकुच्छन्देन तायिना[28]।
सहात्र द्रष्टुमायातः स्वयंभूवं खगाननाम् ॥ ७८ ॥

The king, who was a *bodhisattva,* departed for the place where the Svayambhū and the Goddess Khagānanā resided, to receive the audience of Krakucchanda Buddha.

दूरात्स एनमालोक्य स्वयंभूवं जिनालयम्।
प्रणम्य समुपागत्य चक्रे प्रदक्षिणात्रयम् ॥ ७९ ॥

When he saw the Svayambhū, the residence of the Buddha, he saluted it and did *pradakṣiṇā* around it thrice.

ततोऽभ्यर्च्य महोत्साहैरेनं पञ्जजिनात्मकम्।
सुप्रसन्नो ह्यभूत्तस्मात् बोधिचित्तश्च भूपतिः[29] ॥ ८० ॥

अष्टांगैश्च नमस्कृत्य प्राभजच्छरणाश्रितः[30]।
ततस्तथा स राजेन्द्रो मंजुदेवं च सद्गुरुम् ॥ ८१ ॥

---

28 बुद्धिना इति खपाठः।

29 नास्ति इति घपाठः।

30 शरणंगतैः इति कपाठः।

Approaching the shrine, he worshipped the Lord Svayambhū who was established with the five *buddhas*. He saluted him with eight bodily positions and went to his refuge. Then, he approached the Mañjuśrī and sought his refuge as well.

यथाविधि समभ्यर्च्य प्राभजत् संप्रमोदितः ।
ततस्तथा स राजेन्द्रःखगाननां जिनेश्वरीम् ॥ ८२ ॥

Having procedurally worshipped the Mañjuśrī and having given him the offerings, the king approached the Goddess Khagānanā - that is Tārā (तारा) but some scholars say this is actually Guhyeśvarī (गुह्येश्वरी).

यथाविधि समभ्यर्च्य महोत्साहैर्मुदाभजत् ।
ततोऽष्टौ वीतरागाँश्च सर्वानेतान् स्वयंभुवः ॥ ८३ ॥

He worshipped her according to tradition and afterwards, went towards the eight self-originated *vītarāga* shrines.

दृष्ट्वा प्रमुदितो राजा महोत्साहैस्तथाऽभजत् ।
एतत्पुण्यानुभावैः स महत्पुण्याशयः कृती ॥ ८४ ॥

Then, he worshipped the eight self-originating *vītarāga* with great joy and enthusiasm. The merit he received through the worship gained him great fame all over the world.

सर्वधर्माधिराजेन्द्रः सर्वलोकाधिपो बभौ ।
सर्वविद्याधिपो राजा भद्रश्रीसद्गुणाश्रयः ॥ ८५ ॥

Thus, the worship of the great eight *vītarāga*, the Goddess, the Mañjuśrī and the Svayambhū blessed him with great fortune, the knowledge of all *dharma*, superiority among all kings, attainment of all *dharma* and all great qualities.

धर्माकर इति नाम्ना प्रसिद्धोऽभूद् स भूपतिः ।
ततः सोऽत्रमहाराजः संस्थातुकाम आत्मना ॥ ८६ ॥

Thus the king, who was also a *bodhisattva*, was then named Dharmākara (source or mine of *dharma*). Afterwards, he immediately went to the refuge of Krakucchanda Buddha.

क्रकुच्छन्दं मुनीन्द्रं तं प्रणिपत्य न्यवेदयत्।
भगवन्! कृपया सर्वं विजानीयात् मयेच्छितम्॥ ८७॥

As he reached the residence of the Krakucchanda, he saluted him and did *pradakṣiṇā* around him and prayed to him with hands joined, "O Lord! you are omniscient and you know of the desire that lies in my heart."

तदनुज्ञां पालयामि[31] करोत्वनुग्रहं मयि[32]।
इति संप्रार्थिते तेन भगवान्स मुनीश्वरः॥ ८८॥

"O Lord! please bless me with your immense benevolence." In this way, he prayed to the Buddha.

धर्माकरं नरेन्द्रं तं सम्पश्यन्नेवमादिशत्।
साधु राजन् महासत्त्व! यदेव त्वं समीच्छसि॥ ८९॥

Hearing the prayer, the Lord Buddha, looking at the Dharmākara King, answered so:

"O great King! you are a wise *bodhisattva*. Whatever you desire shall become yours."

तथा त्वमिह सन् स्थित्वा पालय बोधयन् प्रजाः।
तथात्र सकलान् लोकान् संस्थाप्य संप्रबोधय॥ ९०॥

"Your duty is to protect your citizens on the earth and to help instate your subjects on the path of *bodhi*.

बोधिमार्गे प्रतिष्ठाप्य चारयस्व सदा शुभे।
धर्मेण पालयन् सर्वलोकान् स्वयं समाचरन्॥ ९१॥

Establish them into the path of *bodhi* knowledge; serve the citizens of this earth full of *dharma*; and perform good deeds yourself so that everyone would follow the same.

यथाकामसुखं प्राप्य चरस्व त्वं जगत्कृते।
धर्मनीत्या समाधाय कुर्या[33]लोकहितं सदा॥ ९२॥

---

31 नास्ति इति कपाठः।

32 पदत्वामेनुग्रहं कर्तुमर्हति इति कपाठः।

33 कृत्वा इति कपाठः।

Enjoy the pleasures you wish to, constantly gather fast pace for the welfare of the world and work for the world with the principle of *dharma*.

साधय बोधिसम्भारं सदेहोऽत्र निवासतः[34] ।
सदास्य शरणे स्थित्वा धर्मधातोः स्वयम्भूवः ॥ ९३ ॥

Practise the vow of *bodhi* truthfully and in the refuge of Lord Dharmadhātu, reside in his vicinity.

श्रद्धया भजनं कृत्वा संचरस्व जगत्कृते ।
अस्याः खगाननायाश्च देव्याः शरण आश्रितः ॥ ९४ ॥

With devotion in your worship of the Svayambhū, live protecting your citizens. On top of this, go to the refuge of the Goddess Khagānanā.

सर्वदा भजनं कृत्वा चरस्व बोधिसंवरम् ।
अस्यापि मंजुदेवस्य शरणं समुपाश्रयन् ॥ ९५ ॥

Constantly pray this great Goddess so as to climb the steps of greater knowledge. And also worship the good *guru* Mañjuśrī.

बुद्धानुशासनं धृत्वा सद्धर्मे संचरस्व त्वम् ।
एषां च वीतरागाणामष्टानामपि सर्वदा ॥ ९६ ॥

Upholding Buddha's disciplines, walking the path of the good *dharma*, you must worship the eight *vītarāga*s, the forms of Mahādeva, in their refuge.

श्रद्धया भजनं कृत्वा साधय धर्ममुत्तमम् ।
वाग्वतीप्रमुखानाञ्च तीर्थानां समुपाश्रयात् ॥ ९७ ॥

With devotion chant the hymns, practise the ultimate *dharma* and worship the great pilgrimages like the Vāgmatī.

स्नानदानादिकं कृत्वा पितॄन् देवाञ्च तोषयन् ।
लब्ध्वा त्रिकाय-संशुद्धिं धृत्वा संबोधिमानसम् ॥ ९८ ॥

Ablute in the pure rivers; donate, quench the gods and the ancestors

---

34 निवसाश्रिता इति घपाठः ।

and then your words, actions and mind shall consequently get purified and slowly you shall hold all the knowledge in your heart.

सर्वसत्त्वहितं कृत्वा निवस त्वं यथासुखम् ।
एवं राजेन्द्र लोकाँश्च सर्वानपि प्रबोधय ॥ ९९ ॥

Doing the welfare of all beings, O King! live there peacefully. Also try to nudge the other worlds towards the path of knowledge.

एतेषामपि सर्वेषां संस्थाप्य शरणे सदा ।
पूजा-भक्ति-महोत्साहैः चारयित्वा समादरात् ॥ १०० ॥

Urge all these beings to worship the Svayambhū, devote themselves to him and practise the discipline of the Buddha with enthusiasm, as you do.

बोधिमार्गे प्रतिष्ठाप्य चारयस्व सदा शुभे ।
एवं कृत्वा महाराज! संबोधि-निहिताश्रयः ॥ १०१ ॥

Take your subjects to the path of *bodhi,* the good path, so that your actions are filled with *bodhi*.

बोधिचर्याव्रतं धृत्वा संचरस्व जगद्धिते ।
एतत्पुण्याभिलिप्तात्मा भविष्यसि जिनात्मजः ॥ १०२ ॥

In this way, continue your good deeds in this world while practising the *bodhi* vow. Through the merit achieved so, you shall one day become a son of Buddha.

बोधिसत्त्वो महाभिज्ञो भद्रश्री-सद्गुणाश्रयः ।
कदाचिदपि नैव त्वं दुर्गतौ च क्वचित् पतेः[35] ॥ १०३ ॥

You shall become a *bodhisattva* with great knowledge. The essence of all virtues and goodwill shall come to you and you will never reach a state of misery, for you shall be forever bound in the good path.

सदा सद्गतिसंजातः समृद्धिसिद्धिमान्सुधीः ।
श्रीमान् सर्वगुणाधीशः सर्वलोकाधिपः कृती ॥ १०४ ॥

---

[35] पतीन् इति गपाठः ।

You will be wise, able to distinguish the true from the false; you shall have prosperity, wisdom and be the Lord of virtues and all land.

क्रमेण बोधिसंभारं पूरयित्वा समाहितम्।
त्रिरत्नभजनोत्साहैर्महानन्दसुखं सदा ॥ १०५ ॥

Similarly, you shall cross the steps of *bodhi*, gain absolute focus and with devotion towards the Buddha, Dharma and Saṅgha, acquire divine bliss.

भुंजानो निर्मलाचारश्चतुर्ब्रह्म-विहारिणः।
निःक्लेशो निर्जयन् मारान् सर्वानर्हत्वमाप्नुहि ॥ १०६ ॥

The four pleasures – *dharma*, *artha*, *kāma* and *mokṣa* shall be yours. You shall be freed from all misery, victorious against bodily desires and ready to become an *arhant*.

त्रिविधां बोधिमासाद्य संबुद्धपदमाप्नुयाः।
लोकाः सर्वेऽपि चैवं हि परिशुद्धत्रिमण्डलाः ॥ १०७ ॥

Having climbed the three steps of *bodhi*, you shall attain Buddhahood and slowly rise to help purify others in their mind, words and actions.

बोधिसत्त्वा महासत्त्वाः सदा सद्गतिसंभवाः।
बोधिचर्याव्रतं धृत्वा संचरन्ति जगद्धिते[36] ॥ १०८ ॥

You shall forever be in a good state, walk the earth for its welfare and uphold the *bodhicaryā* faithfully, just as the *mahāsattva*s and *bodhisattva*s.

जित्वा मारगणान् सर्वान् चतुर्ब्रह्मविहारिणः
निःक्लेशा निर्मलात्मानः संसारगतिनिःस्पृहाः ॥ १०९ ॥

As the *mahāsattva*s and *bodhisattva*s have conquered their bodily desires to free themselves of all sorrow and with freedom from the mortal cycle and purity in their souls, experience the supreme four pleasures, so shall you.

---

36 जगत्कृते इति कपाठः।

अर्हन्तः त्रिविधां बोधिं प्राप्य बुद्धत्वमाप्नुयुः ।
एषां च वीतरागाणामष्टानामपि साम्प्रतम् ॥ ११० ॥

They, who worship the eight *vītarāga*s, cross the three stages of *bodhi*, become *arhant*s and then proceed towards Buddhahood.

पूजाफलविशेषत्वं वक्ष्यामि शृणु तन्नृप! ।
वाग्वतीसलिले यस्तु स्नात्वा नित्यं समाहितः ॥ १११ ॥

You might wonder what rewards come out of the worship of the eight *vītarāga* and the ablution in the Vāgmatī. Listen carefully, I shall tell you.

अष्टावेतान् महेशाँश्च वीतरागान् सदा भजेत् ।
एतत्पुण्यविशुद्धात्मा श्रीसमृद्धिसुखान्वितः ॥ ११२ ॥

I shall tell you about the rewards, merits and happiness received through the worship of the eight *vītarāga*s, who are manifestations of Śiva himself.

संसारे सर्वदा सौख्यं भुक्त्वा यायाच्छिवालयम् ।
घृतेन स्नापयेत् यस्तु वीतरागान् स्वयंभूवः ॥ ११३ ॥

These forms of Mahādeva – the eight *vītarāga*, shall grant happiness to the world. They must be bathed with *ghee*, which shall bring about great welfare and immense happiness in the world.

शिवालयं व्रजेत् सोऽपि मधुरं ब्रह्ममन्दिरम् ।
दध्ना यः स्नापयेद् देवान् वीतरागान् स्वयंभुवः ॥ ११४ ॥

He, who prays to the eight *vītarāga*s and worships them by bathing them with yogurt and honey, is bound to the realm of Brahmā with great pleasure.

स यायाद् वैष्णवं लोकं श्री समृद्धिसुखाश्रयम्[37] ।
स्नानादिक्षुरसेनापि विद्याधरं पदं व्रजेत् ॥ ११५ ॥

Those that worship these forms of Śiva with sugar cane juice shall reach the *Vaiṣṇava* realm to become a demi-god of the *vidyādhara* kind.

[37] सुखात्मकम् इति कपाठः ।

गन्धोदकेन गान्धर्वं क्षीरेण शशिनःपदम् ।
शीतोदकेन शुद्धात्मा निष्पापो निर्मलेन्द्रियः ॥ ११६ ॥

Those who ablute the eight *vītarāga*s with sandalwood and water, shall reach *gandharva* realm. Those who bathe themselves with milk shall reach *candra* realm. Those who use cold water to cleanse the *vītarāga* shall have their organs purified and sins cleansed off.

एषां पूजां च यःकुर्यान् नानापुष्पैः सुगन्धितैः[38] ।
सर्वकामसुखं भुक्त्वा मोदते मनुजाधिपः ॥ ११७ ॥

They, who worship the eight by offering multitudes of fragrant flowers, shall have their desires fulfilled, become happy and reign as kings among men.

विल्वपत्राणि श्रेष्ठानि रोहणाच्च ह्यतन्द्रितः ।
शिवं सर्वत्र प्राप्नोति यज्ञानां च सहस्रकम् ॥ ११८ ॥

They, who worship the *vītarāga* with *bilva* leaves, shall receive auspiciousness and merit equal to that of a 1,000 *yajña*s (sacrifices).

नैवेद्यं ढोकयेद्यः स दीर्घायुः स्याद् बली नृपः ।
दीपमालां च यो दद्यात्तेजस्वी स्यात्सुदृष्टिमान् ॥ ११९ ॥

The one, who offers food and presents, shall be granted longevity; the one, who lights candles, shall be energetic and have strong eyesight.

गुग्गुलं यो ढौकयति नश्यते सर्वपातकम् ।
तिलपात्रं च यो दद्याद् दुर्गतिं स व्रजेन्न हि ॥ १२० ॥

The one, who offers incense sticks, shall be rid of his sins. The one who offers sesame seeds, shall never reach a bad state of affair and will always be in a good place.

सुवर्णं यः प्रदद्याच्च स यायात् सङ्गतौ सदा ।
तिलधेनुं प्रदद्याद्यो स संयायाच्छिवालयम् ॥ १२१ ॥

The person, who donates gold, will be in a great state and the

---

38 सुबन्धितैः इति गपाठः ।

one who donates cows to the *vītarāga,* shall reach the world of the Śiva.

रौप्यखुरां हेमशृंगीं रणद्घण्ठारवं सुखम् ।
सवत्सां कपिलां दद्याद्यः स यज्ञफलं लभेत् ॥ १२२ ॥

He, who offers a brown cow with hooves, engraved in silver, horns plated with gold, neck adorned with sweet bells, with a calf, shall amass merit equal to that from a great sacrifice.

यो रत्नकंचुकं दद्यात् स भवेद् बहुरत्नवान् ।
वस्त्रवान् वस्त्रदानेन भूमिदानेन भूमिवान्[39] ॥ १२३ ॥

The one, who offers fabric adorned with gems, shall receive gems in plenitude. The one, who offers ordinary fabric, shall never be in scarcity of clothes. The one, who donates land, shall gain great prosperity in terms of land.

तूर्यसंगीति–नृत्यादि–महोत्साहं प्रचारयेत् ।
यः स दिव्यश्रुतिप्राप्तः शिवपार्श्वचरो भवेत् ॥ १२४ ॥

The one, who plays different instruments and dances and conducts festivals, shall receive a divine body and eventually, become an attendant of Śiva.

नीलोत्पलार्कपद्मानि यो दद्यात् स श्रियं लभेत् ।
योऽर्चयेद् विल्वपत्रेण स वलिष्ठो भवेत् कृती ॥ १२५ ॥

The one, who offers blue lotus, shall receive prosperity and fortune. The one, who offers *bela* leaves, shall receive great strength.

धत्तुरकेन निर्वीर्यः पूजनाद् बलवान् भवेत्[40] ।
सुगन्धिकुसुमैः सर्वान् योष्टावपि समर्चयेत् ॥ १२६ ॥

The one, who offers *dhatūrā* plant, shall receive invincibility in strength; and he, who offers the flower of the said plant, shall be undefeatable.

---

39 वीर्यवान् इति कपाठः ।

40 निवार्य केन वीरेण सद् वनो इति कपाठः ।

स श्रीमान् सुभगो धीमान् भवेत्सौगन्धिताश्रयः ।
दिव्यातिसुन्दरः कान्तो भद्रश्री-सद्गुणार्द्धिमान् ॥ १२७ ॥

The one, who offers *dhaturā,* shall be prosperous, beautiful, wise and their speech shall please those who hear it and their actions, filled with virtues and intelligence, shall bring welfare to all.

पुष्पैः पत्रैः फलैर्मूलैः स्तोत्रैर्वा योऽर्चयेच्छिवम्[41] ।
स देवालयमासाद्य भुक्त्वा दिव्यसुखं चरेत् ॥ १२८ ॥

They who offer fruits, leaves and flowers and sing praises of the eight *vītarāga*s, shall reach the realm of Śiva to enjoy divine pleasures.

यश्च प्रदक्षिणाः कृत्वा भजेन्नित्यं समादरात् ।
रूपवान् स भवेदन्ते संप्राप्नुयाच्छिवालयम् ॥ १२९ ॥

They, who constantly perform the *pradakṣiṇā* and chant hymns in reverence, shall be beauteous and ultimately reach the land of Śiva.

यश्च स्तोत्रैः प्रसन्नात्मा भजेदेतान् महेश्वरान् ।
स तु पित्र्यालयं गत्वा महानन्दसुखं लभेत् ॥ १३० ॥

They, who sing prayers and praises of the eight Śivas with joy, reach the realm of ancestors to enjoy boundless happiness.

यश्च नाम समुच्चार्य जपित्वा स समाहितः ।
सोऽपि श्रीमान् महाभिज्ञः प्रान्ते यायाच्छिवालयम्[42]॥ १३१ ॥

They, who utter and chant the name of these eight *vītarāga*s with concentration, become prosperous and wise and ultimately reach the land of Śiva.

अष्टांगैः प्रणतिं कृत्वा यो भजेत् तान् महेश्वरान् ।
स यायात् सङ्गतावेव दुर्गतिं न कदाचन ॥ १३२ ॥

They, who salute the *vītarāga* Maheśvara with eight bodily positions and sing their praises, shall reach a good state and never be in a state of misery.

---

41 शुभम् इति गपाठः ।

42 स्वर्णिमम् इति कपाठः ।

स्मृत्वा ध्यात्वा समुच्चार्य नामापि यो भजेत् सदा ।
स दिव्यामृतभुंजानो रमेद् दिवि यथासुखम् ॥ १३३ ॥

They, who are in constant remembrance and meditation of the *vītarāga*s and sing their praises, shall consume nectar and live happily in celestial realm (heaven).

यश्च दृष्ट्वा प्रसान्नात्मा प्रणमेत् सांजलिर्मुदा ।
सोऽपि दिव्यामृतं भुक्त्वा रमेत् स्वर्गे सुरैः सह ॥ १३४ ॥

They, who receive the auspicious sight of the lords and salute to them with happiness, shall receive elixir and live alongside the gods in heaven.

इत्येषां वीतरागाणामष्टानां भजनाद् ध्रुवम् ।
विशेषफलमाज्ञाय भजस्वैनां यथेच्छया ॥ १३५ ॥

Worship of the eight *vītarāga*s Śiva is certain to grant immense rewards. Therefore, you must all pursue your wishes to worship them and sing their praises full of devotion.

तदत्र भूतले शुद्धं विधाय पुरमाश्रयन् ।
सर्वान् लोकान् प्रतिष्ठाप्य पालयन् सर्वदा वस ॥ १३६ ॥

For that purpose, build homes and *āśrama*s to reside here and invite others and nurture them well, while worshipping these eight forms of Śiva.

तदात्र सर्वदिग्भ्योऽपि सर्वलोकाः प्रमोदिताः ।
आगत्य संस्थितिं कृत्वा निवसेयुः सदा मुदा[43] ॥ १३७ ॥

When you start living here, people from all directions shall follow and gladly start to reside here alongside of you.

तदा जानपादाश्चात्र ग्रामाश्च नागराण्यपि ।
निर्गममागमं चापि प्रवर्तेयुः समन्ततः ॥ १३८ ॥

Then different townsfolk, villagers, people from small cities and

43 ध्रुवम् इति कपाठः ।

villages, shall come here in a procession to live in all directions around you.

तथा देवाः सुरेन्द्राश्च सर्वे लोकाधिपा अपि।
आगत्यात्र समालोक्य धर्मधातोः स्वयंभुवः[44] ॥ १३९ ॥

Similarly, gods and lords of the world, shall come here to live in the auspicious sight of the lords.

गन्धर्वा गुह्यका यक्षाःकिन्नरा राक्षसा अपि।
कुम्भाण्डा गरुडा नागाःसिद्धा विद्याधरा अपि ॥ १४० ॥

साध्याश्च मातृकाश्चापि सभैरवगणा अपि।
ऋषयो योगिनश्चापि यतयस्तीर्थिका अपि ॥ १४१ ॥

श्रावका भिक्षवोऽर्हन्तश्चेलकाश्चाप्युपासकाः।
बोधिसत्त्वा महासत्त्वाः शैवाः कौलाश्च वैष्णवाः ॥ १४२ ॥

Gandharva, *guhyaka*, *yakṣa*, *kinnara*, *kumbhāṇḍa* demi-gods, demons, falcons, serpents, *siddha* and *vidyādhara* demi-gods shall all come. *Sādhya*s, Mātṛkā goddesses, Bhairava groups, sages, *yogī*s, hermits, pilgrims, Vedic brāhmaṇas, initiates, *bhikkhu*, *arhant*, *cailaka*, laymen, laywomen, *bodhisattva*s, *mahāsattva*s, Śaiva and Kaula cultists and Vaiṣṇava shall all come.

आगत्यात्र समालोक्य धर्मधातोः स्वयंभुवः।
देव्याःखगाननायाश्च मंजुदेवस्य सद्गुरोः[45] ॥ १४३ ॥

Upon arrival, they shall worship the Dharmadhātu Svayambhū, the Goddess Khagānanā and the good teacher Mañjuśrī.

एषां च वीतरागाणां तीर्थानां चानुभावताम्।
प्रसादिताः समाश्रित्य भवेयुः सर्वदा मुदा ॥ १४४ ॥

Similarly, they shall worship to please the eight *vītarāga* Śiva and the holy pilgrimages like Vāgmatī and chant their prayers in their refuge.

---

44 स्वयंभुवि इति गपाठः।

45 सद्गुरौ इति कपाठः।

तदात्र सर्वदैतेषां सर्वपुण्यानुभावतः ।
सुभिक्षं मंगलोत्साहं निरुत्पातं भवेद् ध्रुवम् ॥ १४५ ॥

Thanks to the influence of the merit they shall gather, it is certain that prosperity will spread, crops will grow in plenty and all shall be subject to welfare and auspiciousness.

इत्यादिष्टं मुनीन्द्रेण क्रकुच्छन्देन सांप्रतम् ।
धर्माकरः समाकर्ण्य तथेति प्रत्यबुध्यत ॥ १४६ ॥

After the Lord Krakucchanda instructed him, hearing such words highly pleased the King Dharmākara.

ततः स नृप उत्थाय साञ्जलिस्तं मुनीश्वरम् ।
क्रकुच्छन्दं ससंघं तं प्रणिपत्य[46]न्यवेदयत् ॥ १४७ ॥

The King Dharmākara rose from his seat, saluted the Buddha and his Saṅgha and then addressed him.

भगवन्! भगतामाज्ञां धृत्वा मयात्र सर्वदा ।
पुरं विधाय लोकानां हितार्थे निवसिष्यते[47] ॥ १४८ ॥

"O Lord! I accept your command. I will build a great city in this place and reside here for the welfare of the world."

तद् भवान् कृपयालोक्य सर्वदात्र हिमालये ।
ससंघो धर्ममादिश्य विहरेन्नु जगद्धिते ॥ १४९ ॥

"I request you to live with your Saṅgha in the mountains surrounding this land, so that your benevolent sight over our city would bring welfare to the city and as a result, to the whole world."

इति संप्रार्थिते तेन भगवान् स मुनीश्वरः ।
धर्माकरं महासत्त्वं संपश्यन्नेवमब्रवीत् ॥ १५० ॥

Upon hearing the King Dharmākara's humble request, the Krakucchanda Buddha, looking at him, replied:

46 प्रणत्वेवं इति कपाठः ।

47 निवसे खलु इति घपाठः ।

नाहं सदात्र तिष्ठेयं चरेयं सर्वभूतले ।
सर्वसत्त्वहितार्थं हि भवामि धर्मदीक्षकः ॥ १५१ ॥

"O Great King! I cannot eternally reside in this mountain. I have to constantly travel to preach *dharma* for the welfare of the entire world and its sentient beings."

इत्यादिश्य मुनीन्द्रोऽसौ ऋकुच्छन्दः स सांघिकः ।
ततः संप्रस्थितोऽन्यत्र धर्मं संबोधयन् मुदा[48] ॥ १५२ ॥

Having said this, the Krakucchanda Buddha with his Saṅgha, departed for another country to promote the *dharma.*

ततो धर्माकरः सोऽत्र विधाय नगरं तथा ।
राज्यांगानि प्रतिष्ठाप्य राज्यं कृत्वाध्यतिष्ठत ॥ १५३ ॥

The Dharmākara built a magnificent kingdom, established with all seven vital organs of a kingdom and took residence there.

तदात्र सर्व आगत्य मन्दिरेषु समन्ततः ।
आश्रित्य संस्थितिं कृत्वा निवसन्तो मुदाऽचरन् ॥ १५४ ॥

After the city was built near the Svayambhū by the king, people from all over the world came, took up residence and lived there happily.

ततोऽन्येऽपि समायाताः सर्वदिग्भ्योऽत्र मानवाः[49] ।
जानपदे पुरेऽनेकं ग्रामेषु न्यवसन् मुदा ॥ १५५ ॥

People from little towns, small villages, the countryside and other parts of the world all arrived to seek residence.

तथा देवाः सुराद्याश्च सर्वे लोकाधिपा अपि ।
स्वस्वपरिजनैः सार्द्धमागत्यात्र मुदाऽवसन् ॥ १५६ ॥

Even gods and devils, lords of the world, everyone with their families and kinsmen came there to live blissfully.

---

48 धर्मं संबोधयन् मुदा इति घपाठः ।

49 सर्वत इति खपाठः ।

तथा महर्षयश्चापि यतयो ब्रह्मचारिणः ।
योगिनो भिक्षवोऽर्हन्तो व्रतिनश्चाप्युपासकाः ॥ १५७ ॥

बोधिसत्त्वा महासत्त्वाश्चैलकाः श्रावका अपि ।
यथाभिलषिते देशे कृत्वाश्रमं समाश्रयन् ॥ १५८ ॥

Great sages, hermits, *yogī*s, celibates, monks, *arhant*s, vow practitioners, laymen, laywomen, *bodhisattva, mahāsattva*, *cailaka*, *śrāvaka*, everyone arrived from their respective places and built their *āśrama*s to live near the Svayambhū.

तथान्ये तीर्थिकाः शैवा वैष्णवाः कौलिका अपि ।
यथाभिलषिते स्थाने कृत्वाश्रमं समाश्रयन् ॥ १५९ ॥

Everyone from pilgrims and Vedics to devotees of Śiva, Viṣṇu and Kaulikas, all built their homes at the spots they preferred to settle in the town near the Svayambhū.

प्रत्येकसुगताश्चापि समागत्य समन्ततः ।
विविक्ते आश्रमे रम्ये सामाश्रित्य मुदाऽवसन् ॥ १६० ॥

Even novice *buddha*s came there to live in their *āśrama* to meditate in peace and solitude.

मुनीन्द्रा अपि चागत्य विहृत्यात्र ससंघिकाः।
प्राप्य सम्बोधिसद्धर्मं सम्प्रप्यात्र[50]त्वरागताः ॥ १६१ ॥

Other monks and sages came there and gathered their *Saṅgha*s and settled around the Lord Svayambhū to pray for the acquisition of enlightenment.

एवं पुण्यतमा भूमिरियं हिमलयाह्वया ।
सुखावतीनिभा रम्या बोधिसत्त्वसमाश्रया ॥ १६२ ॥

Thus, the land in the laps of the Himalaya was filled with merit and came to be as virtuous a land as the Sukhāvatī realm (the origin of the Buddha).

---

50 समादेश्यन् इति कपाठः ।

बहूनि चात्र तीर्थानि सर्वपापहराण्यपि।
जातानि सन्ति सर्वार्थसमृद्धिसिद्धिदान्यपि ॥ १६३ ॥

The place transformed into a great sacred pilgrimage, complete with a number of holy places and was famed as the land where all sins are removed and divinity is acquired.

तदेतेषु च तीर्थेषु स्नात्वा चरति सद्व्रतम्।
पापं हन्तुं शुभं प्राप्तुं समीच्छन्त्यत्र ये नराः ॥ १६४ ॥

Those, who desire their own good, the removal of sins and prosperity, must bathe, practise holy vows and commit charitable donations in these holy places here.

येऽत्र तीर्थेषु सर्वेषु स्नात्वा नित्यं समाहितः।
जप-यज्ञादि-कर्माणि कृत्वा चरन्ति सम्वरम्[51] ॥ १६५ ॥

Those who come here to bathe in the holy waters, focus and meditate, recite the prayers and perform sacrifices and indulge in good deeds like philanthropy shall amass immeasurable merit.

पितृञ्चापि समभ्यर्च्य देवाञ्च श्रद्धयादरात्।
दत्वा दानं समाधाय ध्यात्वापीशं भजन्ति च ॥ १६६ ॥

Those who give offerings to the gods and ancestors and donate to the poor and then proceed to serve other holy places, shall walk down the path of liberation.

तेऽपि सर्वे विकल्माषाः परिशुद्ध-त्रिमण्डलाः।
श्रीमन्तः सिद्धिमन्तश्च भवेयुः सद्गुणाश्रयाः[52] ॥ १६७ ॥

Such people will slowly be devoid of sins, with purified minds, words and action, and prosperous, full of divine powers and virtues.

ततस्ते सर्वसत्त्वानां हितार्थे धर्मसाधकाः।
बोधिसत्त्वा महासत्त्वा भवेयुः सुगतात्मजाः ॥ १६८ ॥

---

51 बोधिकम् इति गपाठः।

52 सद्गुणान्विताः इति कपाठः।

They will work for the welfare of the whole world and gradually become *bodhisattvas*, *mahāsattvas* and ultimately the sons of Buddha.

ततस्ते बोधिसम्भारं पूरयित्वा यथाक्रमम् ।
त्रिरत्नभजनं कृत्वा संचरेयुर्जगद्धिते[53] ॥ १६९ ॥

Slowly, after climbing all the steps of *Bodhi*, praying to the three-jewels (Buddha, Dharma and Saṅgha), they will wander around for the welfare of the whole world.

ततस्ते विमलात्मानो निःक्लेशा विजितेन्द्रियाः ।
अर्हन्तः त्रिविधां बोधिं प्राप्येयुः सौगतं पदम् ॥ १७० ॥

With minds and souls purified, miseries destroyed, organs conquered, they shall become *arhants*, cross the steps of *bodhi* to be ultimately established into Buddhahood.

एवं मत्वात्र तीर्थेषु सर्वेषु बोधिवाच्छिभिः ।
स्नात्वा दानादिकं कर्म कर्तव्यं सर्वदा भवे ॥ १७१ ॥

Thus, they who desire to seek the *bodhi* knowledge must travel to those pilgrimages and further themselves by bathing, donating, practising *dharma* and good deeds.

इत्यादिष्टं मुनीन्द्रेण समादिष्टं निशम्य ते ।
सर्वे सभाश्रिता लोकाः प्राभ्यनन्दन् प्रबोधिताः ॥ १७२ ॥

Such special knowledge was imparted by the Greatest among the sages. Having heard this great story, all those present in the assembly were pleased; they, in acceptance of his words, saluted the Lord and sang his praises.

॥ इति श्रीस्वयंभूचैत्यसमुत्पत्तिकथा-वीतरागतीर्थ-राष्ट्रप्रवर्तनो
नाम चतुर्थोऽध्यायः समाप्तः ॥

The fourth chapter, called the Vītarāga Tīrtha,
is thus complete.

---

53 जगत्कृते इति खपाठः ।

अथ पंचमोऽध्यायः
(Pañcama Adhyāya)

Story of the Origin of Svayambhū

अथासौ च महासत्त्वो मैत्रेयः साञ्जलिर्मुदा ।
भगवन्तं तमानम्य प्रार्थयेदेवमादरात् ॥ १ ॥

Mahāsattva Maitreya, who was highly pleased upon listening to the stories, saluted the Lord Śākyamuni Buddha with hands joined in reverence and asked him:

भगवन्! तत्र तीर्थानां स्नान-दानादि-कर्मजम् ।
पुण्यफलविशेषत्वं समादिशतु साम्प्रतम् ॥ २ ॥

"O Lord! what are the merits of acts of ablutions and donations at such pilgrimage. Pray tell me."

इति संप्रार्थिते तेन भगवान् स मुनीश्वरः ।
मैत्रेयं तं महासत्त्वं सम्पश्यन्नेवमादिशत् ॥ ३ ॥

When the Maitreya prayed this way, the Lord Śākyamuni looked at him and replied.

साधु श्रृणु महासत्त्व! तीर्थसेवाफलोद्भवम् ।
पुण्यं तत्र विशेषत्वं वक्ष्यामि बोधनाय ते[1] ॥ ४ ॥

"O Mahāsattva! you have posed an appropriate question. Listen carefully, for I shall tell you of the merit received through the service of the pilgrimage sites."

---

[1] सर्व बोधने इति कपाठः ।

तद्यथा मूलतीर्थानि कथ्यन्ते द्वादशैव हि।
महापुण्यानि सर्वेषां तीर्थानां यानि भूतले ॥ ५ ॥

"Listen, there are twelve principle pilgrimages. They are supreme among all others and thereby grant tremendous merit."

अमोघ-फलदायिन्यां वाग्वत्यां यत्र संगमे।
तत्तीर्थशोधनं ख्यातं दशपापविशोधनात् ॥ ६ ॥

Where the River Vāgmatī meets the River Amoghaphaladāyinī, the site is famous as the Śodhana Tīrtha, where a person is relieved of ten kinds of sins.

तत्र नागाधिपो रक्तस्तक्षकाख्यः सुकान्तिमान्।
उज्वालयन् महारत्नं श्रीमत्फणा-विभूषितः ॥ ७ ॥

There resides a serpent-lord named Takṣaka, red skinned, who exudes good energy and is adorned with a brilliant gem and a glorious head.

ये नराःश्रद्धया तत्र पुण्यतीर्थे यथाविधि।
स्नानं कुर्युर्मुदा यावदेकविंशति-वासरम् ॥ ८ ॥

जप-यज्ञादि-कर्माणि कुर्युः सप्तदिनान्यपि।
पितॄन् देवाञ्च संपूज्य कुर्युः संतृप्तमोदितान्[2] ॥ ९ ॥

दद्युर्दानानि चार्थिभ्यो यथेप्सितं समादरात्।
शुद्धशीलाः समाधाय चरेयुश्च व्रतं तथा ॥ १० ॥

एतत्पुण्यविशुद्धास्ते निःक्लेशा निर्मलेन्द्रियाः।
बोधिसत्त्वा महासत्त्वा भवेयुःश्रीगुणाश्रयाः ॥ ११ ॥

ततस्ते बोधिसम्भारं पूरयित्वा यथाक्रमम्।
त्रिविधां बोधिमासाद्य संबुद्धपदमाप्नुयुः ॥ १२ ॥

Those people who joyously bathe in that pious *tīrtha* for twenty-one days, with devotion; those people who perform sacrifice and chant for seven days and please the gods and ancestors to satisfaction through offerings; those people who donate to beggars whatever much they

---

[2] सन्तृप्तकारकान् इति कपाठः।

desire; and practise vows with pure discipline and focus; As a result of the merits amassed, their obstacles and miseries are removed, their organs are purified and they become *bodhisattva*s, *mahāsattva*s, virtuous and prosperous.

Gradually, having fulfilled the vows of *bodhi*, they attain the three types of *bodhi* and ultimately receive Buddhahood.

ततश्चामरदायिन्या वाग्वत्या यत्र संगमः ।
तच्छान्ततीर्थमाख्यातं क्लेश-दोष-विशोधनम् ॥ १३ ॥

At the confluence of the Vāgmatī and the Mardārinī rivers lies the Śānta Tīrtha (the quiet pilgrimage), which removes flaws and obstacles.

तत्र नागाधिपः शुक्लः सोम-शिखीति-विश्रुतः ।
विलसन्मणि-रत्नश्री-फणामण्डल[3]-भूषितः ॥ १४ ॥

There resides a lord of serpents known as the Somaśikhī, white skinned, who is bedecked with a *maṇi* (gemstone) and adorned with many heads.

तत्रापि शान्ततीर्थं च ये क्लेशदुःखिता नराः ।
कुर्युस्नानं तदा यावदेकविंशति-वासरम् ॥ १५ ॥

At the quiet pilgrimage, they, who are defiled and flawed, must bathe for twenty-one days.

जप-यज्ञादिकं कुर्युश्चरेयुश्चाधि-पोषधम्[4] ।
पितॄन् देवाञ्च संपूज्य कुर्युः संतुष्ट-नन्दितान् ॥ १६ ॥

There one must perform sacrifice, incantation and practise *vrata* and satiate and gratify the gods and ancestors.

दद्युर्दानानि चार्थिभ्यो यथाभिलषितं मुदा ।
शुद्धशीलाः समाचारा ध्यात्वा भजेयुरीश्वरम् ॥ १७ ॥

---

3 दीप्तिमण्डल इति खपाठः ।

4 औषधम् इति खपाठः ।

One must donate to beggars according to their desires and must praise the gods with purified conduct.

एतत्पुण्याभिलिप्तास्ते परिशुद्ध-त्रिमण्डलाः ।
बोधिसत्त्वा महासत्त्वा भवेयुःश्रीगुणालयाः ॥ १८ ॥

As a result of the merits amassed, their *tri-maṇḍala* (mind, speech and actions) are purified and they become *bodhisattva*s, *mahāsattva*s and the epitome of prosperity and virtues.

ततस्ते बोधिसम्भारं पूरयित्वा यथाक्रमम् ।
अर्हन्तस्त्रिविधां बोधिं प्राप्नुयुः सौगतं पदम्[5] ॥ १९ ॥

Gradually, having fulfilled the vows of *bodhi*, they consequently become *arhant*s, attain the three types of *bodhi* and ultimately receive Buddhahood.

ततश्च मणिरोहिण्या वाग्वत्या यत्र संगमः ।
तत्रोर्द्धनिःसृता शुद्ध-स्फटिकादारसन्निभा ॥ २० ॥

At the confluence of the Maniromiṇī and the Vāgmatī, another stream, with waters that shine like crystals, flows to merge with them.

रुद्रधारामृताख्याता तस्याश्च तत्र संगमात् ।
त्रिवेणीसंगमस्तेन शंकरतीर्थमुच्यते ॥ २१ ॥

At the junction of the two rivers and a third one known as Rudradhārā, which is famous as the elixir, lies the Triveṇī (three-rivers), called the Śaṅkara Tīrtha.

तत्र नागाधिपःशंखपालो गौरातिसुन्दरः ।
मणिरश्मिसमुद्दिप्तःश्रीमत्फणा-विभूषितः ॥ २२ ॥

There resides a lord of snakes, Śaṅkhapāla, white skinned and immensely beautiful, who is adorned with a glorious head, whose gem exudes light that illuminates the area.

तत्र शंकरतीर्थे ये मानवाश्च यथाविधि ।
स्नानं कुर्युर्मुदा यावदेकविंशतिवासरम् ॥ २३ ॥

[5] उत्तमं पदम् इति ख घपाठः ।

One must procedurally bathe in the Śaṅkara Tīrtha for twenty-one days.

जप-यज्ञादिकर्माणि कुर्युश्च सप्तवासरम्[6] ।
पितॄन् देवाञ्च संपूज्य तर्पयेयुर्यथाविधि ॥ २४ ॥

One must perform sacrifice and incantation for seven days, in order to satisfy the gods and the ancestors through devoted worship.

दद्युर्दानानि चार्थिभ्यःश्रद्धया बोधिमानसाः ।
ध्यात्वा भजेयुरीशं च सञ्चरेयुरुपोषधम्[7] ॥ २५ ॥

One must donate to the poor what they ask and with devotion and *bodhi* in mind, praise the gods.

एतत्पुण्य-विशुद्धात्मनिःक्लेशा निर्मलेन्द्रियाः ।
लभेरन् श्रीमहापुष्टिशान्ति-गुणाश्च कान्त्यपि ॥ २६ ॥

As a result of this merit gained, their souls are purified; miseries are removed, organs are cleansed; they receive great strength, prosperity, virtues and tranquillity.

दुर्गतिं ते न यायुश्च जायन्ते[8] सङ्गतौ सदा ।
बोधिसत्त्वा महासत्त्वा भवेयुर्भद्रचारिणः ॥ २७ ॥

They will never be wretched or miserable; they will be in a good state to eventually become *bodhisattva*s, *mahāsattva*s and famous for their decency in conduct.

ततस्ते बोधिसंभारं पूरयित्वा यथाक्रमम् ।
अर्हन्तस्त्रिविधां बोधिं प्राप्येयुः सौगतं पदम् ॥ २८ ॥

Gradually, having fulfilled the vows of *bodhi*, they consequently become *arhant*s, attain the three types of *bodhi* and ultimately receive Buddhahood.

---

6 सप्ताहाविधिः इति खपाठः ।

7 संचरेञ्चपोषढं इति कपाठः ।

8 संजाताः इति घपाठः ।

ततश्च राजमञ्जर्या वाग्मत्या यत्र संगमः ।
तद्राजतीर्थमाख्यातं राज्यारोग्यसुखप्रदम्[9] ॥ २९ ॥

The confluence of the Vāgmatī and the Rājamañjarī is known as the Rāja Tīrtha, which can grant health and comfort to the kingdom.

तत्र नागाधिपः शुक्लः सुरूपाख्यातिसुन्दरः ।
मणिरत्न-महादीप्ति-श्रीप्रभा-मण्डिताश्रयः ॥ ३० ॥

The lord of serpents that resides there is known as Surūpa, after his beautiful form. He is white of skin, adorned with a great illuminating gemstone and is filled with prosperity and virtues.

तत्र ये मानवा यावदेकविंशतिवासरम् ।
स्नानं दानं जपं ध्यानं कुर्युर्दध्युश्च संवरम् ॥ ३१ ॥

For twenty-one days, one must practise ablution, donation, incantation and meditation and hold *vrata.*

एतत्पुण्य-विशुद्धास्ते निर्दोषा विमलेन्द्रियाः[10] ।
राज्यैश्वर्यं सदारोग्यं भद्रं सौख्यमवाप्नुयुः ॥ ३२ ॥

There, the merit amassed through the *vrata* grants them innocence and purification of organs, as well as royal prosperity, good health, comfort and happiness.

तेऽपि न दुर्गतिं यायुः सदा सद्गति-संभवाः ।
बोधिसत्त्वा महासत्त्वा भवेयुःश्रीगुणाश्रयाः ॥ ३३ ॥

They will never be wretched or miserable, they will always be in a good state to eventually become *bodhisattva*s, *Mahāsattva*s and the epitome of prosperity and virtues.

ततस्ते बोधिसम्भारं पूरयित्वा यथाक्रमम् ।
अर्हन्तस्त्रिविधां बोधिं प्राप्य यान्तु जिनालयम्[11] ॥ ३४ ॥

[9] पदं इति घपाठः ।

[10] शुभकामेन्द्रियाः इति खपाठः ।

[11] बुद्धालयम् इति कपाठः ।

Gradually, having fulfilled the vows of *bodhi*, they consequently become *arhant*s, attain the three types of *bodhi* and ultimately reach Buddhahood.

तथात्र विमलावत्याः केशावत्याश्च संगमे ।
मनोरथं तदाख्यातं स्वेच्छालंकार-संप्रदम् ॥ ३५ ॥

Then the pious meeting point of the Vimalavatī and the Keśavatī is the Manoratha Tīrtha, which is able to fulfil wishes.

तत्र नागाधिपो भीमः कुलिकाख्योऽतिकर्वुरः ।
फणामणि-समुद्दीप्त-श्रीप्रभामण्डिताश्रयः ॥ ३६ ॥

The serpent lord present there is a ferocious serpent named Kulika, who is brown in colour, adorned with brilliant and luminous gemstone on his glorious head and is prosperous.

तत्र मनोरथे तीर्थे मनुजा ये यथाविधि ।
स्नान-दानादिकं कुर्युरेकविंशतिवासरम् ॥ ३७ ॥

A person must perform acts such as bathing and donation at that joyous *tīrtha* following proper procedure for twenty one-days.

तेऽपि न दुर्गतिं यायुः सदा सद्गतिसंभवाः ।
बोधिसत्त्वा महासत्त्वा भद्रश्री-सद्गुणाश्रयाः ॥ ३८ ॥

They will never be wretched or miserable; they will always be in a good state to eventually become *bodhisattva*s, *mahāsattva*s and the epitome of prosperity and virtues.

पट्टसुवस्त्ररत्नादि[12]-स्वेच्छालंकारभूषिताः ।
सर्वसत्त्व-हिताधानं चरेयुर्बोधिसंवरम् ॥ ३९ ॥

Due to the merits received, they will be blessed with golden clothes and jewels and ornaments. They must constantly practise *bodhi* for the welfare of all sentient beings.

ततस्ते बोधिसंभारं पूरयित्वा यथाक्रमम् ।
त्रिविधां बोधिमासाद्य संबुद्धपदमाप्नुयुः ॥ ४० ॥

---

12 सुवर्णवस्त्राणि इति कपाठः ।

Gradually, having fulfilled the vows of *bodhi*, they attain the three kinds of *bodhi* and ultimately reach Buddhahood.

ततश्च कुसुमावत्याःकेशावत्याश्च संगमे ।
निर्मलतीर्थमाख्यातं कल्पनाविघ्ननाशनम् ॥ ४१ ॥

The confluence of Kusumavatī and Keśavatī is famous as the Nirmala Tīrtha, which is able to destroy all obstacles and hindrances.

तत्र नागोपलालाख्यः पीतवर्णो महाकृतिः ।
दिव्यरत्न-प्रभोज्ज्वाल[13]-श्रीमत्फणा-विभूषितः ॥ ४२ ॥

There lives a great serpent named Palāla, who is yellow-skinned, with giant body. He is adorned with glorious heads and divine gems that shine brilliantly.

तत्र ये मानवा यावदेकविंशतिवासरम् ।
स्नानदानादिकं कुर्युस्तथा सर्वे च पूर्ववत् ॥ ४३ ॥

One must go there to bathe and donate for twenty-one days, just as in the previous *tīrtha*s.

तेऽपि न दुर्गतिं यायुः सदा सद्गतिसंभवाः ।
बोधिसत्त्वा महासत्त्वा भद्रश्रीसद्गुणश्रयाः ॥ ४४ ॥

They will never be wretched or miserable; they will be in a good state to eventually become *bodhisattva*s, *mahāsattva*s and the epitome of prosperity and virtues.

कलि-विघ्न-मल-क्लेश-निर्मुक्त-भद्रचारिणः ।
सर्वसत्त्व-हितारक्ता भवेयुर्ब्रह्मचारिणः ॥ ४५ ॥

At that *tīrtha*, they are removed of all obstacles pertaining to the Kali age (evil age); and they shall commit good deeds and become celibate for the welfare of all sentient beings.

ततस्ते बोधिसंभारं पूरयित्वा यथाक्रमम् ।
अर्हन्तो बोधिमासाद्य सम्बुद्धपदमाप्नुयुः ॥ ४६ ॥

---

13 प्रमोदिप्त इति कपाठः ।

Gradually, having fulfilled the vows of *bodhi*, they consequently become *arhant*s, attain *bodhi* and ultimately reach Buddhahood.

तत सुवर्णवत्याश्च वाग्मत्या यत्र संगमः ।
निधानतीर्थमाख्यातं सर्व-सम्पत्तिदायकम् ॥ ४७ ॥

The confluence of Suvarṇavatī and Vāgmatī is the Nidhāna Tīrtha. It is able to grant all wealth and prosperity.

तौ नागौ हरितवर्णौ नन्दोपनन्दनावुभौ ।
नाना-रत्नप्रभाद्दीप्ति-श्री-मत्फणाविभूषितौ ॥ ४८ ॥

Two great serpents reside there, Nanda and Upananda. They are green in colour, bedecked with many luminous jewels and adorned with glorious heads.

तत्र ये मनुजा यावदेकविंशतिवासरम् ।
स्नानादिपूर्ववत्सर्वं कर्म कुर्युर्यथाविधि[14] ॥ ४९ ॥

One must go there to practise acts like bathing and donating (like before), for twenty-one days.

तेऽपि न दुर्गतिं यायुः सदा सद्गतिसंभवाः ।
बोधिसत्त्वामहासत्त्वा भद्रश्री-सद्गुणाश्रयाः ॥ ५० ॥

They will never be wretched or miserable; they will always be in a good state to eventually become *bodhisattva*s, *mahāsattva*s and the epitome of prosperity and virtues.

सर्वसत्त्वार्थ-सम्पन्ना भवेयुर्धर्मचारिणः ।
एतावदस्य माहात्म्यं सर्वं वक्तुं न शक्यते ॥ ५१ ॥

तेऽप्येवं बोधिसंभारं पूरयित्वा यथाक्रमम् ।
अर्हन्तो[15]बोधिमासाद्य सौगतं पदमाप्नुयुः ॥ ५२ ॥

ततश्च पापनाशिन्याःकेशवत्यास्तु संगमे ॥
ज्ञानतीर्थं तदाख्यातं दिव्यभोगसुखप्रदम् ॥ ५३ ॥

---

14 कर्मकामार्थसंभवम् इति खपाठः ।

15 भिक्षवः इति गपाठः ।

तत्र नागाधिपः शुक्लो वाशुकिर्नामभीषणः ।
दिव्य-रत्न[16]प्रभाश्रीमत्फणालङ्कारमण्डितः ॥ ५४ ॥

तत्र ये मानवाःस्नान्ति ह्येकविंशतिवासरम् ।
स्नानदानादि-कर्माणि कुर्युः सर्वाणि पूर्ववत् ॥ ५५ ॥

तेऽपि न दुर्गतिं यायुर्जाताः सदापि सङ्गतौ ।
सर्व-भोग-महासम्पत्सुखवन्तो निरामयाः ॥ ५६ ॥

बोधिसत्त्वा महासत्त्वाश्चतुर्ब्रह्मविहारिणः ।
भद्रश्रीसद्गुणाधारा भवेयुर्बोधिचारिणः ॥ ५७ ॥

तथा ते बोधिसंभारं पूरयित्वा यथाक्रमम् ।
अर्हन्तो बोधिमासाद्य सर्वज्ञ-पदममाप्नुयुः ।
भद्श्री-सद्गुणाधाराः सम्बुद्धगुणसाधिनः ॥ ५८ ॥

Gradually, having fulfilled the vows of *bodhi*, they consequently become *arhant*s, attain *bodhi* and ultimately reach Buddhahood.

At the confluence of Keśavatī and Pāpanāśinī, lies the Jñāna Tīrtha, which grants divine comfort and enjoyments.

There resides a ferocious lord serpent with white skin named Vāsuki, who is adorned with a glorious bejewelled head with a shining gemstone.

One must similarly go there for twenty-one days, to bathe and donate.

They will never be wretched or miserable; they will always be in a good state to receive enjoyments, and happiness, and shall never be sickly or diseased.

They will be *bodhisattva*s, *mahāsattva*s and finally be established in the four highest steps of bodhihood.

Gradually, having fulfilled the vows of *bodhi*, they consequently become *arhant*s, attain *bodhi* and ultimately reach Buddhahood.

---

16 शुभदीप्ति इति खपाठः ।

They will be filled with gentleness and prosperity, and virtues, even the qualities of Buddha.

ततश्च यत्र वाग्वत्याःकेशावत्याश्च संगमः ।
तच्चिन्तामणिरित्याख्यं सर्वकामार्थ-संपदम् ॥ ५९ ॥

At the confluence of the Vāgmatī and the Keśavatī lies the Cintāmaṇi Tīrtha, whose mere sight grants fulfillment to all desires.

गंगा च यमुना चापि तथा देवी सरस्वती ।
पूर्वं प्रत्यागताःतत्र तेन पञ्च-समागमः ॥ ६० ॥

तत्र नागाधिपः शुक्लो वरुणः सर्वनागराट् ।
दिव्यरत्न-प्रभाश्रीमत्फणामण्डलभूषितः ॥ ६१ ॥

The Gaṅga, the Yamunā and the Sarasvatī rivers also come there occasionally and their confluence is known as Pañcasaṅgama. It is inhabited by the lord of serpents named Varuṇa, who has white skin and is adorned with large heads and a divine gemstone.

तत्र ये मानवा[17]यावदेकविंशति-वासरम् ।
स्नानदानादिकं सर्वे कुर्युः पूर्ववदादरात् ॥ ६२ ॥

One must similarly go there, to bathe, donate and worship, for twenty-one days.

तेऽपि न दुर्गतिं यायुः सदा सद्गतिसंभवाः ।
संपूर्णपरमायुष्काः विद्याधिपा विचक्षणाः ॥ ६३ ॥

They will never be wretched or miserable; they will be in a good state. They shall live to the fullest of their lifespans as masters of knowledge and wisdom.

सुसन्ताना महाभोगा धर्मार्थकामभोगिनः ।
बोधिसत्त्वा महासत्त्वाश्चतुर्ब्रह्मविहारिणः ॥ ६४ ॥

They shall receive good children, will enjoy prosperity, *dharma*, wealth and pleasure; they shall become *bodhisattva*s, *mahāsattva*s and finally attain the four highest abodes (*caturbrahmavihāra*s).

---

[17] देवाता इति कपाठः ।

भद्रश्री-सद्गुणाधारा भवेयुःर्बोधिचारिणः ।
ततस्ते बोधिसंभारं पूरयित्वा यथाक्रमम् ।
अर्हन्तो बोधिमासाद्य संबुद्ध-पदमाप्नुयुः॥ ६५ ॥

Gradually, having fulfilled the vows of *bodhi*, they consequently become *arhant*s, attain *bodhi* and ultimately reach Buddhahood.

ततश्च यत्र वाग्वत्या रत्नावत्याः समागमः ।
प्रमोदतीर्थमाख्यातं रतिप्रीतिपदार्थदम्[18] ॥ ६६ ॥

The junction of Vāgmatī and Ratnāvatī is famous as the Pramoda Tīrtha, since the place represents love and affection.

तत्र नागाधिपः पद्मो धवलो दिव्यसुन्दरः ।
दिव्यरत्नमहाकान्तिःफणामण्डलभूषितः ॥ ६७ ॥

तत्र ये मानवा यावदेकविंशतिवासरम् ।
स्नान-दानानि-सर्वाणि कुर्युः कर्माणिपूर्ववत् ॥ ६८ ॥

It is inhabited by the Padma, Lord of serpents, who is white and beautiful, bedecked with a divine gem exuding good energy, adorned with many large glorious heads. One must go there to bathe, donate and do all kinds of good acts for twenty-one days.

तेऽपि न दुर्गतिं यायुः सदा सद्गतिसंभवाः ।
रति-प्रीति-सुखानन्द-महासौख्य-समन्विताः ॥ ६९ ॥

They will never be wretched or miserable; they will always be in a good state. Due to attachment and love, he will be filled with great happiness and satisfaction.

बोधिसत्त्वा महासत्त्वाःपरिशुद्धत्रिमण्डलाः ।
भद्रश्रीसद्गुणाधारा भवेयुर्बोधिसाधिनः ॥ ७० ॥

They shall become *bodhisattva*s, *mahāsattva*s and their mind, speech and bodies shall be purified. They will become gentle, glorious, virtuous and will practise *bodhi*.

---

18 वशार्थदम् इति घपाठः ।

ततस्ते बोधिसंभारं पूरयित्वा यथाक्रमम्।
अर्हन्तश्त्रिविधां बोधिं प्राप्ययायुर्जिनालयम्[19] ॥ ७१ ॥

Gradually, having fulfilled the vows of *bodhi*, they consequently become *arhant*s, attain *bodhi* and ultimately reach Buddhahood.

तत्रैव यत्र वाग्वत्याःचारुवत्याः समागमः ।
तत्सुलक्षणमाख्यातं श्रीतेजो भाग्यसम्पदम् ॥ ७२ ॥

At the junction of the Vāgmatī and the Cārumatī, the place known as the Sulakṣaṇa Tīrtha, it is filled with energy, prosperity and brings good fortune.

तत्र नागो महापद्मोऽतिधवलोऽति सुन्दरः ।
दिव्यरत्न-प्रभाश्रीमत्फणामण्डलमण्डितः ॥ ७३ ॥

There resides a serpent named Mahāpadma, white in colour and beautiful, with a divine gem that is radiating energy and adorned with a group of glorious heads.

तत्र ये मानवा यावदेकविंसतिवासरम्।
स्नानं दानं जपं ध्यानं कुर्युर्यज्ञं च पूर्ववत् ॥ ७४ ॥

A person must go there to bathe, donate, chant, meditate and perform sacrifice as before, for twenty-one days.

तेऽपि न दुर्गतिं यायुः सदा [20]सद्गतिसंभवाः ।
श्रीतेजो [21]भोग्यसंपन्नाः सुरूपलक्षणान्विताः ॥ ७५ ॥

They will never be wretched or miserable; they will always be in a good state. They will be energetic, have plenty of enjoyment, will be beauteous.

बोधिसत्त्वा महासत्त्वाः भद्रश्रीसद्गुणाश्रयाः ।
सर्वसत्त्व-हितोद्युक्ता भवेयुर्बोधिचारिणः ॥ ७६ ॥

---

19 शुभंपदम् इति घपाठः ।

20 पुण्यगति इति कपाठः ।

21 भाग्य इति खपाठः ।

They shall become *bodhisattvas* and *mahāsattvas*, and will always work for the welfare of all sentient beings and practise *bodhi.*

ततस्ते बोधिसंभारं पूरयित्वा यथाक्रमम् ।
अर्हन्तःत्रिविधां बोधिं प्राप्येयुः सौगतं पदम् ॥ ७७ ॥

Gradually, having fulfilled the vows of *bodhi*, they consequently become *arhants*, attain *bodhi* and ultimately reach Buddhahood.

ततश्च यत्र वाग्वत्याः प्रभावत्याः समागमः ।
जयतीर्थं समाख्यातं सर्वशत्रुभयान्तकृत् ॥ ७८ ॥

The point where the Vāgmatī meets the Prabhāvatī is known as the Jaya Tīrtha. It is the destroyer of fear from enemies.

तत्र नागाधिपः शुक्रः श्रीकान्ति-दिव्य-सुन्दरः ।
दिव्यरत्न-प्रभाश्री-मत्फणामण्डलमण्डितः ॥७९ ॥

It is inhabited by the lord serpent Śukra, who has a good energy and divine beauty. He is adorned with a divine gem as well as a group of glorious heads.

तत्र ये मानवा यावदेकविंशतिवासरम् ।
स्नात्वा यज्ञादिकर्माणि कुर्युः सर्वाणि पूर्ववत् ॥ ८० ॥

तेऽपि न दुर्गतिं यायुः सदा सद्गतिसंभवाः ।
निर्भयास्त्रिगुणोत्साहा जयिनो निर्जितारयः ॥ ८१ ॥

One must go there to bathe and perform deeds such as sacrifice like before, for twenty-one days. They will never be wretched or miserable; they will always be in a good state. They will have conquered their enemies, their joy will increase threefold and they will be devoid of all fear.

बोधिसत्त्वा महासत्त्वाश्चतुर्ब्रह्मविहारिणः ।
भद्रश्रीसद्गुणाचारा[22]भवेयुर्बोधिचारिणः ॥ ८२ ॥

They shall become *bodhisattvas* and *mahāsattvas* and attain the four highest divine abodes. They will be gentle, virtuous and practise *bodhi.*

---

22 सद् गुणाधारा इति कपाठः ।

ततस्ते बोधिसंभारं पूरयित्वा यथाक्रमम्।
अर्हन्तस्त्रिविधां बोधिं प्राप्येयुः सौगतं पदम्॥ ८३॥

द्वादशैतानि तीर्थानि महान्त्यत्र हिमालये।
अन्यान्यपि च सन्त्यत्र तानिवक्ष्याम्यहं[23] शृणु॥ ८४॥

Gradually, having fulfilled the vows of *bodhi*, they consequently become *arhants*, attain *bodhi* and ultimately reach Buddhahood.

Thus, I have told the significance and greatness of the twelve pilgrimages in the lap of the Himalayas. There are other pilgrimages as well, of which I shall tell you. Listen.

तद्यथोपरि वाग्मत्याः स्रोतसि द्वारसंनिधौ।
सौन्दर्यतीर्थमाख्यातं सौन्दर्यगुणसंपदम्॥ ८५॥

Above the point of origin of Vāgmatī, near its flow, lies the *tīrtha* named Saundarya, filled with the quality of beauty.

तत्र ये मानवा यावदेकविंशतिवासरम्।
स्नान-दानानि-कर्माणि कुर्युः सर्वाणि पूर्ववत्॥ ८६॥

One must go there for acts such as bathing and donating just as before, for twenty-one days. There is a Saudarya Tīrtha there, which is filled with beauty and qualities. The person who serves and *snānadāna-karma* there twenty-one times will never be *durgati*, always be in *sadgati*.

तेऽपि न दुर्गतिं यायुः सदा सद्गतिसंभवाः।
सुरूपलक्षणोपेताः श्रीमन्तः सद्गुणान्विताः॥ ८७॥

They will never be wretched or miserable; they will always be in a good state. They will be filled with the quality of divine beauty, virtues and prosperity.

बोधिसत्त्वा महासत्त्वाःचतुर्ब्रह्मविहारिणः।
सर्वसत्त्वहिताधानं चरेयुर्बोधिसंवरम्॥ ८८॥

---

23 वदामि ते इति कपाठः।

They shall become *bodhisattvas* and *mahāsattvas*, will practise *bodhi* – which is the cause of the welfare of all sentient beings.

ततस्ते बोधिसंभारं पूरयित्वा यथाक्रमम् ।
अर्हन्तःत्रिविधां बोधिं संप्राप्येयुर्जिनालयम् ॥ ८९ ॥

Gradually, having fulfilled the vows of *bodhi*, they consequently become *arhants*, attain *bodhi* and ultimately reach Buddhahood.

तदुपरिचयत्तीर्थम् अगस्त्येतिमहर्षिणा ।
नित्यस्नानं जपं ध्यानं कृत्वा यज्ञं च सेवितम् ॥ ९० ॥

Above that lies a *tīrtha*, which was served, bathed, meditated, chanted and sacrificed on by the Sage Agastya.

तेनागस्त्यमहत्तीर्थं तदाख्यातं मुनीश्वरैः[24] ।
तत्र ये मनुजाः स्नायुस्ते यायुः परमां गतिम् ॥ ९१ ॥

Thus, it started to be known as the Agastya Tīrtha by sages. Those men who bathe there attain the highest state.

दानं यज्ञं जपादिञ्च कुर्युर्ध्यात्वापि चेश्वरम् ।
तोषं ययुस्तथा पितृन्दद्युर्दानं यथेप्सितम् ॥ ९२ ॥

They must donate, sacrifice, chant and meditate to the god there, satisfy the ancestors and donate what the poor ask for.

सर्वे ते विमलात्मानश्चतुर्ब्रह्मविहारिणः ।
बोधिसत्त्वा महासत्त्वा भवेयुःश्रीगुणाश्रयाः ॥ ९३ ॥

They will have pure soul and take residence in the Four Divine Abodes. They shall become *bodhisattvas*, *mahāsattvas* and they will be the home of the three great qualities.

तथा ते बोधिसंभारं पूरयित्वा यथाक्रमम् ।
अर्हन्तःत्रिविधां बोधिं प्राप्य बुद्धत्वमाप्नुयुः ॥ ९४ ॥

Gradually, having fulfilled the vows of *bodhi*, they consequently become *arhants*, attain *bodhi* and ultimately reach Buddhahood.

---

24 नृपालकैः इति गपाठः ।

तत्रैवानन्तनागेन यदाश्रितं महाह्रदम्[25] ।
तेन तद्ह्रदमाख्यातमनन्ततीर्थमर्थदम् ॥ ९५ ॥

There is a large pond and in that pond lives a great serpent named Ananta, due to which the pond was renowned as the Ananta Tīrtha.

तत्र ये मनुजा यावदेकविंशतिवासरम् ।
स्नानं दानं जपं ध्यानं कुयुर्यज्ञं च पूर्ववत् ॥ ९६ ॥

One must similarly go there for twenty-one days to perform acts such as ablution, donation, incantation and meditation.

तेऽपि न दुर्गतिं यायुःसदा सद्गतिसम्भवाः ।
बोधिसत्त्वा महासत्त्वा भवेयुःश्रीगुणाश्रयाः ॥ ९७ ॥

They will never be wretched or miserable; they will always be in a good state to eventually become *bodhisattva*s, *mahāsattva*s and the epitome of prosperity and virtues.

तथा ते बोधिसम्भारं पूरयित्वा यथाक्रमम् ।
अर्हन्तो[26]बोधिमासाद्य सर्वज्ञपदमाप्नुयुः ॥ ९८ ॥

Gradually, having fulfilled the vows of *bodhi*, they consequently become *arhant*s, attain *bodhi* and ultimately reach Buddhahood.

तत्रैव च महत्तीर्थमार्यतारानिषेवितम् ।
तेनेदं कथितं चार्यतारातीर्थं सुभाग्यदम् ॥ ९९ ॥

There is another great *tīrtha*, which was once served by Āryatārā herself. Therefore, it is famously known as the Āryatārā, which grants good fortune.

तत्रापि ये नरा यावदेकविंशतिवासरम् ।
स्नानं दानं जपं ध्यानं यज्ञं कुर्युर्यथाविधि ॥ १०० ॥

One must similarly go there for twenty-one days to perform acts such as ablution, donation, incantation and meditation following correct procedure.

[25] महत् तोयम् इति कपाठः ।

[26] ज्ञानिनः इति कपाठः ।

तेऽपि न दुर्गतिं यायुःसंजाताः सद्गतौ सदा ।
बोधिसत्त्वा महासत्त्वाः परिशुद्धत्रिमण्डलाः ॥ १०१ ॥

They will never be wretched or miserable; they will always be in a good state to eventually become *bodhisattva*s, *mahāsattva*s and purified in mind, speech and bodies.

[27]सौभाग्याशालिनो धीरा भद्रश्रीसद्गुणाश्रयाः ।
सर्वसत्त्वहितोत्साहा भवेयुर्बोधिचारिणः ॥ १०२ ॥

They shall be fortunate, resilient and the home of gentleness and virtues. For the welfare of all beings, they shall practise the *bodhi*.

तथा ते बोधिसंभारं पूरयित्वा यथाक्रमम् ।
अर्हन्तस्त्रिविधां बोधिं प्राप्येयुः सौगतं पदम् ॥ १०३ ॥

Gradually, having fulfilled the vows of *bodhi*, they consequently become *arhant*s, attain *bodhi* and ultimately reach Buddhahood.

अत उर्ध्वञ्च वाग्वत्याः प्रभवतीर्थमुत्तमम् ।
सर्वेषामपितीर्थानां प्रधानमग्रमुच्यते ॥ १०४ ॥

Above and below the Vāgmatī there is the Prabhava Tīrtha. It is foremost and supreme among all *tīrtha*s.

तत्रैकस्नान-मात्रेण गंगा-स्नान-शताधिकम् ।
पुण्यं महत्तरं सिद्धं वाञ्छितार्थसुखप्रदम् ॥ १०५ ॥

One ablution there is equal to hundred ablutions in the Gaṅgā. It is pious, great and divine and fulfils desire and grants happiness.

तत्र ये मानवा यावदेकविंशतिवासरम् ।
स्नानं दानं जपं ध्यानं यज्ञं कुर्युर्यथाविधि ॥ १०६ ॥

One must go there for twenty-one days to bathe, donate, chant and sacrifice procedurally.

---

27 सुष्टुभाग्येन इति घपाठः ।

सुविशुद्ध-त्रिकायास्ते यथाकामं सुखानि च।
धर्मार्थ[28]-श्रीसमृद्धाः स्युश्चतुर्ब्रह्मविहारिणः ॥ १०७ ॥

They will be pristine, cleansed in mind, speech and body and live happily with all their desires fulfilled.

क्वचिन्न दुर्गतिं यायुः संजाताः सद्गतौ सदा।
स्वपरात्महितं कृत्वा संचरेयुः सदा शुभे ॥ १०८ ॥

They will never be wretched or miserable; they will always be in a good state. They shall be indulged in the auspicious deeds, working for the welfare of themselves and others.

ततस्ते विमलात्मानः सुविशुद्धेन्द्रियाशयाः।
बोधिसत्त्वा महासत्त्वा भवेयुः सद्गुणाकराः ॥ १०९ ॥

Their souls are purified, as are their organs and intentions; so they shall become *bodhisattva*s, *mahāsattva*s and the source of good qualities.

तथा ते बोधिसंभारं पूरयित्वा यथाविधि।
अर्हन्तस्त्रिविधां बोधिं प्राप्येयुः सौगतं पदम् ॥ ११० ॥

Gradually, having fulfilled the vows of *bodhi*, they consequently become *arhant*s, attain *bodhi* and ultimately reach Buddhahood.

तं शंखपर्वतं नाम सर्वशिलोच्चयोत्तमम्।
समारोहण-मात्रेण निष्णातः सिद्धिमान् भवेत् ॥ १११ ॥

There is a mountain named Śaṅkha, which is the highest among mountains. Merely climbing the mountain grants divine powers to anyone.

तत्रापि ये समाश्रित्य स्नात्वा ध्यात्वा समाहिताः।
जपयज्ञादिदानं च कुर्युः संबोधिमानसाः ॥ ११२ ॥

In the refuge of the mountain, having bathed and meditated, one must chant, donate and perform sacrifice rituals with the wish of *bodhi* in mind.

---

28 भावार्थ इति खपाठः।

तेऽपि न दुर्गतिं यायुः सदा सद्गति-संभवाः ।
बोधिसत्त्वा महासत्त्वाः परिशुद्ध-त्रिमण्डलाः ॥ ११३ ॥

They will never be wretched or miserable; they will always be in a good state to eventually become *bodhisattva*s, *mahāsattva*s and purified in mind, speech and bodies.

निःक्लेशा विमलात्मानः सर्व-सत्त्व-हिताशयाः ।
भद्रश्री-सद्गुणाधारा भवेयुर्ब्रह्मचारिणः ॥ ११४ ॥

They will be free of obstacles, have pure souls, intent on helping all beings, gentle, glorious, virtuous and celibate.

ततस्ते बोधिसंभारं पूरयित्वा यथाक्रमम् ।
अर्हन्तो बोधिमासाद्य संबुद्धपदमाप्नुयुः ॥ ११५ ॥

Gradually, having fulfilled the vows of *bodhi*, they consequently become *arhant*s, attain *bodhi* and ultimately reach Buddhahood.

बहूनि[29]चोपतीर्थानि विद्यन्तेऽत्रहिमालये ।
तानि तीर्थानि सर्वाणि भुक्ति-मुक्ति-प्रदायीनि ॥ ११६ ॥

Similarly, in the lap of the Himalayas, there are also other semi-pilgrimages, all of them able to grant enjoyment and salvation.

यत्र यत्र श्रवन्तीनामन्येषां च समागमः ।
तत्र तत्रापि तीर्थानि पुण्य-फल-प्रदायिनि ॥ ११७ ॥

Wherever these streams of water flow and merge with other streams, there *tīrtha*s occur, all of which grant merit.

तेषां चाप्युपतीर्थानां पृथक्पृथक्फलं महत् ।
पाप-संशोधनं पुण्यं सद्धर्मसुखसाधनम् ॥ ११८ ॥

These *upa-tīrtha*s (semi-pilgrimages) grant various forms of merits and rewards respectively; they destroy sins, grant merits and are the instruments of *dharma* and happiness.

---

29 अन्यानि इति कपाठः ।

तेष्वपि ये नराः स्नात्वा चरेयुःपोषधं व्रतम् ।
दद्युर्दानानि चार्थिभ्यःकुर्युर्यज्ञान् च ये मुदा ॥ ११९ ॥

Having taken baths, people must practise *vrata*, donate to the beggars and perform sacrifice happily.

पितॄन् संतर्प्ययेयुश्च पूजयेयुः सुरानपि ।
स्मृत्वा ध्यात्वा त्रिरत्नानां भजेयुर्मन्त्रजल्पनैः[30] ॥ १२० ॥

They must satisfy the ancestors, while also worshipping the gods, must remember and meditate on the Buddha, Dharma and Saṅgha and sing their prayers with devotion.

एवं लोकाधिपानां च स्मृत्वा ध्यात्वा समाहिताः ।
जपित्वा नाममन्त्राणि साधयेयुर्यथाविधि ॥ १२१ ॥

Similarly, one must remember and meditate on the lords of the world with focus and devotion. One must also chant their names and prayers, according to procedure.

तानि सर्वाणि सिध्येयुः साधितानि जगद्धिते[31] ।
दद्युश्चेह शुभोत्साहं परत्र निर्वृतं पदम् ॥ १२२ ॥

They are all powerful, useful for the welfare of the world. They grant good enthusiasm and a path to liberation.

तेऽपि न दुर्गतिं यायुः सदा सद्गतिसंभवाः ।
निःक्लेशा विमलात्मानः परिशुद्धत्रिमण्डलाः ॥ १२३ ॥

They will never be wretched or miserable; they will always be in a good state. They will be freed of obstacles, purified in their souls, cleansed in their mind, speech and bodies.

बोधिसत्त्वा महासत्त्वाश्चतुर्ब्रह्म-विहारिणः[32] ।
भद्रश्री-सद्गुणाधारा भवेयुर्बोधिचारिणः ॥ १२४ ॥

---

30 भजेयुनेमिजल्पनैः इति खपाठः ।

31 लोकहिते इति खपाठः ।

32 महोत्सवा इति गपाठः ।

They shall become *bodhisattvas* and *mahāsattvas* and attain the four highest divine abodes. They will be gentle, virtuous and practise *bodhi*.

ततस्ते बोधिसम्भारं पूरयित्वा यथाक्रमम् ।
अर्हन्तो बोधिं संप्राप्य यायुर्नूनं जिनालयम् ॥ १२५ ॥

Gradually, having fulfilled the vows of *bodhi*, they consequently become *arhant*s, attain *bodhi* and ultimately reach Buddhahood.

एवं विज्ञाय सर्वेषां तीर्थानामपि सत्फलम् ।
भद्रश्री-सद्गुणोत्साहं सौख्यसंबोधिसाधनम् ॥ १२६ ॥

सर्वेष्वेतेषु तीर्थेषु भद्रश्री-गुण-वाञ्छिभिः ।
स्नान-दानादिकं कर्म कर्त्तव्यं बोधि-प्राप्तये ॥ १२७ ॥

Having understood the pious rewards of all *tīrtha*s and knowing them to be the instruments of happiness, knowledge and virtues, those who want such qualities must practise deeds such as ablution, donation and sacrifice for the acquisition of *bodhi*.

ये य एतेषु तीर्थेषु स्नात्वा नित्यं यथाविधि ।
दत्वा दानं व्रतं धृत्वा ध्यात्वा भजेयुरीश्वरम् ॥ १२८ ॥

ते ते सर्वे विकल्माषाः परिशुद्ध-त्रिमण्डलाः ।
निःक्लेशा विमलात्मानो भवेयुर्बोधिभागिनः ॥ १२९ ॥

Having taken baths, donated and prayed to the Lord, those who practise the *vrata* in these *tīrtha*s, shall be freed of their sins and acquire purity in their minds, speech and bodies. Their miseries will be destroyed, souls purified and they will attain *bodhi*.

इति लोकाधिपैः सर्वैर्ब्रह्मेन्द्रप्रमुखैरपि ।
सर्वाण्येतानि[33]तीर्थानि संसेवितानि सर्वदा ॥ १३० ॥

Hence, the lords of the world and gods like Brahmā and Indra were constantly serving these *tīrtha*s.

---

33 सर्वकर्माणि इति कपाठः ।

तथा च मुनिभिः सर्वैस्तापसैर्ब्रह्मचारिभिः ।
यतिभिर्योगिभिश्चापि तीर्थिकैः श्रावकैरपि ॥ १३१ ॥

ब्राह्मणैर्वैष्णवैः शैवैः कौलिकैरपि शक्तिकैः ।
देवैश्च दानवैश्चापि यक्षगन्धर्वकिन्नरैः ॥ १३२ ॥

गुह्यक[34]–सिद्धसाध्यैश्च ग्रहैर्विद्याधरैरपि ।
अप्सरोभिश्च सर्वाभिः सदा संसेवितानि हि ॥ १३३ ॥

नागेन्द्रैर्गरुडैश्चापि कुम्भाण्डै राक्षसैरपि ।
एवमन्यैरपि प्रेत्य सेवितानि शुभार्थिभिः ॥ १३४ ॥

Similarly, sages, hermits, monks, celibates, Hindu monks, *yogīs, ṛṣis*, *śrāvakas*, brāhmaṇas, Vaiṣṇava (followers of Viṣṇu), Śaiva (followers of Śiva), Kaulikas, Śākta (followers of Śakti), gods, demons, demi-gods such as *yakṣas, gandharvas, kinnaras, guhyakas, kumbhāṇḍas, siddhas, sādhyas* and *vidyādharas*, planets, celestial nymphs, falcons, serpent lords, devils and others who sought auspiciousness went to serve these *tīrthas*.

ग्रहैश्च सांधिकैश्चापि व्रतिकैश्चाप्युपासकैः ।
बोधिसत्त्वैर्मुनीन्द्रैश्च सेवितानि जगद्धिते ॥ १३५ ॥

Similarly, planets, *sāndhikas*, *vrata* holders, laymen, laywomen, *bodhisattvas,* supreme sages have all served these *tīrthas* for the welfare of the world.

अहमपि तथैतेषु तीर्थेषु समुपाश्रयम् ।
स्नत्वा दानानि दत्वा च कृत्वा यज्ञं यथाविधि ॥ १३६ ॥

पितॄन् सन्तर्पयित्वापि समभ्यर्च्य सुरानपि ।
त्रिरत्नभजनं कृत्वा प्राचरं पोषधं व्रतम् ॥ १३७ ॥

I, also, took refuge in these *tīrthas*, where I bathed, donated, sacrificed, performed rites to please ancestors, satisfied the gods through worship, sang prayers of the *tri-ratna* (Buddha, Dharma, Saṅgha). This is how I practised the *vrata*.

---

34 चारण इति घपाठः ।

धर्मधातुं समाराध्य स्मृत्वा ध्यात्वा समाहितः ।
जपित्वा धारणी-मन्त्रं प्राचरं बोधिसम्वरम् ॥ १३८ ॥

एतत्पुण्यानुभावेन परिशुद्ध-त्रिमण्डलाः ।
निःक्लेशो निर्मलात्मानःचतुर्ब्रह्मविहारिणः ॥ १३९ ॥

One must, with focus and concentration on the Dharmadhātu, worship, remember and meditate on him and chant the Dhāraṇī *mantras* to maintain the *bodhi* vow. Through the merit amassed so, he becomes purified in his mind, speech and body as well as his soul, becomes freed of misery and attachment, and dwells in the four highest divine abodes.

बोधिसत्त्वा महासत्त्वा भद्रश्री-सद्गुणान्विताः ।
आशु संबोधिसंभारं पूरयित्वा यथाक्रमम् ॥ १४० ॥

जित्वा मारगणान् सर्वान् कलावपि जगद्धिते ।
त्रिविधां बोधिमासाद्य संबुद्धो धर्मराड् भवेत् ॥ १४१ ॥

They who do so become *bodhisattvas*, *mahāsattvas*, gentle, glorious and the source of good qualities. They instantly fulfil the *bodhi* vows to consequently defeat bodily desires; and for the welfare of the world in the Kali era, they attain the three states of *bodhi* to finally acquire Buddhahood.

यूयमपि च ज्ञात्वैव चरत बोधिप्राप्तये ।
यूयं सर्वेषु तीर्थेषु श्रद्धया गच्छत सदा[35] ॥ १४२ ॥

Therefore, to overcome the obstacles that hinder the acquisition of *bodhi,* you all must seek the refuge in these *tīrthas*.

धर्मधातुं समभ्यर्च्य स्मृत्वा ध्यात्वा समाहिताः ।
जपित्वा धारणीमन्त्रं संभजत जगद्धिते ॥ १४३ ॥

You must worship, remember and meditate on the Dharmadhātu and with concentration, sing the Dhāraṇī *mantra*, for the welfare of the world.

---

35 सर्वेषु तेषु तीर्थेषु प्रवध्वं यथाविधि इति कपाठः ।

एतत् पुण्यप्रभावेण परिशुद्धत्रिमण्डलाः ।
दुर्गतिं नैव गच्छेत तिष्ठेत[36] सद्गतौ सदा ॥ १४४ ॥

As a result of this merit, you shall all be purified in your minds, speech and bodies, shall never be wretched or miserable, and will always be in a good state.

तत्र सदा त्रिरत्नानां शरणे समुपस्थिताः ।
सत्कारैर्भजनं कृत्वा संचरेत जगद्धिते ॥ १४५ ॥

You must always be present there to pay homage to the *tri-ratna* (Buddha, Dharma, Saṅgha) and devotedly sing praises and actively work for the welfare of the world.

तेषां हि विमलात्मानां चतुर्ब्रह्मविहारिणाम् ।
बोधिसत्त्वा महासत्त्वा भवेयुर्भद्रचारिणः ॥ १४६ ॥

You would be purified in your souls and dwell in the four highest divine abodes. You shall become *bodhisattva*s, *mahāsattva*s and work for the good.

ततः श्रीसद्गुणाधाराः सर्वविद्याविचक्षणाः ।
सर्वसत्त्वाहिताधानं कुर्वन्तु ते[37]जगद्धिते ॥ १४७ ॥

Then you would become the basis of all good qualities, well-versed in all forms of knowledge and the very reasons for welfare of all sentient beings. Thus, you all must work for the welfare of the world.

ततः संबोधिसंभारं पूरयित्वा यथाक्रमम् ।
आशु त्रिबोधिसामाद्य प्राप्स्यथ सौगतं पदम् ॥ १४८ ॥

Having gradually fulfilled the vows of *bodhi*, you shall instantly attain the three types of *bodhi* to ultimately be established into Buddhahood."

---

36 जायध्वं इति गपाठः ।

37 संचरध्वे इति घपाठः ।

इत्यादिष्टं मुनीन्द्रेण श्रुत्वा सर्वे प्रबोधिताः ।
मैत्रेयादि-सभालोकाःप्राप्यानन्द समाश्रिताः[38] ॥ १४९ ॥

In this way, the king of the sages – *Buddha* instructed everyone. Upon hearing his instructions, everyone present in the assembly including Maitreya, was overjoyed and awakened.

॥ इति श्रीस्वयंभूसमुत्पत्तिकथायाम् अनेकतीर्थसंजातपुण्यमहात्म्यवर्णनं नाम-पंचमोऽध्यायः सम्पूर्णः ॥

Thus, within the story of the origin of Svayambhū, the fifth chapter, on the description of the greatness of the merit received through the service of various *tīrtha*s, ends here.

---

[38] प्रबोधिताः इति कपाठः ।

अथ षष्ठोऽध्यायः
(Ṣaṣṭha Adhyāya)

Dharmādhātu Vāgīśvara

अथासौ च महासत्त्वो मैत्रेयः सुगतात्मजः ।
मुनीन्द्रं श्रीघनं नत्वा साञ्जलिरेवमब्रवीत् ॥ १ ॥

The Mahāsattva Maitreya, son of Buddha, joined his hands in salutation and addressed the Śrīghana.

यदिदं भगवन्! धर्मधातुवागीश्वराभिधम् ।
प्रसिद्धं हेतुना केन तत्समादेष्टुमर्हति ॥ २ ॥

"O Lord! What is the reason for such tremendous fame of the Dharmadhātu Vāgīśvara? Please tell me."

इति संप्रार्थिते तेन मैत्रेयेण स सर्ववित् ।
भगवान् तं महासत्त्वं संपश्यन्निदमादिशत् ॥ ३ ॥

येनात्र हेतुना धर्मधातु-वागीश्वराभिधम् ।
प्रसिद्धं तत्प्रवक्ष्यामि शृणु मैत्रेय सादरम् ॥ ४ ॥

When the Mahāsattva Maitreya prayed to the Lord so, the Lord, looking at him, replied: "O Maitreya! I shall tell you the reason due to which the Dharmadhātu acquired such great fame. Listen carefully!"

तद्यथायुर्यदा नृणां त्रिंशद्वर्षसहस्रकम् ।
शोभावत्यां महापुर्यामुदपादि तदा जिनः ॥ ५ ॥

When the life of man spanned 30,000 years, there was a great city named Śobhāvatī. For the welfare of the world, the Kanakamuni Buddha originated there.

संबुद्धोऽर्हञ्जगच्छास्ता धर्मराजो मुनीश्वरः ।
कनक-मुनीरित्याख्यस्तथागतो विनायकः ॥ ६ ॥

He was the enlightened one, the king of *dharma,* lord of sages, who preached the *dharma* to the world as its *śāstā*. He was famous by the name Kanakamuni and was also called Vināyaka.

तदाहं कुलपुत्रस्तु सुधर्मा नाम आत्मवित्[1] ।
बोधिसत्त्वो महासत्त्वो धर्मश्रीसद्गुणार्थभृत् ॥ ७ ॥

स कनकमुनेः शास्तुः शासने समुपाश्रितः ।
त्रिरत्नभजनं कृत्वा प्राचरं बोधिसंवरम् ॥ ८ ॥

I was present then as a man of noble birth, who understood myself. I was named Sudharma. I was a *mahāsattva* and a *bodhisattva*. I was filled with the glory of *dharma* and virtues manifold. Under the disciple of Kanakamuni Buddha and the service of the *triratna*, I practised *bodhi*.

यदा स भगवाञ्छास्ता शोभावत्या उपाश्रमे ।
विहारे [2]शोभितारामे विजहार ससांघिकः ॥ ९ ॥

तदा तत्र सभालोके ब्रह्मेन्द्र-प्रमुखाः सुराः ।
सर्वलोकाधिपाश्चापि धर्मं श्रोतुं मुदागताः ॥ १० ॥

When Lord Kanakamuni, near the city of Śobhāvatī, in his *mahāvihāra* named Śobhitārāma, dwelled with his Saṅgha, then Brahmā, Indra and other major gods as well as the lords of worlds all arrived there, to hear the sermons of *dharma*.

सर्वे ग्रहाश्च ताराश्च सर्वविद्याधरा अपि ।
सिद्धाः साध्याश्च रुद्राश्च मुनयोऽपि महर्षयः ॥ ११ ॥

गन्धर्वाः किन्नरा यक्षा गुह्यका राक्षसा अपि ।
कुम्भाण्डा गरुडा नागा दैत्याश्चापि समागताः ॥ १२ ॥

---

1 संभवः इति कपाठः ।

2 कुक्कुटारामे इति खपाठः ।

Celestial planets, stars, demi-gods of *vidyādhara*s, *sidhha*s, *sādhya*s, *rudra* kinds, sages and monks also came. So did the *gandharva*s, *kinnara*s, *yakṣa*s, *guhyaka*, *kumbhāṇḍa* demi-gods, serpents, falcons, demons and devils.

यतयो योगिनश्चापि तीर्थिकाश्च तपस्विनः[3] ।
पाखण्डाश्च परिव्राजो निर्ग्रन्था ब्रह्मचारिणः ॥ १३ ॥

Saints, hermits, pilgrims, ascetics, *pākhaṇḍī*, monks, Jainas, celibates, all came.

श्रमणाः श्रावकाश्चापि व्रतिनश्चाप्युपासकाः ।
तत्सद्धर्मामृतं पातुं सादरं समुपागताः ॥ १४ ॥

To hear the teachings of the *dharma*, *śramaṇa*, *śrāvaka*, *vrata* holders, laymen and laywomen all arrived.

ब्राह्मणा क्षत्रियाश्चापि वैश्याश्च मन्त्रिणो जनाः ।
गृहाधिपाश्च[4] श्रेष्ठाश्च भृत्याः सैन्याधिपा अपि ॥ १५ ॥

Brāhmaṇas, kṣatriyas, vaiśyas, courtiers, householders, merchants, servants and military commanders all arrived.

शिल्पिनो वणिजश्चापि सार्थवाहा महाजनाः ।
पौरा जानपदा ग्राम्याः कार्पटिकाश्च शौरिकाः ॥ १६ ॥

Technicians, businessmen, tradesmen with caravans, rich men, townsfolk, people from large cities, villagers, carpenters and wanderers all arrived.

तथान्ये वासिनश्चापि सर्वलोकाः प्रसादिताः ।
तत्सद्धर्मामृतं पातुं सादरं समुपागताः ॥ १७ ॥

Similarly, others from villages and cities and from all over the world, were all happily present in front of the Kanakamuni Buddha, eager to drink the nectar of *dharma*.

---

3 सौगता इति खपाठः ।

4 देवाधिपाश्च इति गपाठः ।

तान् सर्वान् समुपायातान् दृष्ट्वा स भगवान्मुदा ।
सभामध्यासनासीनस्तस्थौ ध्यात्वा प्रभासयन् ॥ १८ ॥

Seeing beings from all the worlds arrive, Lord Kanakamuni was happy. He proceeded to take the central seat in the assembly; all the while he was radiating energy from his form.

तं मुनीन्द्रं प्रभाकान्तं दृष्ट्वा सर्वेऽपि सांघिकाः ।
श्रमणाःश्रावकाः सर्वे भिक्षवो ब्रह्मचारिणः ॥ १९ ॥

भिक्षुण्यो ब्रह्मचारिण्य उपासिकाश्च चैलिकाः ।
चैलका व्रतिनश्चापि धर्मकामा उपासकाः ॥ २० ॥

Sādhakas, śramaṇas, brāhmaṇas, *bhikkhus, bhikkhuṇīs, cailaka, vrata* holders, celibates, maidens and all else who desired *dharma* were happy at the sight of the Kanakamuni who was filled with energy.

सर्वेऽपि ते समागत्य प्रणम्य[5] तं मुनीश्वरम् ।
परिवृत्य पुरस्कृत्य धर्मं श्रोतुमुपाश्रयन् ॥ २१ ॥

The assembled mass surrounded the Kanakamuni Buddha from all directions and went to his refuge to listen to *dharma*, with hands joined in salutation.

ततो ब्रह्मादयो देवाः सर्वे लोकाधिपा अपि ।
तं मुनीन्द्रं समभ्यर्च्य प्रणम्य च यथाक्रमम् ॥ २२ ॥

Brahmā, Indra and other gods and the lords of the world then worshipped and saluted the supreme sage Kanakamuni Buddha.

परिवृत्य पुरस्कृत्य तत्सभायां समन्ततः ।
संपश्यन्तं मुनीन्द्रं तमुपतस्थुः समाहिताः ॥ २३ ॥

Having surrounded him and facing him, everyone sat down in the assembly filled with concentration.

ततस्ते मानवाः सर्वे ऋषि-विप्रनृपादयः ।
तं मुनीन्द्रं[6] समभ्यर्च्य संप्रणम्य यथाक्रमम् ॥ २४ ॥

---

5 प्रणत्वा इति कपाठः ।

6 नागाननम् इति कपाठः ।

The men, gods, brāhmaṇas, sages, kings, everyone present there worshipped the Kanakamuni Buddha and saluted him in a similar procedure.

तत्सभां समुपाश्रित्य परिवृत्य समन्ततः ।
पुरस्कृत्य समुद्वीक्ष्य संतस्थिरे समाहिताः ॥ २५ ॥

Everyone who came there, having surrounded him, looked at the Lord and sat down, with patience and concentration.

ततस्तान् समुपासीनान् दृष्ट्वा स भगवान् मुदा ।
आर्यसत्यं समारभ्य सद्धर्मं समुपादिशत् ॥ २६ ॥

Thus the Supreme Sage Kanakamuni Buddha, who was pleased at the sight of the people sitting patiently and devotedly, commenced the sermons on noble truths and *dharma*.

क्रमेण[7]बोधिचर्याग्रमार्याष्टांङ्गं च तत्पथम् ।
आदिश्य बोधिमार्गे तान् सर्वान् लोकान् नियोजयेत् ॥ २७ ॥

He shared the *bodhicaryā* (the *bodhi* discipline) and described the eightfold paths; he elucidated and thus established all present there into the path of *bodhi*.

तत्सद्धर्मामृतं पीत्वा सर्वे लोकाःप्रबोधिताः ।
सद्धर्मसाधनायुक्ता बभूवुर्बोधिमानसाः ॥ २८ ॥

Everyone, who drank the nectar of the true *dharma* granted by the Kanakamuni Buddha, started to practise the good *dharma* and attained the *bodhi* mind.

तदा विक्रमशिलाख्ये विहारे भिक्षुरात्मवित् ।
ससंघो व्याहरद् धर्मश्रीमित्राख्यः सुधीर्यतिः ॥ २९ ॥

At that moment, a scholar who knew himself, named Dharmaśrīmitra *bhikkhu*, in a *vihāra* named Vikramaśīlā, shared the knowledge of *dharma* to the Saṅgha there.

---

[7] शनैः इति घपाठः ।

स तत्र सर्वलोकानां हितायैव समाश्रितः ।
ससंघो नामसंगीतिं व्याख्यातुमभ्यवाञ्छत ॥ ३० ॥

ततः स सन्मतिः सर्वान् आमन्त्र्य तत्र सादरम्[8] ।
सभामध्यासनासीनस्तस्थौ ध्यानसमाहितः ॥ ३१ ॥

The *bhikkhu*, in the *vihāra* named Vikramaśīlā, for the welfare of all beings, stood at the centre of the gathered Saṅgha and desired to teach them the Nāmasaṅgīti. Thus, the wise *bhikkhu* named Dharmaśrīmitra, happily, took the central seat at the assembly intending to teach the Saṅgha in a meditative state.

तं सभासन आसीनं दृष्ट्वा सर्वेऽपि सांघिकाः ।
तत्सद्धर्मामृतं पातुमिच्छन्तः[9] समुपागताः ॥ ३२ ॥

तत्र तेऽपि यतिं नत्वा परिवृत्य समन्ततः ।
पुरस्कृत्य समीक्षन्त उपतस्थुः समाहिताः ॥ ३३ ॥

When he sat at the assembly, everyone there who was eager to consume the nectar of *dharma* that the venerable *bhikkhu* would shower upon them saluted him, did the *pradakṣiṇā* and with their hands joined, sat there looking at him, with concentration.

तत्राऽऽन्येऽपि समायाता लोका द्विजनृपादयः ।
वैश्याश्च मन्त्रिणोऽमात्या भृत्याः शैन्याधिपा अपि ॥ ३४ ॥

शिल्पिनो वणिजश्चापि सार्थवाहा महाजनाः ।
पौरा जानपदा ग्राम्यास्तथान्ये देशवासिनः ॥ ३५ ॥

सर्वे ते समुपागत्य प्रणम्य तं यतिं मुदा ।
परिवृत्य पुरस्कृत्य संपश्यन्तमुपाश्रयन् ॥ ३६ ॥

Apart from them, others who came, including ordinary men from the world, brāhmaṇas, kings, vaiśyas, courtiers, secretaries, servents, military commanders, carpenters, businessmen, tradesmen with caravans, merchants, townsfolk, villagers and people from

---

8 संघानाम प्रसादरं इति खपाठः ।

9 अमृतज्ञानम् इति गपाठः ।

other countries, saluted the monk with great happiness and having performed the *pradakṣiṇā*, sat around him devotedly.

ततः स यतिरालोक्य सर्वान् तान्समुपाश्रितान् ।
मञ्जुश्रीनामसंगीतिं समाख्यातुं यथाक्रमम् ॥ ३७ ॥

Seeing the people present there, the *bhikkhu* commenced the description of Mañjuśrī Nāmasaṅgīti gradually.

तत्समादिष्टमाकर्ण्य सर्वे लोकाः सभाश्रिताः ।
संबुद्ध-गुणमाहात्म्यं मत्वानन्दप्रबोधिताः ॥ ३८ ॥

Upon hearing his sermons, those mundane people present at the assembly grasped the greatness of the qualities of Buddha and relished in the knowledge.

ततः सर्वेऽपि लोकास्ते ब्राह्मणा भूमिपादयः ।
नत्वा तं यातिमामन्त्र्य स्वस्वालयं मुदाऽऽययुः ॥ ३९ ॥

After listening to the discourse on the Mañjuśrī Nāmasaṅgīti, the brāhmaṇas, the kings and most of the audience, having saluted the *bhikkhu*, returned to their respective abodes.

ततस्ते श्रावका विज्ञा यतयो ब्रह्मचारिणः ।
द्वादशाक्षर-गुह्यार्थं सम्यक् संश्रोतुमीच्छिरे ॥ ४० ॥

Afterwards, the *śrāvaka*s, *bhikkhu*s, celibates and those with greater wisdom in the Saṅgha, wished to know the inner meaning of the Twelve Syllables.

ततस्ते योगिनः सर्वे कृताञ्जलिपुटा मुदा ।
शास्तारं तं यतिं नत्वा समामन्त्र्यैवमब्रूवन् ॥ ४१ ॥

They, who were present there including *yogī*s and the aforementioned groups, joined their hands in reverence and happiness, and saluted the *bhikkhu* who had preached the sermons earlier, and addressed him so:

भदन्त! द्वादशानां यदक्षराणां विशेषतः ।
विशुद्धिं श्रोतुमिच्छामः तत्समादेष्टुमर्हति ॥ ४२ ॥

"O great monk! pray reveal to us the significance of the Twelve Syllables and the procedure for its purification and fulfilment."

इति तैः प्रार्थितो धर्मश्रीमित्रः स सुधीरपि ।
द्वादशाक्षर-गुह्यार्थं विशुद्धिं न समादिशत् ॥ ४३ ॥

When they prayed to him so, the *bhikkhu* Dharmaśrīmitra, despite his scholarliness, was unable to tell the inner meaning and the true form of the Twelve Syllables.

विशुद्धिमनभिज्ञाय विषण्णात्मा स उत्थितः ।
ध्यानागारं समासीनो ध्यात्वैवं समचिन्तयन् ॥ ४४ ॥

He rose up from his seat, distressed due to his inability to answer the question and proceeded to meditate and think simultaneously in concentration.

न ह्येतदक्षरं[10]गुह्यं विशुद्धिश्च न ज्ञायते ।
तत्कथं उपदेक्ष्यामि हाहा कुत्र भ्रमानि वा[11] ॥ ४५ ॥

He thought "Alas! I do not know the true meaning and purity of the Twelve Syllables and thereby cannot teach it to my disciples. What must I do now?"

इति चिन्ता-विषण्णात्मा लज्जा-संमोहिताशयः ।
स्मृत्वा रत्नत्रयं ध्यात्वा तस्थौ धैर्यसमाहितः ॥ ४६ ॥

Agitated, distressed, ashamed and attached, he remembered and mediated on the three jewels (Buddha, Dharma and Saṅgha) as he sat there.

तत्क्षणे स त्रिरत्नानां स्मृति-पुण्यानुभावतः ।
प्राप्तवान् सहसा वीर्यं महोत्साहं च तत्क्षणे[12] ॥ ४७ ॥

As he was meditating, his remembrance of the three jewels brought

---

10 नेतेदक्षरं इति गपाठः ।

11 भ्रमेमहि इति घपाठः ।

12 एवं मतिं महावीर्यं महोत्साहिनिमाप्तवान् इति कपाठः ।

him merit, due to the influence of which he was energized with enthusiasm and strength and filled with bliss.

ततः सन्मतिशौण्डोऽसौ पुनर्ध्यात्वा समाहितः ।
मनसा सर्वलोकेषु विचारयन् व्यलोकयन् ॥ ४८ ॥

Then the *bhikkhu*, with great enthusiasm, started mediating deeper to wonder about the entire world solely through his mind.

तदापश्यन् महाचीन उत्तरस्यां नगोत्तमे ।
मञ्जुश्रियं महाभिज्ञं सर्व-विद्याधिपेश्वरम् ॥ ४९ ॥

बोधिसत्त्वं महासत्त्वं सर्व-धर्माधिपप्रभुम् ।
सर्व-गुह्य-विशुद्ध्यर्थं विज्ञानज्ञानदायकम् ॥ ५० ॥

As he meditated and wondered so, he saw with his divine sight that there is a mountain in the northern part of the world and beyond it is the land known as Mahācīna (China in present day) which is the residence of the Mañjuśrī, who is a great scholar and master of all knowledge, is a *bodhisattva, mahāsattva*, understands the true mystery of *dharma*, knows all secrets, and understands the purity and impurity of incantations and the process of their fulfilment.

तं पश्यन् मनसा धर्मश्री-मित्रःसुसमुत्सुकः ।
सहसोत्थाय तान् संघान् समामन्त्र्यैवमब्रवीत् ॥ ५१ ॥

Having understood the qualities of Mañjuśrī, Dharmaśrīmitra, who was filled with excitement, immediately stood up and went outside towards the Saṅgha assembled there to address them so.

भो भवन्तो गमिष्यामि महाचीने नगोत्तमे ।
मंजुश्रियं महासत्त्वं द्रष्टुमिच्छामि सांप्रतम् ॥ ५२ ॥

"O scholars! *bhikkhus* and others present there! I am departing for the Mahācīna, which lies beyond the great mountain, in order to receive audience from the Mahāsattva Mañjuśrī.

एतस्या नामसंगीत्या गुह्यविशुद्धिविस्तरम् ।
पृष्ट्वा सम्यक् परिज्ञाय ह्यागमिष्याम्यहं द्रुतम् ॥ ५३ ॥

I will ask the deeper meaning of the Nāmasaṅgitī and the purification procedure of the *mantra* and with its good knowledge, I shall return soon.

यावन्नाहमिहायातः तावत्सर्वे समाहिताः ।
त्रिरत्न-भजनं कृत्वा तिष्ठत मा विषीदत ॥ ५४ ॥

Until I return, you all must stay here praising and worshipping the Buddha, Dharma and Saṅgha, without worry.

इत्युक्त्वा स महाभिज्ञस्ततः संप्रस्थितो द्रुतम् ।
सञ्चरन्नत्र नेपालमण्डलं[13] समुपाययौ ॥ ५५ ॥

Having said so, the great scholar *bhikkhu* started walking and gradually reached Nepal on foot.

तमायातं यतिं नत्वा मञ्जुदेवः स सर्ववित् ।
स्वान्तिके समुपाद्रष्टुमैच्छद् ऋद्धिं प्रदर्शयन् ॥ ५६ ॥

As Mañjuśrī saw the *bhikkhu* Dharmaśrīmitra approaching, he recognized him to be the *bhikkhu* who was worried and thus decided, in display of his glory, to invite him closer to teach him.

ततःश्रीमंजुदेवोऽपि भूत्वा कृषिकरः स्वयम् ।
शार्दूल-मृगराजाभ्यां हलेनाकर्षयन् महीम् ॥ ५७ ॥

The Mañjuśrī then took the guise of a farmer and started to plough the field with two tigers.

तं दृष्ट्वा दूरतो धर्मश्रीमित्रो ह्यतिविस्मितः ।
किमेतत् महदाश्चर्यमितिद्रष्टुं समागमत्[14] ॥ ५८ ॥

At the sight of Mañjuśrī from afar, Dharmaśrīmitra was astounded to see the greatly surprising and wondrous sight [of tigers being used to plough fields, instead of traditionally used animals such as oxen or bullocks].

---

13 विषये इति कपाठः ।

14 सुयाचरत् इति खपाठः।

ततः स समुपाश्रित्य दृष्ट्वा तन्महदद्भुतम्।
कृषिकरं तमामन्त्र्य पप्रच्छैवं व्यलोकयन्॥ ५९॥

Then, he approached the farmer indulged in such a wondrous activity and inviting him closer, posed him a question.

अस्मात् स्थानाच्च भो साधो महाचीन-नगोत्तमः।
पंचशीर्षः कियद्दूरे तदुपदेष्टुमर्हति॥ ६०॥

"O gentleman! I seek to reach the great mountain named Mahācīna, which has five peaks. How far is it from here? Pray tell me."

इति संप्रार्थिते तेन श्रुत्वा स हलवाहकः।
सुचिरं तं यतिं पश्यन् सादरमेवमब्रवीत्॥ ६१॥

When he prayed to him so, the farmer considered the *bhikkhu* for the long time before respectfully answering.

यत्त्वं कुत इहायासि किमर्थमुत्तरे पथि।
महाचीनं च गन्तुं त्वं दूरतः[15]परिपृच्छसि॥ ६२॥

"Where have you come from and for what purpose do you seek to reach the land of Mahācīna that lies afar?

अद्य प्रवर्तते सायं तद्विहारे ममाश्रमे।
उषित्वा[16]प्रातरुत्थाय गच्छ मद्देशितात् पथः॥ ६३॥

O friend! the hour is getting late. My household lies nearby. I invite you to spend the night in my residence. When you rise in the morning, I shall direct you towards your path."

इति तेनोदितं धर्मश्रीमित्रस्तु निशम्य सः।
तथेत्यनुमतं धृत्वा तूष्णीं भूत्वा व्यतिष्ठत॥ ६४॥

The *bhikkhu,* upon hearing the words of the farmer, silently accepted his proposal and decided to stay there for the night.

---

15 नास्ति इति खपाठः।

16 अज्भित्वा इति कपाठः।

ततः संबोधितं भिक्षुं मत्वा स हलवाहकः ।
तौ शार्दूलमृगेन्द्रौ द्वौ तत्रैवान्तर्व्यधापयत् ॥ ६५ ॥

The farmer then led his giant tigers away from the monk and eventually willed them to vanish into thin air.

हलं तु सर्वलोकानां संप्रबोधनहेतवे ।
तत्रैवौच्चैः स्थल-क्षेत्रे यूपवदवरोपयत् ॥ ६६ ॥

However, thinking that the plow may be a source of inspiration and an example to the entire world, he placed it on high ground, planting it into the soil there.

अद्यापि तन्महीस्थानं मंजुश्रीभूःप्रसिद्धितः ।
सा वाचेति प्रसिद्धा च यत्रावरोपितं हलम् ॥ ६७ ॥

The spot where he planted the plow is lauded as the place of Mañjuśrī, till this day.

ततस्तं[17]यतिमाहूय सायं स हलवाहकः ।
तत्र प्रविश्यधर्मश्रीमित्रःपश्यति विस्मितः ॥ ६८ ॥

As the night fell, the farmer took the Bhikkhu Dharmaśrīmitra, who had grown suspicious yet intrigued, into his home.

ततो मूल-फल-स्कन्ध-पत्रादिभोगमादरात् ।
दत्वा तस्मै स्वयं भुत्क्वा तस्थौ स हलवाहकः ॥ ६९ ॥

The farmer offered fruits, medicinal herbs, tubers, spinach and salad leaves, and whatever else was available, to the monk respectfully, and they dined together.

ततः स विविधां धर्मश्रीमित्रो रजनीकथाम् ।
भाषित्वा तं महाभिज्ञं कृषिकरो व्यनोदयत् ॥ ७० ॥

The Bhikkhu Dharmaśrīmitra, in return, told various stories that interested the farmer in order to please him.

---

[17] यतेस्तम् इति गपाठः ।

ततः स मंजुदेवस्तं यतिं छात्रालये निशि।
प्रेषयित्वा स्वयं गुह्यागारे शय्यां समाश्रयत्॥ ७१॥

As the night grew, the Mañjuśrī in disguise, arranged to send the *bhikkhu* to sleep in the adjacent building, which was the abode of his students, and he himself went to bed in his own house.

तत्र प्रविश्य धर्मश्रीमित्रः संप्रति विस्मितः।
सुप्त्वाश्रमे समुत्थाय मनसैवं व्यचिन्तयत्॥ ७२॥

As Dharmaśrīmitra entered his shelter, he was still curious regarding the events that day. He slept for a few moments, but then woke up – curiosity did not allow him sleep. He started to think in his mind.

नाद्यात्र शयनीयं यदयं पुमान्महर्द्धिकः।
भार्यया सह कथ्यं किं किं वदेच्च[18]विनोदयन्॥७३॥

He thought, "I must not sleep here tonight. My host seems to be a greatly powerful man, full of glory and prosperity". The monk then, wishing to hear the conversation between the farmer and his wife, rose up from his bed.

इति ध्यात्वा स धर्मश्रीमित्रो यतिः समुत्थितः।
सत्वरं निभृतं तस्य द्वारमूलमुपाश्रितः॥ ७४॥

He rose up and got outside and went to stand right outside the door of the farmer's house.

तत्क्षणे मञ्जुदेवं तं केशिनी सुप्रिया सती।
शय्यासनासमासीना भर्तारमेवमब्रवीत्॥ ७५॥

At that time, the devoted and virtuous wife of Mañjuśrī named Keśinī, addressed her husband who had gone to bed.

स्वामिन्! कोऽयं यतिर्धीमान् किमर्थमस्मदाश्रमे।
इह कुतः समायातःतत्समादेष्टुमर्हति॥ ७६॥

She asked, "O husband! who is this monk? Where does he come from and with what purpose does he come to our house?"

---

18 कुर्यात् इति कपाठः।

इति संप्रार्थितो देव्या मञ्जुदेवो निशम्य सः ।
केशिनीं तां प्रियां भार्यां सम्पश्यन्नेवमब्रवीत् ॥ ७७ ॥

साधु शृणु प्रिये देवि यदर्थं स इहागतः ।
तदर्थं हि महद्धेतुं[19]वक्ष्यामि ते विचारयन् ॥ ७८ ॥

Hearing the questions of his wife, the Mañjuśrī looked at his wife Keśinī and answered, "O wife! listen. I shall tell you the truth about why the monk has come to our home.

अयं भिक्षुर्महाभिज्ञो बोधिसत्त्वो महामतिः ।
विख्यातो यो महाधर्मश्रीमित्राख्यो महान् यतिः ॥ ७९ ॥

"O wife! he is a *bhikkhu*, a great scholar, a *bodhisattva*, with great wisdom. He is greatly renowned as the Dharmaśrīmitra.

विक्रमशिला चाख्याते विहारे स निवासकः ।
नामसंगीतिव्याख्यानं शिष्येभ्यो विस्तरं व्यधात् ॥ ८० ॥

He is the resident of a very famous *vihāra* called Vikramaśilā. He desires to explain the Nāmasaṅgīti and give deep and detailed knowledge to his students.

द्वादशाक्षर-गुह्यार्थं विशुद्धिं ज्ञान-विस्तरम् ।
नाम सम्यगुपाख्यातुं नाशक्नोत्[20] स सुधीरपि ॥ ८१ ॥

There is an incantation of the Twelve Syllables, whose deep meaning and purification procedure, despite being a great scholar, he was unable to teach.

तदायं सुविषण्णात्मा ध्यानागारे समाश्रितः ।
ध्यात्वा[21]लोकेषु सर्वत्र विलोक्यैवं व्यचिन्तयत् ॥ ८२ ॥

When he was unable to do so, he was overcome with worry and anguish and thus went into deep meditation of the world.

---

19 महीज्ञानम् इति गपाठः ।

20 शक्नोति न इति घपाठः ।

21 आलोक्य इति कपाठः ।

मञ्जुश्रीरेव जानीयात्सर्वं गुह्यं विशुद्धिवित्।
[22]द्वादशाक्षरगुह्यार्थं विशुद्धिं समुपादिशेत्॥ ८३॥

In his state of meditation, he discovered that only Mañjuśrī knew the true meaning and purification of the *mantra* of Twelve Syllables.

इति ध्यात्वा समुत्थाय सर्वान् शिष्यान् ससांघिकान्।
बोधयित्वा महोत्साहाद् वीर्येण प्राचरत्ततः॥ ८४॥

With this knowledge, he rose from his meditation and having told this to his disciples, he set out with newfound joy and enthusiasm.

उत्तरस्यां महाचीने पंचशीर्षेऽस्मदाश्रमे।
गन्तुमनेन मार्गेण चरन्निह समागतः॥ ८५॥

Towards the northern country of Mahācīna, at the mountain with the five peaks, lies our *āśrama*, where he set out to reach. On his path, he has come here.

तमिह समये यातं दृष्ट्वा समृद्धिभावतः।
बोधयित्वैवमाहूय ह्यानीतः[23] स्वाश्रमेऽधुना॥ ८६॥

When I knew of his arrival, I, through my powers, saw him and therefore, to grant him knowledge and understanding, I have brought him into our home."

इति भर्त्रा समादिष्टं श्रुत्वा सा केशिनी प्रिया।
स्वामिनं तं समालोक्य पप्रच्छैव समादरात्॥ ८७॥

When he told her so, the wife Keśinī looking at her husband, respectfully asked again.

स्वामिन्नहं न जानामि शृणोमि न कदाचन।
कथमेदद्विशुद्ध्यर्थं समुपादिश मेऽधुना॥ ८८॥

"My Lord, you know everything. What is the purification of the Twelve Syllabled incantation? Pray tell me now."

---

22 तन्मन्त्राक्षर इति खपाठः।

23 नयामि इति गपाठः।

इति संप्रार्थितो देव्या मंजुदेवो निशम्य सः ।
केशिनीं तां प्रियां भार्यां सम्पश्यन्नेवमब्रवीत् ॥ ८९ ॥

When she asked him so, the Mañjuśrī, looking at his wife, answered.

साधु देवि तव प्रीत्या साम्प्रतमुपदिश्यते ।
एतदर्थं महागुह्यं गोपनीयं प्रयत्नतः ॥ ९० ॥

"My Lady, you have asked an excellent question. I will lovingly give you the answers, but understand that this is a matter of great secrecy. You must protect it from others."

इत्युक्त्वा मञ्जुदेवोऽसौ तस्मै देव्यै यथाविधि ।
द्वादशाक्षर-गुह्यार्थ-विशुद्धिं समुपादिशत् ॥ ९१ ॥

Having warned her so, the Mañjuśrī then revealed the true hidden meaning and the purification procedure to his wife.

एतत्सर्वं समाख्यातं विस्तरं स महामतिः ।
धर्मश्रीमित्र आकर्ण्य प्रीत्यानन्देन बोधितः ॥ ९२ ॥

As he was explaining these things to his wife in bed, the *bhikkhu* outside heard their discourse and was filled with joy.

तत्सर्वं मनसि ध्यात्वा धर्मश्रीमित्रः साम्प्रतम्[24] ।
मंजुश्रीरयमेवेति निश्चयं समुपाययौ ॥ ९३ ॥

Having heard all of it, the Dharmaśrīmitra in his heart deduced that his host was in fact Mañjuśrī himself.

ततः स सुप्रसन्नात्मा द्वारमूले कृताञ्जलिः ।
अष्टांगप्रणतिं कृत्वा तस्थौ तद्गतमानसः ॥ ९४ ॥

Then he was overcome with joy, so he saluted the Mañjuśrī with eight bodily positions and stayed at the door all night.

ततःप्रातः समुत्थाय केशिनी मोक्षदायनी ।
द्वारकपाटमुद्घाट्य बहिर्गन्तुमुपाक्रमत् ॥ ९५ ॥

---

24 उत्थिते मुदा इति खपाठः ।

In the morning, the wife Keśinī who was able to grant salvation, opened the door to go outside.

तत्र तं यतिमालोक्य द्वारमूले व्यवस्थितम्।
भीता सा केशिनी देवी द्रुतमुपाचरत्ततः ॥ ९६ ॥

At the sight of the *bhikkhu* lying at the door, bowing down in concentrated reverence, lady Keśinī was so frightened that she recoiled to run back to her husband.

प्रत्यागतां च तां दृष्ट्वा मञ्जुदेवः स सर्ववित्।
विभिन्नास्यां समालोक्य पप्रच्छैवमधीरवत्॥ ९७ ॥

देवि! किं द्वारमुद्घाट्य सत्त्वरं त्वमुपागता।
दृष्ट्वा किं तत्र भीतासि तत्सत्यं वद मे पुरः ॥ ९८ ॥

At the sight of his wife running toward him and her face filled with fright, he asked her, "My lady, when you opened the door, what did you see? What has scared you so? Please tell me."

इति पृष्टं जगच्छास्तुर्भक्ता सा केशिनी तदा[25]।
स्वामिनं तं समालोक्य शनैरेवं न्यवेदयेत्॥ ९९ ॥

When he posed such questions, the frightened Keśinī, looking at her husband, replied so.

स्वामिन् यतिर्नमस्कृत्य द्वारमूले निपातितः।
जीवितो वा मृतो वासौ मया न ज्ञायते खलु॥ १०० ॥

"My lord, the monk that had arrived yesterday is at our door today and is lying down on the floor with hands joined, his head positioned inwards. I do not know if he is breathing and if he is alive or dead. Thus I am scared."

इत्युक्तं भार्यया श्रुत्वा मंजुदेवः स उत्थितः।
उपेत्य द्वारमूले तं संददर्श निपातितम्॥ १०१ ॥

Upon hearing the words of his wife, the Mañjuśrī stood up and went

25 विरात् इति घपाठः।

towards the door to see the *bhikkhu* lying there on the floor, with hands joined in salutation.

दृष्ट्वा स मञ्जुदेवस्तं यतिं नत्वा जितेन्द्रियम् ।
हस्तं धृत्वा समुत्थाप्य संपश्यन्नेवमब्रवीत् ॥ १०२ ॥

At that sight of the monk lying entirely on the floor with head positioned inwards and hands joined in reverence, the Mañjuśrī addressed the monk.

यते किमर्थमत्रैव द्वारं ध्यात्वावतिष्ठसि ।
तन्मम पुरतः सर्वं वद त्वं तु समाहितः ॥ १०३ ॥

"O *bhikkhu*! why are you lying on the floor at the door with your head positioned inwards and hands joined? Pray tell me the reason for this."

इत्युक्त्वा मञ्जुदेवेन धर्मश्रीमित्र उन्मनाः ।
मञ्जुश्रियं तमष्टांगैर्नत्वैवं प्रार्थयन्मुदा ॥ १०४ ॥

Having heard the words of Mañjuśrī, the *bhikkhu* was worried, so he rose up and saluted the Mañjuśrī with eight bodily positions and replied to him:

भगवन्! नाथ! सर्वज्ञ सर्वविद्याधिप प्रभोः ।
भवत्पादाम्बुजे भक्त्या शरणे समुपाश्रये ॥ १०५ ॥

"O Lord! God, Omniscient one, the Master of all Knowledge, I serve at your feet and I seek your refuge.

भवानेव जगच्छास्ता मञ्जुश्रीर्भगवानपि ।
ज्ञायते दृश्यते ह्यत्र ज्ञानरत्ननिधिर्मया ॥ १०६ ॥

You are the ruler of the world, the Mañjuśrī; I recognize you as the ocean of the jewel of knowledge.

तद् भवान् हि विजानाति यदर्थमिह चागतः[26] ।
तन्मेऽभिवांच्छितं शास्ता संपूरयितुमर्हति ॥ १०७ ॥

You know the purpose of my arrival. Pray grant me my desire, with which I have come here."

---

26 व्रज इति कपाठः ।

इति संप्रार्थितस्तेन मञ्जुदेवो निशम्य सः।
विज्ञाय तं महाभिज्ञं संपश्यन्नेवमब्रवीत्॥ १०८॥

Having heard his prayers, the Mañjuśrī then looking at the wise *bhikkhu* said:

कथं विनाऽभिषेकं त्वां मन्त्रार्थमुपदिश्यताम्[27]।
तावदत्राभिषेकं त्वं गृहाणादौ[28]यदीच्छसि॥ १०९॥

"O *bhikkhu*! the mystery of the true meaning of the *mantra* that you seek to know cannot be told without initiation. You must first be initiated and only then I can tell you what you seek to know."

इत्युक्तं मञ्जुदेवेन निशम्य स यतिः सुधीः।
मञ्जुदेवं नमस्कृत्य[29] साञ्जलिरेवमब्रवीत्॥ ११०॥

When the Mañjuśrī said so, the wise *bhikkhu*, with hands joined in reverence, answered so:

सर्वज्ञ! भगवञ्छास्ता निर्धनोऽहमकिञ्चनः।
किं दास्ये भवते शास्त्रे दक्षिणां गुरुभक्तिमान्॥ १११॥

"O Lord! O Omniscient one! O Master! I am but a poor monk. If you granted me initiation, I would not have anything to offer you as *guru-dakṣiṇā*."

इति तेनोदितं श्रुत्वा मञ्जुदेवः स सन्मतिः।
संपश्यन् तं यतिं धर्मश्रीमित्रमेवमब्रवीत्॥ ११२॥

When the monk said so, the wise Mañjuśrī, looking at Dharmaśrīmitra, replied.

यतेः किं धनसंपत्या श्रद्धा ते यदि विद्यते।
तुष्यन्ते गुरवो भक्तिमात्रेणात्र धनेन न॥ ११३॥

"Why do you need wealth or prosperity? You have devotion, which

27 देश्यते इति गपाठः।

28 गृहवाण्हेदं इति गपाठः।

29 तस्य इति कपाठः।

means everything. Devotion satisfies all *gurus*, for they do not have the need for money."

इत्युक्तो मञ्जुदेवेन धर्मश्रीमित्र उन्मनाः ।
अष्टांगैस्तं गुरुं नत्वा प्रार्थयेदेवमादरात् ॥ ११४ ॥

When the Mañjuśrī said so, the Dharmaśrīmitra who was very pleased, saluted him with eight bodily positions before speaking to him.

भगवन्! यदिभक्त्यैव तुष्यतेऽत्र भवान् मम ।
भवतां सुश्रूषामेव करोमि भक्तिमानहम् ॥ ११५ ॥

"O Guru! my lord, if devotion is all that takes to please you, I am very fortunate. I shall serve you full of devotion. Please accept my services.

इति मे कृपया शास्त अभिषेकं यथाविधि ।
दत्वा द्वादशमन्त्रार्थं विशुद्धिं दातुमर्हसि ॥ ११६ ॥

Therefore, O Guru! benevolently grant me initiation and tell me the meaning and the purification of the Twelve Syllables."

इति संप्रार्थितः तेन मञ्जुदेवः स सर्ववित् ।
भक्तिमन्तं तमालोक्य पश्यन्नेवमभाषत ॥ ११७ ॥

दास्यामि ते महाभाग भक्तिः श्रद्धास्ति ते यदि ।
अभिषेकं प्रसान्नात्मा समादत्स्व समाहितः ॥ ११८ ॥

When he prayed like this, seeing the devotion, curiosity and gentleness of the *bhikkhu*, the Mañjuśrī said: "O wise *bhikkhu*! I shall certainly grant you the knowledge and initiation, due to your devotion. Be happy and respectfully accept the knowledge with concentration and respect."

ततः स मञ्जुदेवःश्रीवज्राचार्यं यथाविधि ।
संस्थाप्य मण्डलं धर्मधातुवागीश्वराभिधम् ॥ ११९ ॥

तन्मण्डलं समाराध्य समभ्यर्च्य यथाविधि ।
अभिषेकं प्रसन्नाय तस्मै ददौ स वज्रधृक् ॥ १२० ॥

In this way, the Mañjuśrī who is the *vajracaryā* himself, procedurally created a *maṇḍala* (diagrammatic altar) of the Dharmadhātu Vāgīśvara, worshipped it procedurally and pleased it. The *vajra*-wielding Mañjuśrī then granted knowledge to the *bhikkhu.*

ततस्तान् मण्डले देवान् संदर्शयन् यथाक्रमम् ।
पूजयित्वा यथाशक्ति शरणे समयोजयत् ॥ १२१ ॥

When he initiated the *bhikkhu*, he introduced him to the various gods situated in the *maṇḍala* and worshipped them procedurally, thereby bringing the *bhikkhu* and himself into their refuge.

ततस्तस्मै प्रसन्नाय मञ्जुदेवो यथाविधि ।
द्वादशाक्षर-गुह्यार्थं विशुद्धिं समुपादिशत् ॥ १२२ ॥

Then Mañjuśrī told the hidden meaning of the *mantra* along with its purification process to the *bhikkhu*, who was in bliss having received the knowledge.

ततो लब्धाभिषेकोऽसौ धर्मश्रीमित्र उन्मनाः ।
द्वादशभूमि-गुह्यार्थं विशुद्धिज्ञानमाप्तवान् ॥ १२३ ॥

The Dharmaśrīmitra who had just received initiation was immensely pleased, for he had just learned the true meaning and the purification of the Twelve Syllabled *mantra*.

तस्मै शास्त्रे सभार्याय स्वमात्मानं स दक्षिणाम् ।
संकल्प्य श्रद्धया भक्त्या नत्वैवं प्रार्थयन् मुदा ॥ १२४ ॥

Then the *bhikkhu* pledged himself as offering to the Mañjuśrī and his wife, and worshipfully, with hands joined, said:

भगवन् ! नाथ सर्वज्ञ भवत्कृपाप्रसादतः ।
संप्राप्तपूर्ण-संकल्पो भवामि श्रीगुणार्थभृत् ॥ १२५ ॥

"O Lord! O Omniscient One! due to your benevolence, all my wishes have been fulfilled. I have been endowed with virtues,0 my Lord."

तत्सदाहं भवत्पादशरणे समुपाश्रितः ।
यथात्र भवदादिष्टं तथैव संचरे भवे ॥ १२६ ॥

Therefore, O Guru! I have come into your asylum. I shall wander the world abiding by your instructions.

तन् मेऽनुज्ञादि दत्वात्र संबोधिज्ञानसाधनम् ।
सर्वसत्त्व-हितार्थेन चरेयं बोधिसंवरम् ॥ १२७ ॥

Thus, instruct me, my Lord and tell me the instrument of knowledge, so that I may be able to practise *bodhi* for the welfare of the whole world."

इति संप्रार्थ्य धर्मश्रीमित्रः स समुपाश्रितः ।
श्रद्धाभक्ति-प्रसन्नात्मा गुरुसेवा परोऽभवत् ॥ १२८ ॥

With such prayers, the Dharmaśrīmitra went to the refuge of Mañjuśrī and filled with devotion and joy, started to serve his *guru.*

ततःस मंजुदेवस्तं महासत्त्वं विचक्षणम् ।
मत्वा संबोधि-चर्यायां नियोक्तुं संव्यनोदयत् ॥ १२९ ॥

Then Mañjuśrī, having understood the monk who was *mahāsattva*, *bodhisattva* and the practitioner of *bodhicaryā*, directed him towards the good path.

साधु साधु महाभाग! संचरत्वं जगद्धिते ।
संबोधि-साधनं बोधिचर्याव्रती सदा भव ॥ १३० ॥

"O Bhikkhu! very good, very good! You must travel for the welfare of the world and practise the *bodhi vrata* which is the instrument for *sambodhi*.

एतत्पुण्याभिलिप्तात्मा परिशुद्धत्रिमण्डलः ।
बोधिसत्त्वो महाभिज्ञो भव श्रीसद्गुणाश्रयः ॥ १३१ ॥

The merit you shall receive as a result shall help you purify your mind, speech and body and become a *bodhisattva, mahāsattva,* greatly wise, the residence of virtues; and so you shall wander the world.

ततस्त्वं बोधिसंभारं पूरयित्वा यथाक्रमम् ।
निःक्लेशो बोधिप्राप्तोऽर्हन् सम्बुद्धपदमाप्नुहि ॥ १३२ ॥

Then you shall gradually climb the steps of *bodhi*, be freed of misery, acquire *bodhi* and finally attain Buddhahood.

इति मे शासनं धृत्वा स्मृत्वा ध्यात्वा समाहितः।
त्रिरत्नं समुपाश्रित्य संचर त्वं जगद्धिते ॥ १३३ ॥

In this way, following these instructions in my remembrance, praising the Dharmadhātu, and worshipping the *tri-ratna,* you must constantly strive for the welfare of the world.

यदि जगद्धितं कर्तुं संबोधिं प्राप्तुमिच्छसि।
सद्धर्मं समुपादिश्य सर्वान् लोकान् प्रबोधय ॥ १३४ ॥

If you truly desire the welfare of the world and knowledge, you must sermonize *dharma* to awaken others and bring them from ignorance to knowledge.

ततस्तान् बोधितान् सर्वान् क्रमेण बोधिसाधनम्।
बोधिमार्गे प्रतिष्ठाप्य चारयस्व जगद्धिते ॥ १३५ ॥

Gradually, you must introduce the people you awaken to the instruments of *bodhi* and establish them into the path of *bodhi* and make them work for the welfare of the world.

ततस्तेषां समालोक्य चित्तं संबोधिनिश्चितम्।
त्रियानं समुपादिश्य परमार्थे नियोजय ॥ १३६ ॥

When you see to *bodhi* being stablished into their mind, sermonize the Three Vehicles and lead them towards the ultimate reality.

एवं कृत्वा महद्धर्ममाशु सम्बोधिसाधनम्।
भद्रश्री-सद्‌गुणापन्नं समाप्नुहि जगच्छुभे ॥ १३७ ॥

When you do so, you shall instantly receive the *dharma* that is the instrument for the acquisition of *bodhi* and become filled with virtues manifold.

तेनाशु परिशुद्धात्मा सम्बुद्धपदमाप्नुहि।
जगद्धर्ममयं कृत्वा जिनालयं समाप्नुयाः ॥ १३८ ॥

You shall quickly become purified internally as well as externally, attain Buddhahood and having spread *dharma* all over the world, shall finally reach the realm of Buddha.

इति भद्रव्रतं धृत्वा गत्वा त्वं स्वाश्रमे पुनः ।
व्याख्याय नाम-संगीतिं सद्धर्मं संप्रसारय ॥ १३९ ॥

In this way, practising the highest *dharma,* go to your *aśrama*, explain the Nāmasaṅgīti and preach the true *dharma.*

अहमपि महासत्त्व! श्रोतुं त्वद्धर्मदेशनाम् ।
सांघिकाँश्चापि तान्द्रष्टुमायास्यामि तवाश्रमे ॥ १४० ॥

O Bhikkhu! I shall visit your *āśrama* some day along with people from the Saṅgha to listen to your discourse on *dharma.*"

इति शास्ता समादिष्टं निशम्य स महामतिः ।
धर्मश्रीमित्र आलोक्य तं गुरुमेवमब्रवीत् ॥ १४१ ॥

Upon hearing the instructions of the Mañjuśrī, the monk Dharmaśrīmitra, looking at the Guru and saluting him, said:

महर्द्धिको भवाञ्छास्ता विज्ञास्यते कथं मया ।
इति चिह्नं समाधाय तत्रागन्तुं समर्हति ॥ १४२ ॥

"O Guru! you are a wise god, who grants knowledge to all. If you come there, how do I recognize you? Please give me a sign through which I may be able to know you."

इति तेनोदितं श्रुत्वा मञ्जुदेवः स सन्मतिः ।
धर्मश्रीमित्रमालोक्य पुनरेवमभाषत ॥ १४३ ॥

At this request, the wise Mañjuśrī, looking at Dharmaśrīmitra, said so:

वत्साहमुत्पलं धृत्वा समायास्यामि ते सभाम् ।
तेन चिह्नेन मां तत्र संजानीष्व समागतम् ॥ १४४ ॥

"Child, you shall easily be able to recognize me, for when I come to your residence, I shall come with a blue lotus in my hand.

इति सत्यं समाधाय धृत्वानुशासनं मम।
सद्धर्मं समुपादेष्टुं प्रयाहि तेऽस्तु मंगलम्॥ १४५॥

Follow my instructions and proceed from here to preach the true *dharma*. I wish for your welfare."

इति शास्ता समादिष्टं श्रुत्वा स यतिरुत्सुकः।
शास्तारं तं समालोक्य प्रणम्यैवमभाषत॥ १४६॥

When the Mañjuśrī instructed him so, the *bhikkhu* who was pleased, looked at the *guru*, saluted him, and said:

प्रसीदतु भगवाञ्छास्ता क्षन्तुमर्हति चागसम्।
भवत्प्रसादतः सर्वं सिध्यते मे समीहितम्॥ १४७॥

"O Ruler! please forgive my sins and wrongdoings. It is due to your benevolence that my wishes have been fulfilled. I have been gratified.

तदनुशासनं धृत्वा भवतां च जगद्धिते।
व्याख्यातुं नामसंगीतिं संचरे साम्प्रतं गुरोः॥ १४८॥

I have grasped your teachings and with this knowledge, I shall commence the discourse on Nāmasaṅgīti."

इति संप्रार्थ्य धर्मश्रीमित्रः स संप्रसादितः।
शास्तुस्तस्य पदाम्भोजं नत्वा संप्रस्थितः ततः॥ १४९॥

With such prayers, the Dharmaśrīmitra, having pleased the *guru*, saluted him by placing his head on the *guru*'s feet before leaving.

मात्रोराचार्ययोश्चापि मोक्षदा-वरदाख्ययोः।
पादाम्बुजेषु संनम्य[30] संप्रस्थितःप्रमोदितः॥ १५०॥

Having placed his head on both feet of Mañjuśrī, who was the *ācārya*, the *guru* and had given him knowledge that was able to grant *mokṣa*, the *bhikkhu* departed full of bliss.

ततः स सन्मतिर्धर्मश्रीमित्रः सहसाव्रजत्।
आशु स्वाश्रममासाद्य विहारं समुपाविशत्॥ १५१॥

[30] सनत्वा।

Then, the wise Dharmaśrīmitra immediately returned and thereby, quickly settled down in his *vihāra.*

तत्र तं यतिमायातं दृष्ट्वा सर्वेऽपि सांघिकाः ।
प्रणम्य कुशलं पृष्ट्वा प्रवेशयन् निजालयम् ॥ १५२ ॥

At the sight of the monk's return, everyone present at the *vihāra* saluted the monk, inquired about his well being and then respectfully welcomed him back.

ततः परेद्युरामन्त्र्य सर्वान्संघान् स सन्मतिः ।
व्याख्यातुं नामसंगीतिं सभासने समाश्रयत् ॥ १५३ ॥

The next day, the monk invited everyone to discourse the Nāmasaṅgīti. For that purpose, he took the seat at the assembly.

तं सभासनासीनं दृष्ट्वा सर्वेऽपि सांघिकाः ।
द्विजा भूपादयश्चापि सर्वे लोकाः समागताः ॥ १५४ ॥

Seeing the monk seated at the assembly, those at the *āśrama* and brāhmaṇas, kings and all others approached him.

तत्र सर्वेऽपि ते लोकाःप्रणम्य तं यतिं क्रमात् ।
परिवृत्य पुरस्कृत्य समन्तत उपाश्रयन् ॥ १५५ ॥

All worldly beings, upon arrival, saluted the *bhikkhu*, performed the *pradakṣiṇā* and sat down around him.

तान् सर्वान्समुपासीनान् दृष्ट्वा स यतिरात्मवित् ।
व्याख्याय नामसंगीतिं सविशुद्धिं समादिशत् ॥ १५६ ॥

Seeing everyone sitting there, the wise monk who knew himself, discoursed on the Nāmasaṅgīti and the purification of the *mantra.*

तदा तत्र मनस्तस्य जिज्ञासितुं स मञ्जुवाक् ।
धृत्वोत्पलं विनिन्द्यांगः कुचीवरमुपाचरत् ॥ १५७ ॥

At that time, in order to test the *bhikkhu*'s state of mind, the Mañjuśrī, in the disguise of a body crouched and atrophied with old age, with torn out dirty robes and yet with a lotus in one hand, entered the *vihāra.*

तत्र स मक्षिकान् काये उत्पलेन निवारयन्[31] ।
समागत्य सभैकान्ते पश्यल्लोकानुपाश्रयेत् ॥ १५८ ॥

Using the lotus in his hand to shoo flies that surrounded him away, he went to a corner of the assembly and sat down, as everyone was watching.

समाश्रितं स धर्मश्रीमित्रो दृष्ट्वात्मनो गुरुम् ।
उत्पलेन परिज्ञाय मनसैवं व्यचिन्तयत् ॥ १५९ ॥

Dharmaśrīmitra saw it as well and due to the lotus, deduced the shabby stranger sitting there to be none other than his own *guru* Mañjuśrī and wondered in his mind.

अहो नूनमयं शास्ता मनो जिज्ञासितुं मम ।
कुचरा दुर्भगाकारो धृत्वोत्पलमिहागतः ॥ १६० ॥

"O my *guru* Mañjuśrī! In order to test me, has come here in dirty clothes, ugly figure and a lotus in hand."

कार्यं कथं समुत्थाय प्रत्युत्थानादिकं पुनः[32] ।
अथ पश्यन्नमस्कारं न कुर्यां गुरवे कथम् ॥ १६१ ॥

He thought, "How do I go and bow down to him? It is not possible for me to sit here without saluting my *guru*.

यद्यत्राहं समुत्थाय नमेयमेनमादरात् ।
दृष्ट्वा लोका इमे मां धिक्कुर्युः सर्वे विचारतः ॥ १६२ ॥

If I do not respect, revere and salute my *guru*, those worldly beings that understand the situation would surely reproach and curse me in their thoughts.

एतैर्न ज्ञायते यो हि मञ्जुश्री ऋद्धिमानपि[33] ।
ईदृगेवास्य शास्तायमिति मे स्याद् विहास्यता ॥ १६३ ॥

---

31 प्रदर्शयन् इति गपाठः ।

32 तत्कथमहममुत्थायप्रत्युङ्गम्य न मेय हि इति कपाठः ।

33 शिद्धिमान् इति खपाठः ।

And yet, if I bow down and introduce him as my glorious teacher to the assembly, his shabby appearance might induce ridicule and mockery toward me."

इति ध्यात्वा स धर्मश्रीमित्रो लज्जाभिमोहितः ।
मनसैवं नमस्कृत्य शास्तारं तममानयेत् ॥ १६४ ॥

Such thoughts led the Dharmaśrīmitra into embarrassment and dilemma. He saluted his *guru* solely through his mind and did not stand to physically revere him.

ततः स विमुखीभूय पश्यन्नप्यविभावितः ।
अज्ञातवान्निवापश्यन् पदमात्रमुपादिशत् ॥ १६५ ॥

He faced towards the other direction, avoiding eye contact and pretending to not see or recognize his *guru* as he sermonized his teachings.

ततः सर्वेऽपि ते लोकाःश्रुत्वा सद्धर्मदेशनाम् ।
उत्थाय तं यतिं नत्वा स्वस्वालयमुपाचरन् ॥ १६५ ॥

Then those present at the assembly were pleased to have heard the sermons and rose up to salute the *bhikkhu* before returning to their respective abodes.

ततो लोके गते धर्मश्रीमित्रः स समुत्थितः ।
शास्तारं तं समालोक्य वन्दितुं समुपाचरत् ॥ १६७ ॥

After everyone had left, the Dharmaśrīmitra rose up from his seat and with the intent of saluting his *guru*, approached toward him.

तं दृष्ट्वा मञ्जुदेवोऽसौ वन्दितुं समुपागतम् ।
अपश्यन् विमुखीभूय ततः संप्रस्थितोऽभवत्[34] ॥ १६८ ॥

However, at the sight of his old disciple *bhikkhu* approaching to salute him, the Mañjuśrī faced the opposite direction and slowly walked away.

---

[34] भविष्यति इति गपाठः ।

तं दृष्ट्वा विमुखीभूतो धर्मश्रीमित्र आत्मनः ।
अपराधं महत्पापामनुस्मृत्वापतद् भुवि ॥ १६९ ॥

Seeing the *guru* leave with disregard for him, the Dharmaśrīmitra was filled with remorse and realization of his transgression and he consequently fell to the floor.

निपतन्तं तमालोक्य मञ्जुश्रीः स कृपानिधिः[35] ।
सहसा पाणिना धृत्वा समुत्थाय तथाचरत् ॥ १७० ॥

When he saw him fall to the floor with guilt, the magnanimous Mañjuśrī returned to pick the *bhikkhu* up with his own hands.

तत्र स उत्थितो धर्मश्रीमित्रस्तं महामतिम् ।
प्रचरन्तं समालोक्य नत्वाहैवं मृषा पुनः ॥ १७१ ॥

The Dharmaśrīmitra, seeing his *guru* who had almost left, saluted him and lied to him again.

भगवन्नमया दृष्टो भवानत्र समागतः ।
पश्चादुत्पलचिह्नेन ज्ञायतेऽत्र समाश्रितः ॥ १७२ ॥

"My *guru*, I did not recognize you on arrival. But later, when I saw the lotus in your hand, I came to recognize you then."

इत्युक्त्वा स मृषावादं साञ्जलिस्तस्य सद्गुरोः ।
मञ्जुदेवस्य पादाब्जे प्रणनाम रुदन् पुनः ॥ १७३ ॥

Having lied to him, the monk with his hands joined, placed his head on the feet of his *guru* and started crying.

तत्र तस्य मृषावक्तुरुभेऽपि नयने मुखात् ।
शास्तुः पादाब्जयोरग्रे निपेतं तु महीतले ॥ १७४ ॥

In this way, he speaked false words and shed tears and spoke praises of his *guru* as he fell to his *guru*'s feet.

---

35 महद्धिधृक् इति कपाठः ।

तत्पतितं स धर्मश्रीमित्रो[36]विहतमानसः ।
चिराद्रुदन् समुत्थाय शास्त्रारमेवमब्रवीत् ॥ १७५ ॥

Having lain on the floor for a long time, with a bad state of mind, the *bhikkhu* rose up and addressed the ruler, his *guru*, as such.

भगवन् यन्मयाज्ञानादपराधं कृतं गुरौ ।
भवति तद् भवाञ्छास्ता क्षन्तुमर्हति[37]दुर्मतेः ॥ १७६ ॥

"My Lord, please forgive the offence of my ignorance. You are my teacher and my ruler, pray forgive me."

इति संप्रार्थितं तेन मंजुश्रीः स कृपानिधिः ।
विचक्षुष्कं तमालोक्य कृपादृशैवमब्रवीत् ॥ १७७ ॥

Hearing his pleas, the Mañjuśrī who was an ocean of kindness and benevolence, saw that the monk had become blind due to excessive crying and said to him compassionately:

यदपि लज्जया कर्म ज्ञात्वापि दुष्कृतं त्वया ।
तस्येदं फलमासाद्य भोक्ता त्वमेव वर्तसे ॥ १७८ ॥

"You must suffer the consequence of your misdemeanor that you committed due to shame, despite knowing all too well. You must face blindness as penance.

तथापि ज्ञानदृष्ट्या त्वं सम्पश्य दृष्टिमान् यथा ।
ज्ञानं हि तेऽस्ति यत्तेन ज्ञानश्रीमित्र उच्यसे ॥ १७९ ॥

However, you may view the world with the sight of knowledge, just as a man with actual sight would. You possess knowledge and therefore, are renowned as Jñānaśrīmitra."

इत्युक्त्यैव स मञ्जुश्रीः क्षणादन्तर्हितस्ततः ।
आकाशात् पक्षिवद् गत्वा स्वाश्रमे समुपाययौ ॥ १८० ॥

Having said so, the Mañjuśrī vanished into thin air and through the skies, just as a bird would, flew back to his *āśrama.*

36 मञ्जुश्रीःइति खपाठः ।

37 त्वङ्कृति इति खपाठः ।

अत्रैतत्सर्ववृत्तान्तं भार्ययोः पुरतोर्मुदा ।
समाख्याय स मंजुश्रीस्तस्थौ लोकहितार्थभृत्[38] ॥ १८१ ॥

Having given an account of these events to his two wives named Keśinī and Upakeśinī, the Mañjuśrī then meditated quietly for the welfare of the world.

ततः प्रभृति ज्ञानश्रीमित्रो ज्ञानेन चक्षुषा ।
पश्यन् सद्धर्ममाख्याय प्राचरच्च जगद्धिते ॥ १८२ ॥

Thenceforth, the Jñānaśrīmitra, looking through the eyes of his knowledge, started to promote the good *dharma* for the welfare of the world.

तदा मैत्रेय तेनास्य धर्मधातोः स्वयंभूवः ।
अभूत्प्रसिद्धिस्तद्धर्मधातुवागीश्वराभिधः ॥ १८३ ॥

Thus, O Maitreya!" said Buddha, "the Dharmadhātu Svayambhū came to receive tremendous fame and came to be known as Dharmadhātu Vāgīśvara.

इति मत्वात्र ये धर्मधातुं वागीश्वरं नराः[39] ।
श्रद्धया विधिनाभ्यर्च्य भजन्ति शरणाश्रिताः ॥ १८४ ॥

"With this understanding, they who worship the Dharmādhātu Vāgīśvara and sing praises and pay homage to it, shall receive welfare.

अभिषेकं च संप्राप्य बोधिचित्ता समाहिताः ।
सद्धर्म-धारणी-विद्यामन्त्राणि धारयन्ति ये ॥ १८५ ॥

ते सर्वे विमलात्मानः परिशुद्धत्रिमण्डलाः ।
बोधिसत्त्वा महासत्त्वाश्चतुर्ब्रह्मविहारिणः ॥ १८६ ॥

Similarly, those who receive initiation, acquire *bodhicitta* and with concentration, chant the Dhāraṇī and Vidyā *mantras*, shall become purified in their souls and cleansed in their minds, speech and bodies,

38 लोककर्मकरी इति कपाठः ।

39 मुदा इति घपाठः ।

become *bodhisattva*s, *mahāsattva*s and dwell in the Four Highest Divine Abodes.

भद्रश्रीसद्गुणाधाराः सर्वविद्याविचक्षणाः ।
ऋद्धि-सिद्धि-महाभिज्ञा भवेयुर्भद्रचारिणः ॥ १८७ ॥

They will be the basis for all good qualities, well-versed in all forms of knowledge, recipients of all glory and prosperity, and be transformed into men of good deeds.

आशु सम्बोधिसंभारं पूरयित्वा यथाक्रमम् ।
अर्हन्तस्त्रिविधां बोधिं प्राप्य यायुर्जिनालयम् ॥ १८८ ॥

They will instantly cross the steps of *bodhi*, become *arhant*s and having acquired the three ultimate types of *bodhi*, finally reach the realm of the Buddha.

इति मत्वाऽभिवाञ्छन्ति प्राप्तुं ये सौगतं पदम् ।
तेऽत्र बौद्धालये धर्मधातुवागीश्वरे सदा ॥ १८९ ॥

श्रद्धया भजनं कृत्वा प्राप्याभिषेकमादरात् ।
सधर्मधारणी-विद्यामन्त्र-साधनतत्पराः ॥ १९० ॥

यथाविधि समभ्यर्च्य संबोधि-निहिताश्रयाः ।
बोधिचर्याव्रतं धृत्वा संचरन्ति जगद्धिते[40] ॥ १९१ ॥

[41]आशु ते विमलात्मानः परिशुद्धत्रिमण्डलाः ।
बोधिसत्त्वा महासत्त्वाश्चतुर्ब्रह्मविहारिणः ॥ १९२ ॥

Having said this, those that wish to attain Buddhahood must be present at the area of the Buddha, that is the Dharmādhātu Vāgīśvara, at all times and devotedly sing his praises, receive initiation, practise the good *dharma* and chant the Dhāraṇī *mantra*s. They must procedurally worship the Dharmadhātu and revere their *guru*. They must acquire knowledge in their minds, practise the *bodhicaryā* and wander the earth so.

---

40 त्वमदर्थ इति गपाठः ।

41 अर्थायते इति खपाठः ।

They will instantly become cleansed, with minds, speeches and bodies purified; they will become *bodhisattvas*, *mahāsattvas* and eventually dwell in the Four Highest Divine Abodes.

भद्रश्रीसद्गुणाधाराः सर्वविद्याविचक्षणाः ।
ऋद्धिसिद्धिमहाभिज्ञा भवेयुर्भद्रचारिणः ॥ १९३ ॥

They will be the basis for all good qualities, well-versed in all forms of knowledge, recipients of all glory and prosperity, and be transformed into men of good deeds.

ततः संबोधिसंभारं पूरयित्वा द्रुतं क्रमात् ।
अर्हन्तस्त्रिविधां बोधिं प्राप्य यास्यथ निर्वृतिम् ॥ १९४ ॥

They will instantly cross the steps of *bodhi*, become *arhants* and having acquired the three ultimate types of *bodhi*, finally become liberated."

इत्यादिष्टं मुनीन्द्रेण निशम्य ते सभाश्रिताः ।
सर्वे तथेति विज्ञाप्य प्राभ्यनन्दन् प्रबोधिताः ॥ १९५ ॥

Upon hearing such words of the Buddha, everyone present in the assembly was overjoyed and then praised, saluted and took refuge in Lord Buddha.

॥ इति श्रीस्वयंभूधर्मधातु-वागीश्वराभिधानप्रसिद्धप्रवर्तनो नाम षष्ठोऽध्यायः समाप्तः ॥

Thus, the sixth chapter of the *Svayambhū Purāṇa* named Dharmādhātu Vāgīśvara ends.

अथ सप्तमोऽध्यायः
(Saptama Adhyāya)

Concealment of the Dharmadhātu Vāgīśvara

अथ भूयः स मैत्रेयो बोधिसत्त्वो महामतिः ।
भगवन्तं प्रणम्यैव साञ्जलिरेवमब्रवीत् ॥ १ ॥

The wise *Bodhi*sattva Maitreya saluted the Lord Buddha and with hands joined, started to speak.

भगवन्! शिलयाच्छाद्य धर्मधातुमिमं कदा ।
केनैव हेतुना स्तूपं को व्यधादीष्टिकामयम् ॥ २ ॥

"My Lord, you have granted us enormous knowledge. I have another curiosity. Who covered the Dharmadhātu Svayambhū with bricks and rocks to build the *caitya* as it exists now?

भगवान् तत्समालोक्य सर्वान् लोकान् सकौतुकान् ।
एतद्धेतुं समादिश्य विनोदयितुमर्हति ॥ ३ ॥

"O Lord! everyone in the world is eager to know. Pray tell us the reason for it."

इति संप्रार्थितं तेन मैत्रेयेण मुनीश्वरः ।
भगवान् स महासत्त्वं संपश्यन्नेवमादिशत् ॥ ४ ॥

शृणु मैत्रेय[1]! येनायं गुप्तीकृतःप्रकाशने ।
एतद्धेतुं समाख्यामि सर्वलोकाभिबोधने ॥ ५ ॥

Hearing the Maitreya pray so, the Lord of sages looked at him to answer, "O Maitreya! listen. I shall tell you the reason for the

[1] बोधिमैत्रेय इति घपाठः ।

concealment and seclusion of the Dharmadhātu, so that the whole world may know.

> तद्यथा निर्वृतिं याते संबुद्धे कनके मुनौ ।
> [2]विंशतिवर्षसाहस्रं नृणामायुर्यदाऽभवत् ॥ ६ ॥

By the time Lord Kanakamuni Buddha departed from this world, the life of man spanned 20,000 years.

> तदाभूद् भगवाच्छास्ता धर्मराजो मुनीश्वरः ।
> सर्वज्ञोऽर्हन् महाभिज्ञः काश्यपाख्यस्तथागतः ॥ ७ ॥

Afterwards, the Lord returned again with another form, as the Ruler, the king of *dharma*, the Lord of sages, the Omniscient, the Enlightened, the Master of all knowledge and the *tathāgata*. He was named Kaśyapa.

> स संबुद्धो महापुर्यां वाराणस्यामुपाश्रमे ।
> मृगदावे जिनावासे विजहार ससांघिकः ॥ ८ ॥

The Kaśyapa Buddha resided along with his Saṅgha in his hut situated in the Mṛgadāb (Mṛgadāva) forest near the city of Varanasi.

> तदा संबोधिसत्त्वोऽहं ज्योतिराजाभिधः किल ।
> काश्यपस्य[3]जगच्छास्तुः शरणस्थ उपासकः ॥ ९ ॥

At that time, I was also a *bodhisattva* named Jyotirāja. In his refuge, I served the Kaśyapa Buddha who taught the whole world.

> यदा स काश्यपः शास्ता सर्वत्रैधातुकाधिपः ।
> सद्धर्मं समुपादेष्टुं सभासने समाश्रयत् ॥ १० ॥

Once the Kaśyapa Buddha, who was the master of all three worlds, in order to sermonize the good *dharma*, took the central seat at the assembly.

---

[2] त्रिंशतिवर्ष इति घपाठः ।

[3] ककुच्छन्दस्य इति गपाठः ।

तत्सद्धर्मामृतं श्रोतुं सर्वे लोकाः समागताः ।
ब्रह्मशक्रादयो देवाः सर्वे लोकाधिपा अपि ॥ ११ ॥

ग्रहास्तारागणाश्चापि विद्याधराश्च साप्सराः ।
सिद्धाः साध्याश्च रुद्राश्च यक्षगुह्यककिन्नराः ॥ १२ ॥

कुम्भाण्डा[4] राक्षसाश्चापि नागाश्च गरुडा अपि ।
ऋषयस्तापसाश्चापि तीर्थिका ब्रह्मचारिणः ॥ १३ ॥

यतयो योगिनश्चापि तथान्ये चाप्युपासकाः ।
ब्राह्मणा क्षत्रियाश्चापि राजानोऽपि महीभृतः ॥ १४ ॥

वैश्याश्च मन्त्रिणोऽमात्या भृत्याः सैन्याधिपा अपि ।
शिल्पिनो वणिजश्चापि सार्थवाहा महाजनाः ॥ १५ ॥

Intending to drink the nectar of *dharma*, beings from all the worlds arrived at the assembly, including Brahmā, Indra and legions of gods, Lords of all realms, planets, stars and constellations, celestial nymphs and demi-gods such as *vidyādhara*s, *siddha*s, *sādhya*s, *rudra*s, *yakṣa*s, *guhyaka*s, *kinnara*s, *kumbhāṇḍa*s, demons, serpents, falcons, sages, ascetics, pilgrims, celibates, monks, *yogī*s, laymen and laywomen. brāhmaṇas, kṣatriyas, kings, protectors of the earth, vaiśyas, courtiers, secretaries, servants, military commanders and their soldiers all arrived. So did menials, merchants and tradesmen with caravans and capitalists.

पौरा जानपदा ग्राम्या नैगमाःपार्वता अपि ।
तथान्यदेशिका लोका अपि सर्वे समागताः ॥ १६ ॥

Citizens and townsfolk, villagers, residents of the mountain, forest-dwellers, preachers and ordinary men arrived at the assembly.

तत्र सभासनासीनं संबुद्धं तं मुनीश्वरम्[5] ।
भगवन्तं समालोक्य सर्वे संघाः समाययुः ॥ १७ ॥

---

[4] कर्बुराश्च इति खपाठः ।

[5] महर्द्धिकम् इति कपाठः ।

When the Lord took his seat to start speaking, members of his Saṅgha also saw it and drew closer.

भिक्षवः श्रावकाः सर्वे यतयो योगिनोऽपि च ।
चैलका व्रतिनश्चापि सर्वे उपासका अपि ॥ १८ ॥

Bhikkhus, śrāvakas, monks, *yogīs*, *cailakas,* vow holders and devotees of the Buddha all arrived.

भिक्षुण्योऽपि तथा सर्वा व्रतिण्यश्चैलिका अपि ।
श्राविकाश्चापि तत्रैव[6]तथान्याः समुपागताः ॥ १९ ॥

Bhikkhuṇīs, *Śrāvikās,* nuns, *cailikās*, vow holders and other female devotees of the Buddha also arrived.

बोधिसत्त्वा महासत्त्वा ऋषयो ब्रह्मचारिणः ।
तीर्थिका वैष्णवाः शैवा निर्गन्थाश्च तपस्विनः ॥ २० ॥

Bodhisattvas, mahāsattvas, sages, celibates, Vedic brāhmaṇas, followers of Viṣṇu, followers of Śiva, Jainas and ascetics came too.

तथान्येऽपि समायाताः सद्धर्मगुणलालसाः ।
सर्वेऽपि ते मुनीन्द्रं तं दृष्ट्वा ययुःप्रमोदिताः ॥ २१ ॥

Similarly, others who wished to understand the qualities of the true *dharma* avidly approached the Kaśyapa Buddha.

तत्र सर्वेऽपि ते लोकास्तं मुनीन्द्रं यथाक्रमम् ।
अभ्यर्च्य विधिना नत्वा तत्सभायामुपाश्रयन् ॥ २२ ॥

All who arrived saluted and worshipped the king of sages – the Kaśyapa Buddha – procedurally before taking their seats at the assembly.

तत्र सर्वेऽपि ते लोकाः परिवृत्य समन्ततः ।
पुरस्कृत्य मुनीन्द्रं तं संपश्यन्तः समीहिताः ॥ २३ ॥

They performed the *pradakṣṇā*. Then they surrounded the Kaśyapa Buddha and sat down encircled around him, as they faced towards him with concentration and patience.

---

6 नास्ति इति कपाठः ।

तत्सद्धर्मामृतं पातुं तृषार्ता इव सागरम् ।
साञ्जलयः प्रसन्नास्याः समातस्थुर्यथाक्रमम् ॥ २४ ॥

Just as thirsty men would go to the river to quench their thirst, the gathered mass sat with folded hands with high spirits and concentration before the Buddha.

तान् लोकान् समुपासीनान् सर्वान्संघान्सुरानपि ।
सर्वान् लोकाधिपाँश्चापि दृष्ट्वा स भगवाञ्जिनः[7] ॥ २५ ॥

When Lord Kaśyapa Buddha saw the arrivals from different worlds, *saṅgha*s and legions of gods and lords of realms, he commenced his discourse.

आर्यसत्यं समारभ्य संबोधि-ज्ञानसाधनम् ।
[8]आदि-मध्यान्त-कल्याणं सद्धर्मं समुपादिशत् ॥ २६ ॥

He began with the noble truths and in course of the discourse, told of the instruments for the acquisition of knowledge. His sermons were filled with words of good *dharma* and welfare, in the beginning, middle and the end.

तत्सद्धर्मामृतं पीत्वा सर्वे लोकाःप्रबोधिताः ।
सदा भद्रसुखं प्राप्तुं समीच्छिरे सुसंवरम् ॥ २७ ॥

Upon drinking the nectar of the good *dharma*, everyone was euphoric and reached the state of eternal happiness. They wished to practise the good vow.

ततः सर्वेऽपि ते लोकाः संबुद्ध-गुणवाञ्छिनः ।
बोधिचर्या-व्रतं धृत्वा संचरिरे सदा शुभे ॥ २८ ॥

All of them wished to possess the true qualities of the Buddha and therefore, indulged in auspicious deeds as they practised the *bodhicaryā* discipline.

---

7 भवतां जिनः इति खपाठः ।

8 पूर्व-मध्ये च इति गपाठः ।

तदा सर्वाणि कार्याणि कृत्वा वज्री स योगवित् ।
मञ्जुदेवः[9] सहभार्यां स्वयं निर्वृतिमाययौ ॥ २९ ॥

Meanwhile, having fulfilled his work, the *yogī* Mañjuśrī along with his wives liberated themselves, leaving their bodies in the ground.

ततो गत्वा महाचीने स मञ्जुश्रीर्निजाश्रमे ।
स्वदिव्यवपुराधाय तस्थौ भार्या-समन्वितः ॥ ३० ॥

Then they went to the Mahācīna, to their *āśrama* and started to dwell there, having taken divine forms.

अत्र तेषां शरीराणि शिष्याः सर्वेऽपि पावके ।
संस्कृत्य विधिनास्थीनि गृहीत्वा समशोधयन् ॥ ३१ ॥

However, the bodies they had left behind near the Dharmadhātu were cremated with pure flames and the resultant ashes were respectfully placed in a pious way, by Mañjuśrī's disciples.

ततस्तेऽत्र तदस्थीनि गर्भेस्थाप्य यथाविधि ।
चैत्यं कृत्वा प्रतिष्ठाप्य समभ्यर्च्य सदाभजन् ॥ ३२ ॥

Their bones were cleansed ritually and buried under the earth in a beautiful casket – on top of which they built a *caitya* (shrine) to eternally honour them.

ये चेदं चैत्यमभ्यर्च्य भजन्ति श्रद्धया सदा ।
ते तस्य मञ्जुदेवस्य सद्धर्मगुणमाप्नुयुः ॥ ३३ ॥

They who worship and devote themselves to that shrine shall receive the qualities of *dharma*.

मत्वैवं येऽभिवाञ्छन्ति मञ्जुश्रीधर्मसद्गुणम्[10] ।
अत्र मञ्जुश्रियश्चैत्यं सर्वदा प्रभजन्तु ते ॥ ३४ ॥

Those who seek to possess the virtues of the Mañjuśrī must praise and worship the *caitya* of Mañjuśrī."

---

9 प्रभुदेव इति खपाठः ।

10 सद्गृहम् इति गपाठः ।

इत्यादिष्टं मुनीन्द्रेण निशम्य ते सभाजनाः ।
सर्वे तथेति श्रुत्वैवं प्राभ्यनन्दन् प्रबोधिताः ॥ ३५ ॥

When the Lord of Sages – the Buddha – told them so, the masses concurred in comprehension and therefore, praised the Lord.

अथाऽसौ भगवान् भूयःशाक्यसिंहो मुनीश्वरः ।
मैत्रेयं तां सभाञ्चापि समालोक्यैवमादिशत् ॥ ३६ ॥

Then the Buddha, looking at the sage Maitreya and the whole assembly, addressed them.

ततश्चिराद् गते काले गौडराष्ट्रे नराधिपः ।
अभूत्प्रचण्डदेवाख्यः श्रीमान् वज्रधरांशजः ॥ ३७ ॥

"After a long period of time, in a kingdom named Gauḍa, there was a king named Pracaṇḍadeva who belonged to the Vajradharāṁśa dynasty.

स राजा सुचिरं राज्यं नीतिधर्मेण पालयन् ।
सर्वान् लोकाञ्छुभे धर्मे नियुज्य समचारयत् ॥ ३८ ॥

The king, who was deeply religious, ethically and prudently protected his kingdom and directed his subjects toward the path of the good *dharma*, which he practised himself.

एतद्धर्मानुभावेन सदा तत्र समन्ततः ।
सुभिक्षं मंगलोत्साहं निरुत्पातं प्रावर्तत ॥ ३९ ॥

Due to the influence of his *dharma*, there was adequate, timely rainfall and plenty of harvest, along with joy and auspiciousness; and there was no sorrow or disaster in his kingdom.

तदा सर्वेऽपि ते लोकाः सद्धर्मगुणलालसाः ।
कुलधर्म-सदाचारा दानशीलव्रते रताः ॥ ४० ॥

The subjects in his kingdom would constantly practise the good *dharma*, donate charitably, abide by the principles and uphold their vows.

सत्यसंधानिका धीराश्चतुर्ब्रह्मविहारिणः ।
कुलेशभजनं कृत्वा प्राचरन्त मिथो हिते ॥ ४१ ॥

They held the truth, were very wise, dwelled in the Four Sublime Abodes, praised their lineage lords and partook in the welfare of one another.

दृष्ट्वा स नृपती राजा सर्वान् लोकान् शुभार्थिनः ।
मुदितस्तान् समामन्त्र्य सम्पश्यन्नेवमादिशत् ॥ ४२ ॥

Seeing his subjects engage in such auspicious work immensely pleased the king, who looked at them and addressed them.

भो लोकाः[11]पौरिकाः सर्वे सद्धर्मं यदि वाञ्छथ ।
त्रिरत्नभजनं कृत्वा चरत बोधिसम्बरम् ॥ ४३ ॥

"Dear subjects, if you desire the good *dharma*, serve the Buddha, Dharma and Saṅgha and practise the *bodhi* vow.

तेन यूयं शुभात्मानः परिशुद्धत्रिमण्डलाः ।
बोधिसत्त्वा महासत्त्वा भवत बोधिचारिणः ॥ ४४ ॥

You shall be cleansed into being pure in mind, speech and body and become *bodhisattvas, mahāsattvas* and walk the *bodhi* path.

ततस्ते निर्मलात्मानो निःक्लेशा विमलेन्द्रियाः[12] ।
अर्हन्तो बोधिमासाद्य सम्बुद्धपदमाप्स्यथ ॥ ४५ ॥

Then your souls will be purified, miseries will be removed, organs cleansed. You shall become *arhant*s and then acquire *bodhi* to finally attain Buddhahood."

इत्यादिष्टं नरेन्द्रेण सर्वै र्लोकैश्च संश्रुतम्[13] ।
तथेति प्रतिविज्ञाप्य प्राभ्यनन्दन् प्रबोधिताः ॥ ४६ ॥

Upon hearing the king's instructions, the crowd delightedly accepted them and went on to praise their king.

---

11 भो देवा इति गपाठः ।

12 संयतेच्छितम् इति खपाठः ।

13 निशंम्यते इति कपाठः ।

ततः सर्वेऽपि ते लोका धृत्वा राज्ञानुशासनम् ।
त्रिरत्नभजनं कृत्वा प्राचरन्त शुभं चिरम् ॥ ४७ ॥

They grasped the king's instructions and thereby remained in the service of the *tri-ratna* for a long time.

दृष्ट्वा तान् सकलान् लोकान् बोधिचर्याव्रतारतान् ।
महानन्द-प्रसन्नात्मा पुनरेव व्यचिन्तयन् ॥ ४८ ॥

Seeing his subjects practising the *bodhi* vow greatly satisfied the king and made him wonder.

सफलं जीवितं जन्म ममैतच्छासने रताः[14] ।
सर्वे लोकाः समाधाय प्रचरन्ति सदा शुभे ॥ ४९ ॥

He thought, "The purpose of my subjects lives has been fulfilled, for they have obeyed my instructions to practise the *bodhi* vow and engage in auspicious activities."

अथ प्रचण्डदेवौऽसौ दृष्ट्वा राज्यं महोत्सवम् ।
संसारेऽनर्थं संदृष्ट्वा चिन्तयामास ह्यात्मवित् ॥ ५० ॥

Then the King Pracaṇḍa, seeing the festivities and celebrations going on in his kingdom, worried, "Despite its beauty, the world is bound to the fate of doom all the same.

अत्राहं जालसंक्रान्तो नूनं स्यां जीर्णितेन्द्रियः ।
तदा रोगाभिभूतोऽपि व्रजेयं[15] मरणं ध्रुवम् ॥ ५१ ॥

Senescence is slowly taking hold of me. Gradually my organs will become frail with age; ailments and diseases shall smother me and eventually, my death is to come take me.

तदत्रैव कियत्कालं तिष्ठेयं सन्सुखान्वितः ।
अवश्यं भाविनो भावा भवन्ति भवचारिणाम् ॥ ५२ ॥

So how long am I to sit here, wallowing in comfort and pleasure? For fate is certainly bound to happen.

14 स्थिता इति गपाठः ।

15 व्रजित्वा शरणम् इति खपाठः ।

सदा भवे भवेद् नूनं भद्रं सद्धर्मचारिणाम् ।
दुःखमेव[16] सदा कामचारिणां भवचारणे ॥ ५३ ॥

However, it is assured that those who practise the way of *dharma* shall be subject to welfare, as opposed to those indulgent in the fulfilment of desires, that are eventually bound to harsher fates.

तस्मादहं परित्यज्य कामाश्रयं गृहाश्रमम् ।
निर्जने वन एकाकी विहरेयं समाहितः ॥ ५४ ॥

Therefore I must leave this household, which is the shelter of desires and cravings, to dwell in the forest in absolute solitude and concentration.

स्मृत्वा रत्नत्रयं ध्यात्वा संबोधिनिहिताशयः ।
बोधिचर्याव्रतं धृत्वा संचरेयं जगद्धिते ॥ ५५ ॥

I think it best if I, in remembrance of the *tri-ratna* and intending to acquire knowledge, lived in the forest to practise the *bodhi* vow for the welfare of the world."

इति निश्चित्य स प्राज्ञःप्रचण्डदेव आत्मवित् ।
नृपतिर्मन्त्रिणः सर्वान् समामन्त्र्यैवमादिशत् ॥ ५६ ॥

Having decided so, the scholarly king Pracaṇḍadeva who knew himself, called forth a meeting with his council of ministers and other well-wishers to speak to them.

भो सर्वे मन्त्रिणो यूयं शृणुत मे वचो हितम् ।
अथ यथा मयाख्यातं तथा चरितुमर्हथ ॥ ५७ ॥

"My ministers and well-wishers, please listen to my words carefully, for you must follow my instructions.

तद्यथा जरसाक्रान्तो वृद्धः स्यां जीर्णितेन्द्रियः ।
तथा रोगाभिभूतोऽपि ग्रसिष्ये मृत्युना ध्रुवम् ॥ ५८ ॥

---

16 सुखं स्यात् इति खपाठः ।

It is certain that senescence is getting hold of me. My organs will slowly become frail with age; I shall be diseased and eventually, death will smother me.

इति मे त्रस्यते चित्तं दुर्गति-भयशंकितम् ।
अवश्यं भाविनो भावा भवन्ति भवचारिणम् ॥ ५९ ॥

Hence, my mind is perturbed, crippled with dread of adversity and suffering – for they who dwell in this world must suffer the mortal misery.

भवे भवेत् सदा भद्रं नूनं सद्धर्मचारिणाम् ।
दुःखमेव सदा कामचारिणां भवचारिणे[17] ॥ ६० ॥

However, it is assured that those who practise the way of *dharma* shall be subject to welfare, as opposed to those indulgent in the fulfilment of desires, that are eventually bound to harsher fates.

अनर्थराज्यं विषयोपभोग्यं भयंकरं सर्वभयाकुलं यत् ।
अनित्यमसारमिति विचिन्त्य ह्यागारमध्ये वसितुं न रोचते ॥ ६१ ॥

This circumstance, where we consume materialistic commodities to appease and gratify our desires, is filled with misfortune and doom, just as a chamber full of ferocious snakes is. It is ephemeral and hollow. Knowing this, I no longer wish to stay in this household or this kingdom.

इति मत्वाहमुत्सृज्य कामाश्रयं गृहाश्रमम् ।
वनाश्रमे शुभारामे विहर्तुमुत्सहेऽधुना ॥ ६२ ॥

With this understanding, I am eager to discard and leave my household to seek asylum in the abode of the beautiful forests.

तदहं[18] स्वात्मजं पुत्रं शक्तिदेवं नृपासने ।
प्रतिष्ठाप्य नृपं कर्तुमिच्छामि सांप्रतं खलु ॥ ६३ ॥

---

17 गृहं संगमात् इति खपाठः ।

18 त्वामहङ् इति कपाठः ।

Therefore, I wish to coronate my son and heir, Śaktideva, and place him on the throne before I leave.

तद् भवन्तो निशम्यात्र सर्वेऽपि मम शासनम् ।
अभिषिञ्च्य नृपं कृत्वा भजतैनं ममात्मजम् ॥ ६४ ॥

Listen, you must inaugurate my son to replace me as the regnant and start serving him instead."

इत्यादिष्टं नरेन्द्रेण श्रुत्वा ते मन्त्रिणो जनाः ।
प्रमाणं शासनं भर्तुरित्येवं प्रतिशुश्रुवुः ॥ ६५ ॥

When the king commanded them so, the courtiers and ministers heeded his words in compliance and agreed to obey them and then they bowed to the king.

तदा राजा स तं पुत्रं शक्तिदेवममन्त्रयत् ।
भेदो दण्डः सामदानमित्युपायचतुष्टयम् ॥ ६६ ॥

Then the king invited his son Śaktideva to teach him the four tactics of ruling and politics – *bheda* (to split and separate), *daṇḍa* (to punish and instil fear), *sāma* (to peacefully negotiate and pacify) and *dāna* (to offer value and buy).

अत्राहं जरसाक्रान्तो नूनं स्यां निर्जितेन्द्रियः ।
तदा रोगाभिभूतेऽपि व्रजेयं मरणं ध्रुवम् ॥ ६७ ॥

He then said, "Senescence is getting hold of me. My organs will slowly become frail with age; I shall be diseased and eventually, death will come to me.

तद वनाश्रयमिच्छामि श्रेयःश्लाघेन यन्मया[19] ।
पुरो मृत्यू रिपुं हन्ति गृहसंरक्तमेव वा ॥ ६८ ॥

Thus, I want to seek asylum at the forest, which shall bring me welfare. Or else, seeing me unable to let go of my materialistic attachment, my greatest enemy – death – will come to kill me in my own home.

---

19 तत् कृतम् इति खपाठः ।

तस्मात् संसारभीतो मे बहुधा भयशंकया ।
नात्र स्थातुं मनो रेमे गच्छामि निर्जनं वनम् ॥ ६९ ॥

I am crippled with terror of the world. I am enveloped in fear and mistrust. I do not wish to stay here. I desire to live in an uninhabited forest.

तस्मान् मया यथा प्रोक्तं तथाचरितुमर्हसि ।
प्रजानां पालनं कृत्वा धर्मनीत्या समाचर ॥ ७० ॥

Therefore, heed my instructions carefully. Protect your subjects and live in the discipline of *dharma* and rule with prudence.

लोकान् मा खेद तत्पापं कुलधर्मं समाचर ।
परेष्वपि दयायुक्तैर्दानं हि श्रद्धया कुरु ॥ ७१ ॥

"Never hurt or mistreat the beings of the world; do not commit sins; always follow the *dharma* of our lineage; show compassion and pity even to enemies; and donate devotedly.

प्राणातिपातादत्तादानं काममिथ्यादि मा कुरु ।
मा मृषावाद पैशुन्यं पारुष्यं भिन्नमेव च ॥ ७२ ॥

Never harm any being in the world; never steal or rob; never speak false words; never harass or exploit anyone sexually; never talk maliciously or spread rumours about others; never curse or utter slurs; never discriminate others; and never give them misery.

माभिध्या-व्यापाददोषैर्मिथ्या दृष्ट्यादि संत्यज ।
एतानि तानि सर्वाणि धारय दृढचेतसा ॥ ७३ ॥

Never partake in animal violence; never consume products of violence; never have a malicious sight. Follow these instructions adamantly.

पापानां मूल एष हि सुगतेनेति देशितः ।
इत्थं कृतेऽपि नृपतेर्न भविष्यन्ति हानयः ॥ ७४ ॥

Such actions are the roots of sins, according to Lord Buddha. The king who does not participate in such misdeeds is freed of the six obstacles in governance or regal matters.

धर्मेण प्राप्यते राज्यं धर्मेण धनवर्धनम् ।
धर्मेण कामाः साध्यन्ते धर्मेण मोक्षःसिध्यते ॥ ७५ ॥

Through *dharma*, you shall receive the kingdom, acquire prosperity, have your wishes fulfilled and satisfy your desires.

कामसिद्ध्या हि मोक्षं च प्राप्यते नात्र संशयः ।
अनेन ज्ञानमार्गेण सशास नृपतिः सुतम् ॥ ७६ ॥

When a man is liberated from desires, he proceeds toward the path to salvation. Rule yourself with these principles." In this way, the king educated his son.

ततः स जनको राजा शक्तिदेवं स्वमात्मजम् ।
अभिषिच्य प्रतिष्ठाप्य नृपासने नृपं व्यधात् ॥ ७७ ॥

Then the king inaugurated his son Śaktideva, crowning and enthroning him as the new King.

ज्ञानाङ्कुशभयेनैव कुंचितः स गजो यथा ।
तत्र स जनकः सर्वं पुत्राय सर्वमर्पयत् ॥ ७८ ॥

Like a sharp hook rendering an elephant complicit, the hook of knowledge and wisdom led the king to discipline himself and pass all his fortunes and possessions to his son.

त्यक्त्वा परिग्रहान् सर्वान् पुनरेवमभाषत ।
अद्यारभ्यासि सर्वेषां लोकानामधिपः प्रभुः ॥ ७९ ॥

As he let go of all his possessions, he said to his son, "Henceforth, you have become the ruler of your kingdom, my son.

सर्वधर्मानुशास्ता च सर्वसत्त्वहितार्थभृत् ।
ननाम पितरं तेन श्रुत्वावाक्यं रसानिव ॥ ८० ॥

You are now the preacher of all *dharma* and the source of welfare of all sentient beings." This being said, the son bowed down to his father, consuming his words as if they were medicine.

धृत्वाज्ञां ते यथा तात प्रजानां प्रतिपालने।
इत्याज्ञाप्य ततो भूपःप्रचण्डदेवःसन्मतिः ॥ ८१ ॥

In acceptance of his father's commands, he said, "O father! I shall protect my subjects as per your instructions." Upon hearing this, the old king was immensely pleased.

प्रबोध्य पुत्रपत्न्यादीन् एको ययौ वनाश्रमम्।
तृणेषु निर्जनारण्ये विविक्त उटजाश्रये ॥ ८२ ॥

तृणासनसमासीनः तस्थौ ध्यान-समाहितः।
तत्रैको विहरन् कंचित्कालं स ऋषिधर्मभृत्[20] ॥ ८३ ॥

Having instructed his son and wives, the king proceeded toward the forest alone. In the forest, he built a hut with twigs and started to live in the uninhabited quiet place. He built himself a bed and a seat with grasses and leaves and having adopted the lifestyle of sages, started to meditate with absolute concentration.

सर्वसत्त्वहितोत्साही मनसैवं व्यचिन्तयत्।
किमेवं निर्जनेऽरण्ये ध्यात्वैको[21]विहरन्निह ॥ ८४ ॥

As he was striving for the welfare of all sentient beings, he started thinking to himself, "How long am I to dwell and meditate in this quiet solitary place?

कस्मै समुपदेक्ष्यामि सद्धर्मं बोधिसाधनम्।
दान[22]शीलक्षमावीर्यध्यानप्रज्ञासमुद्भवम् ॥ ८५ ॥

For how long am I going to uphold the instrument for *bodhi* – good *dharma* here? Who am I to teach about donation, principles, forgiveness, resilience, meditation and wisdom in this unpopulated place?

---

20 बुद्धधर्मदृक् इति घपाठः।

21 कृत्वैकाकी इति घपाठः।

22 ज्ञानशील इति गपाठः।

पुण्यं सत्त्वहितार्थाय समाख्यातं मुनीश्वरैः ।
तदेवं निर्जने स्थित्वा किं मे धर्मार्थसाधनम् ॥ ८६ ॥

It has been told that the merit one acquires shall come of use for the welfare of the world. But in this solitary place, what merit am I to amass?

विना सत्त्वहितार्थेन निरर्थं तपसापि हि ।
किमत्र दुष्करेणापि तपसा सिद्धिसाधनम् ॥ ८७ ॥

Austerity without the welfare of beings is futile and meaningless. What is to accomplish here by such extreme penance alone?

केवलं सद्गतौ श्रीमत्सौख्यलाभार्थमेव यत् ।
विना सत्त्वहितार्थेन निष्फलं सिद्धिसाधनम् ॥ ८८ ॥

My penance might be enough for my personal welfare, but such penance without the welfare of beings is in vain.

तदत्र निर्जने स्थित्वा तपसा निष्फलं मम[23] ।
यत्सत्त्वानां हितार्थाय धर्मश्रीगुणसाधनम् ॥ ८९ ॥

Hence, this vow I have been practising in solitude may be fruitless. The real austerity for the welfare of all beings shall bring about increment in *dharma*, glory and virtues.

विद्यासिद्धिः समृद्धिश्च क्षणं वीर्यबलं शुभम् ।
तन्ममैतानि सर्वाणि संसिद्धिसंमितान्यपि ॥ ९० ॥

विना सत्त्वहितार्थेन निरर्थानि पशोरिव ।
तदिदं व्रतमुसृज्य दुष्करं बोधिमानसः ॥ ९१ ॥

I possess knowledge, glory, strength, resilience and auspiciousness already. But these qualities are futile when not employed for the welfare of beings. Therefore, I must discard this severe austerity and leave here, holding *bodhi* in my mind.

23 सुफलं गतम् इति खपाठः ।

बोधिचर्याव्रतं धृत्वा चरेऽहं च जगद्धिते ।
तस्मात् तीर्थेषु तीर्थेषु पीठेषु पुण्यभूमिषु ॥ ९२ ॥

For the sake of all sentient beings, I must travel from one place to another, one pilgrimage to the next and one holy place to another, while practising the *bodhicaryā* vow.

सद्धर्मदेशनां[24]कुर्वन् सत्त्वेभ्यःप्रचराण्यहम् ।
एतत्पुण्यविशुद्धात्मा परिशुद्धत्रिमण्डलः ॥ ९३ ॥

Promoting the good *dharma*, I shall wander the earth, which shall bring merit that purifies soul as well as mind, speech and body.

आशु बोधिं समासाद्य संबुद्धपदमाप्नुयाम् ।
इति निश्चित्य स प्राज्ञःप्रचण्डदेव उत्थितः ॥ ९४ ॥

With this, I shall instantly attain enlightenment and Buddhahood." Having decided so, the Pracaṇḍadeva stood up to leave.

ततः सत्त्वहितार्थेन प्रचचार समाहितः ।
एवं सप्रचरन् धर्ममुपदेश्य समन्ततः ॥ ९५ ॥

He started to travel far and wide for the good of all beings; and he preached and promoted the *dharma* as he reached many lands and countries.

पुण्यक्षेत्रेषु तीर्थेषु पीठेषु प्रागमन् मुदा ।
एवं भ्रमन् स सर्वत्र भूतलेषु यथाक्रमम् ॥ ९६ ॥

During the course of his travels, he reached many pilgrimages, sacred places, shrines of goddesses, various villages and many other parts of this earth.

क्रमेण संचरन्नत्र हिमालयं समाययौ ।
अत्रायातः स संवीक्ष्य सर्वज्ञः संप्रमोदितः ॥ ९७ ॥

He also reached the Himalayas, the sight of which brought him tremendous joy and tranquillity.

---

24 सत्कर्मदेशना इति कपाठः ।

अहो हीदं महापीठमिति प्रोच्याभ्यनन्दत।
ततः स इदमालोक्य धर्मधातुं जिनालयम्[25] ॥ ९८ ॥

He thought, "O! This place is a great pilgrimage, able to grant immense joy". And he was astonished at the sight of the Dharmadhātu.

ज्योतिरूपं प्रसन्नात्मा प्रणत्वैह समाययौ।
अत्र स समुपागत्य समीक्ष्येनं जिनालयम् ॥ ९९ ॥

When he reached the *jinalaya*, the Dharmadhātu, in the form of energy, which had originated itself, he was ecstatic. He joined his hands to salute it in reverence.

यथाविधि समभ्यर्च्य श्रद्धाभक्ति-प्रसन्नधीः।
नैकप्रदक्षिणीकृत्य स्तुत्वा गीतैर्मनोहरैः ॥ १०० ॥

He procedurally worshipped it, expressed his devotion, performed the *pradakṣiṇā* many times, sang various praises, and chanted hymns and prayers.

अष्टांगैः प्रणतिं कृत्वा ध्यात्वा जप्त्वा भजन् मुदा।
ततश्चेदं स संवीक्ष्य मञ्जुदेवस्य निर्मितम् ॥ १०१ ॥

He saluted it with eight bodily positions, meditated, chanted *mantra*s, sang praises to please it.

At the sight of Mañjuśrī*'s caitya*, he was absolutely pleased.

चैत्यमभ्यर्च्य संस्तुत्वा गीतैर्नत्वा भजन् मुदा।
ततोऽसौ च महादेवीं योनिरुपां खगाननाम् ॥ १०२ ॥

When he saw the *caitya,* he praised it and saluted it with hymns and *stotra*s and then proceeded toward the Great Goddess Khagānanā.

समालोक्य प्रसान्नात्मा[26]यथाविधि समर्चयत्।
तत्रापि स महासत्त्वः स्तुत्वा गीतैर्मनोहरैः ॥ १०३ ॥

25 स्वयंभुवि इति खपाठः।

26 स्वचित्तेन इति घपाठः।

He was pleased at the sight of the Goddess Khagānanā and therefore, ritually worshipped and saluted her and praised her through many hymns.

अष्टांङ्गैः प्रणतिं कृत्वा प्रदक्षिणान्येकशः ।
श्रद्धया शरणं गत्वा स्मृत्वा ध्यात्वा समाहितः ॥ १०४ ॥

He saluted her with eight bodily positions, did the *pradakṣiṇā* around her, devotedly paid homage to her and remembered her names, concentrated and meditated on her.

तद्विद्या-धारणीमन्त्रं जपित्वा प्राभ्यनन्दत ।
ततोऽसौ च महासत्त्वो वाग्वतीप्रमुखान्यपि ॥ १०५ ॥

The mystical art of the Dharaṇī *mantra* was practised and worshipped by him, after which the king started to partake in the meditation of pilgrimages near Vāgmatī.

तीर्थान्येतानि सर्वाणि समीक्ष्य प्राभ्यनन्दत ।
ततः स तेषु तीर्थेषु सर्वेष्वपि यथाक्रमम् ॥ १०६ ॥

स्नात्वा दानव्रतादीनि कृत्वाभजन् प्रमोदितः ।
ततोऽष्टौ वीतरागाँश्च दृष्ट्वा स संप्रहर्षितः ॥ १०७ ॥

He received the auspicious sight of all the holy places, worshipped them ritually and offered donations to the best of his abilities. He bathed, donated and practised his vow; and with great joy, he worshipped the eight *vītarāga*s.

यथाविधि समभ्यर्च्य स्तुत्वा नत्वा भजन् क्रमात् ।
ततःप्रचण्डदेवः[27] स बोधिसत्त्वः प्रसादितः ॥ १०८ ॥

He ritually worshipped the eight *vītarāga*s, saluted them and sang their praises. In this way, the Pracaṇḍadeva came to be a *bodhisattva.*

अत्रैव सर्वदाश्रित्य व्रतं चरितुमैच्छत ।
ततः स मञ्जुदेवस्य शिष्यं शासनसम्भृतम् ॥ ११० ॥

---

27 नृपाल इति खपाठः ।

सद्गुरुं समुपाश्रित्य प्रार्थयेदेव मानतः ।
भदन्तात्र पुण्यक्षेत्रे महापीठे हिमालये ॥ १११ ॥

Then, practising and listening to the good *dharma*, he went to the disciple of Mañjuśrī and bowed to him, paid homage and said to him, "O *bhante*! this is great holy place. I desire to dwell here alongside you.

प्रव्रज्यासम्वरं धृत्वा संस्थातुमुत्सहे सदा ।
तद् भवान् कृपया मह्यं संबोधिज्ञानसाधनम् ॥ ११२ ॥

O Guru! I seek inauguration to reside with you forever. Therefore, with your benevolence, bestow the instrument of *bodhi* upon me."

प्रव्रज्यासम्वरं दातुं समर्हति जगद्धिते[28] ।
इति संप्रार्थितं तेन निशम्य स गुणाकरः ॥ ११३ ॥

"After being ordained at the initiation, I shall work for the welfare of all sentient beings." On hearing such words come from the king, the *bhikkhu* started to speak.

बोधिसत्त्वं सुविज्ञं तं सम्पश्यन्नेवमब्रवीत् ।
एहि भद्र समिच्छा ते यद्यस्ति बौद्धसम्वरे ॥ ११४ ॥

प्रवज्याव्रतमाधाय संचर त्वं समाहितः ।
इत्युक्त्वा स महाभिज्ञःप्रव्रजितं विधाय तम् ॥ ११५ ॥

When he heard such words come from the king, he replied, "O son! come here. I shall grant you your wish for inauguration, through which you may be able to walk for the welfare of the world." Having said this, he ordained the king into the *dharma*.

बोधिचर्याव्रतं दत्वा प्रचारयज्जगद्हिते ।
तत्र स मुण्डितपात्री सुरक्तचीवरावृतः ॥ ११६ ॥

ब्रह्मचारी यतिर्भिक्षुर्निःक्लेशोऽर्हन् सुधीरभूत् ॥
तस्य नाम तदा शान्तश्रीभिक्षुरिति कल्पितम्[29] ॥ ११७ ॥

---

28 स्वयम्भुव इति घपाठः ।

29 नामोऽभूत् इति कपाठः ।

स देवासुरलोकानामपि वन्द्यार्चितोऽभवत्।
तदारभ्य स शान्तश्रीर्धर्मधातोर्जिनालये ॥ ११८ ॥

त्रिरत्नभजनं कृत्वा तस्थौ बोधिव्रतं चरन्।
स एकस्मिन् दिने चेमं ज्योतिरूपं प्रभास्वरम् ॥ ११९ ॥

Upon doing so, he told the king, "Practise the *bodhicaryā* vow and walk for the welfare of the world". He shaved his head, clad him in good *cīvara* robes and so he turned celibate, into a great monk, who has conquered obstacles. He became scholarly as well and was then named Śāntaśrī Bhikkhu. With the desire to teach the whole world, he started to wander in all four directions as a *bodhisattva*. Even gods, demons and lords of the worlds saluted him. Thenceforth, the Śāntaśrī took up residence near the Dharmadhātu Jinālaya. He remained in constant service of the *tri-ratna* through praises and thus upheld the *bodhi* vow. One day, he delved into deep thought about the illuminating Svayambhū.

रत्नपद्मासनासीनं पश्यन्नेवं व्यचिन्तयत्।
अहो ह्ययं स्वयं जातो ज्योतिरूपःप्रभास्वरः ॥ १२० ॥

रत्नपद्मासमासीनः संतिष्ठते जगद्धिते।
कियत्कालमयं श्रीमान् धर्मधातुर्जिनालयः ॥ १२१ ॥

He started to wonder at the sight of the Dharmadhātu, atop a lotus with red petals. He wondered at how it self-originated, at how it exuded divine light, at how it is surrounded by red lotuses and how it exists for the welfare of the world. He wondered how long the Dharmadhātu would exist so.

एवं संभासयन् लोकान् संस्थास्यते जगद्धिते।
यतःकलौ समयाते लोके पंचकषायिते[30] ॥ १२२ ॥

सर्वे लोका दुराचारा भविष्यन्ति दुराशयाः।
मदाभिमानिनो दुष्टा लोभिनःकामचारिणः ॥ १२३ ॥

---

30 पञ्चपालने इति घपाठः।

Filled with wonder, he thought to himself, "The Dharmadhātu must exist for a long time for the good of the world. For the Kali age shall soon dawn upon us, when man shall be corrupted with five great sins. They will all be filled with malice, and indulge in atrocities. They will be overcome with vanity, greed, lust and wickedness.

ईर्ष्यालवःप्रमत्ताश्च मात्सर्यव्याकुलाशयाः ।
क्लेशाहंकारगर्वान्धा निर्विवेकाः प्रमादिनः ॥ १२४ ॥

They would be envious, intoxicated, filled with jealousy and resentment, wretched and proud, foolish and negligent.

कामभोगातिसंरक्ता दशाकुशलचारिणः ।
तदा कथमयं श्रीमान् ज्योतिरूपःप्रभास्वरः ॥ १२५ ॥

रत्नपट्टा[31]समासीन एवं तिष्ठेज्जगद्धिते ।
नूनं ये लाभिनो दुष्टाः क्लेशव्याकुलमानसाः ॥ १२६ ॥

इमं चैत्यं प्रतिक्षिप्य रत्नानि हरेयुस्तदा ।
मूर्खाः तथान्येऽपि जना दुष्टाः क्लेशाभिमानिनः ॥ १२७ ॥

In the Kali era, they would be indulged in desires, partaking in inauspicious and wicked deeds. How can the self-originating and illuminating Lord Svayambhū, who sits atop a red lotus for the welfare of all sentient beings, exist so in such a time? The greedy, wicked and men with troubled minds would surely come to destroy the *caitya* to steal the jewels of the Dharmadhātu and thereby bring harm to the Svayambhū.

ज्योतिरूपमिमं चैत्यं ध्वंसयिष्यन्ति सर्वथा ।
एवं तदा कलौ काले ध्वंसितेऽस्मिन् जिनालये ॥ १२८ ॥

महापातकसंभूतं महोत्पातं भवेद् ध्रुवम् ।
इति हेतोरहं धर्मधातोरस्य सुरक्षणे ॥ १२९ ॥

गुप्तिकर्तुं शिलाच्छाद्य चैत्यं कुर्यां महोच्छ्रयम् ।
तदा सर्वेऽपि लोकास्ते इमं स्तूपं महोच्छ्रितम् ॥ १३० ॥

31 कौशेयवस्त्र इति गपाठः ।

समीक्ष्य श्रद्धया भक्त्या भजिष्यन्ति प्रसादिताः[32] ।
तदैतत् पुण्यभावेन सर्वदात्र समन्ततः ॥ १३१ ॥

The men in the Kali age would destroy the *caitya* that exudes light and energy. When the *jinālaya* (home of the Buddha) is destroyed in that age, sins would spread through all lands; there would be chaos all around. Therefore, the Dharmadhātu must be protected and preserved. I must secretly hide it under a massive rock and build a tall *caitya* on top of it. Thenceforth, everyone would come to see, worship and please the great *caitya*; and the received merit would bring welfare.

सुभिक्षं मङ्गलोत्साहं निरुत्पातं भवेद् ध्रुवम् ।
इति ध्यात्वा स शान्तश्रीः शास्तारं तं पुनर्मुदा ॥ १३२ ॥

उपेत्य साञ्जलिर्नत्वा प्रार्थयेदेवमादरात् ।
भदन्त सद्गुरोः शास्तुर्यदिच्छामीह साम्प्रतम् ॥ १३३ ॥

Through the merit received, there would be adequate rainfall, plenty of harvest and auspiciousness all around; chaos would cease to exist." With this thought, the Śāntaśrī Bhikkhu goes to the *guru* to speak to him, "O Guru! you must bless me with benevolence".

धर्मधातुमिमं चैत्यं गुप्तिकर्तुं सुरक्षणे ।
तदूर्ध्वं शिलयाच्छाद्य स्वीष्टिकाभिः समुच्छ्रितम्[33] ॥ १३४ ॥

स्तूपं कृत्वा प्रतिष्ठाप्य स्थिरीकर्तुं समुत्सहे ।
इत्यत्र मे भवाञ्छास्ता गुप्तिं कृत्वाभिरक्षणे ॥ १३५ ॥

"*Guru*, I wish to build a *caitya* on the Dharmadhātu and conceal it secretly inside the earth and obscure it through a large rock and build a tall *stūpa* with bricks – inside of which the Lord Dharmadhātu will exist, undisturbed. This is my wish."

धर्मधातोः जगद्भर्तुरनुज्ञां दातुमर्हति ।
इति संप्रार्थिते तेन शान्तश्रिया निशम्य सः ॥ १३६ ॥

---

32 प्रभञ्जने इति खपाठः ।

33 समुद्घृतम् इति कपाठः ।

महामतिर्महासत्त्वं तं पश्यन्नेवमब्रवीत् ।
भद्र! स्वयम्भुवस्तस्य गुप्तीकर्तुं यदीच्छसि[34] ॥ १३७ ॥

प्रत्येकं श्रावकं यानं मुक्त्वा महति संश्रितः ।
वज्राभिषेकमादाय चरं वज्रव्रतं पुनः ॥ १३८ ॥

"I seek your permission to conceal the Dharmadhātu." When the Śāntaśrī Bhikkhu prayed to the *guru* residing in Mañjuśrī*'s* shrine near the Svayambhū, he replied: "O Mahāsattva! very well, your desire to seclude the Svayambhū shall come true. To accomplish it, you must acquire the *vajra* ordinance and practise the *vajra* vow. You must discard other paths and practise the Vajrayāna.

इति शास्ता समादिष्टं निशम्य स प्रमोदितः ।
शास्तारं तं प्रणम्यैवं[35]प्रार्थयदेवमादरात् ॥ १४० ॥

In this way, having received instructions from the *guru*, the Śāntaśrī Bhikkhu delightedly saluted him and spoke:

सद्गुरुर्मे भवाञ्छास्ता धर्मधातुसुरक्षणे ।
वज्रचर्याव्रतं दत्वा चारय मां जगद्धिते ॥ १४१ ॥

"You are my revered *guru* and the ruler of the world. In order to fulfil my desire to preserve the Dharmadhātu, pray grant me the *vajracaryā* vow, after which I shall wander for the welfare of the world."

इति संप्रार्थिते तेन शान्तश्रिया निशम्य सः ।
महामतिर्महासत्त्वं तं समीक्ष्यैवमब्रवीत् ॥ १४२ ॥

Upon hearing the prayers of the Śāntaśrī, the Mahāmati Vajrasattva looked at him to reply.

यदि श्रद्धास्ति ते भद्र! वज्रचर्या–महाव्रतम् ।
यथाविधि प्रदास्यामि तद् गृहाण जगद्धिते ॥ १४३ ॥

"You have devotion. Therefore, I shall ritually grant you the *vajracaryā* vow, which you must uphold for the welfare of the world."

---

34 त्वमन्तरा इति घपाठः ।

35 प्रणत्वा च इति खपाठः ।

इत्युक्त्वा स महाचार्यस्तस्मै शान्तश्रिये क्रमात् ।
साभिषेकं महायाने वज्रचर्याव्रतं ददौ ॥ १४४ ॥

Having said this, the great teacher provided the Vajrayāna inauguration and ordinance to the Śāntaśrī Bhikkhu.

स शान्तिश्रीवज्राचार्य इति नाम स्थापितं तदा[36] ।
ततःप्राप्ताभिषेकः स शान्तश्रीर्वज्रयोगवित् ॥ १४५ ॥

He was then inaugurated as the Śāntaśrī Vajrācārya. He was blessed with instant knowledge and had become a scholar of *vajra-yoga.*

स्वात्मानं दक्षिणां तस्मै गुरवे प्रददौ मुदा ।
ततः स वज्रधृग् योगी महाभिज्ञः सुसिद्धिमान् ॥ १४६ ॥

He immediately gave an offering to his *guru* – the offering being himself. Then he became the yielder of the *vajra* and a great scholar with divine powers.

स्वकुलेशं समाराध्य सगणं प्राभजन् मुदा ।
ततः सवज्रधृग् योगी महाभिज्ञः सुसिद्धिमान् ॥ १४७ ॥

He then worshipped and sang praises of the patron-deity and his entourage. The divine *vajra* yielding *yogī* was joyous.

सद्धर्मसाधनोत्साही सर्वविद्याधिपोऽप्यभूत् ।
ततःशास्तुरनुज्ञां स समासाद्य प्रसादितः ॥ १४८ ॥

He became the lord of all knowledge and enthusiastic to practise the good *dharma*. He then decided to follow the instructions of his *guru*.

धर्मधातुं समाराध्य प्रार्थयेदेव मानतः ।
भगवन् नाथ सर्वज्ञ भवतां रक्षणाय यत् ॥ १४९ ॥

ज्योती रूपं समाच्छाद्य चैत्यं कर्त्तुमिहोत्सहे ।
तद् भवान् त्रिजगन्नाथ ! कृपया मे प्रसीदतु ॥ १५० ॥

36 चाधिज्ञप्राप्तोऽभूत् । तत्क्षणे नयज्ञानमपि तेनैव प्राप्तम् इति खपाठः ।

He approached the Dharmadhātu and started his prayers, "O Lord! O Omniscient One! in order to perpetually protect you, I seek to cover your illuminating form and build a *caitya* on top. O *jinālaya*! please be pleased."

यदत्राप्यपराधं मे तत्सर्वं क्षन्तुमर्हति ।
इति संप्रार्थ्य स प्राज्ञो ज्योतीरूपं जिनालयम् ॥ १५१ ॥

स रत्नपद्मैराछाद्य शिलया समगोपयत्[37] ।
तदुपरीष्टिकाभिश्च विधाय चैत्यमुच्छ्रितम् ॥ १५२ ॥

यथाविधि प्रतिष्ठाप्य महोत्साहैः सदाभजत् ।
तत इदञ्च पुच्छाग्रं मञ्जुदेवस्य निर्मितम् ॥ १५३ ॥

चैत्यं स शिलयाछाद्य स्तूपं व्यधान्महोत्तमम् ।
इदं स्तूपं च शान्तश्रीः प्रतिष्ठाप्ययथाविधि ॥ १५४ ॥

"My Lord, please forgive any crimes and offences I may inadvertently commit." Having said this, he fetched a giant rock to cover the Svayambhū that lay on a red lotus; and on top of it, he built a tall *caitya* with bricks. He ritually established it and celebrated with constant hymns.

Then on the Pucchāgra mountain, the shrine of Mañjuśrī was also covered with rocks and a great *stūpa* was built on top of it. The Śāntaśrī ritually established the *stūpa* as well.

सर्वदा श्रद्धया भक्त्या महोत्साहैर्मुदाभजत् ।
ततश्चासौ महाचार्य आराध्य पंचदेवताः ॥ १५५ ॥

With immense devotion, servitude and enthusiasm, while celebrating with hymns, the great *ācārya* Śāntaśrī established five gods in five directions.

पंच सुराः पुरेष्वेवं प्रतिष्ठाप्य सदाभजत् ।
तद्यथा देवता-पंच-प्रथमं वायुदेवताम् ॥ १५६ ॥

---

37 समाच्छादितम् इति कपाठः ।

वायुपुरे प्रतिष्ठाप्य वह्निपुरेऽग्निदेवताम् ।
नागपुरे च नागेन्द्रं वसुपुरे वसुन्धराम् ॥ १५७ ॥

शान्तिपुरे महाश्रीमत्सम्वरं सुगणं तथा ।
एतान् सर्वान् समाराध्य स आचार्यो यथाविधि ॥ १५८ ॥

Five gods were allocated five spots (*pura*). Among them, the first was the Wind God, who was placed in the Vāyupura. The Fire God was placed at the Agnipura, the Serpent God at the *Nāgapura*, the Earth Goddess at the Vasupura and the virtuous Mahāśrīmatsambara was placed at the Śāntipura. Having established these gods, he proceeded to procedurally worship them.

महोत्साहैः समभ्यर्च्य प्राभजत् सर्वदा मुदा ।
एवं कृत्वा स आचार्य शान्तश्रीश्च महर्द्धिकः ॥ १५९ ॥

With immense joy, the Śāntaśrī worshipped the gods till he was content. As a result, he received great prosperity.

भद्रश्रीमन्त्रसंसिद्धः सर्वविद्याधिपोऽभवत् ।
ततो भूयः स आचार्यो बोधिसत्त्वो महामतिः ॥ १६० ॥

He received tremendous gentleness, prosperity and divinity of incantations, became the lord of all knowledge, a great *ācārya*, a *bodhisattva* and a *mahāmati*.

सर्वसत्त्वहितोत्साही ध्यात्वैवं समचिन्तयत् ।
अत्रैवमहमाराध्य सर्वान् देवान् यथाविधि ॥ १६१ ॥

प्रतिष्ठाप्य समभ्यर्च्य महोत्साहैर्भजे मुदा ।
तथात्र सर्वदा धर्मधातुवागीश्वरं सदा ॥ १६२ ॥

स्मृत्वा ध्यात्वा समाराध्य संतिष्ठेयं जगद्धिते ।
इति ध्यात्वा स शान्तश्रीराचार्यस्त्रिगुणार्थ[38]भृत् ॥ १६३ ॥

He was enthusiastic for the welfare of all sentient beings and thus started to meditate. He decided to stay there to ritually worship the gods and joyously sing their praises. Similarly, the Śāntaśrī Ācārya who

---

38 त्रिबोधिकृत् इति कपाठः ।

was complete with all three virtues sang praises of the Dharmadhātu Vāgīśvara, with the desire to stay there in remembrance, meditation and service of the Dharmadhātu, for the welfare of all beings.

सर्वसत्त्वहितार्थेन तस्थावत्रैव नन्दितः ।
एवं ता देवता भक्त्या भजन्ति ये यथाविधि ॥ १६४ ॥

ते भद्रश्रीगुणापन्ना भवेयुर्बोधिचारिणः ।
तद्विशेषफलं चापि शृणु मैत्रेय सांप्रतम् ॥ १६५ ॥

He resided there for the sake of all sentient beings, with immense pleasure. In this way, they who praise the gods ritually become prosperous, gentle and the source of all virtues and established in *bodhi*.

I shall tell you of the special fruit of residing there, Maitreya, listen carefully.

सर्व-सत्त्वानुबोधार्थं वक्ष्याम्यत्र समासतः ।
तद्यथा ये समाराध्य सगणां वायुदेवताम् ॥ १६६ ॥

यथाविधि समभ्यर्च्य संभजन्ते समादरात् ।
तेषां वातमहोत्पातभयं क्वापि न विद्यते ॥ १६७ ॥

For the knowledge of all beings, I shall tell you in brief about the benefits of the worship of each God. Listen quietly. They, who procedurally praise the God of Wind and his followers, shall never suffer from the wind or storm.

निरोग्य[39]श्रीसमापन्नं कामभोग्यं सदा भवे ।
ये चाप्येवं समाराध्य सगणां वह्निदेवताम् ॥ १६८ ॥

Similarly, those who worship the God of Fire would be free of diseases, prosperous and all their wishes would be fulfilled.

यथाविधि समभ्यर्च्य संभजन्ते समादरात् ।
तेषां वह्निमहोत्पातं भयं क्वापि न विद्यते ॥ १६९ ॥

---

[39] सुकृत्यम् इति खपाठः ।

They who procedurally praise the Fire would never suffer from fire or arson.

परिपुष्टेन्द्रि[40]यारोग्यं महासौख्यं सदा भवेत्।
ये चाप्येवं समाराध्य सगणां नागदेवताम्[41] ॥ १७० ॥

They who worship the Serpent God along with his followers, receive happiness and comfort, as well as development in their organs.

यथाविधि समभ्यर्च्य प्रभजन्ते[42] सदा मुदा।
तेषां न विद्यते क्वापि दुर्भिक्षोत्पातजं भयम् ॥ १७१ ॥

Those who praise the Serpent God regularly would never have affliction or fear.

भद्रश्रीरत्नसंपत्तिकामभोग्यं सदा भवे।
ये चाप्येवं समाराध्य सगणां श्रीवसुन्धराम् ॥ १७२ ॥

यथाविधि समभ्यर्च्य सम्भजन्ते समादरात्।
तेषां दारिद्र्यदुःखादि भयं नास्ति कदाचन ॥ १७३ ॥

They who worship the Goddess Earth (Vasundharā) would be filled with virtues and prosperity and their wishes would be fulfilled. Ritualistic worship and praise of the Goddess removes poverty and brings fortune.

भद्रश्रीसद्गुणापन्नमहासंपत्सुखं सदा।
ये चाप्येवं समाराध्य सगणं सम्बरं जिनम् ॥ १७४ ॥

They who worship the Śambara Jina would be rewarded with immense prosperity, gentleness, virtues, as well as great comfort and happiness.

यथाविधि समभ्यर्च्य सम्भजन्ते समादरात्।
तेषां मारोपसर्गं च भयं क्वापि न विद्यते ॥ १७५ ॥

They who procedurally worship and pay homage to the God shall never suffer from communicable diseases.

40 परिपूर्णेन्द्रिये इति गपाठः।

41 वासुदेवताम् इति घपाठः।

42 कुर्वन्ति इति खपाठः।

सद्धर्मरत्नसंपत्तिमहैश्वर्यसुखं सदा ।
ये चेदं चैत्यमाराध्य मञ्जुदेवेन निर्मितम् ॥ १७६ ॥

यथाविधि समभ्यर्च्य सम्भजन्ते समादरात् ।
ते दुर्भगा दुराचारा दुष्टाः स्युर्न कदाचन ॥ १७७ ॥

They who worship the *caitya* of Mañjuśrī would receive *dharma*, prosperity and happiness. Procedural worship would destroy their misfortunes and misconducts and they would be freed of enemies.

सर्वे धर्माधिपा नाथा भवेयुःश्रीगुणाकराः ।
ये चापीदं समाराध्य धर्मधातुं जिनालयम्[43] ॥ १७८ ॥

यथाविधि समभ्यर्च्य संभजन्ते समादरात् ।
ते सर्वे विमलात्मानो भद्रश्रीसद्गुणाश्रयाः ॥ १७९ ॥

They who worship the Dharmadhātu jinālaya – the Svayambhū, would be lords of *dharma*, masters of virtues; their souls would be cleansed; they would be filled with virtues manifold.

बोधिसत्त्वा[44]महाभिज्ञा भवेयुर्बोधिचारिणः ।
य एता देवताः सर्वाः स्मृत्वा ध्यात्वापि सर्वदा ॥ १८० ॥

They who remember, meditate and worship these Gods would become *bodhisattva*s, *mahāsattva*s and upholders of *bodhi*.

नामापि च समुच्चार्य संभजन्ते समाद्रिताः ।
तेऽपि सर्वे न यास्यन्ति दुर्गतिं च कदाचन ॥ १८१ ॥

They who chant the names of these gods with reverence would never be wretched or miserable.

सदा सद्गतिसंजाता भवेयुःश्रीगुणाश्रयाः ।
ततस्ते सुकृता रक्ताः सद्धर्मगुणलालसाः ॥ १८२ ॥

They would always reach a good state and be the sources of prosperity and virtues. They would be decorated with merits. They would receive the qualities of the good *dharma*.

---

43 शुभालये इति गपाठः ।

44 महासत्त्वा इति घपाठः ।

त्रिरत्नशरणं कृत्वा[45] संचरेयुः सदा शुभे।
ततस्ते विमलात्मानः परिशुद्धेन्द्रियाशयाः ॥ १८३ ॥

In the refuge of *tri-ratna*, they would have to take part in auspicious activities so that their souls be purified, and organs and intentions cleansed.

बोधिसत्त्वा महासत्त्वाश्चतुर्ब्रह्मविहारिणः।
सर्वसत्त्वहिताधानं चरेयुर्बोधिसम्वरम् ॥ १८४ ॥

They would become *bodhisattva*s, *mahāsattva*s and would dwell in the Four Sublime Abodes. They would become the foundation for the welfare of all sentient beings and they would be in constant practise of the *bodhi*.

ततस्ते बोधिसंभारं पूरयित्वा यथाक्रमम्।
दशभूमीश्वरा नाथा भवेयुः सुगतात्मजाः ॥ १८५ ॥

They would complete the steps of *bodhi* and would conquer the ten highest stages of trance (*daśabhūmi*) to finally become the sons of Buddha.

ततस्ते निर्मलात्मानः संसारगतिनिःस्पृहाः।
अर्हन्तः सबलं मारं निर्जित्य स्युर्निरंजनाः ॥ १८६ ॥

Then their souls are cleansed; their worldly attachments are removed. They would become *arhant*s. They would be filled with strength and be victorious against bodily desires. Finally, they would be separated from the cycles of birth and death.

त्रिविधां बोधिमासाद्य सद्धर्मगुणभास्कराः[46]।
सर्वसत्त्वहितार्थेन संबुद्धपदमाप्नुयुः ॥ १८७ ॥

Having received the three types of *bodhi*, they would be the suns of the qualities of the good *dharma*. For the welfare of sentient beings, they would attain Buddhahood.

---

45 शरणे गत्वा इति कपाठः।

46 गुणलालसाः इति खपाठः।

येऽप्येतद् गुणमाहात्म्यं श्रुत्वा तत्रानुमोदिताः ।
तथा तत्पुण्यमाहात्म्यं प्रशंसन्ति समादरात् ॥ १८८ ॥

Those who listen to the discourse on these qualities and concur with their importance, shall receive boundless merit and would be lauded by great men.

तेऽपि सर्वे विकल्माषाः परिशुद्धत्रिमण्डलाः ।
श्रीमन्तः सद्गुणाधारा भवेयुर्बोधिमानसाः ॥ १८९ ॥

Their sins would be destroyed; they would be purified in mind, body and speech; they would become prosperous and virtuous; and *bodhi* would reside in their minds.

न ययुर्दुर्गतिं क्वापि सदा सद्गतिसम्भवाः ।
सर्वसत्त्वहितं कृत्वा संचरेरञ्जगद्धिते ॥ १९० ॥

They would never be wretched or miserable, but always in a good state. They would start wandering the world for the sake of all sentient beings.

ततः सर्वाधिपास्ते स्युर्धर्मार्थ–संप्रपूरकाः ।
बोधिसंभारं संपूर्य संबुद्धपदमाप्नुयुः ॥ १९१ ॥

They would become lords of everything, they would be complete in *dharma* and *artha* and having fulfilled their *bodhi* steps, they would ultimately reach the Buddha position.

इति सत्यं परिज्ञाय बौद्धं पदं यदीच्छथ ।
एतान् देवान् समाराध्य भजत सर्वदा भवे ॥ १९२ ॥

Having learnt this, if you desire the position of Buddhahood, you must worship the gods and the Dharmadhātu.

एतत्पुण्यानुभावेन यूयमप्येवमाभवम् ।
दुर्गतिं नैव गच्छेत[47]कदाचित् कुत्रचिद् ध्रुवम् ॥ १९३ ॥

---

47 यायात् इति कपाठः ।

Through the influence of the merit you will have received by listening to this sermon, may you never reach a state of wretchedness or misery and always be in a good state.

सदा सद्गतिसंजाता भद्रश्रीसद्गुणाश्रयाः ।
बोधिसत्त्वा महासत्त्वा भवत बोधिचारिणः ॥ १९४ ॥

In this way, I wish for you to acquire all these qualities and to become *bodhisattva*s, *mahāsattva*s and the upholders of *bodhi*.

ततः संबोधिसंभारं पूरयित्वा यथाक्रमम् ।
त्रिविधां बोधिमासाद्य संबुद्धपदमाप्स्यथ ॥ १९५ ॥

Having fulfilled the steps of *bodhi* and having acquired the three ultimate types of *bodhi*, may you receive Buddhahood!

इति मत्वात्र ये लोका वाच्छन्ति सौगतं पदम् ।
स देवान् सगणान् सर्वान् समाराध्य भजन्तु च ॥ १९६ ॥

Those who understand this and desire Buddhahood must worship and please the gods and their followers."

इत्यादिष्टं मुनीन्द्रेण निशम्य ते सभाश्रिताः ।
सर्वे तथेति विज्ञाप्य प्राभ्यनन्दन् प्रबोधिताः ॥ १९७ ॥

Upon hearing such instructions from the Lord, the assembly was internally awakened and thus praised the Lord Buddha.

तदा शान्तश्रिया योऽसौ[48]गुप्तीकृतो जिनालयः ।
इत्यादिश्य मुनीन्द्रोऽपि समाधिं गतःतत्क्षणम्[49] ॥ १९८ ॥

In this way, after talking about the Śāntaśrī Vajrācāryā concealing the Svayambhū below the *stūpa*, the Lord went into a state of trance.

॥ इति श्रीस्वयंभूधर्मधातु-वागीश्वर-गुप्तीकृत-प्रवर्तनो नाम सप्तमोऽध्यायः सम्पूर्णः ॥

Thus, the seventh chapter of the *Svayambhū Mahāpuranam* on the "Concealment of the Dharmadhātu Vāgīśvara" ends.

---

48 यस्सं इति कपाठः ।

49 विद्धेक्षणं इति घपाठः ।

अथ अष्टमोऽध्यायः
(Aṣṭama Adhyāya)

Instrument for Good Rainfall

अथ स भगवाञ्छास्ता समाधेरुत्थितःपुनः ।
मैत्रेयं तां सभां चापि समालोक्यैवमादिशत् ॥ १ ॥

The Lord Buddha came out of his trance again and thus addressed Maitreya and the assembly.

शृणु मैत्रेय भूयो स्यादेतद् देवानुभावतः[1] ।
सिद्धभूमेः प्रवक्ष्यापि महत्सिद्धिप्रभावताम् ॥ २ ॥

"Maitreya, listen further, for I shall tell you of the divine land and beings, through gods' grace.

तद्यथात्रोपछन्दोहे सिद्धलोके हिमालये ।
नेपाल इति विख्यात एतद् देवानुभावतः[2] ॥ ३ ॥

सदा भद्रमहोत्साहं सुभिक्षं निरुपद्रवम् ।
सर्वद्रव्यसमापन्नं समृद्धं धाम राजते ॥ ४ ॥

On the lap of the Himalaya, there is a divine land called Nepal, where there is always an abundance of welfare, constant celebration, adequate rainfall and absence of chaos. The land is prosperous and thriving.

तदा सर्वत्र लोकाश्च दशकुशलचारिणः ।
त्रिरत्नभजनारक्ताः प्राचरन्त सदा शुभम् ॥ ५ ॥

---

1 बुद्धानुभवति इति गपाठः ।

2 बुद्धानुभाविता इति खपाठः ।

All beings there perform auspicious deeds. They dwell together, in eternal refuge of the Buddha, Dharma and Saṅgha and in harmony.

एतत्पुण्यानुलिप्तास्ते चतुर्ब्रह्मविहारिणः।
भद्रश्रीसद्गुणाधारा बभूवुर्बोधिचारिणः ॥ ६ ॥

As a result of their merits, they dwell in the Four Sublime Abodes. They are virtuous and prosperous and they practise the *bodhi* vow.

एवमेषां प्रसिद्धाभूद् ऋद्धिसिद्धिगुणार्थदा।
ऋद्धा स्फीता सुभिक्षाश्रीसमाश्रयाभिशोभिता ॥ ७ ॥

They acquired fame, for they possessed the qualities of prosperity and divinity. They had plenty of reap, great fortune and tranquillity.

तेनात्र योगिनो विज्ञा यतयो ब्रह्मचारिणः।
स्मृत्वा[3]ध्यात्वा कुलेशानं समाराध्य समाश्रयत् ॥ ८ ॥

Yogīs, scholars, monks, celibates live there in remembrance of god, meditation and auspicious deeds.

तथान्येऽपि सुलोकाश्च समागत्य प्रसादिताः।
धर्मधातुमिमं भक्त्या भजमानाः समाश्रयन् ॥ ९ ॥

Similarly, beings from other worlds go there as well to live in devoted prayer of the Dharmadhātu.

सर्वेष्वपि च तीर्थेषु स्नानदानादि संवरम्।
कृत्वाष्टौ वीतरागांश्च भजन्तः समुपाश्रयन् ॥ १० ॥

Pilgrims arrive to bathe, donate and practise vows in various pilgrimages. The eight *vītarāga*s are praised and served as well.

एताश्च देवताःपञ्च समाराध्य यथाविधि।
भजमानाः[4] सदोत्साहैः प्राचरन्त समाहिताः ॥ ११ ॥

The five gods are also praised with hymns and enthusiastic offerings as well as devoted worship.

---

3 कृतं इति गपाठः।

4 विज्यमाने इति खपाठः।

तदा खगाननां देवीं समाराध्य यथाविधि।
भजमाना महोत्साहैः प्राचरन्त सदा शुभम् ॥ १२ ॥

They procedurally serve and praise the Goddess Khagānanā, filled with joy.

एवमिमं च पुच्छाग्रं चैत्यं मञ्जुश्रियोऽपि ते।
सर्वे लोकाः समाराध्य प्राभजन्त प्रसादिताः ॥ १३ ॥

The *caitya* on the grave of Mañjusrī named Pucchāgra is also visited, where they worship and sing praises of him.

एवं सर्वेऽपि लोकाश्च सद्धर्माभिरता मुदा।
सदा भद्राणि कर्माणि कृत्वात्र सर्वदाश्रयन् ॥ १४ ॥

Similarly, all sentient beings living there practise the good *dharma*. They constantly gain welfare and live in happiness and comfort through their good deeds.

एवमेषां महासिद्धि-भूमिःश्रीसंप्रशोभिता[5]।
महाजन-समाकीर्णा सर्वभूम्युत्तमा बभौ ॥ १५ ॥

This great divine land is where prosperity resides, where great men dwell. It is supreme among all land.

ततःकालान्तरेणात्र राजा भूमिर्यतिर्नृपः।
श्रीगुणकामदेवाख्यःशास्ता लोकाधिपोऽभवत् ॥ १६ ॥

At a certain time, there arose a king named Guṇakāmadeva, whose duty was to protect and foster the place.

तदा स नृपतिःप्रौढो युवा कामातिलालसः।
यथा कामरसं भुक्त्वा प्राचरन् स्वेच्छया रमन् ॥ १७ ॥

As the king gained maturity, he got attracted to indulgences of desires. For the fulfilment of his desires, he started wandering incessantly.

ततः स क्षत्रियास्वेवं कामभागाभिमोहितः।
प्रमदागुणसंरक्तो नीतिधर्मे निरादरः ॥ १८ ॥

[5] प्रमोदिता इति गपाठः।

He was lecherously attracted to women and held no difference between kṣatriya women and non-kṣatriya women. He disrespected prudence and morality to pursue his wanton desires.

दृष्ट्वा स सुन्दरीं कान्तामगम्यामपि मोहतः[6] ।
बलेनापि समाकृष्य बुभुजे स्वेच्छया तदा ॥ १९ ॥

Whenever his sight fell on any beautiful woman, whether she was worthy of him or not, he took her by force to satisfy his lust.

एवं स नृपती राजा कामधर्मातिलालसः ।
मन्त्रिषु सर्वराज्याङ्गं निवेश्य स्वेच्छयारमत् ॥ २० ॥

Thus, in his incessant pursuit of desire, he left his kingdom in the hands of courtiers and ministers.

ततस्ते मन्त्रिणः सर्वे नृपं तं प्रमदावशे[7] ।
प्रतिष्ठाप्य यथाकामं भुक्त्वाऽचरन् यथेच्छया ॥ २१ ॥

Knowing that his own lust could control the king, the ministers provided him with further women so they could run the country to their own wishes.

तथा भृत्या जनाश्चापि सर्वेऽपि क्लेशिताशयाः ।
सद्धर्मं तं प्रतिक्षिप्य प्राचरन् कामभोगिनः ॥ २२ ॥

His servants and subjects were greatly saddened, for *dharma* was disparaged and desire was encouraged.

ब्राह्मणाश्च तथा सर्वे दशाकुशलचारिणः ।
स्वकुलधर्ममर्यादां त्यक्त्वाऽचरन् यथेच्छया ॥ २३ ॥

Brāhmaṇas started abandoning their auspicious traditions. They discarded their good *dharma* and ethics and behaved according to their own desires.

---

6 कामत इति खपाठः ।

7 प्रमनाग्रहे इति घपाठः ।

वैश्याश्चापि तथा धर्मद्रव्यसंग्रहलालसाः ।
स्वकुलवृत्तिमुत्सृज्य भुक्त्वाऽचरन् यथेप्सितम्[8] ॥ २४ ॥

Vaiśyas focused solely on the accumulation of wealth and capital, discarded the laws of their family and took what they wanted.

महाजनास्तथा सर्वेऽप्यन्यायद्रव्यसाधिनः ।
स्वकुलधर्ममुत्सृज्य भोगात्ते प्राचरन् सुखम् ॥ २५ ॥

Capitalists sought only money and having forgotten their integrity and morality, wallowed in their comfort.

वणिजोऽपि तथा सर्वे मिथ्यार्थसाधनोद्यताः ।
सत्यधर्मं प्रतिक्षिप्य चेरुः क्लेशाभिमानिताः ॥ २६ ॥

Merchants employed falsehood and trickery to earn easy money. They discarded truth and honesty and spent their lives in pride and vanity.

शिल्पिनोऽपि तथा सर्वे कवलभृतिलालसाः ।
अविधिज्ञाःप्रमादान्धाश्चक्रुःकर्म यथेच्छया ॥ २७ ॥

Artists were overcome by gluttony – and lacked artistic proficiency. They were blinded by carelessness and did as they liked.

तथा नारीजनाश्चापि कामक्लेशाकुलाशयाः[9] ।
स्वकुलधर्ममुत्सृज्य प्राचरन्त यथेप्सितम् ॥ २८ ॥

Womankind also succumbed to desires; they discarded their *dharma* to do what they liked.

एवं सर्वेऽपि लोकाश्च दशाकुशलसंरताः ।
स्वकुलाचारमुत्सृज्य प्राचरन्त यथेच्छया ॥ २९ ॥

In this way, everyone got involved in the Ten Inauspicious Deeds and discarded the pious deeds of their ancestors to act on their own desires.

तीर्थिकाश्चापि ये दुष्टास्ते दृष्टैवं जिनालयम् ।
निन्दित्वा परिभाषन्तःप्राचरन्त यथेच्छया ॥ ३० ॥

---

8 अथेच्छिता इति गपाठः ।

9 विलासिता इति कपाठः ।

Vedic scholars forsook their rituals and became wicked. Despite seeing the glory of the *jinālaya*, they denounced him; they started to wrongly define *dharma* how they wanted.

तदात्र बहवो दुष्टा चौरा धूर्ताः प्रगल्भिकाः ।
साधुजनान् प्रतिक्षिप्य चेरु मत्तद्वीपा इव ॥ ३१ ॥

Similarly, wicked ones, thieves, cunning men, liars rose to besmirch and defame saints while they wandered like wild elephants.

साधवः[10] सज्जनाश्चापि नीचकर्मानुचारिणः ।
सद्धर्मविरतोत्साहाश्चेरु भुक्त्वैव नीचवत् ॥ ३२ ॥

Saints and noblemen discarded the good *dharma* and started to misbehave like lower base born men.

तदैवं पापसंचारात् सर्वत्राप्यचरत् कलिः[11] ।
सद्धर्मो दुर्बलीभूतो नीचवद्विलयं ययौ ॥ ३३ ॥

When such sins and evil increased all around, Kali himself appeared and *dharma* was weakened and diminished.

तदात्रप्रवरीभूते कलेः संचारतां गते ।
दृष्ट्वा लोकाधिपाः सर्वेऽभवन् धर्मपराङ्मुखाः ॥ ३४ ॥

Then seeing the world engulfed with Kali, the lords of the world turned their backs on *dharma*.

ततोऽत्र विमुखीभूय सर्वलोका धिपा अपि ।
धिग्नृपमिति निन्दन्तो द्रष्टुमपि न चेच्छिरे[12] ॥ ३५ ॥

When the lords of the world turned their backs, the citizens chastized their king.

तदात्र लोकपालानां सुदृष्टिविरतोत्सवे ।
ईतयः[13] समुपाक्रम्य प्रावर्त्तितुमुपाचरन् ॥ ३६ ॥

---

10 पुराश्च इति खपाठः ।

11 किल इति गपाठः ।

12 समन्तात् इति गपाठः ।

13 इयतः इति कपाठः ।

The protectors perceived the world badly and therefore, disruptions and catastrophes such as flood and drought arose.

ततो देवा अपि क्रूरा ये दुष्टा मारपक्षिकाः[14] ।
सर्वे तत्र समागत्य महोत्पातं प्रचक्रिरे ॥ ३७ ॥

The gods turned ruthless – they partook in the chaos. Misery and chaos engulfed the land.

वह्निरपि तथालोक्य दुष्टवत् कोपिताशयः ।
धूमाकुलार्चिषादग्धो महोत्पातं व्यधादिह ॥ ३८ ॥

Fire was angered at the condition of the world and consequently thick black smoke covered the air in a disastrous manner.

धर्मराजोऽपि रुष्टोभून् निर्दयी निरुजानपि ।
निहन्तुं प्राणिनः सर्वान् महामारीमचारयत् ॥ ३९ ॥

In his fury, Dharmarāja (God of death) turned cruel – he started to kill those that were healthy and young and so the world was hit by a devastating plague.

नैऋत्यो राक्षसेन्द्रोऽपि प्रकोपितोऽतिनिर्दयः ।
सर्वत्रापि प्रविष्टोऽत्र महोत्पातं व्यधात्सदा ॥ ४० ॥

The Lord of Demons – Nairr̥tya – was also infuriated into cruelty. As a result, disaster and catastrophe afflicted the land everywhere.

वरुणो नागराजोऽपि प्रदुष्टः क्रूरचक्षुषा ॥
दृष्ट्वा वारिवहान् मेघान् सर्वान् वृष्टिं न्यवारयत् ॥ ४१ ॥

The king of snakes – Varuṇa – looked through cruel eyes filled with malice and seeing the clouds carrying water, forbade them to shower upon earth.

मरुतोऽपि[15]तथालोक्य प्ररुष्टा निर्दयाःस्थिराः ।
असाध्यं प्राचरन्तात्र महोत्पातं प्रचक्रिरे ॥ ४२ ॥

---

14 गारपक्षका इति खपाठः ।

15 मन्यतापि इति घपाठः ।

The Wind God – Mārut – was also wrathful and in his ruthlessness he caused disastrous catastrophes.

तथा यक्षाश्च ये दुष्टाःकिन्नरा गुह्यका अपि ।
गृहे गृहे प्रविश्यापि रोगोत्पातं प्रचक्रिरे ॥ ४३ ॥

Demi-gods such as *yakṣa*s, *kinnara, guhyaka*s started breaking into households and causing disease and damage.

तथा भूताःपिशाचाश्च वेतालाःकटपूटिनाः[16] ।
डाकिण्यःप्रमथाश्चापि शाकिन्यः सगणास्तथा ॥ ४४ ॥

So did ghosts, phantoms, zombies, vampires and witches, Ḍakīnī and Śakīnī demi-goddesses and attendants of Śiva.

रुद्रा अपि सगन्धर्वाःकुम्भाण्डा गरुडा अपि ॥
सर्वत्र प्रचरन्तोऽत्र महोत्पातं प्रचक्रिरे ॥ ४५ ॥

*Rudra*s, *gandharva*s, *kumbhāṇḍa* demi-gods, as well as falcons, all arrived to cause chaos.

मातृका अपि सर्वांश्च सगणा अप्रसादिताः ।
सुदुष्टं तं समालोक्य द्रष्टुं च न समाहिरे ॥ ४६ ॥

Mātṛkās (mother goddesses) were displeased, so instead of protecting the people, they started to inflict harm upon them.

ग्रहास्तारागणाः सर्वे विरुद्धा अप्रसादिताः ।
अनुसंदर्शनं वापि कर्तुं नैवाववाञ्छिरे ॥ ४७ ॥

Planets and stars turned against the world and in their displeasure, did not appear at all.

कुलेशा[17]अपि सर्वाश्च देवता अप्रसादिताः ।
संत्रासाय समर्थास्तान् पश्यन्त्य एव तस्थिरे ॥ ४८ ॥

Patron deities and gods were not happy. Instead of proving protection, they inflicted further harm.

---

16 कठपूटका इति खपाठः ।

17 कौलिका इति गपाठः ।

एवमन्येऽपि देवाश्च सर्वत्राणपराङ्मुखाः ।
तेषां संदर्शनं कर्तुमपि नैव ते वांछिरे ॥ ४९ ॥

Other gods stopped protecting the people; they refused to even gaze at them.

तेषां त्राणं तदेकापि न शशाक कथञ्चन ।
एवमत्र महोत्पातं प्रावर्तत समन्ततः ॥ ५० ॥

No one was able to protect the people, for chaos and disaster came from all directions.

एकमत्रमहोत्पातं प्रावर्ततापि सर्वतः ।
सर्वक्लेशहतात्मानः प्रचक्रुर्विग्रहं मिथः ॥ ५१ ॥

Chaos and disaster came from all directions. Those ridden with afflictions started fighting each other.

तदेवं कलिसंरक्तान् सर्वान् लोकान् विलोक्य सः ।
नृपतिः सुचिरं ध्यात्वा मनसैवं व्यचिन्तयत्[18] ॥ ५२ ॥

हा कष्टं पापजं घोरं जायतेऽत्राधुना मम ।
तत्पापशमनायैवं को दद्यान्मे हिताशयः[19] ॥ ५३ ॥

Kali engulfed the land. Seeing atrocities, afflictions and catastrophes everywhere, the king wondered what caused it all. "Tremendous misery has been caused by sins. Who would destroy the sins and remove the sorrow, poverty and pain? Who would help me?" he wondered.

कथमिह महद्दुःखं शमीकर्तुं विधास्यते ।
पश्यन्नेवमुपेक्ष्यैव रमेयं साम्प्रतं च किम् ॥ ५४ ॥

"Do I forget this wretchedness and continue to wallow in my indulgences, unaffected? Or do I strive to remove this misery?

---

18 कृतं कृतम् इति गपाठः ।

19 कृताशये इति खपाठः ।

यो हि राजा प्रजादुःखमुपेक्ष्य रमते सुखे ।
स किं राजा प्रभुर्भर्ता दुष्टाहिवद्विगर्ह्यते ॥ ५५ ॥

The king who neglects the suffering of his citizens and revels in his pleasures is not a worthy ruler and would be compared to an evil snake in disgrace.

यत्र राजा प्रजादुःखहानाय न विचारयेत् ।
स्वयमेव सुखं भुक्त्वा रमंश्चरेद् यथेच्छया[20] ॥ ५६ ॥

तत्र सर्वप्रजालोकाः क्लेशव्याकुलमानसाः ।
सत्यधर्मकुलाचारं हित्वा चरेयुरौद्धताः ॥ ५७ ॥

Where the king ignores the misery of his subjects and instead enjoys his delights, there all subjects become distressed with suffering. Then having discarded the truth, the law, and the ethics of the family, they become undisciplined and perverse.

ततस्ते दुरितारक्ता दशाकुशलचारिणः ।
महापापेऽपि निर्लज्जाः संचरेरन् यथेच्छया ॥ ५८ ॥

Then they become involved in various crimes and shamelessly commit sins as they fancy.

एतत् सर्वं महोत्पातं भुञ्जीयान्नृपतिर्ध्रुवम् ।
इति सत्यं समाख्यातं नीतिविज्ञैर्महर्षिभिः ॥ ५९ ॥

Eventually, the sins find their way back to the king; and he ultimately has to suffer the consequences. Those who know the *niti* (policies) and *dharma* know of this.

इत्येतत्पापवैपाक्यं भोक्तव्यं हि मया भवे ।
तदत्र किं[21]करिष्यामि यदुपायं न चिन्त्यते ॥ ६० ॥

One day I shall have to suffer the fruit of these sins. Where shall I go? Who could tell me the ways to redemption and absolution?

---

20 शुखेच्छता इति खपाठः ।

21 तदानी कि इति गपाठः ।

धिग् जन्म मेऽत्र संसारे यस्य राज्ये सदा कलिः ।
दुर्भिक्षादिमहोत्पातं प्रवर्तते दिवानिशम् ॥ ६१ ॥

Curse my birth! Despite being the king, I have been sinning and misbehaving and so I have let Kali take over. Chaos is running riots and disaster lurks everywhere. There is no peace, at day or night.

धन्यास्ते पुरुषा ये हि निःक्लेशा विमलाशयाः ।
विमुक्त-भव-संचारा भिक्षवो ब्रह्मचारिणः ॥ ६२ ॥

Bless those great men who are untroubled, whose minds are at peace and intentions are of good. They will be liberated one day, for they are *bhikkhu*s and celibates.

किं मेऽत्र जन्म संसारे सुकुलमपि तन्नृणाम् ।
यदहं पशुवद् भुक्त्वा काममेव रमे गृहे ॥ ६३ ॥

What good have I accomplished since my birth in this land? I have only acted as an animal, indulging in unrestrained pleasures.

तदेतत्पापलिप्तोऽहं क्लेशव्याकुलमानसः ।
नरकेषु भ्रमन् दुःखं भुंजीयां विविधं सदा ॥ ६४ ॥

Now I am overcome by sins, my heart tormented by misery. I shall certainly dwell in hell someday, suffering tremendously.

तदा को मे सुहृन् मित्रं संरक्षितुमुपाचरेत् ।
धर्मादेव तदा त्राणं सर्वदुःखापहं भवेत् ॥ ६५ ॥

Who would protect me then? Only *dharma* could come as a friend to remove my sins and miseries.

धर्माणां प्रवरो बौद्धो धर्मः सर्वभयापहः[22] ।
सर्वार्थसाधनं सिद्धमित्याख्यातं जगद्धितम् ॥ ६६ ॥

Among *dharma*s, the Bauddha Dharma is the foremost; it removes fear, provides prosperity and brings welfare to the world, according to ancestors.

[22] सर्वपुरान् इति कपाठः ।

इत्यहं साम्प्रतं गत्वा गोशृङ्गे पर्वते स्थितम् ।
शान्तश्रियं महाचार्यं प्रार्थयेयं समादरात् ॥ ६७ ॥

Therefore, I must immediately depart for the Go-śṛṅga Parvata to respectfully pray to the Śāntaśrī Bhikkhu."

स एव हि महाचार्य एतदुत्पातशान्तये ।
विधानं समुपादिश्य कुर्यान्मेऽत्र हितं सदा ॥ ६८ ॥

To discover the way to pacify the chaos and the atrocities of Kali, he was determined to set out, knowing it was the only chance for welfare.

इति निश्चित्य भूपालः पुरोहितं समन्त्रिणम् ।
महाजनान् सपौरांश्च समामन्त्र्यैवमादिशत् ॥ ६९ ॥

With this determination, he called an assembly of his priests, courtiers and citizens to address them.

भो भवन्तो यदत्रैवं महोत्पातं प्रवर्तते ।
तच्छान्तिकरणं धर्मं कर्तुमिच्छामि सांप्रतम् ॥ ७० ॥

"It is my greatest duty to pacify all the misery that has befallen our land; and I desire to do so.

तदाचार्यं महाभिज्ञं शान्तिश्रियं समादरात् ।
प्रार्थयित्वा तदादेशात् कर्तुमिच्छामि सदृशम् ॥ ७१ ॥

Therefore, I must respectfully pray to the wise Ācārya Śāntaśrī to remove this sorrow from our lands.

इति सर्वे वयं तत्र गोशृङ्गाग्रे समादरात् ।
शान्तश्रियं महाचार्यं प्रार्थनाय व्रजामहै ॥ ७२ ॥

Let us all go to the Go-śṛṅga Parvata to respectfully pray to the Śāntaśrī Ācārya."

इत्यादिष्टं नरेन्द्रेण श्रुत्वा पुरोहितादयः ।
सर्वे तथेति विज्ञाप्य प्राभ्यनन्दन् प्रबोधिताः ॥ ७३ ॥

Upon hearing the command of the king, the priests and others concurred and they were pleased, so they praised the king.

ततः स नृपती राजा समन्त्रिजनपौरिकाः ।
पुरोहितं पुरोधाय गोशृङ्गाग्रे मुदाचरत् ॥ ७४ ॥

Then the king, along with his priests, courtiers and secretaries, departed for the Go-śṛṅga mountain.

तत्र दृष्ट्वा तमाचार्यं नृपतिः संप्रमोदितः ।
समेत्य साञ्जलिर्नत्वा पादाब्जे समुपाश्रयत् ॥ ७५ ॥

As they reached the mountain, the king and his company saw the *ācārya* and immediately bowed at the feet of the *bhikkhu* and paid homage to him.

तथा सर्वेऽपि लोकाश्च समीक्ष्येनं[23] प्रसादिताः ।
समेत्य पादयोर्नत्वा समुपतस्थिरे मुदा ॥ ७६ ॥

The whole world was pleased at the sight of it, for they knew that welfare was imminent. Having saluted the *bhikkhu*, everyone sat down.

तान् सर्वान् समुपासीनान् समीक्ष्य स महामतिः ।
शान्तश्रीस्तं महीपालं सम्पश्यन्नेवमादिशत् ॥ ७७ ॥

Seeing everyone sitting around him, the Mahāmati Śāntaśrī faced towards the king and said:

राजन् सदास्तु वो भद्रं सर्वत्रापि निरन्तरम्[24] ।
किमर्थमिह प्रायातः तन्मेऽग्रे वक्तुमर्हसि ॥ ७८ ॥

"O king, may you be blessed! Pray tell me the purpose of your arrival."

इति शान्तश्रिया प्रोक्ते नृपतिः स कृताञ्जलिः ।
प्रणम्य तं महाचार्यं पश्यन्नेवं न्यवेदयत्[25] ॥ ७९ ॥

भो गुरोस्तद् यदर्थेऽहं भवच्छरणमाव्रजे ।
तदर्थं प्रार्थयाम्यत्र समुपादेष्टुमर्हति ॥ ८० ॥

---

23 संप्रदाने इति खपाठः ।

24 सुभंकृतर इति गपाठः ।

25 प्रकल्पिता इति घपाठः ।

When the Śāntaśrī asked so, the king joined his hands and bowed to the king again before replying to him, "O *bhante*! I have come to your asylum, to pray for wisdom and guidance.

यन्मेऽत्र पापतो राज्ये महोत्पातं प्रवर्तते।
तच्छान्तिकरणोपायं समुपादेष्टुमर्हति ॥ ८१ ॥

Tremendous mayhem has come to my kingdom. I have come to you to pray for a solution so peace and order may be restored."

इति संप्रार्थिते राज्ञा शान्तश्रीर्मन्त्रवित् सुधीः।
नृपतिं तं महासत्त्वं समालोक्यैवमादिशत् ॥ ८२ ॥

When the king prayed so, the wise Śāntaśrī looked at the king and his company as he answered.

नृपते पापतोऽत्रैवं महोत्पातं प्रवर्तते।
तत्पापशमनोपायं वक्ष्यापि ते शृणुष्व तत् ॥ ८३ ॥

"O king! this chaos is a result of sins. I shall tell you the way to atone for these sins.

यः त्वमत्र[26] नृपो राजा सर्वधर्मानुपालकः।
नीतिधर्मनुसारेण संपालयसि न प्रजाः ॥ ८४ ॥

As a king, you should have abided by the law and *dharma* to protect your subjects. But alas! you have not done so.

मन्त्रिणोऽपि तथा सर्वनीतिधर्मपराङ्मुखाः।
भुक्त्वा कामसुखान्येव प्रचरन्ति यथेच्छया ॥ ८५ ॥

Your ministers disobey law and *dharma* and incessantly pursue pleasures that they desire.

तथा भृत्या जनाश्चापि पौराश्चापि महाजनाः।
स्वकुलधर्ममुत्सृज्य प्रचरन्ति यथेच्छया[27] ॥ ८६ ॥

---

26 यत्त्यागात् इति खपाठः।

27 शुभात्मता इति घपाठः।

Your servants, subjects, townsfolk, villagers and capitalists discard the laws of the families to do as they like.

एवं सर्वेऽपि लोकाश्च दशाकुशलचारिणः ।
सद्धर्माणि[28]प्रतिक्षिप्य प्रचरन्ति प्रमादतः ॥ ८७ ॥

The men of the world are involved in the Ten Inauspicious Deeds and have cast *dharma* aside in an intoxicated behaviour.

तदैतत् पापवैपाक्यं भोक्तव्यमेव हि भवे ।
येनैव यत्कृतं कर्म भोक्तव्यं तेन तत्फलम् ॥ ८८ ॥

Those who commit the sins must suffer their consequences in this world.

एवं मत्वा नृपः स्वामी स्वयं नीत्या विचारयन् ।
बोधयित्वा प्रयत्नेन लोकान् संपालयेत् सदा ॥ ८९ ॥

Understanding this, a king must always lawfully and prudently strive to protect the world. Then the entire world follows the king to indulge in wanton desires, as they like.

यद्यत्र नृपतिः सम्यगविचार्य प्रमादतः[29] ।
स्वयं कामसुखान्येव प्रचरेयुर्यथेच्छया ॥ ९१ ॥

तदा तत्र महोत्पातं ध्रुवं पापात् प्रवर्तते ।
प्रवर्तिते महोत्पाते लोका स्युःपापदुःखिताः ॥ ९२ ॥

If a king works against it and always engage, himself in sexual pleasures, surely, mayhem is then certain, as a result of such sins. The chaos caused by the sins brings misery to all.

तत्र तान् नृपतिःपश्यन्नुपेक्ष्य निर्दयँश्चरत् ।
लोकसंरक्षणेऽशक्तः स सर्वपापभाग् भवेत् ॥ ९३ ॥

Having seen all of this, the king, who cruelly disregards his kingdom and is unable to protect it, is considered guilty of all the sins.

---

28 सधर्मे इति कपाठः । यद्यपि धर्माणिप्रयोगो वेदेषु दृश्यते । तथाप्यत्र ग्रन्थकृता लौकिकव्याकरणनियमान् अविचार्यैव तथा कृतमिति प्रतीयते ।

29 प्रमोदतः इति गपाठः ।

सर्वाण्यपि हि पापानि सर्वलोकैः कृतान्यपि ।
पतित्वा नृपतेरग्रे प्रदद्युस्तत्फलानि हि ॥ ९४ ॥

No matter who commits the crimes, they find their way to the king who ultimately suffers the fruit of the crimes.

इति सत्यं समाख्यातं सर्वैरपि मुनीश्वरैः ।
मत्वा राजा स्वयं नीत्या विचारयन् समाचरेत् ॥ ९५ ॥

This has been preached by various ancient sages and scholars. It is wise for a king to act on the principles provided by the sages."

इति तेन समादिष्टं शान्तश्रिया समन्त्रिणा[30] ।
श्रुत्वा स नृपतिर्भीत्या संतापतापिताशयः ॥ ९६ ॥

When the Śāntaśrī solemnly spoke such words, the king felt immensely agitated by fear and remorse.

शान्तश्रियं तमाचार्यं समीक्ष्य शरणं गतः ।
नत्वा पदाम्बुजे भूयःप्रार्थयेदेवमादरात् ॥ ९७ ॥

The king sought the refuge of the *bhikkhu* and saluting his feet, prayed to him again.

शास्तः सदा चरिष्यामि भवदाज्ञां शिरोवहन् ।
तन् मे यदुचितं धर्मं तं समादेष्टुमर्हति ॥ ९८ ॥

"My Lord, I shall act on your commands. Pray instruct me the suitable path for welfare and *dharma*."

इति संप्रार्थिते राज्ञा श्रुत्वाचार्यः स सन्मतिः।
नृपतिं तं महासत्त्वं सम्पश्यन्नेवमादिशत् ॥ ९९ ॥

Hearing such prayers, the wise *bhikkhu* looked at the great king and his companions as he commenced his address.

राजञ्छृणु समाधाय वक्ष्यामि शुभकारणम् ।
यद्यस्ति ते कृपालोके तत् कुरु यन्मयोदितम् ॥ १०० ॥

---

30 सहलोकिकैः इति खपाठः ।

"O king! listen carefully. I shall provide you the auspicious solution, which shall bring welfare to the world when implemented.

तद्यथैतेषु तीर्थेषु स्नात्वा नित्यं यथाविधि[31] ।
शुचिशीलसमाचारः समाहितत्रिमण्डलः ॥ १०१ ॥

Bathe in these sacred pilgrimages, ritually and regularly. Practise good conduct and cleanse your mind, speech and body.

सम्बोधिप्रणिधानेन सर्वसत्त्वहितार्थभृत् ।
त्रिरत्नभजनं कृत्वा चरस्व पोषधं व्रतम् ॥ १०२ ॥

Practise the vow for the acquisition of *sambodhi* and the welfare of all sentient beings, while praising and serving the *tri-ratna*.

तत इमं जगन्नाथं[32]धर्मधातुं जिनालयम् ।
यथाविधि समाराध्य संभजस्व सदादरात् ॥ १०३ ॥

Thereafter, ritually worship the lord of the world – the Dharmadhātu Jinālaya and devotedly sing his praises.

तथा सर्वा इमा पंचदेवताश्च यथाविधि ।
समाराध्य समभ्यर्च्य संभजस्व समादरात् ॥ १०४ ॥

Similarly, you must regularly worship, praise and serve the five gods established here, with respect and devotion.

इमं मञ्जुश्रियश्चापि चैत्यमाराध्य सर्वदा ।
यथाविधि समभ्यर्च्य संभजस्व महोत्सवैः ॥ १०५ ॥

Worship the *caitya* of Mañjuśrī and chant praises of him ritually and joyously.

तथाष्टौ वीतरागांश्च समाराध्य यथाविधि ।
समभ्यर्च्य महोत्साहैः संभजस्व सदादरात्[33] ॥ १०६ ॥

You must also worship and celebrate the eight *vītarāga*s who reside here and praise them devotedly.

---

31 यथेप्सितम् इति गपाठः ।

32 खगाननाम इति घपाठः ।

33 समाकृतात् इति खपाठः ।

तथा माहेश्वरीं देवीं खगाननां समादरात्।
समाराध्य समभ्यर्च्य संभजस्व यथाविधि ॥ १०७ ॥

You must revere the Great Goddess Khagānanā; worship, pray, serve and sing her praises ritually.

एते सर्वेऽपि देवा हि सर्वलोकाधिपेश्वराः।
सर्वसत्त्वहितार्थेन प्रादुर्भूताः स्वयं खलु ॥ १०८ ॥

Similarly, there are other gods and lords of the world, who have self-originated; for the welfare of all sentient beings, you must worship them.

तदत्रैतेषु देवेषु सर्वेषु श्रद्धया सदा।
विधिना भजनं कृत्वा संचरस्व जगद्धिते[34] ॥ १०९ ॥

You must be devoted to all of these gods and ritually sing their praises, for the welfare of all sentient beings.

लोकांश्चापि तथा सर्वान् बोधयित्वा प्रयत्नतः।
सर्वेष्वेतेषु तीर्थेषु स्नानदानादिकं सदा ॥ ११० ॥

Similarly, you must preach the entire world. Go to pilgrimages to bathe, donate and so on.

कारयित्वा महत्पुण्यं जगद्भद्रसुखार्थदम्।
संबुद्धगुणसत्सौख्यं चारय पोषधं व्रतम् ॥ १११ ॥

Involve others in the auspicious work and ask them to practise the good *vrata* for the welfare and happiness of the world. The merit shall spread the qualities of Buddha.

एतेषां च त्रिरत्नादिदेवानां भजनं सदा।
कारयित्वा महोत्साहैर्बोधिमार्गे प्रचारय ॥ ११२ ॥

Always praise the *tri-ratna* and the other gods and make others do it as well. Promote the path of *bodhi* with great enthusiasm.

---

34 शुभात्मके इति गपाठः।

तदैतत्पुण्यभावेन सर्वत्रापि चरच्छुभम् ।
तदा सर्वमहोत्पातं सर्वत्र विलयं व्रजेत् ॥ ११३ ॥

Through the influence of this merit, order and auspiciousness shall be restored; chaos and mayhem would be removed.

तदा ब्रह्मामरेन्द्राद्याः सर्वे लोकाधिपा अपि ।
सुदृशात्र समालोक्य पालयेयुः सदा मुदा ॥ ११४ ॥

When they see you doing this, Brahmā, Indra and the gods, as well as lords of other realms, shall come to your aid.

तदा संपालितेऽस्मिन् तैः सर्वैर्लोकाधिपैः पुनः ।
सुभिक्षं श्रीशुभोत्साहं प्रवर्तयेद्धि सर्वदा ॥ ११५ ॥

And so, the lords of the world shall protect your country. There will be adequate rainfall and plenty of reap. There will be prosperity and celebrations.

तदा सर्वेऽपि लोकाश्च नीरोगाःश्रीगुणाश्रयाः ।
विरम्य[35]पापमार्गेभ्यः संचरेरन् सदा शुभे ॥ ११६ ॥

People would become healthy and vigorous, virtuous and prosperous. They would discard the path of crime and would partake in the auspicious.

एवं धृत्वा सदा राजन् महापुण्यप्रभावतः ।
अन्ते बोधिं समासाद्य संबुद्धपदमाप्नुयुः ॥ ११७ ॥

Immense merit will be generated, which will influence people to eventually acquire *bodhi* and attain Buddhahood.

एवं महत्तरं पुण्यं त्रिरत्नभजनाद् भवम् ।
विज्ञायादौ त्रिरत्नानि भजस्व श्रद्धया स्मरन्[36] ॥ ११८ ॥

Even greater merit will be amassed through the praise and worship of the *tri-ratna*. With this understanding, you all must devotedly pray, worship and remember the *tri-ratna*.

---

35 विरचय्य इति कपाठः ।

36 खगाम् इति खपाठः ।

ततः सर्वेषु तीर्थेषु स्नात्वा शुद्धेन्द्रियाशयः।
त्रिरत्नशरणं गत्वा भजस्व पोषधं व्रतम्॥ ११९॥

In this way, bathe in all the sacred places to purify your organs and in the refuge of the *tri-ratna*, practise the excellent vow.

ततः सर्वानिमान् देवान् धर्मधातुमुखान् सदा।
यथाविधि[37] समाराद्य संभजस्व समर्चयन्॥ १२०॥

Ritually worship, praise and devote yourself to the gods, among whom the Dharmadhātu is supreme.

लोकानपि तथा सर्वान् बोधयित्वा प्रयत्नतः।
सर्वेष्वेतेषु यत्नेन स्नापयित्वा यथाविधि॥ १२१॥

Teach your subjects this and send them to the pilgrimages to bathe ritually.

त्रिरत्नशरणे स्थाप्य संबोधिज्ञानसाधनम्।
भद्रश्रीसद्‌गुणाधारं चारय पोषधं व्रतम्[38]॥ १२२॥

Establish them all into the refuge of the *tri-ratna*, provide them the instrument for *sambodhi.* Influence them to cultivate good virtues and gentleness and ask them to practise the good *vrata*.

एतेषामपि देवानां कारयित्वा सदार्चनम्।
बोधिमार्गे प्रतिष्ठाप्य यत्नतःपालयञ्छुभे॥ १२३॥

Make them worship to please the gods. Establish them into the path of *bodhi* and motivate them for good.

एवं कृत्वा महत्पुण्यं प्राप्य श्रीसद्‌गुणाश्रयः।
बोधिसत्त्वो महासत्त्वो महाभिज्ञो भवेद् धुवम्॥ १२४॥

Having done this, great merit will be generated, along with the prosperity of virtues. You would become a *bodhisattva, mahāsattva* and a wise scholar.

---

37 यथेच्छयै इति खपाठः।

38 औषधं वृति इति खपाठः।

ततः संबोधिसंभारं पूरयित्वा यथाक्रमम् ।
अर्हन् बोधिं समासाद्य संबुद्धपदमाप्नुयाः ॥ १२५ ॥

Having crossed the steps of *bodhi*, you would attain *arhant* position, acquire *bodhi* and finally become Buddha."

इति शान्तश्रिया शास्ता समादिष्टं निशम्य सः ।
नृपस्तथेति विज्ञाप्य कर्तुमेवं समैच्छत ॥ १२६ ॥

When the Śāntaśrī commanded the king, he promised to obey and abide by his instructions.

ततः स नृपतिः सर्वान् मन्त्रिणः सचिवाञ्जनान् ।
पौरान्[39]महाजनाँश्चापि समामन्त्र्यैवमादिशत् ॥ १२७ ॥

The king then gathered his courtiers, secretaries, townsfolk and merchants to instruct them accordingly.

भो मन्त्रिणो जनाः सर्वेऽमात्याःपौरा महाजनाः ।
आचार्येण यथादिष्टं तथा चरितुमर्हथ ॥ १२८ ॥

"Ministers, priests, citizens and merchants, you all must act on the instructions of the *guru*.

अहमपि तथा धृत्वा सर्वदा भद्रकारणम्[40] ।
त्रिरत्नशरणं कृत्वा व्रतं चरितुमुत्सहे ॥ १२९ ॥

I shall also abide and work for a good cause. I shall take refuge of the *tri-ratna* and practise the vows joyously."

इत्यादिष्टं नरेन्द्रेण श्रुत्वा ते मन्त्रिणो जनाः ।
पौरा महाजनाः सर्वे तथेति प्रतिशुश्रुवुः ॥ १३० ॥

Upon hearing the king's instructions, the ministers, townsfolk, priests and merchants present there all pledged to obey.

ततः स नृपतिः सर्वैः सपुरोहितमन्त्रिभिः ।
अमात्यैः सचिवैः पौरैर्महाजनैः समन्वितः ॥ १३१ ॥

---

39 पुरवास्या इति गपाठः ।

40 भद्रकल्पका इति गपाठः ।

सर्वेष्वेतेषु तीर्थेषु स्नात्वा यथाविधि क्रमात् ।
शुद्धशीलः[41] समाधाय प्राचरत् पोषधं व्रतम् ॥ १३२ ॥

The king, along with the gathered priests, ministers, secretaries, merchants and villagers, proceeded to the pilgrimages and ritually bathed, purified conduct and practised vows.

ततस्ते विमलात्मानःत्रिरत्नशरणं गताः ।
धर्मधातुं समाराध्य समभ्यर्च्याभजन्मुदा ॥ १३३ ॥

Then their souls became purified; they went to the refuge of the *tri-ratna*; and they were pleased to worship and serve the Dharmadhātu.

तथा वायुपुरे वायुदेवतां च यथाविधि ।
अग्निपुरेऽग्निदेवं च नागपुरे फणेश्वरम् ॥ १३४ ॥

They went to the Vāyupura (shrine of the Wind God) to ritually worship him and then proceeded to the Agnipura (shrine of Fire God) and Nāgapura (shrine of the Serpent God).

वसुपुरे वसुन्धरां सद्धर्मश्रीगुणप्रदाम् ।
शान्तपुरे महेशानं सम्वरं सगणं क्रमात् ॥ १३५ ॥

They worshipped at the Vasupura (shrine of the Earth Goddess) that provided the good *dharma*, prosperity and virtue. Finally, they went to the Śāntapura (shrine of the Saṁbara and his attendants).

यथाविधि समभ्यर्च्य श्रद्धया समुपाश्रितः ।
तथा मञ्जुश्रियश्चैत्यं समभ्यर्च्याभजन् तदा ॥ १३६ ॥

Having ritually worshipped and prayed to everyone devotedly, the company went to the Mañjuśrī *caitya* to worship and serve him.

तथाष्टौ वीतरागांश्च श्रीदेवीं च खगाननाम्[42] ।
यथाविधि समाराध्य समभ्यर्च्याभजन् तदा ॥ १३७ ॥

They went to ritually worship the eight *vītarāga*s and then the Great Goddess Khagānanā.

---

41 युद्धशिल इति खपाठः ।

42 महोत्तमी इति गपाठः ।

तथा सर्वेऽपि लोकास्ते नृपवृत्तानुचारिणः ।
स्नात्वा सर्वेषु तीर्थेषु शुद्धशीलाः समादरात् ॥ १३८ ॥

The men of the world followed the king by bathing at every pilgrimage site and purifying their conduct respectfully.

त्रिरत्नशरणं कृत्वा चरन्तःपोषधं व्रतम् ।
धर्मधातुमुखान् सर्वान् देवाँश्चाभ्यर्च्य प्राभजन् ॥ १३९ ॥

They practised their good *vrata* at the refuge of the *tri-ratna*. Then they praised and served the gods along with the Dharmadhātu.

तदैतत्पुण्यभावेन सर्वत्र शुभमाचरत् ।
ततः सर्वं महोत्पातं क्रमेण प्रशमं ययौ ॥ १४० ॥

Due to the influence of the merit received, auspiciousness spread everywhere and chaos was slowly pacified.

तदा सर्वेऽपि ते लोका नीरोगाःपुष्टितेन्द्रियाः[43] ।
महानन्दं सुखं प्राप्य बभूवुर्धर्मलालसाः ॥ १४१ ॥

The citizens were freed from diseases, their organs became vigorous. They experienced divine ecstasy and happiness, and strived for *dharma*.

तद् दृष्ट्वा स नृपो राजा प्रत्यक्षं धर्मसत्फलम् ।
अहो सद्धर्ममाहात्म्यमित्युक्त्वा नन्दितोऽचरत् ॥ १४२ ॥

Seeing this, the king directly witnessed the influence and rewards of *dharma*. He was pleased at this and thus lauded the greatness of the good *dharma*.

किन्तु सुवृष्टिरेवात्र न बभूव कथंचन ।
तद् दृष्ट्वा स नृपश्चासीद् दुर्भिक्षशंकिताशयः ॥ १४३ ॥

However, seeing that there was still no rainfall, the king anticipated drought and famine.

---

43 पुरुषेन्द्रिया इति गपाठः ।

ततः स करुणाविष्टहृदयःस नृपःपुनः।
शान्तश्रियं तमाचार्यं नत्वैवं प्राह साञ्जलिः ॥ १४४ ॥

Overcome with compassion in his heart, the king again went to the Śāntaśrī Bhikkhu and addressed him with hands joined in devotion.

आचार्य कृपया तेऽत्र चरते शुभताधुना।
सर्वदापि महोत्पातं संशाम्यत समन्ततः ॥ १४५ ॥

"Ācārya, I have followed your benevolent advice, due to which chaos has been solved.

सुवृष्टिरेव नाद्यापि प्रवर्त्तते कथंचन।
सुवृष्टिकरणोपायं तत् समादेष्टुमर्हति ॥ १४६ ॥

However, the kingdom has not seen adequate rainfall. Pray teach me the method to bring good rainfall."

इति संप्रार्थितं राज्ञा श्रुत्वाचार्यः स सन्मतिः[44]।
नृपतिं तं महासत्त्वं संपश्यन्नेवमब्रवीत् ॥ १४७ ॥

Upon hearing the prayer of the king, the wise *bhikkhu* looked at the king and answered.

साधु राजञ्छृणुष्वात्र सदा सुभिक्षकारणम्।
सुवृष्टिकरणोपायमुपदेक्ष्यापि सांप्रतम् ॥ १४८ ॥

"King, listen carefully, I shall tell you the way to achieve good rainfall and plenty of reap.

लिखित्वा मण्डलं नागराजानां तद्यथाविधि।
तत्र नागाधिपान् सर्वानावाह्याराधय स्वयम् ॥ १४९ ॥

First, create a *maṇḍala*; then draw the images of the kings of serpents to summon them within.

तदत्र त्वं[45]महावीरो भवस्वोत्तरसाधकः।
यथा मयोपदिष्टानि तथा सर्वाणि साधय ॥ १५० ॥

44 ऋद्धिका इति खपाठः।

45 त्वञ्चात्र इति कपाठः।

O king! heed my words carefully and act upon them to perform rigorous *sādhanā* so as to achieve good rainfall."

> इत्याचार्यसमादिष्टं श्रुत्वा स नृपतिर्मुदा ।
> तथेति प्रतिविज्ञाप्य तथा भवितुमैच्छत ॥ १५१ ॥

Upon hearing the instructions of the *ācārya*, the king was gladdened and thus promised to follow them.

> ततः स वज्रधृग् विद्वान् नागपुरं यथाविधि ।
> लिखित्वा मण्डलं रम्यं प्रतिष्ठाप्य समर्चयत् ॥ १५२ ॥

The king then drew a *maṇḍala* of the abode of the serpents (Nāgapura) to summon the serpent lords and thus he commenced the worship.

> तत्र नागाधिपान् सर्वानाचार्यः स यथाक्रमम् ।
> समाराध्य समावाह्य पूजयितुं समालभत्[46] ॥ १५३ ॥

As for the instructions of the *ācārya*, the king summoned all the lords of serpents by performing rituals and worship.

> तत्र नागाधिपाः सर्वे समागत्य यथाक्रमम् ।
> स्वस्वासनं समाश्रित्य संतस्थिरे प्रसादिताः ॥ १५४ ॥

The serpent lords materialized and sat at their respective seats that had been laid out and were pleased.

> कर्कोटकोऽहिराडेक एव न लज्जयागतः ।
> तत्समीक्ष्य स शान्तश्रीर्महाचार्यो महर्द्धिमान्[47] ॥ १५५ ॥

However, the great serpent Karkoṭa did not appear, due to embarrassment. The wise Śāntaśrī assessed this situation.

> नृपतिं तं महावीरं महासत्त्वं महर्द्धिकम् ।
> महाभिज्ञं[48] समालोक्य समामन्त्र्यैवमादिशत् ॥ १५६ ॥

Addressing the courageous, prosperous, learned and great king, the *bhikkhu* said:

---

46 समाकृतम् इति खपाठः ।

47 महत्कृत इति घपाठः ।

48 महाकरम् इति कपाठः ।

राजन् नागाधिपाः सर्वे समागता इहाधुना ।
एकःकर्कोटको नागराज एवेह नागतः ॥ १५७ ॥

"King, the serpent lords all answered your summon and arrived. One serpent lord named Karkoṭaka, however, did not come.

विरूपोऽहं कथं नागराजमहासभासने ।
गत्वा तिष्ठेयमित्येवं ध्यात्वा नायाति लज्जया ॥ १५८ ॥

'How can I attend the glorious assembly with my hideous appearance?' he must have thought in shame.

अतस्तं सहसा राजन् गत्वा तत्र महाह्रदे ।
कर्कोटकं तमामन्त्र्य संप्रार्थ्येह समानय[49] ॥ १५९ ॥

Therefore, dear King, go to the great lake where the Karkoṭaka resides, invite him with prayers, and return together.

यदि संप्रार्थ्यमानोऽपि नागच्छेदिह सोऽहिराट् ।
तदा बलेन धृत्वापि सर्वथा तं समानय ॥ १६० ॥

In case the serpent does not comply, despite your prayers, you must use force to capture and bring him here."

इत्याचार्यसमादिष्टं श्रुत्वा स नृपतिः सुधीः ।
शान्तश्रियं तमाचार्यं पश्यन्नेवं न्यवेदयत् ॥ १६१ ॥

Upon hearing the instructions of the Śāntaśrī, the king looked at him and prayed:

आचार्य! कथमेकोऽहं तत्र गाढमहाह्रदे ।
गत्वा बलेन नागेन्द्रं धृत्वा नेतुं प्रशक्नुयाम् ॥ १६२ ॥

'Teacher, how would I go to the great lake alone and single-handedly take on and capture the mighty serpent and bring him back?'

इति निवेद्य तं राजा श्रुत्वाचार्यः स मन्त्रवित् ।
नृपतिं तं महावीरं सम्पश्यन्नेवमब्रवीत् ॥ १६३ ॥

When he said so, the wise *ācārya* looked at the valiant king and said:

---

49 सुसंस्कार इति खपाठः ।

हरिदश्वं समारुह्य पुष्पं मन्मन्त्रशोधितम् ।
धृत्वा व्रज प्रशक्नोषि मम मन्त्रानुभावतः ॥ १६४ ॥

'Mount a strong and fleet-footed horse and carry my enchanted flower as you go; with the influence of my enchantment, you shall be able to carry out your task.

दुर्वाकाण्डमिदं[50]पुष्पं तत्रादौ क्षिप मां स्मरन् ।
भ्रमन् यत्र चरेत् पुष्पं तद् यथानुसरन् व्रज ॥ १६५ ॥

This enchanted flower contains a strand of sacred grass; take it with you and cast it into the great lake. When it floats, follow its track on your horse.' "

इत्युपदेश्य दुर्वाकं काण्डं मन्त्राभिशोधितम् ।
पुष्पं दत्वा नरेन्द्राय पुनरेवमुपादिशत् ॥ १६६ ॥

Having said this, the *bhikkhu* gave the flower with a strand of sacred grass *dūrvā*, before he continued his instruction.

गत्वैवं नृपते तत्र नागपुरे समेत्य तम् ।
कर्कोटकं समामन्त्र्य मद्गिरैवं निवेदय ॥ १६७ ॥

"When you reach the abode of the Karkoṭa, call upon him with these words:

भो कर्कोटक नागेन्द्र यदर्थमहमिहागतः ।
तद् भवानपि[51]जानीयात् तथापि वक्ष्यते मया ॥ १६८ ॥

"O Karkoṭa! Lord of serpents, you are aware of the reason for my arrival. Nevertheless, I beseech you again.

गोशृङ्गेस्ति महाचार्यः शान्तश्रीर्वज्रभृत् कृती ।
दुर्भिक्षशमनं कर्त्तुं सुवृष्टिचारणे सदा ॥ १६९ ॥

On the mount Go-śṛṅgā lives the wise teacher Śāntaśrī who wields the *vajra*. He is able to remove the drought and famine and bring adequate rainfall.

---

50 दुर्वेपुष्पम् इति गपाठः ।

51 त्वमेवगमनम् इति कपाठः ।

तत्र नागपुरे सर्वान् नागाधिपान् यथाविधि ।
समाराध्य समावाह्य पूजयितुं समारभत् ॥ १७० ॥

For that purpose, I created a shrine for the serpent lords and summoned them to commence the ritual of worshipping them in this Nāgapura.

सर्वे नागाधिपास्तत्र वरुणाद्याः समागताः ।
त्वमेव नागतःकस्मात् सहसागन्तुमर्हसि ॥ १७१ ॥

Varuṇa and all other serpent lords arrived but you. Why? I have come to escort you."

एवं संप्रार्थ्यमानोऽपि नागच्छेत् सोऽहिराड् यदि ।
बलेनापि समाकृष्य सहसानीयतां त्वया ॥ १७२ ॥

Even then if the serpent refuses to come, you must capture him and bring him here by force."

इति शान्तश्रिया शास्ता समादिष्य समादरात् ।
प्रेषितोऽहं[52]तदर्थेऽत्र तत् समागन्तुमर्हति ॥ १७३ ॥

The Śāntaśrī Bhikkhu instructed the king to reiterate to the serpent that he had been sent by the *bhikkhu* and therefore must come along.

इत्यादिश्य स आचार्यः पुष्पं मन्त्राभिशोधितम् ।
दत्वा तं नृपतिं वीरं प्रैषयत् तत्र सत्वरम् ॥ १७४ ॥

Having said this, the *bhikkhu* gave him the enchanted flower and sent the brave king on his mission.

इत्याचार्यसमादिष्टं निशम्य स महामतिः ।
दुर्वाकुण्डं समादाय तथेत्युक्त्वा ततोऽचरत् ॥ १७५ ॥

Having received the instructions from the *bhikkhu*, the great king took the flower with the grass strand and left for the lake.

ततः स नृपतिर्वीरः शास्तुराज्ञां शिरोवहन् ।
हरिदश्वं समारुह्य संचरन्तद् ह्रदं ययौ[53] ॥ १७६ ॥

---

52 प्रेषयित्वेह इति गपाठः ।

53 गृहं ययौ इति खपाठः ।

Heeding the *guru*'s commands, the valiant king mounted a strong horse and rode it to the lake.

तत्र तीरं समासाद्य पश्यन् नृपः स तं ह्रदम् ।
नत्वा चार्यमनुस्मृत्वा दुर्वाकाण्डं जलेऽक्षिपत् ॥ १७७ ॥

As he arrived at the bank, the king looked at the lake and remembering the *guru*'s words, cast the flower and the strand of grass into the water.

तत्प्रक्षिप्तं जलेऽगाढे भ्रमन् नागपुरेऽचरत् ।
राजाप्यश्वं समारुह्य तत्पुष्पानुसरन् ययौ ॥ १७८ ॥

The flower started floating at the surface of the deep waters. The king also followed its path on his horse.

एवं नागपुरे गत्वा नृपतिः स विलोकयन् ।
कर्कोटकं[54]महीन्द्रं तं सहसा समुपाचरत् ॥ १७९ ॥

When he reached far into the abode of the serpents, the king saw the ferocious serpent-lord Karkoṭa lying there.

तत्र समेत्य स वीरः कर्कोटकमहीश्वरम् ।
यथाचार्येण संदिष्टं तथा सर्वं न्यवेदयत् ॥ १८० ॥

Having reached the ferocious Karkoṭa, the valiant king implored the serpent as his *guru* had taught him.

तत् सन्निवेदितं सर्वं श्रुत्वा नागाधिपोऽपि सः ।
किञ्चिदप्युत्तरं नैव ददौ तस्मै महीभुजे ॥ १८१ ॥

Despite hearing the pleas and prayers of the king, the Lord of serpents gave no response.

ततः स नृपतिश्चैव निवेद्य तं महीश्वरम् ।
संपश्यन् समुपामन्त्र्य प्रार्थयेदेवमादरात् ॥ १८२ ॥

Having pleaded to the serpent, the king invited him again and prayed to him so.

54 कर्कोदके इति खपाठः ।

नागेन्द्रोऽत्र प्रसीद त्वं शास्तुराज्ञां शिरोवहन्[55] ।
त्वदामन्त्रण एवाहं प्रागतस्तत् समाव्रज ॥ १८३ ॥

"Be pleased, O serpent Lord! for I have come heeding the instructions of my ruler to invite and bring you with me."

इति संप्रार्थ्यमानोऽपि राज्ञा स भुजगाधिपः ।
किञ्चित्प्रत्युत्तरं नैव ददौ तस्मै महीभुजे ॥ १८४ ॥

Even when he pleaded so, the king of serpents still gave no response whatsoever.

ततोऽसौ नृपतिर्वीरः शास्त्रादिष्टं यथा तथा ।
सर्वं निवेद्य तस्याग्रे पुनरेवमभाषत ॥ १८५ ॥

Then the valiant king pleaded again as his *guru* had instructed them and then proceeded to say:

नागेन्द्र नापराधं[56] मे यत्त्वया न श्रुतं वचः ।
तन्मे शास्त्रा यथादिष्टं तथा नूनं चरेय हि ॥ १८६ ॥

"O serpent Lord! it is not my transgression that I am about to act on my *guru*'s instructions.

इत्युक्तेऽपि नरेन्द्रेण कर्कोटकोऽहि योऽपि सः ।
किञ्चिदप्युत्तरं नैव ददौ राज्ञे महीभृते ॥ १८७ ॥

And yet, the Karkoṭa serpent did not give the king any reply.

ततः स नृपतिवीरः शास्तुराज्ञां शिरोवहन् ।
धृत्वा तमहिमाकृष्य गरुत्मानिव प्राचरत् ॥ १८८ ॥

Then the valiant king, remembering his *guru*'s instructions, captured the serpent with force, just as a falcon would capture a snake.

ततो हयात् समानीतो गुणकामदेवेन सः ।
आनीतो येन मार्गेण वशिकाचल उच्यते ॥ १८९ ॥

---

55 स्वयं वहे इति गपाठः ।

56 नराधिप इति कपाठः ।

The King Guṇakāmadevā then brought the serpent back. The path he travelled while doing so has been named the Vaśikācala.

एवं धृत्वा समाकृष्य स वीरस्तं महीश्वरम्।
तदा नागपुरे[57]नीत्वा शास्तुरग्रे समाचरत्॥ १९० ॥

Pulling the serpent with force to the Nāgapura, the king put him before his *ācārya* and said:

आचार्य भवदादेशात् तथा कर्कोटकोऽहिराट्।
धृत्वाकृष्य मयानीतस्तं समीक्ष्य प्रसीदतु॥ १९१ ॥

"Guru, on your instructions, I have captured and brought the serpentine king Karkoṭa before you. Be pleased!"

इति निवेदितं राज्ञा श्रुत्वाचार्यः समादितः[58]।
नृपतिं तं महावीरं सम्पश्यन्नेवमादिशत्॥ १९२ ॥

Upon hearing the words of the king, the *bhikkhu* who was pleased looked at the king and said:

साधु राजन्! महावीर! यदानीतस्त्वयाहिराट्।
तदेनमासने नीत्वा संस्थापय यथाक्रमम्॥ १९३ ॥

"Valiant king, you have done a good job on bringing the great serpent here. Now place him on his seat ritually."

इत्याचार्यसमादिष्टं श्रुत्वा स नृपतिस्तथा।
नागराजं तमामन्त्र्य स्वासने संन्यवेशयत्॥ १९४ ॥

Having heard the *guru's* instructions, the king invited the Serpent Lord to take the seat designated for him.

तं दृष्ट्वा स्वासनासीनमाचार्यः स यथाविधि।
नागेन्द्रान् तान् समावाह्य समाराध्य समर्चयत्॥ १९५ ॥

Seeing this, the *ācārya* called forth the assembled Serpent Lords to greet and worship them.

57 कनकपुरे इति कपाठः।

58 स्वयेच्छया इति खपाठः।

ततः सवज्रधृग् विद्वान् आचार्यः स महीपतेः ।
सर्वान् नागाधिपान् स्तुत्वा प्रार्थयच्चैवमादरात् ॥ १९६ ॥

भो भवन्तो महानागराजाः सर्वे मयाग्रतः ।
समाराध्य समावाह्य यथाविधि समर्चिताः ॥ १९७ ॥

The *vajra*-wielding *ācārya*, along with the king, praised, prayed and respected the serpents and said, "King of serpents, I have summoned and ritually worshipped you.

तन्मे सदा प्रसीदन्तु दातुमर्हन्ति वाञ्छितम् ।
सर्वलोकहितायैव आराधयामि नान्यथा ॥ १९८ ॥

Be pleased and grant me my wish, for I pray to you for the sake of the whole world and no other cause.

यदत्र पापसंचाराद् दुर्भिक्षं वर्ततेऽधुना ।
तेन सर्वेऽपिदुःखार्ता लोकाश्चरन्ति पातकम् ॥ १९९ ॥

The crimes in the world led to drought and famine. The men in the world suffered tremendous misery and again resorted to sinning.

तद्दुर्भिक्षाभिशान्त्यर्थं सुभिक्षकरणं सदा ।
सुवृष्टिचरणोपायं करोमीदं जगद्धिते ॥ २०० ॥

I strive for the welfare of the world by the satiation of famine and achievement of plenty and adequate rainfall.

ते भवन्तोऽत्र सर्वेऽपि सर्वसत्त्वाभिरक्षणे ।
चारयितुं समर्हन्ति सुवृष्टिमत्र सर्वदा ॥ २०१ ॥

Therefore, for the sake of sentient beings, I request you to grant adequate rainfall to the world."

इति संप्रार्थितं तेन शान्तश्रिया निशम्य[59]तत् ।
सर्वे नागाधिपास्तस्य तथेति प्रतिशुश्रुवुः ॥ २०२ ॥

When the Śāntaśrī prayed to the serpent lords thus, all of them pledged to comply.

---

59 नियम्यते इति कपाठः ।

तैस्तथेति प्रतिज्ञातं नागराजैर्निशम्य सः ।
शान्तश्रीर्नागराजान् तान् प्रार्थयदेवमादरात् ॥ २०३ ॥

Upon hearing the pledge of the serpent lords, the Śāntaśrī respectfully said to them:

भवन्तो मे प्रसीदन्तु यदहं प्रार्थये पुनः ।
सर्वसत्त्वहितायैव दातुमर्हन्ति वाञ्छितम् ॥ २०४ ॥

"Pray be pleased, my lords, I pray to you, grant us what we seek, for the sake of sentient beings."

इति संप्रार्थिते तेन शान्तश्रिया निशम्यते ।
सर्वनागाधिपाः तस्मै तथेति प्रतिशुश्रुवुः ॥ २०५ ॥

When they heard the Śāntaśrī Bhikkhu pray so, the serpent lords again agreed to grant rainfall.

सर्वैर्नागाधिपैस्तैस्तैःप्रतिज्ञातं निशम्य सः ।
आचार्यस्तानहीन्द्राँश्च प्रार्थयेदेवमादरात् ॥ २०६ ॥

After hearing the serpents' agreement, the *ācārya* again respectfully prayed to them and said:

भवन्तःश्रूयतां वाक्यं यन् मया प्राथ्यर्ते पुनः ।
तद्भवद्भिः प्रतिज्ञातं संध्यातव्यं तथा सदा ॥ २०७ ॥

"Listen to me, my lords, I pray to you once again. I ask you to fulfil what you have pledged.

यदात्र पापसंचाराद् दुर्वृष्टिश्चाभवद् ध्रुवम् ।
तदा सुवृष्टिसंसिद्धिसाधनं तत् प्रणीयताम् ॥ २०८ ॥

Due to the wide spread of crimes, famine and drought have taken place. Thus, pray grant us the instrument for adequate rainfall.

तद्यथा भवतां पट्टे लिखित्वा मण्डलं[60]शुभम् ।
यथाविधि प्रतिष्ठाप्य स्थापयितुं समुत्सहे ॥ २०९ ॥

60 सुपटं तदा इति गपाठः ।

दुर्वृष्टिः स्याद्यदाप्यत्र तदेवं पट्टमण्डलम् ।
प्रसार्य विधिनाराध्य समावाह्य समर्चयेत् ॥ २१० ॥

एवं प्रसार्य पट्टेस्मिन् संपूजिते यथाविधि ।
सुवृष्टिरत्र युष्माभिः संभर्तव्या जगद्धिते ॥ २११ ॥

Hence, at the event of draught and famine, if your images are established in a *mandala* drawn on cloth and are ritually worshipped, pray grant good rainfall for the sake of the world."

इति संप्रार्थिते तेन शान्तश्रिया निशम्यते ।
सर्वनागाधिपास्तस्मै तथेति प्रतिशुश्रुवुः ॥ २१२ ॥

Upon hearing the prayers of the Śāntaśrī, the serpents all agreed to comply.

ततः स मन्त्रवित् प्राज्ञः सर्वनागाधिपाज्ञया ।
लिखित्वा मण्डलं पट्टे प्रतिष्ठाप्य यथाविधि ॥ २१३ ॥

Then the wise Śāntaśrī, with the permission of the serpents, drew a *mandala* on cloth and ritually established them onto it.

पश्चात्[61]कालेऽत्र दुर्वृष्टिर्वृत्ते सुवृष्टिसाधने ।
नागपुरेऽत्र संस्थाप्य निर्दग्धं संप्रगोपितम् ॥ २१४ ॥

For the future when there will be drought and famine, he secretly preserved the *maṇḍala* in the Nāgapura, so it may be an instrument to bring rainfall and plenty.

ततो वज्री स आचार्यः सर्वान् तान् भुजगाधिपान् ।
संप्रार्थ्य विनयं कृत्वा विससर्ज विनोदयन् ॥ २१५ ॥

Then the *vajra*-wielding *ācārya,* having worshipped and honoured the serpent lords, sent them off pleased.

ततः सर्वेऽपि ते नागराजाः स्वस्वालयं गताः ।
मेघमालां समुत्थाप्य सर्वज्ञः समवर्षयन् ॥ २१६ ॥

When the serpents returned to their respective abodes, clouds gathered in the sky and showered rain upon earth.

---

61 ततोऽपि इति कपाठः ।

तदा सुवृष्टिसंचाराद् दुर्भिक्षं विलयं ययौ ।
सुभिक्षमंगलोत्साहं प्रावर्तत समन्ततः ॥ २१७ ॥

Due to the rainfall, drought and famine were removed. Plenty, auspiciousness and celebration spread all around.

तदा सर्वेऽपि लोकास्ते महानन्दप्रमोदिताः ।
त्रिरत्नभजनं कृत्वा प्राचरन्त सदा शुभे ॥ २१८ ॥

All the beings of the world were ecstatic. They started praising the *tri-ratna* and practising good conduct.

ततः स नृपती राजा दृष्टसत्यः प्रसादितः ।
शान्तिश्रियं तमाचार्यं समभ्यर्च्य यथाविधि ॥ २१९ ॥

Having seen the truth, the king was pleased. He then ritually worshipped his Ācārya Śāntaśrī.

नत्वाष्टांङ्गैः प्रसान्नात्मा कृत्वा प्रदक्षिणानि च ।
कृताञ्जलिपुटः पश्यन् प्रार्थयच्चैवमादरात् ॥ २२० ॥

He saluted the *bhikkhu* with eight bodily positions and pleased him with *pradakṣiṇā*. With hands joined in reverence, he then addressed the *bhikkhu*.

भो भगवन् महाचार्य भवद्धर्मानुभावतः ।
सर्वोत्पातं शमीभूतं सुवृष्टिः संप्रवर्तते ॥ २२१ ॥

"O Lord! Great Teacher! due to your benevolence, chaos has been removed and good rainfall has started.

तदत्र सर्वदा नूनं निरुत्पातं समन्ततः ।
धर्मश्रीमंगलोत्साहं भवेदेव निरन्तरम् ॥ २२२ ॥

Chaos has been removed from all directions; *dharma*, auspiciousness, glory and celebration are constant.

एवं सदा कृपा दृष्ट्या संपश्यन् विषमे मम ।
निरुत्पातं[62]शुभोत्साहं कर्तुमर्हति सर्वथा ॥ २२३ ॥

---

[62] कदोत्पातम् इति खपाठः ।

May your benevolent sight always be upon me; and may there never be mayhem, but always celebration.

साम्प्रतं सफलं जन्म संसारजीवितं च मे।
यल्लोकाश्च सुखीभूताः संचरन्ते सदा शुभे॥ २२४॥

The purpose of my birth has been fulfilled, for the people are happily engaged in good activities.

तदहं साम्प्रतं शास्तर्भवदाज्ञां शिरोवहन्।
स्वराज्याश्रममाश्रित्य चरेयं पालयञ्जगत्॥ २२५॥

Therefore, O Guru! heeding your words, I shall take shelter in the hermitage that is my kingdom and dwell there protecting my subjects.

तन्मेऽनुग्रहमाधाय कृपया संप्रसादितः।
संबोधिसाधने चित्तं सुस्थितिं कर्तुमर्हति॥ २२६॥

Grace me your kindness and benevolence, and establish my mind into the instrument of *sambodhi*."

इति विज्ञाप्य भूपालस्तस्य शास्तुःपदाम्बुजे।
नत्वानुज्ञां समासाद्य महोत्साहैः पुरं ययौ॥ २२७॥

Having said this, the king laid his head on the *bhikkhu*'s feet and having received permission to depart, left happily.

तत्र स नृप आश्रित्य समन्त्रिसचिवो मुदा।
बोधिचर्याव्रतं धृत्वा तस्थौ कुर्वन् सदा शुभम्॥ २२८॥

Along with his ministers and secretaries, the king reached his kingdom and practised the *bodhicaryā* and good deeds.

॥ इति श्रीस्वयंभूचैत्याश्रमसाधनसुवृष्टिचारणो नामाष्टमोऽध्यायः समाप्तः॥

Thus ends the eighth chapter of the *Svayambhū Purāṇa*
named "Instrument for Good Rainfall"

अथ नवमोऽध्यायः
(Navama Adhyāya)

The Glory of the Qualities of Śāntikara

अथ मैत्रेय आलोक्य समुत्थाय कृताञ्जलिः ॥
भगवन्तं तमानम्य प्रार्थयच्चैवमादरात् ॥ १ ॥

Then Maitreya stood from his seat, joined his hands in salutation to the Lord Buddha, and asked:

कदा शान्तिकरो[1]नाम तस्याभवत् कथं पुनः ।
तद्धेतुं श्रोतुमिच्छामि समुपादेष्टुमर्हति ॥ २ ॥

"My Lord, how did the name Śāntikara come to be? I wish to hear the story. Pray tell."

इति संप्रार्थिते तेन मैत्रेयेण स सर्ववित्[2] ।
भगवान् तं महासत्त्वं सम्पश्यन्नेवमादिशत् ॥ ३ ॥

When he prayed to the Lord so, the omniscient Buddha looked at the Mahāsattva Maitreya and said:

शृणु मैत्रेय वक्ष्यामि शान्तश्रियो महद्‌गुणान् ।
सद्धर्मसाधनोत्साहान् भद्रश्रीसद्‌गुणार्थदान् ॥ ४ ॥

"Maitreya, listen, I shall tell you of the virtues of Śāntaśrī, that are the instruments for the joyful practise of the good *dharma* and the acquisition of gentleness, prosperity and good qualities.

---

1 शान्तिकृतो इति खपाठः ।

2 सर्वज्ञते इति घपाठः ।

योऽसौ राजा महासत्त्वः सद्धर्मगुणलालसः ।
त्यक्त्वा कामसुखं राज्यं तीर्थयात्रामुपाचरत् ॥ ५ ॥

The once king, who was inspired by the qualities of the good *dharma*, renounced his kingdom and left his pleasures to venture on a pilgrim's journey.

स सर्वेष्वपि तीर्थेषु स्नात्वा दानं विधाय[3] च ।
त्रिसमाधिं समाधाय संचरन् पोषधं व्रतम् ॥ ६ ॥

He bathed and ritually donated at every pilgrimage; he attained the three concentrations (*tri-samādhi*) and practised good vow.

एवं सर्वेषु पीठेषु भ्रमन् सद्धर्ममानसः ।
योगचर्याव्रतं धृत्वा प्रचचार समाहितः[4] ॥ ७ ॥

With his mind in the true *dharma*, he wandered every shrine, and practised and preached *yoga*.

पुण्यक्षेत्रेषु सर्वेषु भ्रमन्नेवमिहागतः ।
दृष्ट्वैमं मण्डलं रम्यं विस्मितं समुपाययौ ॥ ८ ॥

He wandered from one holy place to another, and seeing its magnificence, arrived at the *maṇḍala* (the Nepal Valley, present-day Kathmandu).

अत्रैमं दूरतो दृष्ट्वा धर्मधातुं[5] जिनालयम् ।
मुदाष्टाङ्गैः प्रणम्याशु संद्रष्टुं समुपाययौ ॥ ९ ॥

He saw the Dharmadhātu Jinālaya from afar, saluted it with eight bodily positions, and then came closer to behold the auspicious sight.

समेत्य स महासत्त्वो ज्योतिरूपं जिनालयम् ।
धर्मधातुमिमं दृष्ट्वा प्रणम्य समुपाश्रयत् ॥ १० ॥

---

[3] कृत्वेति इति खपाठः ।

[4] महाकृते इति कपाठः ।

[5] खगेश्वरम् इति गपाठः ।

Upon arrival, he bowed and paid homage to the great Dharmadhātu Jinālaya that existed in the form of light.

ततः समुदितो राजा नेपालेऽत्र मनोरमे ।
सर्वत्रापि च संद्रष्टुं प्रचचार विलोकयन् ॥ ११ ॥

Pleased by the beauty of Nepal, he travelled around the country preaching the *dharma.*

तेषु सर्वेषु तीर्थेषु स्नात्वा दत्वा यथेप्सितम् ।
यथाविधि समाधाय व्रतं चचार योगतः ॥ १२ ॥

Performing ritualistic ablution and donating charitably, he began to live in practise of good conduct and vows.

ततोऽष्टौ वीतरागाँश्च दृष्ट्वा स संप्रमोदितः ।
यथाविधि[6] समाराध्य समभ्यर्च्य सदाभजत् ॥ १३ ॥

The sight of the eight *vītarāga*s gave him great joy, so he worshipped, praised and served them ritually.

ततश्चासौ महादेवीं खगाननां महेश्वरीम् ।
यथाविधि समाराध्य समभ्यर्च्याभजन्मुदा ॥ १४ ॥

He then ritually served and worshipped the Great Goddess Khagānanā, and paid homage to her.

ततो मञ्जुश्रियश्चैत्यं समीक्ष्य तं प्रमोदितः
यथाविधि समभ्यर्च्य प्राभजत् समुपस्थितः ॥ १५ ॥

He proceeded to the shrine of Mañjuśrī and procedurally worshipped and praised him devotedly.

ततश्चैतत्महत्पुण्यैः शान्तिश्रीशुभितेन्द्रियः[7] ।
प्रव्रज्या-संवरं धृत्वा ब्रह्मचारी बभूव सः ॥ १६ ॥

Through the influence of the merit amassed in doing so, he acquired tranquillity; his organs became auspicious. Upholding his ordinance, he practised celibacy.

---

[6] सुष्ठु विद्ये इति खपाठः ।

[7] शुभकामता इति घपाठः ।

यत्तस्य सुप्रशान्तश्री–शोभितानीन्द्रियानि षट्।
तस्य नामप्रसिद्धं च शान्तश्रीरित्यभूद्यतः ॥ १७ ॥

He became calm from within, his organs as well. Thus, he came to be known as the Śāntaśrī.

ततोऽसौ सन्मतिर्विज्ञो बोधिसत्त्वो जगद्धिते[8] ।
वज्रचर्याव्रतं गृह्य प्रचचार समाहितः ॥ १८ ॥

Then the wise Bodhisattva Śāntaśrī, who had a great mind, started to dwell practising the *vajrācārya* vow for the welfare of sentient beings.

ततश्च शिलयाच्छाद्य धर्मधातुमिमं जिनम्।
इष्टिकाभिर्महत्स्तूपं विधाय समगोपयत्॥ १९ ॥

He covered the Dharmadhātu Jinālaya with a massive rock, and went on to build a tall brick *stūpa* on top of it.

ततः पंचपुरेष्वत्र स्थापिताःपञ्चदेवताः ।
मञ्जुश्रियमिदं चैत्यमनेन च महत्कृतम्॥ २० ॥

He then established the five gods in the five spots, and also built the shrine of Mañjuśrī.

एवं कृत्वात्र कार्याणि सर्वाणि स महीपतिः ।
बोधिसत्त्वो महाभिज्ञःप्रचचार जगद्धिते॥ २१ ॥

Having done all this work, he became a very wise lord, a *bodhisattva* and constantly strived for the sake of the world.

ततश्चात्र महत्पातं शमीकृत्य समंततः ।
भद्रश्रीमङ्गलोत्साहं स शान्तश्रीः सदाव्यधात्॥ २२ ॥

Having pacified the great chaos emerging from all directions, the Śāntaśrī spread the auspicious glory, celebration and joy.

ततश्चासौ महाभिज्ञो दुर्वृष्टिः परिवर्तते।
नागराजान् समाराध्य सुवृष्टिं समचारयत्॥ २३ ॥

---

8 जगत्कृति इति खपाठः ।

Then the great scholar, in famine and drought, worshipped the serpent lords to bring good rainfall and plenty.

एवं स त्रिगुणाभिज्ञो महोत्पातप्रशान्तिकृत् ।
शुभंकरः सदा तेन शान्तिकर इति स्मृतः[9] ॥ २४ ॥

He knew the three qualities, pacified the disasters, constantly brought happiness, and is therefore remembered as the Śāntikara.

ईदृग्मन्त्री महाभिज्ञो वज्राचार्यो महामतिः ।
समृद्धिसिद्धिसंपन्नो न भूतो न भविष्यति ॥ २५ ॥

He acquired tremendous divinity, immense wisdom, the position of the *vajrācārya* and greatness. He acquired such enormous prosperity and divinity that no one ever had in the past and no one ever would in the future.

एवं विधाय सर्वज्ञो निरुत्पातं शुभोत्सवम् ।
बोधिसत्त्वः स शान्तश्रीस्त्रैलोक्यमहितोभवत् ॥ २६ ॥

Having removed chaos and misery, and brought happiness and celebration everywhere, the Bodhisattva Śāntaśrī was famously lauded in all three worlds.

एवमस्य महत्पुण्यं भद्रश्रीगुणसाधनम् ।
विज्ञाय शरणं गत्वा सेवितव्यं शुभार्थिभिः[10] ॥ २७ ॥

Many people, who sought the auspicious, went to his refuge to serve him, knowing that the merit received would be the instrument for virtue and prosperity.

विज्ञाय शरणं गत्वा श्रद्धया समुपाश्रिताः ।
यथाविधि समाराध्य भजेयुः सर्वदा मुदा ॥ २८ ॥

He, who takes up his refuge and devotedly serves him and ritually worships him, shall receive great happiness.

---

[9] कृत इति कपाठः ।

[10] शुभं करं इति खपाठः ।

ते सर्वे विमलात्मानो निःक्लेशा विजितेन्द्रियाः ।
भद्रश्रीगुणसंपत्तिं सर्द्धिसिद्धिं समाययुः ॥ २९ ॥

Their souls would be purified and freed of misery, they would have complete control over their organs; and they would be filled with great virtues, prosperity and divinity.

ते च तस्य सदा स्मृत्वा ध्यात्वापि च समाहितः ।
नामापि च समुच्चार्य भजेयुःश्रद्धया[11] सदा ॥ ३० ॥

तेऽपि सर्वे विकल्माषाः परिशुद्धत्रिमण्डलाः ।
सद्गुणश्रीसमापन्ना भवेयुर्बोधिचारिणः ॥ ३१ ॥

They who meditate and remember him, and chant his name with devotion, have their sins destroyed; their mind, speech and body become divine, they acquire virtues manifold and finally become established into *bodhi*.

इत्येवं तन्महत्पुण्यं विज्ञाय तद्गुणार्थिनः ।
तस्यैव शरणंगत्वा भजन्तु ते सदा मुदा ॥ ३२ ॥

The virtuous men who wish to acquire merit may go to his refuge and praise him constantly."

इत्यादिष्टं मुनीन्द्रेण सर्वेऽपि ते सभाश्रिताः ।
लोकास्तथेतिविज्ञाप्य प्राभ्यनन्दत् प्रबोधिताः ॥ ३३ ॥

When the Lord of sages preached to the assembly so, everyone, having received the knowledge, was pleased and thus praised the Śākyamuni.

एवमसौ महासत्त्वो भद्रश्रीसद्गुणार्थभृत् ।
सर्वसत्त्वहितं कृत्वा संतस्थे सुचिरं[12]तथा ॥ ३४ ॥

"The great king Guṇakāmadeva who was the mine of all virtues, stayed there for a long time doing the welfare of sentient beings.

---

11 भार्यया इति खपाठः ।

12 सुपूर्वम् इति गपाठः ।

ततःकाले गते राजा वृद्धोऽभूज्जीर्णितेन्द्रियः।
निःक्लेशो विरतरागो ध्यात्वैवं समचिन्तयत्॥ ३५॥

After a long time had passed, his body became frail with age, organs atrophied with senility. Yet he was unperturbed and he started to think and meditate.

अहं वृद्धोऽतिजीर्णाङ्गः स्थास्याम्येवं कियच्चरम्।
अवश्यं दैवयोगेन यास्यामि मरणं ध्रुवम्॥ ३६॥

He thought, "My body has become old and frail, how long am I to live in this body? My death is certain, according to God's laws.

तदत्राहं स्वपुत्राय यूने लोकानुपालने।
साभिषेकमिदं राज्यं दातुमर्हामि साम्प्रतम्॥ ३७॥

Therefore, for the protection of the kingdom, I must pass the kingdom to my son and crown him king."

इति ध्यात्वा स भूपालो नरेन्द्रदेवमात्मजम्।
अभिषिच्य नृपं कृत्वा बोधयन्नेवमादिशत्॥ ३८॥

With these thoughts, the king inaugurated his son Narendradeva into the throne, and gave him advice.

राजन्! पुत्र! समाधाय धर्मनीत्या समाचरन्।
त्रिरत्नभजनं कृत्वा संचरस्व सदा शुभे॥ ३९॥

"Dear son, you must prudently practise and uphold the principles of *dharma*, and praise the *tri-ratna*, in order to bring happiness and prosperity.

अद्यारभ्यासि सर्वेषां लोकानामधिपःप्रभुः[13]।
सर्वधर्मानुशास्ता च सर्वसत्त्वहितार्थभृत्॥ ४०॥

Henceforth, you are the king of the entire world. You must practise the discipline of *dharma* and work for the welfare of all sentient beings.

---

[13] गुरुः इति गपाठः।

तदत्र सकलान् लोकान् धर्मनीत्यानुपालयन् ।
त्रिरत्नभजनं कृत्वा संचरस्व सदा शुभे ॥ ४१ ॥

Protect your people in accordance to the *dharma*, and praise the *tri-ratna*, in order to maintain happiness and prosperity."

इत्यनुशास्य तं पुत्रं पिता स भवनिस्पृहः ।
सर्वपरिग्रहान् त्यक्त्वा वानप्रस्थं समाश्रयत्[14] ॥ ४२ ॥

Having disciplined his son, the old king who was now detached, renounced all his possessions and left for the forest.

तत्रस्थोऽसौ महाभिज्ञः परिशुद्धत्रिमण्डलः[15] ।
समाधिनिहितः स्वान्तःसंचरेद् ब्रह्मसंवरम् ॥ ४३ ॥

Then the wise man, who had been purified in mind, speech and body, went into sublime trance in solitude.

ततःकाले गते मृत्युसमये स समाहितः ।
त्रिरत्नं संस्मरन् त्यक्त्वा देहं ययौ सुखावतीम् ॥ ४४ ॥

After a long time had passed, his mortality caught up to him; and in remembrance of the *tri-ratna*, he abandoned his body and transcended into the *sukhāvatī* realm (Realm of the Buddha).

ततः स नृपती राजा नरेन्द्रदेव इन्द्रवत् ।
संबोधयन् प्रयत्नेन सर्वान् लोकानपालयत् ॥ ४५ ॥

Then the king Narendradeva protected his subjects with wisdom and prudence just as Indra protects the heavens.

सोऽपि राजा विशुद्धात्मा सद्धर्मगुणलालसः ।
शान्तिकरं तमाचार्यं समेत्य शरणं ययौ ॥ ४६ ॥

The king's soul was purified, for he sought the qualities of the good *dharma*. So he went to the refuge of the Śāntikara Ācārya.

---

[14] समाधिहि इति कपाठः ।

[15] त्रिधातुकः इति कपाठः ।

तत्र स समुपाश्रित्य शास्तुराज्ञां शिरोवहन्[16] ।
त्रिरत्नभजनं कृत्वा प्राचरत् सर्वदा शुभे ॥ ४७ ॥

In his asylum, the king obeyed every command of the *ācārya*. He perpetuated good deeds while praising the *tri-ratna*.

सदा सर्वेषु तीर्थेषु स्नानं कृत्वा यथाविधि ।
पितृभ्यःप्रददौ पिण्डमर्थिभ्योऽपि यथेप्सितम् ॥ ४८ ॥

He went on pilgrimages to every holy place, where he bathed ritually and provided lavish offerings to please his ancestors.

तथाष्टौ वीतरागाँश्च क्षेत्रलोकाधिपानपि ।
यथाविधि समाराध्य समर्चयेत् स पर्वसु ॥ ४९ ॥

He visited the eight *vītarāga*s (protectors of the world) and ritually worshipped and served them occasionally.

तथा च श्रीमहादेवीं खगाननां यथाविधि ।
समाराध्य समभ्यर्च्य महोत्साहैर्मुदाभजत् ॥ ५० ॥

He ritually worshipped, sang praises, served and celebrated the great Goddess Khagānanā to please her.

तथा मञ्जुश्रियश्चैत्ये पूच्छाग्रेऽस्मिन्नुपाश्रयत् ।
यथाविधि समाराध्य समभ्यर्च्याभजत् सदा ॥ ५१ ॥

At the *caitya* of the Mañjuśrī that lay on the Pucchāgra Mountain, he ritually worshipped, served and sang praises of him.

तथा वायुपुरे वायुदेवताः सगणा अपि[17]।
यथाविधि समाराध्य समभ्यर्च्याभजत् सदा ॥ ५२ ॥

At Vāyupura where the Wind God lived with his attendants, the king ritually worshipped and sang praises of the Wind God.

तथा वह्निपुरे वह्निदेवाताः सगणा अपि ।
यथाविधि समाराध्य समभ्यर्च्याभजत् सदा ॥ ५३ ॥

---

16 सुधावहा इति कपाठः ।

17 सलाजाअपि इति खपाठः ।

At Vahnipura, he ritually worshipped and sang praises of the Fire God and his attendants.

तथा नागपुरे नागदेवताः सगणा अपि ।
यथाविधि समाराध्य समभ्यर्च्याभजत् सदा ॥ ५४ ॥

At Nāgapura, where the serpent lords lived with their attendants, he ritually worshipped, served and sang their praises.

तथा वसुपुरे देवीं वसुन्धरां समण्डलाम्[18] ।
यथाविधि समाराध्य समभ्यर्च्य सदाभजत् ॥ ५५ ॥

At Vasupura, where the Goddess Earth lived with the *maṇḍala*, he ritually worshipped, served and sang her praises.

तथा शान्तिपुरे श्रीमत्सम्वरं सगणं जिनम् ।
यथाविधि समाराध्य समभ्यर्च्य सदाभजत् ॥ ५६ ॥

At Śāntipura, where the Lord Saṁbara lived with his attendants, he ritually worshipped, served and sang his praises.

तथा तस्य धर्मधातोः नरेन्द्रः समुपाश्रितः ।
यथाविधि समाराध्य प्राभजत् सर्वदार्चयन् ॥ ५७ ॥

Then the king went to pay homage to the Dharmadhātu and thus worshipped, praised and served him devotedly.

एवं स नृपती राजा सद्धर्मगुणलालसः।
त्रिरत्नभजनं कृत्वा संप्राचरत् सदा शुभे ॥ ५८ ॥

In this way the king who sought the qualities of the good *dharma* constantly praised the Three Jewels, and practised and preached the good and the auspicious.

एवं स नृप एतेषु तीर्थयात्रादिकर्मसु ।
बोधयित्वा प्रयत्नेन सर्वान् लोकान् यथाजयत्[19] ॥ ५९ ॥

The king who went on pilgrimages and performed good deeds also attempted to enlighten all his subjects onto the path of *bodhi*.

---

18 सभाकृते इति गपाठः ।

19 यथाकृतम् इति खपाठः ।

तथा सर्वेऽपि ते लोका धृत्वा नृपानुशासनम्[20] ।
एतेषु तीर्थयात्रादिकर्मसु संप्रचेरिरे ॥ ६० ॥

The people heeded the discipline of the king by performing auspicious deeds and going on pilgrimages.

तथाष्टौ वीतरागांश्च देवीं खगाननामपि ।
पञ्चैता देवताश्चापि चैत्यं मञ्जुश्रियोऽपि च ॥ ६१ ॥

Therefore, they worshipped the eight *vītarāgas*, the Goddess Khagānanā, the five gods and the shrine of the Mañjuśrī.

जगदीशं जगन्नाथं धर्मधातुं जिनालयम्[21] ।
यथाविधि समभ्यर्च्य प्राभजन् ते सदा मुदा ॥ ६२ ॥

They worshipped and sang praises to please the Lord of the world – the Dharmadhātu Jinālaya.

एतद्धर्मानुभावेन सर्वदात्र सुमङ्गलम् ।
निरुत्पातं महोत्साहं प्रावर्तत समन्ततः ॥ ६३ ॥

Due to the influence of such profound *dharma*, auspiciousness spread everywhere. There was no disaster, only celebration in all directions.

एवं स नृपती राजा नरेन्द्रदेव आत्मनः[22] ।
बोधिचर्याव्रतं धृत्वा संप्राचरद् जगद्धिते ॥ ६४ ॥

Thus, the king Narendradeva practised the *bodhicaryā* vow and preached it for the sake of the world.

पुरानपि तथा सर्वान् लोकान् यत्नेन बोधयन् ।
बोधिमार्गे समायुज्य प्राचारयज्जगद्धिते ॥ ६५ ॥

He preached the path of *bodhi* to his subjects as well as outsiders, teaching them that the path of *bodhi* would bring welfare to the whole world.

---

20 याचनम् इति गपाठः ।

21 जिनेश्वरी इति घपाठः ।

22 आत्मजा इति गपाठः ।

एवं स इन्द्रवद् राजा बोधिसत्त्वो जगत्प्रभुः[23] ।
सर्वसत्त्वहितं कृत्वा तस्थौ चिरं शुभे रमन् ॥ ६६ ॥

In this way, the *bodhisattva* king, who was the Lord of the world, indulged in the welfare of all sentient beings and spread auspiciousness for a long time.

ततःश्रीमान् स आचार्यः शान्तिकरो महर्द्धिकः ।
कृतकृत्यःप्रबुद्धोऽपि निर्वातुं नाभिवाञ्छति ॥ ६७ ॥

The Ācārya Śāntikara, who was prosperous, virtuous and divine, did not seek to attain final *nirvāṇa* even though he was of an advanced age.

सर्वसत्त्वहिताकांक्षी शान्तिपुराग्रसंस्थिते ।
ध्यानागारे महाचैत्ये योजनैकप्रमाणिके ॥ ६८ ॥

Because he wished to establish peace and desired welfare of all sentient beings, he started to meditate in solitude.

आरोप्य श्रीमहाज्वाले चिन्तामणिमहाध्वजम् ।
स प्राज्ञः स महासत्त्वो बोधिसत्त्वो जिनात्मजः ॥ ६९ ॥

In a great flame, he, who was a *bodhisattva*, *mahāsattva* and son of Buddha, planted a wish-fulfilling flag named Cintāmaṇi.

समाधिधारणीविद्यायोगध्यानसमाहितः ।
सम्बोधिप्रणिधिं धृत्वा तस्थौ निश्चलमानसः ॥ ७० ॥

He meditated, chanted Dhāraṇī *mantra*s and other incantations, performed *yoga* and went into trance and practised *sambodhi* with a steady mind.

यदा सद्धर्महीनेऽत्र लोकपंचकषायिते ।
तदोत्थाय समाधेः स सद्धर्मं देशयिष्यति ॥ ७१ ॥

When good *dharma* is absent and the world resorts to the five crimes, the *Ācārya* shall rise from his trance to teach the good *dharma*.

---

23 जगत्कृते इति खपाठः ।

यदा यदात्र सन्मित्रः शास्ता विद्याधिपो न हि।
तदा तदा स सन्मित्रः शास्ता विद्याधिपोऽभवेत् ॥ ७२ ॥

"During times when *buddha*s and enlightened ones are not present to provide knowledge, I must rise to grant knowledge.

सर्वान् लोकान् प्रयत्नेन निवार्य पापमार्गतः ।
बोधिमार्गे प्रतिष्ठाप्य चारयिष्यति धर्मकम् ॥ ७३ ॥

I must divert the people from the path of crime and bring them onto the path of *bodhi*, and thus preach the good *dharma*."

एवं ध्यात्वा स आचार्यः शान्तिकरः समाधिभृत्।
सर्वसत्त्वहितार्थेन तस्थौ योगसमाहितः ॥ ७४ ॥

With these thoughts, the Ācārya Śāntikara went into trance and remains in trance for the sake of all sentient beings.

एवं स त्रिगुणाचार्यः सर्वसत्त्वहितार्थभृत्।
बोधिसत्त्वमहाभिज्ञःतिष्ठतेऽत्र जगद्धिते ॥ ७५ ॥

Thus, the Master of three qualities, the wise *bodhisattva*, who had vowed for the welfare of sentient beings, still exists for the sake of the world.

ये तस्य शरणं गत्वा स्मृत्वा ध्यात्वा समादरात्[24] ।
नामापि च समुच्चार्य भजन्ति श्रद्धया सदा ॥ ७६ ॥

तेऽपि सर्वे महाभिज्ञा बोधिसत्त्वा विचक्षणाः ।
भद्रश्रीगुणसंपन्ना भविष्यन्ति सदा भवे ॥ ७७ ॥

They who go to his refuge and remember and meditate on him with respect and chant his names and sing his praises with devotion, become *bodhisattva*s and are filled with wisdom, prosperity and virtues.

ततस्ते विमलात्मानश्चतुर्ब्रह्मविहारिणः ।
बोधिचर्याव्रतं धृत्वा चरिष्यन्ति जगद्धिते ॥ ७८ ॥

---

24 समाचर इति खपाठः ।

With their organs purified, they start to dwell in the Four Sublime Abodes, and practising the *bodhicaryā vrata*, they work for the welfare of the world.

ततस्ते बोधिसंभारं पूरयित्वा यथाक्रमम् ।
अर्हन्तो बोधिमासाद्य प्राप्स्यन्ति सौगतं पदम् ॥ ७९ ॥

Having gradually fulfilled the steps of *bodhi*, they become *arhants*, acquire *bodhi* and ultimately receive Buddhahood.

ये च तद्गुणमाहात्म्यं शृण्वन्ति श्रद्धया मुदा ।
तेऽपि तद्गुणसंपत्ति-संसिद्धिं समवाप्नुयुः ॥ ८० ॥

They who carefully listen to the glory of these qualities in return receive prosperity, divinity and virtues.

इति विज्ञाय वाञ्छन्ति ये तस्य गुणसंपदः ।
ते तु सद्गुणमाहात्म्यं श्रोतुमर्हन्ति सादरम् ॥ ८१ ॥

With this knowledge, they who desire the acquisition of such great virtues must respectfully listen to the glory of such qualities."

इत्यादिष्टं मुनीन्द्रेण श्रुत्वा सर्वसभाश्रिताः ।
लोकास्तथेति संज्ञाप्य प्राभ्यनन्दन् प्रबोधिताः ॥ ८२ ॥

Upon hearing such commands of the *Munīndra* (Buddha), they, who were present at the assembly, were highly pleased and thus lauded the Lord.

॥ इति श्रीमहाचार्यशान्तिकरगुणसंसिद्धिमाहात्म्यानुभावप्रकथनप्रवृत्तो नाम नवमोऽध्यायः सम्पूर्णः ॥

The ninth chapter of the *Svayambhū Mahapurāṇa* that discusses the glory of the qualities of Śāntikara thus ends.

अथ दशमोऽध्यायः
(Daśama Adhyāya)

The Glory of Svayambhū

अथासौ भगवान् भूयो मैत्रेयं तं महामतिम् ।
समालोक्य[1] सभां चापि समामन्त्र्यैवमादिशत् ॥ १ ॥

Then the Lord Buddha, facing towards the assembly, addressed the wise Maitreya.

शृणु मैत्रेय वक्ष्यामि मञ्जुश्रियो जगद्गुरोः ।
सद्धर्मगुणमाहात्म्यं संबोधिज्ञानदायकम्[2] ॥ २ ॥

"Maitreya, listen carefully, I shall speak of the Mañjuśrī, who is the world's *guru*, who grants the *sambodhi* and the great qualities of the *dharma*.

यदियं भिक्षुणी चूडा सुशीला ब्रह्मचारिणी ।
इदं मञ्जुश्रियश्चैत्यं श्रद्धया समुपाश्रिता ॥ ३ ॥

The *bhikkhuṇī* present here named Cūḍā is virtuous in conduct, and practises maidenhood. She has devotedly worshipped the shrine of Mañjuśrī.

शुद्धोत्पलस्रजा नित्यं समभ्यर्च्य यथाविधि ।
स्मृत्वा ध्यात्वा समाराध्य सभक्त्या श्रद्धया सदा ॥ ४ ॥

Each day, she offers a pure garland of lotuses to the *caitya*. She expresses her devotion through constant remembrance, meditation, prayer and worship.

---

[1] सभालाक्य इति कपाठः ।

[2] ज्ञानजननम् इति कपाठः ।

आद्यां चले चुले वन्दे स्वाहेति नवमाक्षरम्[3] ।
धारणीं परमां विद्यां पठन्ती भजने सदा ॥ ५ ॥

She chants the great Dhāraṇī *mantra* of the nine syllables – *auṁ cale cule vande svāhā*.

एतत्पुण्यानुभावेन चुडेयं भिक्षुणी सती ।
पंचाभिज्ञावती वर्षैर्द्वादशभिर्भवेद् ध्रुवम् ॥ ६ ॥

Due to the merit amassed in doing so, the *bhikkhuṇī* has acquired the five knowledges in twelve years.

ततश्चेयं महाभिज्ञा श्रीसमृद्धिगुणाश्रया ।
सर्वसत्त्वहितं कृत्वा प्रचरेद् बोधिसंवरम् ॥ ७ ॥

She has acquired perfected wisdom, plenitude of wealth, prosperity and virtues manifold. She practises the *bodhi* vows for the sake of sentient beings.

ततोऽर्हन्ती महाप्राज्ञा परिशुद्धत्रिमण्डला ।
त्रिविधां[4]बोधिमासाद्य संबुद्धपदमाप्स्यति ॥ ८ ॥

She has become an *arhant*, a great scholar, pure in mind, speech and body. Having received the three types of *bodhi*, she shall attain Buddhahood.

एवमन्येऽपि लोकाश्च चैत्यमञ्जुश्रियः स्थले ।
पठन्ति धारणीमेनां भजन्ति श्रद्धया सदा ॥ ९ ॥

तेऽपि सर्वे विकल्माषाः परिशुद्धत्रिमंडलाः ।
भद्रश्रीसद्‌गुणाधारा बोधिसत्त्वा जितेन्द्रियाः ॥ १० ॥

If the worldly beings take refuge at the shrine of Mañjuśrī and chant the Dhāraṇī incantations with devotion, they will be freed of their sins; their mind, speech and body will be purified; they will acquire prosperity and virtues; and having conquered their organs, they become *bodhisattva*s.

3 दशमाक्षरे इति घपाठः ।

4 ततोऽत्र इति खपाठः ।

पञ्चाभिज्ञपदप्राप्ताश्चतुर्ब्रह्मविहारिणः ।
सर्वतत्त्वहिताधारा चरेयुर्बोधिसम्वरम् ॥ ११ ॥

They will receive the five types of knowledge and dwell in the Four Sublime Abodes. They will practise the *bodhi* vows for the sake of all sentient beings.

ततस्ते बोधिसंभारं पूरयित्वा[5] यथाक्रमम् ।
जित्वा मारगणान् सर्वान् निःक्लेशा विमलेन्द्रियाः ॥ १२ ॥

Having duly fulfilled the vow of *bodhi*, they will defeat bodily desires, be freed from obstacles and have their organs cleansed.

अर्हन्तोऽपि महाभिज्ञाः संबोधिसाधनारताः ।
त्रिविधां बोधिमासाद्य संबुद्धपदमाप्नुयुः ॥ १३ ॥

They would become *arhant*s, and receive perfected wisdom as a result of their *bodhi* practises. Having acquired the three types of *bodhi*, they would ultimately attain Buddhahood.

यूयमपीति मत्वात्र चैत्यं मञ्जुश्रियस्तथा ।
पठन्तो[6]धारणीमेनां भजध्वं बोधिमानसाः ॥ १४ ॥

You all must take refuge at the shrine of Mañjuśrī, and chant the Dhāraṇī incantations with a *bodhi* mind.

एतत्पुण्याभिलिप्ता हि परिशुद्धत्रिमण्डलाः ।
यूयमपि तथा सर्वे भवेयुः सुगतात्मजाः ॥ १५ ॥

Through the merit received, your mind, body and speech will be purified. You all shall become the children of Buddha.

बोधिसत्त्वा महासत्त्वा भद्रश्रीसद्गुणाश्रयाः ।
महाभिज्ञा जगन्नाथा भवेयुर्भद्रचारिणः॥ १६ ॥

You shall become *bodhisattva*s and *mahāsattva*s, acquire gentleness, prosperity and virtues, and perfected wisdom.

---

5 पर्यन्त इति घपाठः ।

6 पठ्यन्ते इति कपाठः ।

ततः संबोधिसंभारं पूरयित्वा यथाक्रमम् ।
जित्वा मारगणान् सर्वान् चतुर्ब्रह्मविहारिणः ॥ १७ ॥

Having completed the steps of *sambodhi*, you shall conquer bodily desires and dwell in the four sublime abodes.

अर्हन्त[7]स्त्रिविधां बोधिं प्राप्य बुद्धा भविष्यथ ।
इति सत्यं परिज्ञाय यदि संबोधिमिच्छथ ॥ १८ ॥

You shall become *arhant*s, and after the acquisition of three types of *bodhi*, attain Buddhahood. If you desire enlightenment, heed my words, for they are true."

एतन्[8]मञ्जुश्रियश्चैत्यं भजध्वं सर्वदा मुदा ।
इत्यादिष्टं मुनीन्द्रेण निशम्य ते ससांघिकाः ॥ १९ ॥

As the Lord of sages commanded the assembly, the audience assented to abide and praised the Lord happily.

सर्वलोकास्तथेत्युक्त्वा प्राभ्यनन्दन् प्रबोधिताः ।
ततः सर्वेऽपि ते लोका ब्रह्मशक्रादयो ऽमराः ॥ २० ॥

Then the men and the gods, Brahma, Indra and the rest, as well as the lords of other realms, along with their kinsmen, were all pleased.

सर्वे लोकाधिपाश्चापि सार्द्धं परिजनैर्मुदा ।
भगवन्तं मुनीन्द्रं तं ससंघसंप्रसादिताः ॥ २१ ॥

Having saluted and venerated the Lord Buddha and his Saṅgha with *pradakṣiṇā*, they returned to their respective abodes.

नत्वा प्रदक्षिणीकृत्य स्वस्वालयं मुदा ययुः ।
सर्वे मर्त्या नृपाद्याश्च समन्त्रिजनपौरिकाः ॥ २२ ॥

Mortals, kings with their courtiers and subjects, having saluted the Lord of the sages along with his Saṅgha, returned to their own homes.

---

7 बुद्धातथेति इति खपाठः ।

8 नत्वैनम् इति घपाठः ।

ससांघिकं मुनीन्द्रं तं नत्वा स्वस्वालयं ययुः ।
हारीति यक्षिणी सापि सात्मजा बौद्धरक्षिणी।
गता सापि च तत्सर्वं स्वीकृत्यैव मुदा तदा॥ २३ ॥

The demi-goddess Hārīti, who was the protector of the *dharma*, who was the daughter of Buddha, venerated the *tri-ratna* with praises and worshipped the Dharmadhātu.

त्रिरत्नभजनं कृत्वा धर्मधातोरुपाश्रयात् ।
ततः स[9] भगवांश्चापि समुत्थाय ससांघिकः
प्रभासयञ्जगद्भासैर्जटोद्याना श्रमं ययौ ॥ २४ ॥

Then the Lord Buddha, along with his Saṅgha, rose up, and illuminating the atmosphere with his locks, returned to his abode.

ततः परञ्च भगवान् लोककल्याण-मानसः ।
तायित्वात् त्रिजगन्नाथो विहारं सह सांघिकैः ।
सद्धर्मं समुपादिश्य विजहार जगद्धिते ॥ २५ ॥

Then the Lord of all three worlds, who lived with his Saṅgha, in order to preach the *dharma* for the sake of the world, started wandering."

इति मे गुरुणादिष्टं श्रुतं मया तथोच्यते ।
श्रुत्वाप्येतन्महाराज श्रद्धयाभ्यनुमोदय ॥ २६ ॥

I have narrated the story told to me by my own *guru*, king. Act in accordance, and be pleased.

इति शास्त्रार्हतादिष्टं निशम्य स नराधिपः[10] ।
प्रसादितं तमर्हन्तं नत्वा प्राहैवमादरात् ॥ २७ ॥

Upon hearing such commands from his *guru*, the king Aśoka, who was pleased, saluted his *guru* and said:

भदन्तोऽहं समिच्छामि संद्रष्टुं तं स्वयंभुवम् ।
तन्नेपालं प्रगच्छामि तदनुज्ञां प्रदेहि मे[11] ॥ २८ ॥

---

9 तत्र सर्बा इति गपाठः ।

10 कृपया इति खपाठः ।

11 ददस्वतु इति कपाठः ।

"O Guru! I certainly wish to behold the Svayambhū. Therefore, I ask you to grant me permission to depart for Nepal."

इति संप्रार्थितं राज्ञा श्रुत्वा सोर्हन्यतिर्मुदा ।
नृपतिं तं महासत्त्वं संपश्यन्नेवमादिशत् ॥ २९ ॥

Having heard the prayers of the king, the monk Upagupta was pleased, and looking at the great king, answered:

साधु राजन्! समिच्छा ते यद्यस्ति तं स्वयम्भूवम् ।
द्रष्टुं गच्छ समाराध्य भज श्रद्धासमन्वितः ॥ ३० ॥

"Very well, king, proceed to behold the Lord Svayambhū; praise and venerate him devotedly.

सर्वतीर्थेषु च स्नात्वा दत्वा दानं यथेप्सितम् ।
वीतरागान् समाराध्य समभ्यर्च्य समादरात् ॥३१॥

Bathe and donate at every sacred pilgrimage; praise, venerate and worship the eight *vītarāga*s.

धर्मोदयां महादेवीं खगाननां जिनेश्वरीम् ।
श्रद्धया समुपाश्रित्य समभ्यर्च्य भजादरात् ॥ ३२ ॥

Go to the refuge of the mother of Buddha – the Great Goddess Khagānanā and pray, praise and pay homage to her.

पञ्चपुरस्थिताःपञ्च देवताश्च यथाविधि[12] ।
समाराध्य समभ्यर्च्य भज भक्त्या समादरात् ॥ ३३ ॥

Visit the abodes of the five elemental deities, and worship, serve and praise those gods.

मञ्जुदेवस्य चैत्यं च समालोक्य यथाविधि ।
समाराध्य समभ्यर्च्य भजैनां धारणीं पठन् ॥ ३४ ॥

Then visit the shrine of Mañjuśrī to worship and serve him, and chant the Dhāraṇī *mantra*s.

---

12 तथेतितम् इति खपाठः ।

आचार्यं च गुहासीनं समाधिध्यानसंस्थितम् ।
ध्यात्वाराध्य समभ्यर्च्य नत्वा भज समादरात् ॥ ३५ ॥

You will find an *ācārya*, inside a cave, in a state of trance; worship, serve, salute and praise him devotedly.

एवमन्यान् महासत्त्वान् धर्मधातोरुपासकान् ।
सर्वानपि समाराध्य समभ्यर्च्य समादरात् ॥ ३६ ॥

Similarly, there are other great beings in service of the Dharmadhātu, that you must venerate and serve with respect.

एतत्पुण्यविशुद्धात्मा भद्रश्रीसद्गुणाश्रयः ।
बोधिसत्त्वो महासत्त्वो जगद्भर्ता भवेदपि[13] ॥ ३७ ॥

Through this merit, your soul will be purified, you shall be the source of all virtue, glory and auspiciousness; you shall become a *bodhisattva*, a *mahāsattva*, and the protector of the world.

ततः संबोधिसंभारं पूरयित्वा यथाक्रमम् ।
अर्हन् सम्बोधिमासाद्य संबुद्धपदमाप्स्यसि ॥ ३८ ॥

You shall cross the steps of *bodhi*, become an *arhant*, receive the *bodhi* knowledge and ultimately attain Buddhahood.

इति सत्यं परिज्ञाय संबोधिं यदि वाञ्छसि ।
प्राप्स्यसि तन् महत्सौख्यं धर्मधातोः प्रसादतः ॥ ३९ ॥

With the knowledge of this truth, if you seek the *sambodhi* knowledge and contentment, follow my instructions and you shall receive great happiness due to the grace of the Dharmadhātu.

गत्वा तत्र महोत्साहैर्धर्मधातुं विलोक्य तम् ।
यथाविधि समाराध्य भजस्व समुपाश्रितः ॥ ४० ॥

Go there joyously to behold the Dharmadhātu and ritually worship, praise and pay homage to him.

---

13 भवेष्व च इति कपाठः ।

गच्छ ते मङ्गलं भूयात् सिध्यतु ते समीहितम् ।
यथेच्छया समालोक्य समायाहि प्रमोदितः ॥ ४१ ॥

Go, and may you be blessed; may your wishes come true. Worship the Svayambhū according to your desires, and be pleased."

इतिशास्त्रा[14] समादिष्टं श्रुत्वा स नृपतिर्मुदा ।
तं गुरुं साञ्जलिर्नत्वा प्राप्यानुज्ञामनन्दत ॥ ४२ ॥

Upon hearing the commands of his *guru* Upagupta, the wise king, who was pleased to have received permission to depart, thereby saluted the monk.

ततः स नृपती राजा समन्त्रिजनपौरिकाः ।
राजदर्धि[15]–मंगलोत्साहैः संप्रस्थितो मुदाचरत् ॥ ४३ ॥

Then the king gathered his courtiers and subjects and departed in a celebratory manner.

तत्र मार्गे स राजेन्द्रः सर्वान् लोकान् प्रसादयन् ।
महोत्साहैश्चरन्नाशु नेपालं समुपाययौ ॥ ४४ ॥

During the journey, the king delighted the people with festivities and celebrations; and he reached Nepal.

तत्र प्राप्तः समालोक्य दूरात् तं श्रीस्वयम्भुवम् ।
साञ्जलिः प्रणतिं कृत्वा प्रमनाः सहसाचरत् ॥ ४५ ॥

As he caught the auspicious sight of the Svayambhū from afar, the king, who was pleased, saluted the *caitya* with his hands.

तत्र सर्वत्र संवीक्ष्य शुभोत्साहप्रवर्तितम् ।
विस्मयानन्दितान् सर्वान् नृपतिः समुपाचरत् ॥ ४६ ॥

Seeing the celebratory mood surrounding him, the king delightedly approached closer.

---

14 गुर्वा इति कपाठः ।

15 राज्येन इति गपाठः ।

तत्र सर्वेषु तीर्थेषु क्रमेण स नराधिपः ।
स्नात्वार्थिभ्यो यथाकामं ददौ दानं चरन् व्रतम् ॥ ४७ ॥

The king bathed and donated at each sacred site, and practised his vows.

ततोऽष्टौ वीतरागान् स नृपतिर्वीक्ष्य हर्षितः ।
यथाविधि समाराध्य भजत्यर्च्य यथाविधि ॥ ४८ ॥

Contented at the sight of the eight *vītarāga*s, the king worshipped, praised and served them in order.

ततो मुदाचरन् वीक्ष्य धर्मधातुं जिनालयम् ।
यथाविधि समाराध्य समभ्यर्च्याभजत् क्रमात् ॥ ४९ ॥

He, who was highly pleased as he auspiciously beheld the Dharmadhātu, worshipped, served and paid homage to the *jinālaya*.

ततो वायुपुरे वायुदेवतां सगणां मुदा ।
यथाविधि समाराध्य समभ्यर्च्याभजत् क्रमात् ॥ ५० ॥

He then visited the abode of the Wind God and his attendants, and worshipped, served and praised the deity orderly.

ततश्चाग्निपुरे वह्निदेवतां सगणामपि ।
यथाविधि समाराध्य संपूज्याभजदरात् ॥ ५१ ॥

At the abode of the Fire God and his attendants, the king ritually prayed to, worshipped and praised the God.

ततो नागपुरे नागदेवताः सगणा अपि ।
यथाविधि समाराध्य समभ्यर्च्य मुदाभजत् ॥ ५२ ॥

Then he went to the abode of the serpent Lord and his attendants, and in order, prayed to and worshipped them, and joyously sang their praises.

ततो वसुपुरे देवीं सगणां श्रीवसुन्धराम्[16] ।
यथाविधि समाराध्य भजत्यर्च्य समादरात् ॥ ५३ ॥

16 श्रीधुरेणे इति घपाठः ।

At the abode of the Earth Goddess and her attendants, he procedurally worshipped, praised and venerated her.

ततःशान्तिपुरे श्रीमत्सम्वरं सगणं तथा ।
यथाविधि समाराध्य समभ्यर्च्य मुदाभजत् ॥ ५४ ॥

At the peaceful abode of the Śrīmatsamvara and his entourage, the king venerated, prayed to and lauded the deity.

ततःशान्तिकराचार्यं समाधिध्यानसंस्थितम् ।
ध्यात्वाराध्य समभ्यर्च्य प्राभजत् संप्रमोदितः ॥ ५५ ॥

The king then visited the Ācārya Śāntikara who remains in a state of trance, and was happy to venerate him with meditation, prayers and devoted worship.

ततो धर्मोदयां देवीं खगाननां महेश्वरीम्[17] ।
यथाविधि समाराध्य समभ्यर्च्य मुदाभजत् ॥ ५६ ॥

In order, he venerated the upholder of *dharma*, the Great Goddess Khagānanā, with devoted worship, servitude and laudation.

सम्बुद्धं पुण्डरीकाक्षं सर्वज्ञ–करुणास्पदम् ।
समन्तभद्र–शास्तारं शाक्यसिंहं नमाम्यहम् ॥ ५७ ॥

He bowed to the omniscient one, whose eyes are like lotuses, who is the epitome of compassion, who is the enlightened one, who is gentle and kind, who is the lion of the Śākya dynasty, who is the ruler of the world.

श्रीघनं श्रीगुरुं श्रेष्ठं शीलराशिं शिवंकरम् ।
श्रीमन्तं श्रीकरं शान्तं शान्तिमूर्तिं नमाम्यहम् ॥ ५८ ॥

"I bow to him who is dense with glory, the prosperous, the supreme, the upholder of principles, the benevolent, the one who grants prosperity, the idol of peace, the tranquil."

नैरात्मवादिनं सिंहं निरवद्यनिराश्रवम् ।
नीतिज्ञं निर्मलात्मानं निष्कलंकं नमाम्यहम् ॥ ५९ ॥

---

17 विनायकीम् इति खपाठः ।

"I bow to him who discards the existence of soul, who does no wrong, who does not accumulate possessions, who is well-versed in law and prudence, whose mind is pure and pristine, who is unblemished."

निर्द्वन्द्वं निरहंकारं निर्विकल्पं तथागतम्[18] ।
निर्धूतनिखिलक्लेशं निष्प्रपञ्चं नमाम्यहम् ॥ ६० ॥

"I bow to him who is not in conflict, who is selfless, who is irreplaceable, who knows the reality of form, who removes all misery, who is free of the five worldly elements."

विश्वेश्वरं विशेषं तं विश्वरूपं विनायकम् ।
विश्वलक्षणसंपूर्णं वीतरागं नमाम्यहम् ॥ ६१ ॥

"I bow to the Lord of the whole world, the special one, within whom the form of the world resides, who is the protector of all, who is complete with the virtues of the world, who is devoid of worldly attachments."

विद्यावरेण सम्पन्नं विश्वेशं विमलप्रभम् ।
विनीतवेगं विमलं वीतमोहं नमाम्यहम्[19] ॥ ६२ ॥

"I bow to him who possesses knowledge, who is the master of the world, who exudes a calm energy, who is humble, who is unblemished, who is free of delusions."

दुर्दान्तदमकं शान्तं शुद्धं पञ्चजिनालयम् ।
सुगतिं सुश्रुतं शुभ्रकीर्तिं चापि नमाम्यहम् ॥ ६३ ॥

"I bow to him who pacifies the wild, who brings calm and peace, who is pure, who is the abode of the five *buddha*s, who is gentle, auspicious, whose fame has spread in all directions."

योगीश्वरं दशबलं लोकज्ञं लोकपूजितम् ।
लोकाचार्यं लोकमूर्तिं लोकनाथं नमाम्यहम् ॥ ६४ ॥

"I bow to the Lord of *yogī*s, who possesses the ten strengths, who understands the world, who is revered by the world, who is the teacher

---

18 महोत्सवम् इति कपाठः ।

19 प्रनमामि इति घपाठः ।

of the world, who is the idol of the world, who is the master of the world."

कलंकमुक्तिं[20]कामारिं सकलैकं कलाधरम् ।
कान्तमूर्तिं दयापात्रं कनकाभं नमाम्यहम् ॥ ६५ ॥

"I bow to him who is free of blemishes, who is the enemy of desire, who is the sole teacher of the world, who is the source of all art and skill, whose aura is of energy, who is compassionate, whose body is golden."

ततो मञ्जुश्रियश्चैत्यं धर्मधातुमुपाश्रयन् ।
यथाविधि समाराध्य समभ्यर्च्यानतोऽभजत् ॥ ६६ ॥

He then proceeded towards the Mañjuśrī *caitya*, which lies close to the Dharmadhātu and venerated the shrine with worship, service and praises.

ततो मुदा चरन् वीक्ष्य धर्मधातुं जिनालयम् ।
यथाविधि समाराध्य समभ्यर्च्याभजन् मुदा ॥ ६७ ॥

To his pleasure, he again worshipped the Dharmadhātu Jinālaya, and joyously paid homage to him with praises and salutations.

भक्त्या परमयास्तौषीज्जिनालयं स्वयंभुवम् ।
ज्योति रूपाय चैतन्यरूपाय भवते नमः ॥ ६८ ॥

"I bow to the Svayambhū, the abode of the Buddha, who exists in the form of light, who is the embodiment of wisdom and consciousness."

मुरादिनिधनायश्रीदात्रे प्रणवरूपिणे ।
विश्वतोमुखरूपाय भक्तवत्सल! ते नमः ॥ ६९ ॥

"I bow to him who removes bodily desires, who grants prosperity, who is the embodiment of the life force, who is the face of the world, who is kind to his devotees."

पृथ्व्यादिभूतनिर्मात्रे जगद्वन्द्याय ते नमः।
जगत्स्रष्टे जगत्पात्रे जगद्धर्त्रे नमो नमः ॥ ७० ॥

---

20 कङ्कालिमूर्ति इति कपाठः ।

"I bow to him who conjures the five elements, who understands the world, who creates the world, who protects the world, who destroys the world."

ध्यानगम्याय ध्येयाय चतुर्वर्गप्रदायिने ।
एवं स्तुत्वा ह्यशोकः स पुनः क्षमापनं व्यधात् ॥ ७१ ॥

"I bow to him who can be attained through meditation, who is the goal of meditation, who grants *dharma, artha, kāma, mokṣa*." In this way, the Aśoka repeatedly prayed to the Lord and also asked for forgiveness.

एवं स नृपतिः सर्वान् धर्मधातोरुपासकान् ।
महासत्त्वान्[21] समभ्यर्च्य सत्कृत्य समतोषयत् ॥ ७२ ॥

Then the king praised the devotees of the Dharmadhātu, who were divine beings, and served them respectfully.

एवं स नृपराजः श्रीधर्मधातोरुपाश्रितः ।
त्रिरत्नभजनं कृत्वा प्राचरद् बोधिसम्वरम् ॥ ७३ ॥

In this way, the king Aśoka went to the refuge of the Dharmadhātu, and praising the *tri-ratna*, practised and preached the *bodhi* path.

ततः स नन्दितो राजा समन्त्रिजनपौरिकः ।
नत्वा प्रदक्षिणीकृत्य धर्मधातुं मुदाचरत् ॥ ७४ ॥

Then the merry king, along with his courtiers and subjects, was pleased to salute and venerate the Dharmadhātu with *pradakṣiṇā*.

ततश्चरन् स भूमीन्द्रो महोत्साहैः प्रमोदितः ।
सहसा पुरमासाद्य विहारं समुपाचरत् ॥ ७५ ॥

The king returned to his city with great enthusiasm and visited the *vihāra*.

तत्रोपेत्य तमर्हन्तमुपगुप्तं ससांघिकम् ।
समीक्ष्य[22] साञ्जलिर्नत्वा सभैकान्तं समाश्रयत् ॥ ७६ ॥

---

21 बुधानेति इति खपाठः ।

22 प्रह्लाय इति कपाठः ।

Upon reaching the *vihāra*, the king saw the Arhant Upagupta, who was with his fellow *bhikkhus*, and having saluted the monk, sat at a corner of the gathering.

तं समायातमालोक्य सोऽर्हन् शास्ता प्रसन्नदृक् ।
स्वागतं कुशलं कच्चिन्नृपतिं पर्यपृच्छत ॥ ७७ ॥

At the sight of his arrival, the monk with a happy heart welcomed the king and asked him of his well-being.

तच्छ्रुत्वा स महीपालः शास्तारं तं कृताञ्जलिः ।
प्रणम्य सुप्रसन्नाश्यः संपश्यन्नेवमब्रवीत् ॥ ७८ ॥

On hearing such words, the Protector of the World joined his hands venerating the teacher, and happily bowing to him, commenced his address:

समागतोऽस्म्यहं शास्तर्भवत्कृपानुभावतः ।
कुशलं मे कथं न स्यात् सर्वत्रापि सदापि हि ॥ ७९ ॥

"*Guru*, due to your benevolence and grace, I have returned in a good state. I am well.

भवत्कृपानुभावेन नेपालेऽहं मुदाचरन् ।
दृष्ट्वा सर्वेषु तीर्थेषु स्नात्वा दानं यथेप्सितम्[23] ॥ ८० ॥

Due to your benevolence, I journeyed to Nepal to behold the sacred sites where I bathed and donated lavishly.

तथाष्टौ वीररागाँश्च समालोक्य प्रमोदितः ।
यथाविधि समाराध्य समभ्यर्च्य जिनं क्रमात् ॥ ८१ ॥

Then I visited the eight *vītarāgas*, and pleased them with rigorous worship, veneration and laudation.

ततः समीक्ष्य तं श्रीमद्धर्मधातुं स्वयं भुवम् ।
यथाविधि समाराध्य समभ्यर्च्याभजन् मुदा ॥ ८२ ॥

---

[23] यथोत्तरम् इति घपाठः ।

I auspiciously beheld the Dharmadhātu Svayambhū, whom I worshipped, venerated and praised in order.

ततो वायुपुरे वायुदेवताभ्यर्च्चिता मया।
ततश्चाग्निपुरे वह्निर्देवतापि मयार्चिता॥ ८३॥

I visited the abode of the Wind God to venerate him, then went to the abode of the Fire Deity to worship him as well.

तथा नागपुरे नागराजा चापि मयार्च्चितः।
तथा वसुपुरे देवी वसुन्धरा समर्चिता॥ ८४॥

At the abode of the Serpent God, I worshipped the Serpent Lord. At the abode of the Earth Goddess, I worshipped the goddess devotedly.

ततःशान्तिपुरे श्रीमत्सम्वरश्च समर्चितः।
ततःशान्तिकराचार्यः समालोक्य मयार्चितः[24]॥ ८५॥

I went to the abode of the Śrīmatsambara to venerate him. Then I visited the Ācārya Śāntikara, whom I ritually worshipped.

देवी खगाननां चापि समाराध्य समर्चिता।
मञ्जुदेवस्य चैत्यं च यथाविधि समर्चितम्॥ ८६॥

I then venerated and served the Goddess Khagānanā and went to the shrine of Mañjuśrī to ritually worship him.

एवं भदन्त! तत्रोपच्छन्दोहे पुण्यभूतले।
यथाविधि समाराध्य सर्वदेवा मयार्चिताः॥ ८७॥

Guru, at the pious land of Nepal, I ritually worshipped, served and praised all the deities that resided there.

एतत्पुण्यं मयालब्धं भवत्कृपानुभावतः।
तदत्र जन्मसाफल्यं जीवितं चापि मेऽधुना॥ ८८॥

Due to your grace, I have received immense merit. The purpose of my birth has been served, and my life has been blessed.

---

24 निगद्यता इति खपाठः।

तथात्र[25] सर्वदा शास्त! धर्मधातुं जिनालयम्।
स्मृत्वा नाम समुच्चार्य ध्यात्वा भजेयमाभवम्॥ ८९॥

Therefore, may I be able to eternally venerate the Dharmadhātu Jinālaya through constant remembrance, chanting of his name, meditation and laudation!"

इति राज्ञा समाख्यातं श्रुत्वा सोऽर्हन् प्रसादितः।
नृपतिं तं समालोक्य पुनरेवं समादिशत्॥ ९०॥

Upon hearing such words of the king, the monk Upagupta was highly pleased, and looked at him and said:

धन्योऽसि यन्महाराज! धर्मधातुं जिनालयम्।
स्मृत्वा ध्यात्वापि संभक्तिमिच्छसेऽत्र सदा भज॥ ९१॥

"O king! you are blessed, for you have visited the Dharmadhātu Jinālaya, and you must constantly remember, meditate and praise the Svayambhū.

एतत्पुण्यविशुद्धात्मा भद्रश्रीसद्गुणाश्रयः।
बोधिसत्त्वो महासत्त्वः सर्वधर्माधिपो भवेः॥ ९२॥

Through this merit, may your soul be purified, may you receive gentleness, glory and virtues manifold, and become a *bodhisattva, mahāsattva* and the Lord of *dharma*.

ततः संबोधिसंभारं पूरयित्वा यथाक्रमम्।
अर्हन् स्त्रिबोधिमासाद्य ध्रुवं बुद्धपदं[26] लभे॥ ९३॥

Having crossed the steps of *bodhi*, may you become an *arhant* and having received *bodhi*, may you attain Buddhahood.

समुत्पत्तिकथां तस्य धर्मधातोः स्वयंभुवः।
श्रुत्वापि यन्महत्पुण्यं संबोधिसाधनं लभेत्॥ ९४॥

The one who listens to the origin story of the Svayambhū Dharmadhātu

25 एहिशास्तृ इति गपाठः।

26 स्वयम्भुवपदे इति खपाठः।

shall receive tremendous merit and the instrument for the acquisition of *sambodhi*.

इति मत्वा समुत्पत्तिकथां तस्य स्वयंभुवः।
सत्कृत्य श्रद्धया मर्त्याः श्रोतुमर्हन्ति सर्वथा॥ ९५॥

Having understood this, human beings must, therefore, listen to the origin story of Lord Svayambhū with reverence and devotion.

समुत्पत्तिकथां तस्य धर्मधातोः स्वयंभुवः[27]।
शृण्वन्ति ये नरा भक्त्या सत्कृत्य श्रद्धया मुदा॥ ९६॥

दुर्गतिं ते न गच्छन्ति कुत्रापि हि कदाचन।
सदा सद्गतिसंजाताः भद्रश्रीसद्गुणाश्रयाः॥ ९७॥

They who listen to the origin story of the Svayamabhū Dharmadhātu and express reverence and devotion enthusiastically shall never be wretched or miserable; they shall never be disparaged. They will always reach a good state and become adorned with virtue, glory and prosperity.

सर्वसत्त्वहिताधानबोधिचर्याव्रते रताः।
महाभिज्ञा जगन्नाथा भवेयुः सुगतात्मजाः॥ ९८॥

They shall practise the *bodhi* vow for the sake of sentient beings, and become perfectly enlightened, lords of the world and the children of Buddha.

क्रमेण बोधिसम्भारं पूरयित्वा जगद्धिते।
अर्हन्तः त्रिविधां बोधिं प्राप्येयुः सौगतं पदम्[28]॥ ९९॥

Having crossed the steps of *bodhi* for the sake of the world, they shall become *Arhant*s. After the acquisition of three types of *bodhi*, they shall finally attain Buddhahood.

इति मत्वा महाराज! श्रोतव्यं श्रद्धयादरात्।
स्वयंभूगुणमाहात्म्यं दुर्लभं बोधिवाञ्छिभिः॥ १००॥

---

27 खगेश्वराम् इति घपाठः।

28 सुगतां तथा इति खपाठः।

Having understood this, king, you must regularly listen to and tell of the greatness of Svayambhū, for it is rare and is able to grant the *bodhi* knowledge.

शृण्वन्ति ये नरा भक्त्या सत्कृत्य श्रद्धया मुदा।
स्वयंभूगुणमाहात्म्यं सद्धर्मश्रीगुणार्थदम् ॥ १०१ ॥

They who worshipfully and devotedly listen to the great qualities of Svayambhū shall receive virtue and glory of the *dharma*.

तेऽपि न दुर्गतिं यायुः सदा सद्गतिसंगताः।
भद्रश्रीसद्गुणाधारा भवेयुर्बोधिलाभिनः ॥ १०२ ॥

They shall never be wretched or miserable and will always be in a good state. They shall gain glory, prosperity, and virtue; and be rewarded with *bodhi*.

तस्मादेतन्महत्पुण्यं श्रुत्वा ध्यात्वा सदादरात्।
स्मृत्वा नाम समुच्चार्य संभक्तव्यं स्वयंभुवम् ॥ १०३ ॥

Therefore, you must listen and meditate to the pious story with joy; and remember and chant the name of Svayambhū with immense veneration.

अहमपि पुरा राजन् धर्मधातोः स्वयंभुवः।
श्रुत्वा सद्गुणसांकथ्यं बभूव संप्रमोदितः ॥ १०४ ॥

I, too, once listened to the story of the great qualities of the Dharmadhātu Svayambhū to my pleasure.

ततोऽहं सहसा तत्र नेपाले समुपाचरम्[29]।
स्नात्वा सर्वेषु तीर्थेषु ददौ दानं यथेप्सितम् ॥ १०५ ॥

I then immediately went to Nepal, and bathed and lavishly donated at the sacred sites.

अष्टौ तान् वीतरागाँश्च समाराध्य मयार्चिताः।
देवीं खगाननां चापि समाराध्य समर्चिता ॥ १०६ ॥

---

29 उपदिश्यताम् इति कपाठः।

I worshipped the eight *vītarāga*s with devotion; and I devotedly worshipped the Great Goddess Khagānanā as well.

मञ्जुदेवस्य चैत्यं च समाराध्य समर्चितम् ।
पञ्चपुरे स्थिताःपञ्चदेवताश्च समर्चिताः[30] ॥ १०७ ॥

I worshipped the shrine of Mañjuśrī and the abodes of the five elemental deities.

तथा शान्तिकराचार्यः समालोक्य समर्चितः ।
ततः शरणमाश्रित्य धर्मधातोः स्वयंभुवः ॥ १०८ ॥

I visited and beheld the Śāntikara Ācārya to serve him, and then I went to the refuge of the Dharmadhātu Svayambhū.

सत्कृत्य श्रद्धया नित्यं समाराध्य मुदाऽभजम् ।
एवं तत्र सदाश्रित्य धर्मधातोरुपासकः ॥ १०९ ॥

I devoted myself to the joyful worship, veneration and praise of the Svayambhū. In his asylum, I became a devoted servant of his.

त्रिरत्नभजनं कृत्वा प्राचरं बोधिसंवरम् ।
एतत्पुण्यविशुद्धात्मा परिशुद्धत्रिमण्डलः ॥ ११० ॥

I sang praises of the Three Jewels, practised the path of *bodhi*, and through this merit, received purification of the soul and cleansing of the mind, speech and body.

अहं बोधिं समासाद्य जिनात्मजो भवेऽधुना ।
इति विज्ञाय मनुजा वाञ्छन्ति ये सुनिर्वृतिम्[31] ॥ १११ ॥

Then I attained the *bodhi* knowledge and became a son of Buddha. Knowing this, one who seeks salvation must follow my instructions.

धर्मधातुं समाराध्य भजन्तु ते सदा मुदा ।
स्मृत्वा ध्यात्वा च नामापि समुच्चार्य समादरात् ॥ ११२ ॥

One must worship and praise the Dharmadhātu regularly and with

30 शुभे हनि इति घपाठः ।

31 धर्मधात्व इति खपाठः ।

joy and venerate him with remembrance, meditation and chanting of his names.

समालोक्य प्रणम्याऽपि भजन्तु तं जिनालयम् ।
ये भजन्ति सदा स्मृत्वा ध्यात्वा नत्वा जिनालयम् ॥ ११३ ॥

They must visit the *jinālaya* to praise him, and constantly remember, praise, salute and meditate on the *jinālaya*.

द्रुतं संबोधि[32]मासाद्य संबुद्धपदमाप्नुयुः ।
इति सत्यं समाख्यातं सर्वैरपि मुनीश्वरैः ॥ ११४ ॥

Consequently, they shall receive *bodhi* enlightenment and attain the Buddhahood. The Lord Buddha has preached this fact.

श्रुत्वानुमोद्य तं धर्मधातुं स्मृत्वा भजन्त्वलम् ।
सुभाषितमिदं येपि श्रुत्वानुमोदिताशयाः ॥ ११५ ॥

You must listen and fathom the Dharmadhātu, remember him and chant his praises; and you must use sweet words to speak of it to others.

धर्मधातुमनुस्मृत्वा ध्यात्वा भजन्ति सर्वदा ।
तेऽपि चैतत्महत्पुण्यपरिशुद्धत्रिमण्डलाः ॥ ११६ ॥

They who remember, meditate on and praise the Dharmadhātu forever shall receive the merits of a *caitya* and their minds, speech and body shall be cleansed.

भद्रश्रीसद्गुणाधाराश्चतुर्ब्रह्मविहारिणः ।
बोधिसत्त्वा महासत्त्वा महाभिज्ञाः शुभेन्द्रियाः[33] ॥ ११७ ॥

They would become the epitome of goodness, glory and virtue and would dwell in the four sublime abodes. They would become *bodhisattva*s, *mahāsattva*s and enlightened ones with vigorous organs.

द्रुतं संबोधिमासाद्य संबुद्धपदमाप्नुयुः ।
इति मे गुरुणादिष्टं श्रुतं मया तथोच्यते ॥ ११८ ॥

They would quick acquire *bodhi* and ultimately attain Buddhahood.

---

32 तत्रेति सद्रुते इति गपाठः ।

33 शुकिङ्कृति इति गपाठः ।

I have told you this as my *guru* had once told me. You too must preach this to your people.

त्वमपीदं सदालोकान् श्रावयित्वानुमोदय ।
एतत्पुण्यानुभावेन सर्वत्र सर्वदापि ते ॥ ११९ ॥

Due to the merit you have received, there shall certainly be no disaster or chaos; there shall always be merry celebration everywhere."

निरुत्पातं शुभोत्साहं भवेन्नूनं नराधिपः ।
इति तेनार्हतादिष्टं श्रुत्वाशोको नृपो मुदा ॥ १२० ॥

Having heard such commands of the *arhant*, the king Aśoka was pleased; and assenting to abide, he, along with his entourage, lauded and venerated the monk.

तथेति प्रतिविज्ञाप्य प्राभ्यनन्दत् सपार्षदः ।
ततः सर्वेऽपि ते लोका निशम्यैतत्सुभाषितम्[34] ॥ १२१ ॥

Having heard such sweet words, the people accepted, celebrated and always performed auspicious activities.

अनुमोद्य महोत्साहैः संचेरिरे शुभे सदा ।
तदैतत्पुण्यभावेन सर्वत्र तत्र सर्वदा ॥ १२२ ॥

Due to the influence of the merit so amassed, there was no disaster or chaos, there was only celebration everywhere."

निरुत्पातं शुभोत्साहं प्रावर्तत निरन्तरम् ।
इत्यादिश्य महाभिज्ञो जयश्रीः स महामतिः ॥ १२३ ॥

When the wise Mahāmati Jayaśrī had spoken so, he looked at the gathered assembly and again, said:

सर्वान् तान् सांघिकान् पश्यन् पुनरेवं समादिशत् ।
यत्रेदं धर्मसांकथ्यं प्रावर्तयेत् कलावपि ॥ १२४ ॥

भाषेत् यःशृणुयाद्यश्च श्रावयेद्यः प्रचारयेत् ।
एतेषां तत्र सर्वेषां सम्बुद्धाः सकलाः सदा ॥ १२५ ॥

---

34 शुभेहति इति घपाठः ।

"In the Kali age, they who discourse this story of *dharma* and they who listen to, preach and propagate it, shall all be looked upon with benevolence by all *buddhas* and be granted life-long welfare.

कृपा–दृष्ट्या समालोक्य प्रकुर्युर्भद्रमाभवम् ।
सर्वाः पारमिता देव्यस्तेषां तत्र सदा शिवम्[35] ॥ १२६ ॥

The Pāramitās (Goddesses of perfection) shall grant them welfare and gradually fulfil their *bodhi* vows.

कृत्वा संबोधिसंभारं[36] पूरयेयुर्यथाक्रमम् ।
सर्वेऽपि बोधिसत्त्वाश्च प्रत्येकसुगता अपि ॥ १२७ ॥

Similarly, all *bodhisattvas*, *pratyeka buddhas*, *arhants* and *yogīs* shall grant them benediction.

अर्हन्तो योगिनस्तेषां प्रकुर्युमङ्गलं सदा ।
सर्वे लोकाधिपाश्चापि सर्वे चापि महर्षयः ॥ १२८ ॥

The lords of the worlds and great sages shall look after them and grant them felicity.

तत्र तेषां हि सर्वेषां कुर्युः समीक्ष्य मङ्गलम् ।
सर्वे देवाधिपाश्चापि सर्वदैत्याधिपा अपि ॥ १२९ ॥

तथा सर्वेऽपि गन्धर्वाः सर्वयक्षाधिपा अपि ।
गरुडा नागराजाश्च कुम्भाण्डाधीश्वरा अपि[37] ॥ १३० ॥

As shall the gods and the demons, as well as the *yakṣa* and *gandharva* demi-gods, falcons and serpents as well as lords of *kumbhāṇḍa* demi-gods shall look after such people and protect them from harm.

समीक्ष्य सर्वदा तेषां रक्षां कुर्युः समन्ततः ।
सर्वाश्च मातृका देव्यः सभैरवगणा अपि ॥ १३१ ॥

The mother goddesses (Mātṛkās) and Bhairava gods would provide protection and grant them welfare and felicity.

---

35 शुभम् इति गपाठः ।

36 कर्मान्त इति कपाठः ।

37 महोत्तमा इति गपाठः ।

कृत्वा रक्षां सदा तेषां कुर्युर्भद्रं समन्ततः ।
सर्वे ग्रहाश्च ताराश्च सिद्धा विद्याधरा अपि ॥ १३२ ॥

Planets, stars, *siddha* demi-gods, *vidyadhara* demi-gods and *sādhya* demi-gods would take care of them and grant benediction.

साध्याश्चापि सदालोक्य तेषां कुर्युः सुमङ्गलम् ।
भूतप्रेतपिशाचाश्च दुष्टा मारगणा अपि ॥ १३३ ॥

Ghosts, phantoms, wraiths, wicked ones and manifestations of bodily desires, would look at them with happiness, and provide them protection.

वीक्ष्य तेषां प्रसन्नास्ते रक्षां कुर्युः सदा मुदा ।
स्वयंभूगुणमाहात्म्यं सांकथ्यं यो लिखेत् मुदा[38] ॥ १३४ ॥

He who writes of the glory of Svayambhū writes but the sweet words of Mahāyāna.

तेनापि लिखितं सर्वं महायानसुभाषितम् ।
लेखापितं च येनेदं धर्मधातुसुभाषितम् ॥ १३५ ॥

When he gets the sweet words of the Dharmadhātu written, he is getting the Sūtra literature written.

तेनापि सकलं सूत्रं लेखापितं भवेद् ध्रुवम् ।
लिखितं चापि येनेदं प्रतिष्ठाप्य यथाविधि ॥ १३६ ॥

शुद्धस्थाने गृहे स्थाप्य पूजाङ्गैः सर्वदार्चितम् ।
तेनार्हन्तो जिनाः सर्वे प्रत्येकसुगता अपि ॥ १३७ ॥

After writing and inaugurating it on a sacred altar at home, in worshipping it, he worships the *Arhants, pratyeka buddhas,* and *bodhisattvas* with their *saṅghas*.

ससंघा[39]बोधिसत्त्वाश्च भवन्ति पूजिताःखलु ।
यश्चापीदं स्वयं धृत्वा परेभ्योऽपि समादिशत् ॥ १३८ ॥

---

38 लिख्य इति गपाठः ।

39 सर्वसत्त्वा इति खपाठः ।

भावयेत् सततं स्मृत्वा ध्यात्वापि प्रणमेन्मुदा।
तस्य सर्वमुनीन्द्रो हि प्रत्येकसुगता अपि ॥ १३९ ॥

When one holds and makes others hold it, and remembers, meditates on it, and salutes it with joy, *buddhas, pratyeka buddhas, arhants* and *bodhisattvas*, pleased with him, grant his wishes.

अर्हन्तो बोधिसत्त्वाश्च तुष्टा दद्युः समीहितम्।
यश्चैतदुपदेष्टारं सर्वांश्च श्रावकानपि ॥ १४० ॥

यथाविधि समभ्यर्च्य भोजनैः समतोषयेत्।
तेन सर्वेऽपि संबुद्धाः प्रत्येकसुगता अपि॥ १४१ ॥

अर्हन्तो भिक्षवः सर्वे योगिनो ब्रह्मचारिणः।
बोधिसत्त्वाश्च सर्वेऽपि व्रतिनो यतयोऽपि च ॥ १४२ ॥

When one feeds and ritually worships the preacher of the story and its listeners, the *bodhisattvas, pratyeka buddhas, arhants, bhikkhus, yogīs,* celibates, vow holders and monks shall all have been fed, venerated and pleased.

अर्चिता भोजितास्तुष्टा भवेयुरनुमोदिताः।
किमेवं बहुनोक्तेन सर्वे बुद्धा मुनीश्वराः ॥ १४३ ॥

सर्वास्ताराश्च देव्योऽपि सर्वसंघा जिनात्मजाः।
नित्यं तेषां कृपा–दृष्ट्या समालोक्यानुमोदिताः ॥ १४४ ॥

रक्षां विधाय सर्वत्र वरं दद्युः समीहितम्।
तुष्टाः स्युः पूजया सर्वे देवा देव्यश्च निश्चितम्[40] ॥ १४५ ॥

Need I say more? The *buddhas* and sages, stars and goddesses, children of Buddha and the Saṅgha would always view such people with compassion and appreciation; they would provide protection and grant their wishes as well.

सर्वे लोकाधिपाश्चापि सर्वे देवा सुराधिपाः।
रक्षां कृत्वा वरं दद्युस्तेषां सद्धर्मसाधने ॥ १४६ ॥

---

40 मङ्गला इति कपाठः।

The lords of the world and of gods would protect them and grant them the instrument of *dharma*.

राजानोऽपि सदा तेषां रक्षां कृत्वानुमोदिताः ।
यथाभिवाञ्छितं दत्वा पालयेयुः सदादरात् ॥ १४७ ॥

Kings would protect and praise them, grant their wishes and nurture them.

मन्त्रिणोऽपि सदा तेषां सामात्यसचिवानुगाः ।
सभृत्यसैन्यभट्टाश्च भवेयुर्हितकारिणः ॥ १४८ ॥

Ministers, along with secretaries, servants and soldiers, would favour them.

सर्वे वैश्याश्च सर्वार्थभर्तारः स्युः सुहृत्प्रियाः ।
श्रेष्ठिमहाजनाः सर्वे भवेयुर्हितकारिणः ॥ १४९ ॥

Vaiśyas would guard them and hold them dear; capitalists would become benefactors.

द्विषोऽपि दासतां यायुर्दुष्टाश्च स्युर्हिताशयाः ।
एवमन्येपि लोकाश्च सर्वे स्युर्मैत्रमानसाः ॥ १५० ॥

Foes would become servants; wicked ones would intend welfare. All would develop a friendly attitude toward, them.

पशवःपक्षिणश्चापि सर्वकीटाश्च जन्तवः[41] ।
नैव तेषां विरुद्धाः स्युर्भवेयुर्हितशंसिनः ॥ १५१ ॥

Animals, birds, insects and beings would never antagonize them and would always be helpful.

एवं सर्वत्र लोकेषु तेषां सद्धर्मसाधिनाम् ।
निरुत्पातं शुभोत्साहं सौमाङ्गल्यं सदा भवेत् ॥ १५२ ॥

Wherever they may be in the world, there would never be disaster, only celebration and happiness.

41 जैत्रका इति खपाठः ।

एवं भद्रतरं पुण्यं स्वयंभूभवनोद्भवम् ।
नत्वा तं त्रिजगन्नाथं भजध्वं सर्वदा मुदा ॥ १५३ ॥

You must, therefore, revere the auspicious and pious story of the Svayambhū, and venerate the Lord of three worlds.

ये तस्य शरणे स्थित्वा स्मृत्वा ध्यात्वा समाहिताः ।
नामापि च समुच्चार्य भजन्ति श्रद्धया सदा ॥ १५४ ॥

तेषां त्रिण्यपि रत्नानि सुप्रसन्नानि सर्वदा[42] ।
कृपा-दृष्ट्या समालोक्य कृत्वा देयुः सदा शुभम् ॥ १५५ ॥

They, who take the refuge of Svayambhū and remember, meditate, chant his name and praise him with reverence and devotion, shall please the Three Jewels; they would be looked upon with benevolent sight, and granted felicity."

इति शास्त्रा समादिष्टं जयश्रिया निशम्यते ।
जिनेश्वरीमुखाः संघाः सर्वेऽनन्दन् प्रबोधिताः ॥ १५६ ॥

Upon hearing the commands of Jayaśrī, the monk Jineśvara and the rest of the Saṅgha were pleased.

सर्वावती सभा सापि श्रुत्वैतत् संप्रसादिता ।
तथेति प्रतिविज्ञाप्य प्राभ्यनन्दन् प्रबोधिताः ॥ १५७ ॥

The audience was pleased – they were in agreement and in happiness.

ततस्ते सकला लोकाः समुत्थाप्य प्रसादिताः ।
जयश्रियं ससंघं तं नत्वा स्वस्वाश्रमं ययुः[43] ॥ १५८ ॥

The people stood up, happy, and, bowing to Jayaśrī and the Saṅgha, returned to their own abodes.

तत्र नित्यमुपेत्यासौ ससंघ-सजिनात्मजः ।
स्नात्वा सर्वेषु तीर्थेषु धृत्वा व्रतं यथाविधि ॥ १५९ ॥

The Saṅgha, along with the children of Buddha, proceeded to bathe at the holy rivers and practise their vows ritually.

42 अस्यानि इति घपाठः ।

43 स्वालये तदा इति खपाठः ।

ततोऽष्टौ वीतरागाँश्च देवीं चापि खगाननाम्।
पञ्च ता देवताश्चापि यथाविधि समर्चयन्[44] ॥ १६० ॥

They worshipped the eight *vītarāgas*, the Goddess Khagānanā and the five elemental deities ritually.

तथा शान्तिकराचार्यं चैत्यं मञ्जुश्रियोऽपि च।
धर्मधातुं समाराध्य ध्यात्वाभ्यर्च्य सदाभजन् ॥ १६१ ॥

They worshipped the Ācārya Śāntikara and the shrine of Mañjuśrī and then they venerated the Dharmadhātu in meditation, with praise and worship.

तदैतत्पुण्यभावेन विषये तत्र सर्वदा।
निरुत्पातं शुभोत्साहं प्रावर्तत समन्ततः ॥ १६२ ॥

The influence of that merit removed disaster and brought celebration and happiness in all directions.

ततश्चासौ महाभिज्ञो जयश्रीः सुगतात्मजः।
सर्वान् तान् सांघिकान् पश्यन् पुनरेवं समादिशत्[45] ॥ १६३ ॥

Jayaśrī, the wise son of Buddha, looked at the devotees present and spoke again.

यत्रेदं धर्मसांकथ्यं प्रचारितं स्वयंभुवः।
तत्रैतत्पुण्यभावेन भवतु सर्वदा शुभम् ॥ १६४ ॥

"Where we preach the pious story of Svayambhū, may the merit bring eternal happiness there!"

सम्बुद्धास्तत्र सर्वेऽपि प्रत्येकसुगता अपि।
अर्हन्तो बोधिसत्त्वाश्च कुर्वन्तु मंङ्गलं सदा ॥ १६५ ॥

"May the *buddhas*, *arhants*, *bodhisattvas* and *pratyeka buddhas* there do good!"

सर्वे लोकाधिपाश्चापि सर्वे चापि महर्षयः[46]।
समालोक्य सदा तत्र प्रकुर्वन्तु सुमङ्गलम् ॥ १६६ ॥

---

44 समुन्नये इति घपाठः।

45 भविष्यति इति कपाठः।

46 सुमङ्गला इति खपाठः।

"May the lords of the world and the great sages always look after and bless the land!"

काले वर्षन्तु मेघाश्च भूयाच्छस्यवती मही।
निरुत्पातं सुभिक्ष्यं च भवन्तु तत्र सर्वदा ॥ १६७ ॥

"May clouds shower timely, may land be covered with paddy; may there never be famine, and plenty be always!"

राजा भवतु धर्मिष्ठो मन्त्रिणो नीतिचारिणः[47]।
सर्वे लोकाः सुवृत्तिस्था भवन्तु धर्मसाधकाः ॥ १६८ ॥

"May the king be lawful, ministers prudent, and people practise *dharma* with good conduct."

सर्वे सत्त्वाः समाचाराः संबोधिविहिताशयाः।
त्रिरत्नभजनं कृत्वा संचरन्तु सदा शुभे ॥ १६९ ॥

"May all sentient beings practise good conduct and be endowed with *sambodhi*; may they praise the Three Jewels and do good."

इति जयश्रियादिष्टं श्रुत्वा सर्वेऽपि सांघिकाः।
एवमस्त्विति प्राभाष्य प्राभ्यनन्दन् प्रसादिताः[48] ॥ १७० ॥

Thus, having heard the teachings of Jayaśrī, the people of the Saṅgha were pleased and they expressed happiness.

देयधर्मोऽयं प्रवरमहायायिनःश्रीमत्रुद्रवर्णमहाविहारावस्थितस्य।
परमोपासकश्रीशाक्यवंशोद्भवेनश्रीरामानन्देन लिखितोऽगमत् संपूर्णताम् ॥

Rāmānanda, born into the noble Śākya family, a devout worshipper of the gods, practitioner of the Mahāyāna way, and resident of the Rudravarṇa mahāvihāra, for the purpose of a gift, has finished transcribing this text.

॥ इति श्रीधर्मधातुस्वयम्भूत्पत्तिधर्ममाहात्म्यसुभाषितसूत्रं नाम दशमोऽध्यायः सम्पूर्णः ॥

Thus, the tenth chapter with the origin and glory of
the Svayambhū Dharmadhātu ends.

---

47 धारिणः इति कपाठः।

48 प्रसन्नता इति खपाठः।

उपसंहारः
(Epilogue)

असंस्कृतं च्युतं भ्रष्टं पुराणं रत्नपूरितम् ।
संस्कृतं श्रद्धया सर्वं युक्त्या बुद्ध्या श्रमेण च ॥

This Purāṇa, found rough, corrupted, and full of errors, yet so full of gems, has now been polished with devotion, acumen, intellect and toil.

अनेन कर्मणा प्रापि यच्च पुण्यं मयाऽधुना ।
तेन पुण्येन लोकोऽयं भवेत् सौख्यपरायणः ॥

By the merit that I may have amassed through this deed, may the whole world be immersed in happiness.

योगीन्द्रानन्दशिष्येण काशीनाथेन धीमता ।
संस्कारैर्भूषितं पुस्तं रत्नं कीटानुविद्धवत् ॥

Previously akin to a gem eaten away by insects, this book has now been skilfully adorned by [Acharya] Kāśinātha [Nyaupane], the disciple of Svāmī Yogindrānanda.

शुभमस्तु सर्वदा ॥

May there be auspiciousness always!